Study Guide

GLEITMAN, REISBERG, GROSS

Psychology

Seventh Edition

JOHN JONIDES
UNIVERSITY OF MICHIGAN

PAUL ROZIN
UNIVERSITY OF PENNSYLVANIA

W • W • NORTON & COMPANY • NEW YORK • LONDON

Printed in the United States of America

Layout and composition by Roberta Flechner Graphics

ISBN 978-0-393-93029-0

W. W. Norton & Company, Inc., 500 Fifth Avenue, New York, NY 10110
www.wwnorton.com

W. W. Norton & Company Ltd., Castle House, 75/76 Wells Street, London W1T 3QT

3 4 5 6 7 8 9 0

CONTENTS

ACKNOWLEDGMENTS

The authors would like to thank Caroline Arnold, Jason Fabozzi, Elizabeth Gross, Georgia Larounis, Jennifer Lerner, Laura Lowery, Maureen Markwith, Linda Millman, Deborah Reyher, Amanda Thomas, Nathan Witthoft, Jeff Moher, and Barbara Zeeff for their contributions and valuable suggestions.

In the course of developing the sections entitled "Investigating Psychological Phenomena" for each chapter, we have had occasion to seek the advice of colleagues and students who have particular expertise in the areas in question. We would like to acknowledge the help of Lyn Abramson, Henry Gleitman, Aaron Katcher, Charles G. Morris, Lorraine Nadelman, Harriet Oster, Christopher Peterson, Martin E. P. Seligman, W. John Smith, Marjorie Speers, and Edward Stricker. We also thank Walter Love and Jeannie Morrow for special assistance in field testing a number of the activities that we have included.

TO THE STUDENT

This study guide is designed to help you to understand and apply the material presented in *Psychology*, Seventh Edition, by Henry Gleitman, Daniel Reisberg, and James Gross. Each chapter in the study guide corresponds to one in the textbook. There are four sections in each study guide chapter: Learning Objectives, Programmed Exercises, Self-Test, and Investigating Psychological Phenomena. The first three sections will help you determine the essential ideas of the chapter as well as give you experience with possible test questions. The fourth section, Investigating Psychological Phenomena, allows you to extend your knowledge of some issues raised in the text. This section will also give you a feeling for how the data used by psychologists are collected, and how theories are tested in psychology. Let us briefly review the function of each of these sections.

LEARNING OBJECTIVES

We have provided an outline of the key issues discussed in each chapter. Each entry in the outline refers to a basic fact, theory, or relationship that you should have learned from the chapter. These entries are listed in order of occurrence in the chapter and are arranged under the same headings used in the chapter. It may be useful to read the learning objectives before reading the chapter, as well as after. They will help to orient you to the major issues, or the "big picture," of the chapter.

PROGRAMMED EXERCISES

For each chapter of the text, we have provided fill-in-the-blank questions. These questions test your basic knowledge of the key words and concepts of the chapter. These questions are very straightforward and can be looked up and verified in the text. So that you will know whether you are correct, the answer has been provided on the right side of the page. Be sure to cover that side of the page with your hand or a piece of paper as you do the exercises.

To facilitate locating the answers in the text, the programmed exercises are also arranged under the major headings of the textbook, and they follow the order of presentation in the text. This allows you to see which fact or theory pertains to which major point of the chapter.

SELF-TEST

For each chapter in the text, we have prepared a self-test composed of multiple-choice questions. They also follow the order of the text. In general, these questions are more difficult than the fill-ins, though both types of questions cover the range of materials presented in the text. The multiple choices sometimes highlight subtle distinctions, ask for some amount of integration, or test your ability to apply some of the material in the text.

Since multiple-choice questions are commonly used in examinations, and since they can also be very instructive, we will spend some time in this section discussing how to answer them. We will also describe and illustrate some different types of multiple-choice questions used in this study guide.

First, some basic strategies. Most multiple-choice questions on examinations, and in this study guide, have four or five choices. On most examinations there is a penalty of –1/3 point for wrong answers of four-choice questions, and –1/4 point for wrong answers on five-choice questions. This would mean that wild guessing should net a score of zero. But if you can eliminate even one choice, it pays to guess among the remaining alternatives.

Read each question carefully. Try to understand the *point* of the question. Read through the alternatives. The answer may be obvious to you. If not, try to eliminate some of the choices. You may be able to eliminate choices on the following grounds:

1. The choice is inherently inconsistent, illogical, or actual nonsense (e.g., word salad: a bunch of usually relevant terms combined in a meaningless way).

2. The choice makes sense and may even be true, but it is not an *answer* to the question.

3. On the basis of your knowledge, the choice is just the wrong answer to the question.

Get used to sorting out sense from nonsense and relevant from irrelevant answers. These skills will stand you in good stead in many of your activities outside of this course. Work with the remaining choices (if more than one choice remains), and do the best you can to determine the best fit between the question and the answer.

We will illustrate a number of different types of multiple-choice questions, all represented in this study guide. For each example we will indicate the correct answer and add comments on some of the incorrect choices.

Straight factual questions. Many multiple-choice questions simply ask for your knowledge of facts: names, definitions, and basic concepts.

1. The Prime Minister of Great Britain at the end of World War II was
   a. Neville Chamberlain.
   b. Winston Churchill.
   c. Harold Wilson.
   d. Sir D. Winter.
   e. Anthony Eden.

Comment: This is a very straightforward question. You know it or you don't. The answer is *b*, Winston Churchill. The other names were selected to make the question somewhat difficult: three of the other choices were prime ministers of Great Britain at the beginning or after the war, and one, Sir D. Winter, is a fictitious name.

2. The best way to describe inflation is
   a. increase in the gross national product not accompanied by increased unemployment.
   b. a general increase in prices.
   c. a decrease in the money supply.
   d. a decrease in the value of the monetary system, when associated with a gross national product.
   e. another form of recession.

Comment: This question is more difficult than 1. This is in part because the choices are more difficult. The correct answer is *b*. Answers *a*, *c*, and *e* are just wrong. Though *a* is consistent with inflation, it does not define it. Item *d* is inherently wrong; that is, it is sort of nonsense. What does it mean to decrease the value of the monetary *system* as opposed to money? And everything is associated with some gross national product. Keep your eyes open for nonsense. There is a lot of it in the world.

Evaluating evidence for a theory. In this type of question you are asked to judge whether particular results (real or hypothetical) support a particular theory (or which theory would be supported or opposed by a particular result). The theory and/or results may have been presented in the text, or they may be introduced in the question. The question tests both your knowledge of the materials, and your progress in understanding how to evaluate evidence. This type of question is often formulated in the negative—"Which of the following would be evidence against theory X?"—simply because it is usually easier to come up with results supporting major theories than results opposing them. We will assume, for the next sample question, that you have read in some text or other that Yentzel claimed that the crime rate increases as population mass and density increase. (Yentzel is a fictitious name.)

3. Which of the following would be evidence against Yentzel's theory? (Note: We assume that New York is larger than Philadelphia, which is larger than Tucson.)
   a. Philadelphia has a crime rate higher than Tucson.
   b. A few cities with increasing population also have increasing crime rates.
   c. A few cities with decreasing population have an increase in crime rate.
   d. Philadelphia has a lower crime rate than New York.
   e. The ratio of murder to robberies is lower in New York than in Tucson.

Comment: The correct answer is *c*, because this result is opposite to what would be predicted by Yentzel's theory. Answers *a*, *b*, and *c* are supporting evidence for the theory. Answer *e* is irrelevant: the theory says nothing about the types of crime, and *e* says nothing about the overall crime rate. (Note another clue to the right answer: *b* and *c* are opposites, so it is likely that one is evidence against the theory. However, clever exam writers know about this and sometimes put in opposites that are irrelevant to the question to keep you on your toes.)

Extending a principle or theory to a new situation. This type of question tests your understanding of a principle, theory, or concept by asking you to apply it to a situation other than those presented in the text.

4. If the saying "a stitch in time saves nine" were applied to medicine, one would recommend
   a. reducing the amount of sewing in surgery.
   b. increasing the cost of medical insurance.
   c. increasing the frequency of checkups.
   d. increasing the number of physicians.
   e. making prescription drugs available over the counter.

Comment: The correct answer is *c*. To answer the question, one must understand the saying and translate it into medical terms. This translation would be something like, Medical precautions can lead to avoidance of major illnesses. Alternative *a* is irrelevant to the *real* meaning of the saying and simply follows the *literal* meaning. Answer *b* would not lead, in any direct way, to avoidance of illness. But *b* is a sort of correct answer, since one might assume that increasing the cost of medical insurance would lead to increased coverage. The answer says increasing the cost, not the amount of insurance. Answer *c* relates directly to the saying, More checkups should lead to early discovery of illnesses that might prove harmful if allowed to develop. While *d* might well cut down the rate of illnesses, it is not a direct way of arriving at prevention. Lastly, *e* is irrelevant to the issue raised in the saying.

Relating different ideas or facts, or integrating materials. This type of question often involves materials from different sections of a chapter, or perhaps from different chapters (we have refrained from the latter, since we don't know the order in which you will be reading the chapters in the book).

5. The president of the United States is related to the electoral college as a U.S. Senator is related to*
   a. his or her own college faculty.
   b. the voters of his or her state.
   c. the members of the House of Representatives.
   d. the state of his or her electors.
   e. the state of his or her voters.

Comment: The correct answer is *b*. The electoral college is the group of people who actually elect the president. The voters of a senator's state are the people who elect the senator. Item *a* is totally wrong and simply a play on the word college. Item *c* is factually wrong. Item *d* is wrong and doesn't make too much sense, and item *e* is a reversal of the correct answer and has no relation to the question.

INVESTIGATING PSYCHOLOGICAL PHENOMENA

For each chapter of the text, we have presented one or two activities or experiments. These activities build upon concepts or theories presented in the chapter and extend and deepen your knowledge and understanding of these concepts or theories.

*This type of relation is often stated as "president of the U.S.: electoral college::U.S. Senator: ___________."

The activities give you an opportunity to understand something about the progress of psychology as a science. While the text emphasizes our current understanding of psychology, the activities emphasize the process through which we arrive at this understanding. How is the theory tested? How do psychologists get data to describe basic relations or test theories? How do they analyze the data? We hope to give you a feeling for how progress is made, while at the same time indicating the problems and difficulties associated with the serious study of something as complex as the human mind.

We have attempted to provide you with a variety of activities. Some emphasize the generation or testing of theories, others emphasize data collection or analysis. We have tried to cover the major methods of data collection used by psychologists: among all the activities are included examples of the experiment, the questionnaire, direct observation, and the interview. In many cases we provide data from studies we have done with introductory psychology students as a base for comparison with the data you collect. In each activity in which you collect data, we guide you through some analysis of the data and get you to try to interpret the data and relate it to issues raised in the text. If your instructor wishes to include the activities as part of the course, he or she may ask you to tear out the report (data) sheet pages, and hand them in. These sheets are duplicated at the end of the book in Appendix 2. Otherwise, you may consider these activities as a less formal extension of your education in psychology.

We have tried out all of these activities on undergraduate students like yourselves. We have included only studies that work out for the great majority of students. Of course, with people as variable as they are, all the studies that you do on one or a few students will not show the same results. But we expect that most of you will get most of the predicted results.

Many of the most important phenomena in psychology cannot be included in these activities because they must be measured under controlled conditions that you could not easily arrange. Some involve expensive equipment, like timers that can time thousandths of a second, or panels of lights and switches. Some important relations are not striking enough to be seen in one or a few participants. We have tried to find, for each chapter, at least one activity that can be appreciated within the limits under which you will be working. We require no equipment other than pencil, paper, some sort of second indicator (stopwatch, digital watch with second indicator, or a watch with a second hand), and materials presented within this study guide. We have limited the time demands on you for any activity to less than one hour. In all but a few cases, we have limited the number of participants to a very few. At the beginning of each activity, we indicate the equipment involved and the time demands it will make on you and the participants.

These activities are designed to be both educational and entertaining. We hope that you find that they meet these goals.

CHAPTER 1

Introduction

Learning Objectives

THE SCOPE OF PSYCHOLOGY

1. What is psychology? What is it a science of?

Watching the living brain

2. What makes the measurement of metabolic activity relevant to the study of the brain?

Memory errors

3. Be able to cite a factor that can render an eyewitness's memory false.

Innate capacities

4. What technique has been used to tell us about the innate perceptual abilities of infants?

Displays and the evolution of communication

5. How is social interaction in animals mediated by displays? How do displays differ from one animal to another? Give examples.

Complex social behavior in humans

6. How are humans more complex in their social behavior than other animals?

A SCIENCE OF EATING

7. Discuss the range of eating phenomena studied by psychologists.

The biological basis for eating

8. Describe the mechanisms behind self-regulation.

9. What different parts of the body are involved in the process of deciding when to eat?

Cultural influences on eating

10. Give examples of different eating habits in different parts of the world.

11. How can ideal body weights differ?

Eating and the social world

12. How can the behavior of others influence our eating habits?

13. Describe the possible causes of anorexia nervosa.

Cognitive control over eating

14. Describe Rozin's study of clinical amnesia patients and their eating habits.

The development of food preferences

15. What are the primary factors in the development of food preferences?

WHAT IS IT THAT UNITES PSYCHOLOGY?

16. What differentiates psychology from the other approaches used to answer the same questions in the past?

17. What are the three factors that unify the field of psychology?

THE SCIENTIFIC METHOD

18. Give some examples of problems that can be approached by the scientific method.

19. What are some of the characteristics of the scientific method? What is a hypothesis? a prediction? a disconfirmation? What happens to hypotheses that are disconfirmed? What is the role of publication?

Designing a persuasive experiment

20. Be able to describe what makes a hypothesis testable.

21. Describe some of the characteristics of data collection that would make the evidence systematic. Do anecdotes count?

22. Know what a report bias is and how it might taint results.

23. What is the danger in relying on memory as the basis of data collection?

24. Be able to define a dependent and an independent variable.

25. Why is it sometimes necessary to have a panel of raters to assess the dependent variable?

26. What is a control group and how does it differ from an experimental group?

27. What is a danger of "before/after" designs?

28. Explain what we should keep in mind in designing a treatment for a control group.

29. What is a placebo, and what does it have to do with expectations?

30. How would subjects behave if they were being influenced by the demand characteristics of an experiment?

31. What is a double-blind design and how does it help assure the purity of an experimental design?

32. Be able to describe what a confound is and to give an example of a confounding variable.

An overview of an experiment's design

33. Name some quantitative measures that can be used as dependent variables.

34. What is the significance of causation, and why is it often hard to identify?

Evaluating evidence outside the laboratory

35. How might knowledge of good experimental design be applied outside of the laboratory?

OBSERVATIONAL STUDIES

36. What is the key difference between an experimental study and an observational one?

Correlational studies and causal ambiguity

37. Understand that the defining feature of a correlational study is understanding the relationship between an independent variable and a dependent variable.

38. Describe a case in which the direction of causality is unclear between two variables.

39. What type of experiment can best determine causality?

40. Explain how a third variable might cause a spurious correlation between variables A and B in which there is no direct link between A and B at all.

Matching the experimental and control groups

41. Understand that in principle, experiments and correlational studies have a similar structure, with independent and dependent variables. So what permits experiments to escape some of the ambiguities of correlational studies?

42. What is the special property that random assignment confers on an experiment? How does this help establish causation? How does it mitigate the third-variable problem?

43. There are advantages and disadvantages to within-subject designs. Describe some. How does counterbalancing help to relieve some disadvantages?

Studies of single participants

44. Why would we ever study just a single participant when we are trying to learn about general laws of behavior?

45. What safeguards might we introduce to add rigor to the study of single cases?

TYPES OF DATA

46. What is the strength in using multiple methods to approach a problem?

GENERALIZING FROM RESEARCH

47. What is meant by external validity and how is this related to the problem of generalizing from research?

Selecting participants

48. How must participants be selected so that results from a sample can be generalized to the population of interest?

49. Describe a random sample and why it is preferable to a nonrandom sample.

50. Why is it important to gather a representative sample of responses?

External validity

51. Be aware of the issues involved in assessing the external validity of a study.

RESEARCH ETHICS

52. What are some of the protections that must be afforded to human and animal research participants?

53. What mechanisms exist for implementing these protections?

Programmed Exercises

THE SCOPE OF PSYCHOLOGY

1. Psychology involves not only the study of the mind but also the study of ___________. — behavior

2. Studying which parts of the brain show _________ activity helps us understand which part of the brain is active at a particular moment. — metabolic

3. Many phenomena are best studied not at the _________ level but at the ___________ level by focusing on the person's behavior and thinking, rather than the underlying nervous mechanisms. — biological, psychological

4. _________ questions can cause a piece of information to become implanted in a previous memory. — Leading

5. Studies showing that infants understood the concepts of _________ and _________ suggest that some perceptual knowledge may not be _________, but is built into us from the start. — addition, subtraction, learned

6. In animals, social interactions depend largely on _________ forms of communication. — innate

7. Many types of animal communication are based on signals called _________. — displays

8. The behavior of rioting crowds is determined not only by each individual but also by the individual's __________ interaction. social (group)

A SCIENCE OF EATING

9. Psychology often has a need for __________ approaches even when considering a single phenomenon. diverse
10. When food is freely available, animals usually eat the __________ amount. right
11. In one study, animals ate __________ food if it was adulterated with nonnutritive cellulose. more
12. The blood sugar __________ helps animals self-regulate eating habits, and much of it is converted to __________ for later use. glucose glycogen
13. The __________ sends satiety signals to the __________ in the brain. liver, hypothalamus
14. The __________ setting often determines the ideal weight toward which people strive. cultural
15. Bayer's experiment showed that a hen who is already full will resume her meal if joined by other hens who are __________. hungry
16. One study showed that images of fat people lead to __________ associations. negative
17. Our body weight goals are often influenced by how other people __________ us and what they expect from us. perceive
18. __________ __________ is defined as the pursuit of thinness through self-starvation. Anorexia nervosa
19. People's desire to be thin can lead to __________ disorders which can cause serious health problems. eating
20. Whether we eat is influenced by our __________ of recent meals. memory
21. In one study, patients with __________ __________ continued eating meals as they were presented, even though they had already eaten. clinical amnesia
22. These patients also claimed to be __________ shortly after eating their first meal. hungry
23. The development of food preferences is influenced by both learning and __________. biology
24. The overall message is that if we are going to understand what, when, and how much people eat, we need to understand eating from multiple __________. perspectives

THE SCIENCE OF PSYCHOLOGY

25. When we conduct investigations with specific hypotheses that are subject to rigorous test, we are using the __________ method. scientific

THE SCIENTIFIC METHOD

26. Testable hypotheses allow us to make specific __________ about what we expect to find in an experimental test. predictions
27. Two forms of gathering data are __________ and __________. experimentation, observation
28. __________ data for any reason where those data did not arise directly from experimentation, inventing, or observation is fraud. Fudging
29. If results are not consistent with a prediction, then the underlying hypothesis is __________. disconfirmed
30. Scientists often want to rerun the same study with new participants, a process called __________. replication
31. The written public presentation of results appears in a __________. publication
32. A __________ hypothesis is one for which we can identify the results that would confirm or disconfirm it. testable
33. __________ evidence, often in the form of a testimonial by a single person, is often dismissed by scientists because it is not systematic. Anecdotal

34. A report __________ arises when some observations are more likely to be reported than others. bias

35. The __________ problem is one example of report bias in which unsuccessful results are suppressed. file-drawer

36. In an experiment, the __________ variable is the one that is a function of some other factor, the __________ variable. dependent independent

37. Sometimes, dependent variables cannot be measured directly, so one must enlist a panel of __________ to rate the variable. judges

38. If judges on a panel agree to a certain extent, then an investigator can be confident that their assessments are not __________ or __________. arbitrary, idiosyncratic

39. In an experiment, the __________ group is administered the critical manipulation (e.g., the subliminal self-help tape described in the text), while the __________ group is deprived of this manipulation. experimental control

40. It is important to __________ and control experimental groups in all respects except for the experimental manipulation. match

41. Participants' expectations can have a profound influence on a study's results. This is the basis for __________ effects. placebo

42. Sometimes there are cues in an experiment called __________ __________ that signal that one response is more desirable than another. demand characteristics

43. __________ designs are ones in which neither the investigator nor the study participants know who is in the experimental and control groups. Double-blind

44. A __________ is an uncontrolled factor that could influence the results and result in __________ ambiguity. confound causal

OBSERVATIONAL STUDIES

45. In many cases, variables can't be experimentally controlled (as in a person's height), so we must turn to a(n) __________ study. observational

46. One type of observational study involves an assessment of the relationship between an independent and a dependent variable; this is called a __________ study. correlational

47. The direction of causality is not always easily determined in __________ studies. correlational

48. Sometimes, correlations arise because a __________ variable is related to each of the two variables being correlated. third

49. Experiments escape the ambiguity about causality because the experimental and control groups start out __________ to each other. identical

50. Often the reason that experimental and control groups are identical to each other is that participants have been __________ assigned to one or the other group. randomly

51. If you use the very same participants for experimental and control groups, this is a __________ comparison. Using different groups makes it a __________ comparison. within-subject between-subject

52. Within-subject designs can result in a __________ __________ confound. test sequence

TYPES OF DATA

53. In a __________ study, psychologists investigate a single individual in great detail. case

GENERALIZING FROM RESEARCH

54. Whether we can generalize outside the bounds of a particular study to a wider group of people depends on the external __________ of the study. validity

55. Almost always, we want the conclusions of a study to apply to a __________ even though the subjects in the study were drawn from a __________. population sample

56. Generalization to a population depends on how __________ the sample is. representative

57. A __________ sample is one in which every participant has an equal and unpredictable chance of being picked. random

58. Questions of external validity must be resolved through __________ and not be based on __________. research assumptions

RESEARCH ETHICS

59. Psychological research must be conducted __________, in a way that protects the rights, well being, and confidentiality of the research participants. ethically

60. In the United States, psychological research with humans must follow the guidelines of the __________ __________ __________. American Psychological Association

61. Before a study may begin, we must obtain __________ __________ from the subjects. informed consent

Self-Test

1. Psychology is
   a. the science of the mind.
   b. the science of behavior.
   c. a and b
   d. none of the above.
2. Psychology covers a large range of topics including
   a. topics that touch on anthropology and sociology.
   b. behavior in humans.
   c. behavior in animals.
   d. all of the above.
3. Studying psychological processes has been helped significantly by the development of techniques that assess which parts of the brain are active during psychological tasks. This is possible because we can measure
   a. the activity of individual neurons in the living human brain.
   b. the direct neural activity of sets of neurons when they are active in the human brain.
   c. changes in metabolic activity that accompany changes in regional neural activity.
   d. all of the above.
4. The memories of eyewitnesses are open to question because
   a. their memories can be altered by leading questions that are presented after an event has occurred.
   b. they can be influenced to remember details of an event that never really happened.
   c. they can forget incidents that might have really happened.
   d. all of the above.
5. The fact that children are able to understand concepts such as addition and subtraction at a young age suggests that perceptual skills
   a. are learned.
   b. are innate.
   c. could be innate.
   d. all of the above.
6. The displays that animals use to communicate
   a. are innate and have arisen through selection.
   b. are almost always threat signals that ward off predators.
   c. will rarely involve parts of the body other than the head.
   d. all of the above.
7. Human social interactions differ from those of other animals because
   a. humans are less variable in their interactions.
   b. humans are more flexible in their interactions.
   c. human social behavior is always rational and reasoned.
   d. human behavior in groups is predictable from knowing the responses that individual humans will make in a given situation.
8. What self-regulates eating in humans?
   a. Glucose
   b. The liver
   c. The hypothalamus
   d. All of the above
9. Across different cultures, mealtimes tend to be
   a. varied.
   b. the same.
   c. the same, but the size of the meal varies.
   d. none of the above.
10. Anorexia nervosa may be a result of
    a. an intense psychological fear of becoming fat.
    b. a genetic predisposition.
    c. a fear of sexuality.
    d. any of the above.
11. In a study, patients with clinical amnesia were given a full meal, and a few minutes after they finished, given another full meal without being told they just ate. When this happened, they
    a. declined the second meal.
    b. ate the second meal.
    c. ate the second meal, but commented on how full they felt afterward.
    d. none of the above.

12. Food preferences develop because of
    a. biology.
    b. learning.
    c. a and b
    d. none of the above.

13. The discussion of emotion in the text indicates that this and many other psychological phenomena can be profitably studied by
    a. studying cases where they go wrong (psychopathology).
    b. studying their representations across cultures.
    c. studying their underlying neurological representation in the brain.
    d. all of the above.

14. The scientific method requires
    a. collecting anecdotes about some phenomenon.
    b. creating testable hypotheses.
    c. making specific predictions that can be tested.
    d. b and c.

15. Perhaps the worst sin we can commit when using the scientific method is
    a. devising a hypothesis that turns out to be incorrect.
    b. making a prediction that is later disconfirmed when tested.
    c. concocting data that have not been collected.
    d. confirming a hypothesis that is under test.

16. For a hypothesis to be testable, it must be
    a. specific enough that it can be confirmed.
    b. specific enough that it can be disconfirmed.
    c. broad and all-inclusive so that any data collected will show that it is confirmed.
    d. a and b

17. Report bias arises when
    a. an observer reports only some of the data relevant to a situation but not others.
    b. an observer publishes encouraging results but not ones that are inconsistent with a hypothesis.
    c. the file-drawer problem is present in some situation.
    d. all of the above.

18. Imagine an experiment in which you give students in a course both an easy and a difficult examination on some topic. All students take the easy exam and the difficult exam, and you record each student's score on each exam. The purpose of your experiment is to determine whether students who score high on the easy exam are the same ones who score high on the difficult exam, and students who score low on one exam are also those who score low on the other. In this experiment,
    a. the difficulty of the exam is the dependent variable.
    b. the difficulty of the exam is the independent variable.
    c. the exam scores are the independent variable.
    d. none of the above; there are no independent and dependent variables in this experiment.

19. For the experiment described in question 18, what sort of experimental design was used?
    a. A within-subject comparison
    b. A between-subject comparison
    c. A double-blind design
    d. A causally ambiguous design

20. When we use a panel of judges to rate some measure, it is important to
    a. explain to them what the independent variable is in the experiment.
    b. get them to agree to a reasonable extent in order to use their judgments.
    c. have them blind to what the dependent variable is.
    d. all of the above.

21. Suppose you are interested in the effect of creating images of a list of words on the memorability of those words (an interesting question, as you will see in the section on "Investigating Psychological Phenomena" in Chapter 7). You instruct one group of subjects to create images of each word in a list, and another group of subjects to repeat each word as it is presented. In this experiment,
    a. the group instructed to repeat the words is the experimental group.
    b. the group instructed to create images is the control group.
    c. the design is an observational one, not an experimental one.
    d. none of the above.

22. Whenever you want to assess the effect of a placebo, you want to be sure that
    a. you have included demand characteristics in your experiment.
    b. you have included confounds in your experiment.
    c. you have designed the experiment in a double-blind way.
    d. your experiment is causally ambiguous.

23. Suppose you are interested in the effect of age on memory. You test memory by presenting participants a list of words after which they have to recall the words in any order. Your experiment includes two groups of participants, ones aged 18 to 25 and ones aged 65 to 72. As it happens the younger participants are rarely awake early in the morning, so you test them in the afternoon. Conveniently, the older participants like to awake early, so you test them in the morning. You discover that the younger participants remember more words from the lists. This experiment suffers from
    a. not having an independent variable.
    b. not having a dependent variable.
    c. having confounded age and time of testing (morning versus afternoon).
    d. being double-blind.

24. For the experiment described in question 23,
    a. there is causal ambiguity if the younger participants remember more than the older participants.
    b. there is causal ambiguity if the older participants remember more than the younger participants.
    c. either time of day or age was a cause of any differences in memory performance.
    d. all of the above.

25. A correlational study would be needed if you wanted to measure the effect of
    a. shoe size on intelligence.
    b. age on depression.
    c. alcoholism on memory.
    d. all of the above.

26. Suppose you conducted a study of shoe size and its relationship to intelligence among people aged 8 to 12. To conduct this study, you measure the shoe size of each of the participants, and you give each participant an identical test of intelligence. Your results tell you that there is a positive relationship between shoe size and intelligence: the larger the shoe size, the higher the score on the intelligence test. For this study, there is
   a. a third-variable problem: larger shoe size is related to age.
   b. a third-variable problem: larger shoe size is related to intelligence.
   c. no causal ambiguity because there are no confounds in the study.
   d. none of the above.

27. We are told often that a correlation by itself does not permit us to draw causal inferences. By contrast, a properly designed experiment does permit causal inferences. This is because
   a. in an experiment, we randomly assign participants to experimental and control groups.
   b. in an experiment, the experimental variable can be causally attributed to it.
   c. assigning participants to experimental and control groups randomly ensures that the two groups are matched at the beginning of the experiment.
   d. all of the above.

28. One problem with the design of the experiment in question 18 is that students are given both the easy exam and the difficult exam. If these exams are always given with the easy exam first and the difficult one second, or vice versa, there might be a learning effect so that students would do better on the second exam they take, regardless of whether it is easy or difficult. You could solve this problem by
   a. randomly assigning half the students to take the easy exam first, and the other half to take the difficult exam first.
   b. using a within-subject comparison.
   c. using a correlational study rather than an experimental one.
   d. using a double-blind procedure in which the experimenter and the participants do not know which exam is easy and which is difficult.

29. Single-case studies are
   a. typically preferred to studies with multiple participants because we simplify the testing by having fewer participants.
   b. sometimes necessary when the object of study is precisely the case in question.
   c. not approachable by standard experimental methods.
   d. all of the above.

30. When we conduct an experiment, we typically want to generalize the results to a whole population of people. That is, we would like to draw conclusions about the entire population, but we often cannot afford to test an entire population. To solve this problem, we might
   a. test a random sample of the population.
   b. test as many people from that population as we can.
   c. a or b; either would allow generalization to the entire population.
   d. none of the above; neither a nor b would allow generalization to the entire population.

31. The concept of the external validity of an experiment refers to whether
   a. the results of the experiment can be generalized to phenomena in the outside world.
   b. an experiment was properly controlled in its design.
   c. an experiment has confounds in it that prevent a proper interpretation of the results.
   d. none of the above.

32. In conducting an experiment on human participants, we must assure
   a. the safety of the participants.
   b. the confidentiality of the results.
   c. that informed consent is obtained from participants before they are tested.
   d. all of the above.

Answer Key for Self-Test

1.	c	17.	d
2.	d	18.	b
3.	c	19.	a
4.	d	20.	b
5.	c	21.	d
6.	a	22.	c
7.	b	23.	c
8.	d	24.	d
9.	a	25.	d
10.	d	26.	a
11.	b	27.	d
12.	c	28.	a
13.	d	29.	b
14.	d	30.	c
15.	c	31.	a
16.	d	32.	d

Investigating Psychological Phenomena

CONSISTENCY OF JUDGMENTS OF FACIAL EXPRESSION

It is time to put some of what you learned in this chapter into practice. You have an idea now about how to conduct an experiment, and so we shall apply what you have learned to the development of an experiment on facial expressions. There is reason to suspect that some emotions are universally expressed. For example, when people of various cultures encounter a happy face, they often perceive it as happy. This is in contrast to other expressions, for which the agreement among different observers may be as little as 30 to 40%. It would be quite interesting to conduct this experiment using a very wide range of emotional expressions on a very wide array of participants from multiple cultures. Of course, it is difficult for the average college student to have access to such a wide array of participants. However, the average student does have access to students of both genders, and so the question we shall ask is whether judgments of facial expressions differ as a function of gender and, further, whether the judgments of one gender are more concordant with faces of that gender than with faces of the other gender.

To conduct this experiment, you will need an array of faces that you can use as stimuli. Fortunately, in these days of widely available digital cameras and personal computers, it should be relatively easy to construct a stimulus array and organize it into a systematic set of faces about which to collect judgments. First you need to capture the images. Select a friend of each gender whose face is plain (e.g., no facial hair, no facial ornaments, no facial tattoos). Then pose each of these two "actors" in front of a digital camera set to collect images at an average resolution. In turn, ask each volunteer to pose as if he is

Ecstatic	Happy
Sad	Shocked
Frightened	Disgusted
Calm	Resigned
Disappointed	Angry
Resolute	

Take one picture of each pose for each actor. You should now have a collection of 22 images, 11 of the male actor and 11 of the female. Import these images into a presentation program such as Microsoft PowerPoint such that each slide of the presentation has just one image and the images are in a random order. (You can determine this by making up 22 slips of paper, writing a description of one slide [e.g., happy male] on each slip, and then picking them out of a bowl [without looking]. The sequence in which you pick the slips of paper is your random order.) In addition, make up 20 answer sheets, each of which has the numbers 1 to 22 in order with a line next to each on which the participant can write his or her answer.

Next, you should choose 10 male and 10 female participants. You will be testing them one by one. When each participant is sitting in front of the computer on which the presentation is programmed (be sure that your presentation begins with a blank page so that the participant cannot see the first face), give him or her the following instruction:

"We are interested in examining how universally people are able to recognize facial expressions. So, we have prepared a set of 22 faces, each of which is posed with some expression. On the sheet in front of you, there are 22 lines, and for each expression, you should enter a one-word description of that expression. If you are in doubt about some face, enter your best guess. Once you have written an answer and moved on to the next face, do not change any prior answers. Do you have any questions?"

Set the program so that it presents each slide for 5 seconds cycling through all the slides. After the last slide is shown, collect the answer sheet and thank the participant.

Now you need to score the sheets. If a judgment about a face matches one of the judgments that you used to create the face originally, count that correct. If it is close to the correct label (e.g., neutral for calm or depressed for sad), count that correct also. Now you want to create a table for all the subjects and all the stimuli; you can do this in the following template. The template has a place to record each answer from each subject about each face. Having done this, you now want to score the correct answers by each gender group for each face. Simply count down each column per stimulus and note (out of a maximum possible score of 11 for each gender) how many of the faces were judged correctly (of course, "correct" here is judged by definition, that is, by the instruction you gave the actor before you took his or her picture; it is not an absolute criterion).

Now you are ready to examine the data by gender. You can do this on the summary table templates that are available. First, create a total accuracy score for the female subjects and for the male subjects by totaling all their respective judgments. Are males overall more or less accurate than females in judgments of facial emotion? Previous research gives little reason for this to be so, but it is possible that females and males will differ in their judgments when they are judging the emotions on female versus male faces. So, calculate the total accuracy for females on the female faces, for females on the male faces, for males on the female faces, and for males on the male faces. Once again, do a comparison to see whether there are any gender effects that might differ according to the gender of the face. There are hypotheses that might predict that people may be different in judging the expressions on faces of their own gender compared to those on faces of the other gender.

Popular lore suggests that males are just not as sensitive in judging certain emotions in women as women are in judging them in women. To get an informal test of this lore, examine each of the individual expressions to see whether there are any cases of large discordance between the accuracy of males and the accuracy of females (large would be, for example, a score of 7/11 for one gender but only 3/11 for the other gender).

We should note that all the comparisons you accomplished were qualitative ones. It might be that a small difference for any of them could be due to statistical fluctuation that does not reveal any true differences. The text's appendix, which concerns statistical analysis, will give you an idea about how to overcome this limitation. For now, though, you should examine your data to see whether you found any systematic differences that might be revealing about gender differences in the identification of facial expression.

	Female Subjects	**Male Subjects**
Total accuracy		

	Female Subjects	**Male Subjects**	**Total**
Female faces			
Male faces			
Total			

	Female Subjects	Male Subjects
Female ecstatic		
Female happy		
Female sad		
Female shocked		
Female frightened		
Female disgusted		
Female calm		
Female resigned		
Female disappointed		
Female angry		
Female resolute		

	Female Subjects	Male Subjects
Male ecstatic		
Male happy		
Male sad		
Male shocked		
Male frightened		
Male disgusted		
Male calm		
Male resigned		
Male disappointed		
Male angry		
Male resolute		

CHAPTER 2

Evolution and the Biological Roots of Behavior

Learning Objectives

1. Indicate which domains of human life are particularly likely to be informed by a biological science approach.
2. Differentiate among three types of biological approaches: the search for mechanisms, the comparative approach, and the evolutionary perspective.

THE EVOLUTIONARY ROOTS OF MOTIVATED BEHAVIOR

The basic principles of natural selection

3. Explain the Darwinian principle of natural selection, and indicate how it presumes there is variation.

Genes

4. Define genes and DNA. What are chromosomes? What is the genome?
5. About how many genes do humans have?
6. Distinguish between dominant and recessive genes, giving an example.
7. What is meant by polygenic inheritance?
8. Distinguish between genotype and phenotype.

Personal and genetic survival

9. Distinguish personal from genetic survival. Give examples in which they seem to be opposed to one another.

Evolution of behavior

10. Indicate the types of evidence that would suggest that a given human feature can be traced to the evolutionary history of humans, and is hence represented in some way in human genes.
11. Evaluate the claim that some important aspects of human behavior have an evolutionary-genetic basis.

THE ACHIEVEMENT OF HOMEOSTASIS

Homeostasis

12. Define homeostasis and give an example of homeostasis in action.
13. Describe the role of negative feedback in homeostasis.

The autonomic nervous system

14. Distinguish endotherms and ectotherms.
15. Describe the autonomic nervous system, including its two parts, the sympathetic and parasympathetic branches.
16. What are the functions of the parasympathetic and sympathetic systems?
17. Describe the way the two branches of the autonomic nervous system function in temperature regulation.
18. Describe how the hypothalamus is involved in thermoregulation.

EATING

Set points

19. Explain the meaning of *set point* and review evidence suggesting that humans and other animals have a weight set point.

The role of the liver

20. Indicate how the liver regulates energy expenditure and storage internally, through the conversion of glucose to glycogen and of glycogen to glucose.
21. Explain how the liver provides signals for eating or ceasing eating, and how liver activity can anticipate energy deficits.

Other control signals for feeding

22. Describe how signals from the brain (glucoreceptors), stomach, and duodenum influence food intake.

23. Distinguish between short-term and long-term control of food intake, and describe long-term regulation in terms of adipose cells and leptin, and the effect of leptin on the neuropeptide Y.

Why so many control systems?

24. Offer two different explanations for why there are many different systems that influence food intake.

25. Explain the idea that some signals potentiate the influence of other signals, rather than having a direct effect on food intake.

Hypothalamic control centers

26. What is the dual-center theory? What are the main lines of evidence for and against it?

27. Indicate evidence that brain areas outside of the hypothalamus are involved in feeding (e.g., neuropeptide Y studies).

Obesity

28. Define body mass index.

29. Discuss the definition, incidence, and disadvantages of obesity.

30. Review evidence that establishes a role for genes in obesity.

31. Review evidence that indicates an important environmental and/or cultural influence on obesity.

32. Consider and evaluate different possible causes of obesity.

33. Is being overweight a disorder? Consider this in the light of the idea of the thrifty gene.

34. What is anorexia nervosa, and what might be some possible causes?

THREAT AND AGGRESSION

35. Compare threat and eating in terms of the relative importance of internal and external causes.

Threat and the autonomic nervous system

36. Review the functions of the parasympathetic and sympathetic systems.

37. Indicate how sympathetic nervous system activation and adrenaline secretion prepare an animal for action.

The emergency reaction

38. Describe the emergency reaction. What role does the sympathetic arousal system play in the flight-or-fight response? Understand the biological survival value of the emergency reaction.

Disruptive effects of autonomic arousal

39. Describe the immediate disruptive effects of sympathetic arousal and the possible long-term effects on health.

Aggression and predation

40. Is aggression related to predatory attack? Explain.

Male aggression and hormones

41. Discuss the relation between testosterone and aggression.

Territoriality

42. What is a territory, and how does it function to control aggression?

43. What is the evidence for territory or personal space in humans? Discuss the contributions of our genes and of individual and cultural experience to the manifestations of territory.

Patterns of human aggression

44. Illustrate the way humans express aggression, both physically and symbolically.

45. List some aspects of personality that account for some individual differences in aggression.

46. Describe how culture influences the expression of aggression.

Learning to be aggressive

47. Discuss the evidence supporting and arguing against an effect of violence in the media on actual levels of violence.

Is aggression inevitable?

48. Explain mechanisms for limiting aggression, including sizing up the strength of the "enemy" and dominance hierarchies.

SEX

49. Discuss and compare the roles of biological, experiential, and cultural factors in accounting for human eating, threat/aggression, and sexual behavior.

Hormones and animal sexuality

50. Describe the mammalian female hormonal cycle.

51. Indicate how sex hormones affect behavior, and the role of the hypothalamus.

52. Illustrate how behavior affects hormones.

53. Indicate how sex hormone effects are different in humans.

Selecting a mate

54. What is the perspective of the subfield of evolutionary psychology on human sexual behavior?

55. Review arguments for the importance of physical attractiveness in human mate selection.

56. Describe the dating-dance study that shows the importance of physical attractiveness in mate choice.

57. Discuss the effects of physical attractiveness on the perception of other traits (the halo effect).

58. Indicate universal or near-universal features of physical attractiveness, including some differences in the criteria for physical attractiveness of males and females.

59. What are the evolutionary or adaptive justifications for some of the near-universal criteria for physical attractiveness? Make sure to include symmetry and waist-hip ratio in this answer.

60. Explain the matching hypothesis.

61. Explain why the costs of mating are usually much higher for females than for males.

62. Relate the cost difference of mating between males and females to differences in the degree to which males and females advertise their sex and desirability as mates.

63. Indicate differences in the major criteria for mate selection in human males and females, and relate these differences to differences in the investment in offspring.

64. Suggest cultural conditions that might reduce the differences between human male and female mating strategies.

65. Describe the difference between human males and females in the importance of commitment in mating relationships, and offer an evolutionary account for this.

66. Explain differences in the way human males and females may manifest jealousy in terms of reactions to different types of infidelities.

67. Indicate how these differences may depend on what question is asked, and on the status of males and females in a particular culture.

The evolutionary perspective in perspective

68. Summarize the relative importance of evolutionary and environmental or cultural influences on sexual behavior, especially in humans.

SOME FINAL THOUGHTS: REFLECTIONS ON THE CONTRIBUTION OF THE BIOLOGICAL PERSPECTIVE

69. Compare the influence of genetic/evolutionary and cultural/environmental factors on animal and human function in the domains of eating, threat-aggression, and sex.

Programmed Exercises

1. A _________ science approach to psychology is particularly apt for basic survival needs, including food, protection, and reproduction.	biological
2. The biological approach has three components: the search for _________ of behavior, the _________ approach, and the _________ perspective.	mechanisms comparative, evolutionary

THE EVOLUTIONARY ROOTS OF MOTIVATED BEHAVIOR

3. The evolutionary approach originated with Charles _________ and his great book, _________.	Darwin, *The Origin of Species*
4. According to Darwin, evolution proceeds because _________ of a species with superior characteristics are more likely to survive. This process is called _________ _________.	variants natural selection
5. The unit of hereditary transmission is the _________. The set of all of these in an individual or a species is called the _________.	gene genome
6. The basic chemical constituent of genes is called _________.	DNA
7. Genes are arranged and stored in pairs of structures called _________.	chromosomes
8. A gene that exerts its effect regardless of the identity of the other member of its pair is called _________.	dominant
9. A gene that will express itself only if the other member of its pair is comparable is called _________.	recessive
10. When an attribute is determined by multiple genes, this is called _________ inheritance.	polygenic
11. The observed characteristics of an organism are called its _________, while the underlying genetic blueprint is called its _________.	phenotype genotype
12. Essentially, natural selection is not about literal survival, or _________ survival, but about reproductive success, which amounts to _________ survival.	personal genetic
13. Evolution of behavior is likely, according to evolutionary theory, if there is evidence for _______ based variation in that behavior, and the behavior in question has some _________ advantage over alternative behaviors.	genetically, selective (fitness, adaptive)
14. Evidence that a particular human behavior has some basis in human evolution can be gained from studies of pairs of _________ and from _________ of the behaviors of humans and other mammals, particularly primates.	twins, comparison

15. The period from about 1.8 million years ago to about 10,000 years ago, called the _________ epoch, is the period in which many distinctively human traits evolved. Pleistocene

THE ACHIEVEMENT OF HOMEOSTASIS

16. The maintenance of a stable equilibrium in the body is called _________. homeostasis

17. In a _________ feedback system, the feedback stops, or even reverses, the original change. negative

18. As opposed to _________, _________ can control their temperature internally. ectotherms, endotherms

19. Temperature regulation and many other body functions are controlled by the _________ nervous system. autonomic

20. The autonomic nervous system operates by controlling the _________ _________ and the _________. smooth muscles glands

21. The _________ branch of the autonomic nervous system is involved in mobilizing the body to deal with vigorous action. sympathetic

22. The _________ branch of the autonomic nervous system is involved in maintaining normal body functions such as digestion. parasympathetic

23. The _________ and _________ divisions of the autonomic nervous system work in opposite directions to control temperature. The _________ division acts to generate heat to counteract low temperatures. parasympathetic sympathetic (in either order), sympathetic

24. With respect to controlling body temperature by affecting blood vessels, the parasympathetic system dissipates higher temperature by causing _________, whereas the sympathetic branch, to conserve or generate heat, causes _________. vasodilation vasoconstriction

25. The part of the brain that is most involved in thermoregulation is called the _________. hypothalamus

EATING

26. The fact that animals and humans tend to maintain the same weight over long periods suggests that there is a weight _________ _________. set point

27. Receptors sensitive to the metabolic state (energy need) of the organism have been postulated to exist in the _________ and _________. liver, brain

28. These receptors respond to blood levels of the basic source of short-term energy, which is _________. The liver controls the level of blood _________ by reversibly converting it to the stored animal starch, _________. glucose, glucose glycogen

29. There is evidence that the glucose-glycogen balance in the liver changes in _________ of a decrease in available energy, signaling an increase in food intake. anticipation

30. Satiety signals also originate in the gastrointestinal system, from nutrient receptors in the _________ and _________. stomach, duodenum

31. The brain may also be informed about the state of long-term energy stores (fat) in the body, by detecting the level of _________, a secretion of _________ cells, in the blood. leptin, adipose

32. The _________ secreted by full adipose cells may block the activity of the neurochemical _________ _________, a major food intake stimulant. leptin neuropeptide Y

33. The attractiveness of food can influence the amount ingested, but its effectiveness depends on the metabolic state of the organism, which may _________ the reaction to the food. potentiate

34. According to the dual-center theory, activity in the _________ hypothalamus stimulates eating, and activity in the _________ hypothalamus inhibits it. lateral ventromedial

35. The dual-center theory is supported by the fact that lesions in the lateral hypothalamus produce _________ eating, while lesions in the ventromedial hypothalamus produce _________ eating. less more

36. The ventromedial hypothalamus affects eating directly but also indirectly by affecting _________ storage. fat

37. The potent appetite stimulant __________ __________ seems to act outside of the hypothalamus. neuropeptide Y (NPY)

38. The standard measure of heaviness is weight (in kilograms) divided by height in meters squared. This is called the __________ __________ __________. body mass index (BMI)

39. A BMI greater than 30 defines obesity. Presently, about __________% of American adults qualify as obese by this criterion. 30

40. The high resemblance in obesity and body distribution of fat in __________ __________ argues for a __________ determinant of obesity. identical twins genetic

41. Obese people may have, on the average, higher __________ __________ than the rest of the population. set points

42. Increasing obesity rates in many developed countries over recent decades argues for an important __________ influence on obesity. environmental

43. According to the __________ gene hypothesis, what we now see as perhaps maladaptive obesity may have been part of an adaptive strategy to store extra energy when it was available in the human ancestral environment. thrifty

44. __________ __________ is a life-threatening disorder in which a person eats very little and loses a great deal of weight. Anorexia nervosa

THREAT AND AGGRESSION

45. The sympathetic system has a(n) __________ function. activating

46. Sympathetic action is supported or amplified by the secretion of the hormone __________. adrenaline

47. As originally described by Walter Cannon, the __________ reaction results from activation of the __________ nervous system. emergency sympathetic

48. __________ arousal can have disruptive effects, which, if maintained, can compromise health. Sympathetic

49. The generally higher level of aggression seen in the males of most species has been attributed in part to higher levels of the male hormone __________. testosterone

50. Animals often defend a particular area against other members of their species. This area probably serves to guarantee them essential __________ and is called a __________. resources, territory

51. A person walks up to a stranger, approaching her until their bodies are just inches apart. This can be considered a violation of __________ __________. personal space

52. In humans, aggression is not only physical, but also __________. symbolic

53. Aggression seems to be more likely in persons with high __________-__________. self-esteem

54. Personality traits associated with increased aggression include __________ __________ and __________. sensation seeking impulsivity

55. Aggression occurs at different levels and in different contexts, depending on the __________. culture

56. Many but not all investigators believe that violence portrayed in __________ encourages actual violence in individuals. the media (television)

57. The problem in determining causality is partly that a correlation between TV and actual violence can result from violence on TV causing violence or from people who are already more __________ preferring to watch violence on TV. violent

58. Aggression is limited in animals and humans by a number of mechanisms, including __________ hierarchies, __________ gestures, and withdrawal from conflict by one party after its assessment that it is __________ than its adversary(ies). dominance, appeasement, weaker

SEX

59. Except for primates, mammals mate only when the female is in heat, or __________. estrus

60. The most important hormones involved in the mammalian female reproductive cycle are __________ and __________. estrogen, progesterone

61. The principal mammalian male sex hormone is __________. testosterone

62. In most adult mammals, removal of the ovaries or testes produces a major decline in sexual behavior, but this can be reversed by injection or implantation of the appropriate sex __________. hormones

63. Although the biological aspects of the human female reproductive cycle are controlled by hormones, in the human female, __________ __________ is relatively independent of hormones. sexual activity (sexual behavior)

64. __________ __________ examines the influence of the evolutionary history of humans and mammals on human sexual behavior and other human behaviors. Evolutionary psychology

65. Perhaps the most important initial feature that attracts one potential human mate to another is __________ __________. physical attractiveness

66. People tend to believe that good traits go together, so physically attractive people are thought to be, for example, more intelligent. This is called the __________ __________. halo effect

67. It is a near universal that physically attractive people are often a little more __________ in the desirable direction than the __________-appearing people of their group. extreme average

68. Some universal features contributing to physical attractiveness in both sexes are __________ and __________. clear skin, symmetry, near-average features (any two)

69. A feature that nearly universally appears to contribute to female attractiveness is a __________ ratio of about 7:10. waist-hip

70. Some of the universal features of physical attractiveness may be adaptive because they are predictive of __________ or __________. health, fertility (reproductive success)

71. People tend to link up with and mate with others who are at about the same level of physical attractiveness. This is called the __________ __________. matching hypothesis

72. In most species, the __________ (male or female) has the major role in deciding whether to mate. female

73. In mammals, birds, and some other groups, the female is usually more selective in mating because the __________ of mating are greater for the female. costs

74. Because of differences in offspring investment, in humans, females emphasize __________ in selecting mates more than males do, and males emphasize __________ and __________ more than females do. status (socioeconomic level, wealth, loyalty), youth, physical attractiveness

75. The optimal male mating strategy, from an evolutionary point of view, is to mate with __________ partners. many

76. Because of limitations on her opportunities to produce offspring, the human female will typically value __________ in a relationship more than the human male will. commitment

77. There is evidence that human males and females think differently about __________, and hence that their jealousy is different. infidelity

78. In some situations, human females are more jealous about __________ infidelity, and males are more jealous about __________ infidelity. emotional sexual

Self-Test

1. The biological science perspective in psychology is particularly appropriate for the study of which aspects of human function?
   a. Sports
   b. Eating
   c. Sex and reproduction
   d. b and c
   e. All of the above

2. In order for Darwinian evolution to occur, it is necessary to have
   a. variation on some relevant characteristic.
   b. a difference in survival value among the variants.
   c. a wide selection of natural products.
   d. a and b
   e. all of the above.

3. DNA is to genes as
   a. sodium chloride is to table salt.
   b. chromosomes are to genes.
   c. sex is to reproduction.
   d. natural selection is to variation.
   e. b and d

4. The ability to taste a certain chemical called PTC is genetically determined and is controlled by a single pair of genes. All children of nontasters are nontasters, but some of the children with two taster parents are also nontasters. This suggests that the gene that codes for tasting is
   a. polygenic.
   b. on at least four chromosomes.
   c. dominant.
   d. recessive.
   e. genomic.

5. Phenotype is to genotype as
   a. building is to building plan.
   b. maturation is to motor development.
   c. recessive is to dominant.
   d. chromosome is to gene.
   e. embryo is to fetus.

6. Cynthia raccoon lives a long life, and has 8 baby raccoons. These have altogether 12 raccoon children (Cynthia's grandchildren). Emily raccoon does not live as long as Cynthia, and has 7 baby raccoons. These 7 have 14 raccoon children (Emily's grandchildren). We can say that __________ has more personal survival and that __________ has more genetic survival.
   a. Cynthia, Cynthia
   b. Cynthia, Emily
   c. Emily, Cynthia
   d. Emily, Emily
   e. Not enough information is provided to make these classifications.

7. The period in which many distinctively human characteristics evolved is
   a. the last 10,000 years.
   b. the Pleistocene epoch.
   c. more than 3 million years ago.
   d. spread more or less evenly across the last 3 million years.
   e. b and c

8. An investigator claims that a particular human behavior, nail biting when tense, has a genetic-evolutionary basis. Which of the following hypothetical observations would be evidence for this claim?
   a. Nail biting only exists in humans.
   b. Identical twins are more likely to both be nail-biters than nonidentical twins.
   c. Nail biting under tense conditions is seen in some nonhuman primates.
   d. a and b
   e. b and c

9. The constancy of the internal environment is maintained by
   a. negative feedback.
   b. Claude Bernard.
   c. identical twins.
   d. the sympathetic nervous system.
   e. none of the above.

10. The sympathetic and parasympathetic branches of the autonomic nervous system
    a. both work in the same direction.
    b. are both parts of the autonomic nervous system.
    c. work reciprocally.
    d. a and b
    e. b and c

11. The sympathetic branch of the autonomic nervous system is responsible for
    a. decreased heart rate.
    b. vasoconstriction in most blood vessels.
    c. vegetative functions, such as digestion.
    d. emptying of the colon and bladder.
    e. none of the above.

12. A rat's hypothalamus is cooled, and it shows vasoconstriction of blood vessels that serve the skin. This illustrates
    a. activation of the sympathetic branch of the autonomic nervous system.
    b. that directly manipulating hypothalamic temperature can cause an animal to make a response that is inappropriate to its actual body temperature.
    c. activation of both branches of the autonomic nervous system.
    d. an effect of the hypothalamus on smooth muscles.
    e. all of the above except c.

13. When its body temperature drops, a particular animal species shows shivering and vasoconstriction. These responses suggest that the animals in this species
    a. are endotherms.
    b. are ectotherms.
    c. have a hypothalamus.
    d. show temperature regulation or homeostasis.
    e. a and d

14. When rats are given a great deal of exercise, their intake of food increases; that is, they eat a larger amount of food. Rats also decrease their intake of a food if it is enriched so that it contains more calories per gram. These findings suggest that
   a. stomach fullness must be critical in regulating the rat's food intake.
   b. the rat is regulating the volume of food consumed.
   c. the rat is regulating the caloric or energy value of the food consumed.
   d. all of the above.
   e. a and c

15. The fact that rats, humans, and other animals maintain their weight rather constantly over long periods, and return to this weight when forced to depart from it by food restriction or overfeeding, suggests that
   a. the hypothalamus plays a major role in food intake regulation.
   b. neuropeptide Y is a major stimulant of eating.
   c. there are many influences, both internal and external, on food intake.
   d. there is a weight set point.
   e. the liver plays a central role in food intake control.

16. Leptin and blood glucose have in common that
   a. they are both produced by the liver.
   b. they can both be converted to glycogen.
   c. when levels are high in the blood, they promote satiety.
   d. all of the above.
   e. a and b

17. Initiation of eating is most likely to be associated with
   a. high blood glucose.
   b. excitation of the ventromedial hypothalamus.
   c. inhibition of the lateral hypothalamus.
   d. high liver glycogen.
   e. a compensatory increase in glucose production by the liver.

18. Which of the following statements best summarizes the way that internal and external signals influence food intake?
   a. Signals from various internal structures (brain receptors, liver, etc.) determine the amount eaten; external factors have almost no effect.
   b. Metabolic information from receptors in the brain controls about half of food intake, and external stimulation the other half.
   c. Metabolic information from receptors in the liver, brain, and possibly other locations interacts with external stimulation to determine the amount eaten.
   d. Internal signals determine levels of leptin and glucose; external signals determine levels of glycogen.
   e. Hypothalamic receptors for internal and external events have a dual role in maintaining caloric intake.

19. Which of the following assumptions or predictions does the dual-center theory *not* make?
   a. The liver is the primary source of information concerning the metabolic state of the organism.
   b. Activation of the lateral hypothalamus should produce eating.
   c. The two hypothalamic feeding centers perform opposite functions.
   d. Damage to the "on" center should produce reduced eating.
   e. Damage to the "off" center should produce overeating.

20. Evidence suggests that hypothalamic control of eating operates
   a. partly by stimulating or inhibiting eating directly.
   b. partly by control of metabolism.
   c. by producing NPY in the hypothalamus.
   d. only in response to signals from the liver.
   e. a and b

21. Two rats (or people) differ greatly in weight and fatness, but each of them holds its weight rather constant over a period of months. This suggests that the two differ in
   a. set point.
   b. stomach size.
   c. the amount of NPY in the hypothalamus.
   d. the ability to regulate food intake.
   e. the size of the hypothalamus.

22. A person who is 2 meters tall and weighs 100 kilograms would have a body mass index of
   a. 20.
   b. 21.
   c. 22.
   d. 25.
   e. 30.

23. Which one of the following is a very *unlikely* cause of obesity in humans?
   a. Damage to the lateral region of the hypothalamus
   b. High digestive efficiency
   c. A high set point
   d. Genetic predisposition
   e. Insensitivity to leptin

24. Which of the following findings supports a set point account of obesity?
   a. Obese people eat relatively more of highly palatable foods.
   b. Obese people tend to maintain a steady weight.
   c. Obese individuals who lose weight on diets tend to return to their previous obese weight.
   d. b and c
   e. All of the above.

25. Which of the following suggests an important environmental contribution to obesity?
   a. Anorexia nervosa exists.
   b. BMI is more similar in identical than fraternal twins.
   c. Even obese individuals tend to remain at a stable weight.
   d. Obesity levels have been increasing markedly in recent decades.
   e. Leptin insensitivity may be a cause of obesity.

26. The sympathetic branch of the autonomic nervous system is responsible for
   a. decreased heart rate.
   b. increased blood flow to the muscles.
   c. increased digestive activity.
   d. b and c
   e. none of the above.

27. Which of the following is *not* associated with activity of the sympathetic system?
    a. The emergency reaction
    b. Increased blood flow to the muscles
    c. Secretion of adrenaline by the adrenal medulla
    d. Increased heart rate
    e. Secretion of digestive enzymes

28. Short-term activation of the sympathetic branch of the autonomic nervous system can mobilize for __________, but long-term activation may lead to __________ effects.
    a. emergencies, emergency
    b. immunity, activity
    c. action, disruptive
    d. disruption, disruptive
    e. action, immune

29. Aggression is increased in most mammals by
    a. higher levels of testosterone.
    b. parasympathetic activation.
    c. lower levels of adrenaline.
    d. a and b
    e. a and c

30. Aggressive encounters between members of the same species are often concerned with the establishment of
    a. distributed testosterone levels.
    b. territories.
    c. predation.
    d. appropriate defense mechanisms.
    e. a and c

31. The adaptive value of territories is that they
    a. increase the aggressiveness of the territory holder.
    b. provide resources for the territory holder.
    c. prevent threat displays.
    d. decrease personal space and allow for greater reproduction.
    e. c and d

32. Human territories
    a. have a biological basis.
    b. are transformed and elaborated by cultures.
    c. must be distinguished from personal space.
    d. a and b
    e. b and c

33. Human aggression
    a. is often verbal.
    b. is often symbolic.
    c. is culturally channeled, as in the culture of honor.
    d. may be physical.
    e. all of the above.

34. Human aggression can be promoted by
    a. high self-esteem.
    b. sensation seeking.
    c. impulsivity.
    d. certain cultures.
    e. all of the above.

35. Many studies on TV violence and actual violence report that they are positively correlated. From this we can conclude that
    a. TV violence almost always causes actual violence.
    b. people who are actually violent prefer to watch violence on TV.
    c. human aggression is entirely generated by culture.
    d. b and c
    e. none of the above.

36. Which of the following does *not* serve as a mode of limiting aggressive interactions in humans or animals?
    a. The development of morality and legal systems
    b. Dominance hierarchies
    c. Appeasement gestures
    d. High self-esteem
    e. b and d

37. During estrus, the female (nonprimate) mammal is
    a. secreting estrogen.
    b. most receptive to sexual approach of males.
    c. fertile.
    d. all of the above.
    e. none of the above.

38. In some species in which the female has a clearly defined estrus cycle, the male is always ready for sexual activity. This would make sense if in these species,
    a. all females came into estrus at the same time.
    b. estrus were dependent on the season.
    c. estrus occured throughout the year and females were not synchronized in their cycles.
    d. hormonal factors were especially important in determining the receptivity of the female.
    e. a and b

39. Unlike most other mammals, for humans
    a. hormones have no effect on sexual behavior.
    b. hormones have effects on only male sexual behavior.
    c. sexual receptivity in females is relatively independent of the fertile period in the sexual cycle.
    d. sex is a social activity.
    e. b and c

40. A feature(s) that contribute to physical attractiveness more or less universally in humans include(s)
    a. clear skin.
    b. symmetrical face.
    c. small nose.
    d. long hair.
    e. a and b

41. Which of the following statements about the waist-hip ratio is *false?*
    a. It is a critical factor in selection of males as well as females.
    b. For females, in most cultures, the ideal is about 7:10.
    c. There are some cultures in which the ratio is quite different from that in others.
    d. A larger hip than waist is indicative of fertility, in terms of a mature pelvis.
    e. A ratio less than 1 indicates a desirable amount of fat stored in the area of the hips.

42. An argument(s) for biological determinants in some features of physical attractiveness in humans is(are)
    a. the matching hypothesis.
    b. the existence of variation in most features.
    c. the universality of attractiveness of some features.
    d. the fact that hair length attractiveness may vary with gender.
    e. a and b

43. In a particular culture, relatively thin males tend to marry relatively plump females. According to the matching hypothesis, this implies that
    a. relative thinness in males is as desired (attractive) as relative plumpness in females is.
    b. physical attractiveness is not important in this culture.
    c. body shape is not important in this culture.
    d. the plumpness and thinness of relatives is important in this culture.
    e. c and d

44. Predictions about male-female differences in mammalian mate selection are based on the fact that female mammals have a greater investment in reproduction because they
    a. carry the offspring during pregnancy.
    b. take the greater responsibility for the early care of infants.
    c. account for a greater part of the genetic material of their offspring.
    d. all of the above.
    e. a and b

45. There is a tendency for human males to seek more variety in mates (male promiscuity) than females. Which of the following is *not* evidence that this difference has a biological basis?
    a. Males have higher economic and social status in almost all cultures.
    b. Male promiscuity appears cross-culturally.
    c. Male promiscuity occurs in most mammalian species.
    d. Male mammals have a lower investment than females in any particular offspring.
    e. Female mammals carry and nurse their young.

46. According to the evolutionary account, a human female is inclined to emphasize financial/social security in selecting a mate because
    a. this improves the prospects for a successful upbringing of her children.
    b. males with higher status are more likely to be fertile.
    c. she is likely to give birth to more children.
    d. males with higher status have higher waist-hip ratios.
    e. b and c

47. In terms of enhancing their ability to pass on their genes, males in most species, including humans, give prime importance in mate selection to
    a. loyalty of the mate.
    b. physical attractiveness of the mate.
    c. youth of the mate.
    d. b and c
    e. a and b

48. In a culture in which male and female opportunities to accumulate wealth and status on their own are about equal, we might expect the biggest reduction in male-female mating strategy differences in the area of:
    a. desire for physical attractiveness.
    b. importance of commitment in a mate.
    c. importance of youth in a mate.
    d. variety seeking in males.
    e. none of the above.

49. An evolutionary perspective predicts that males should be more concerned about infidelity involving the female mate's having intercourse with other males, whereas females should be more concerned about their mate's emotional commitment to another female. Evidence so far suggests that
    a. in many cases, this is true.
    b. usually both sexes are more concerned about intercourse than emotional attachments.
    c. this is the case for how people think about infidelity, but less so about how they actually behave and feel in real infidelity situations.
    d. b and c
    e. a and c

50. Overall, whether thinking about eating, aggression, or sex, it is fair to say that
    a. biological/evolutionary factors are the main accounts of human function.
    b. cultural/environmental factors are the main accounts of human function.
    c. both biological and evolutionary factors are very important, and the degree of importance depends to some degree on the culture in question.
    d. the effects of evolutionary factors are more important for eating and least important for sex.
    e. there are important biological/evolutionary effects, but cultural/environmental forces can erase any of them.

Answer Key for Self-Test

1. d
2. d
3. a
4. c
5. a
6. b
7. b
8. e
9. a
10. e
11. b
12. e
13. e
14. c
15. d
16. c
17. e
18. c
19. a
20. e
21. a
22. d
23. a
24. d
25. d
26. b
27. e
28. c
29. a
30. b
31. b
32. d
33. e
34. e

35. e
36. d
37. d
38. c
39. c
40. e
41. a
42. c
43. a
44. e
45. a
46. a
47. d
48. b
49. e
50. c

Investigating Psychological Phenomena

EFFECTS OF MENTAL PROCESSES ON AUTONOMIC ACTIVITY

Equipment: Stopwatch or with swatchecond indicator
Number of participants: Three
Time per participant: Ten minutes
Time for experimenter: Forty minutes

As part of its role in the control of bodily functions, the autonomic nervous system (ANS) controls heart rate. In this way it can influence the rate of delivery of oxygen and nutrients to the cells of the body. In times when the body is stressed, increased heart rate (and other changes) increases the delivery of nutrients to cells, as well as increasing the rate of disposal of waste products. The changes in heart rate are produced directly by nerve impulses sent to the heart. They are also produced indirectly by stimulation, through autonomic pathways, of the release of epinephrine (adrenaline) and related substances from the adrenal glands.

Arousal of the sympathetic system, and hence increased heart rate, occurs when the organism is undergoing physical exertion. But it can also be produced by mental events. Such a pathway would allow an organism to mobilize its physiological resources in anticipation of a physical stress. On the other hand, it also allows for high and ultimately damaging levels of sympathetic arousal based on chronic anxiety or mental tension.

In this study we will demonstrate the effectiveness of the sympathetic nervous system link between mental activity and heart rate. Participants will be asked to increase their heart rate by thinking about either a strenuous physical activity or something that is mentally exciting.

Make sure that your participant is seated comfortably, has been relaxing for at least ten minutes, and did not engage in any strenuous activity in the last half hour. Before reading the instructions make sure you can find the participant's pulse on his or her wrist. The unit of recording for heart rate will be a thirty-second interval. You will record the number of beats every thirty seconds on the data sheet on the next page. Allow fifteen seconds to pass between each thirty-second interval or recording so that you will have enough time to record the pulse and give the instruction. If you have an instruction to give the participant (e.g., "Relax," "Increase mental activity"), give the instruction as soon as you have recorded the pulse rate, but wait the full fifteen seconds before counting heartbeats.

Instructions to read to the participant:

This is a short, ten-minute experiment to determine whether you can control the rate of beating of your heart. When I say "Begin," you should close your eyes and relax while I take your pulse. After a minute I will say "Increase physical activity," and you should try to increase your heart rate by thinking about some physical activity in which you are personally engaged and which requires a lot of exertion. After I record your pulse I will say, "Relax," and you should stop trying to increase your heart rate and relax again. I will take your pulse for another minute and then I will say "Increase mental activity." This time you should try to increase your heart rate by thinking of something that is exciting but that does not involve a lot of physical activity. This could be a fearful experience that you have had, the excitement from watching a sports event, preexamination anxiety, and so on. Following this one-minute episode I will say, "Relax," and you should stop trying to increase your heart rate and relax. I will take your pulse for one final minute. Before you begin the experiment decide on each image you will think about for the physical activity and the mental activity. After you have decided, stop thinking about the images until I give you the instruction during the actual experiment.

Give the participant a few minutes to decide on images and then to stop thinking about them before you begin the experiment. Wait one minute after the participant has selected the two images, to allow any excitation that this may have produced to go away.

DATA FROM THREE PARTICIPANTS (A, B, C)

Instruction and time	A	B	C
"Begin and relax"			
00:00–0:30			
0:45–1:15			
"Increase physical activity"			
1:30–2:00			
2:15–2:45			
"Relax"			
3:00–3:30			
3:45–4:15			
"Increase mental activity"			
4:30–5:00			
5:15–5:45			
"Relax"			
6:00–6:30			
6:45–7:15			

List for each participant the basic situation that he or she imagined in the "increase" minutes.

	Physical	Mental
A	____________	____________
B	____________	____________
C	____________	____________

Plot the data for each participant on the graph below. Use a different symbol for each participant, and connect the symbols for each participant by lines. Since heart rate is usually expressed as beats per minute, double each of the numbers you have recorded (since you recorded beats per thirty seconds) before plotting. We have plotted the results from ten undergraduates (mean). In our study, nine of the ten undergraduates showed the increased heart rate effect.

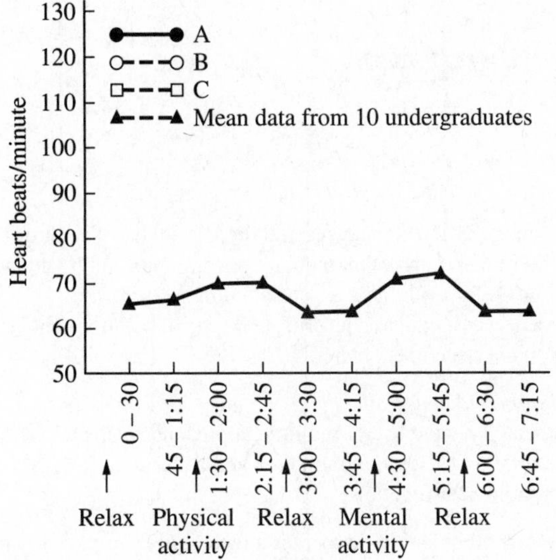

Do all of your participants show an ability to increase heart rate by mental activity? Which procedure, thinking of physical activity or something mentally exciting, is more effective? *(If your instructor collects the data, fill out the report sheet in Appendix 2.)*

FURTHER PROJECTS

Lowering heart rate is much more difficult than raising it. You might see if you can get some participants to do that.

Some people have great difficulty in raising their heart rate. If one of your participants is such a person, you could try to get an increase by having the participant talk about physical activity or something exciting during a one-minute period.

You could also explore whether certain kinds of "exciting thoughts" (e.g., fear, excitement of a spectator at a sports event) are more effective in raising heart rate.

CHAPTER 3

The Brain and the Nervous System

Learning Objectives

THE ORGANISM AS A MACHINE

Descartes and the reflex concept

1. Be familiar with Descartes' conception of the reflex and how it was encouraged by scientific advances in Europe prior to Descartes.
2. Indicate how Descartes integrated the explanation of human choice and values into his mechanical model.

HOW THE NERVOUS SYSTEM IS STUDIED

3. Describe the new discipline of neuroscience and the more traditional disciplines that contribute to it.
4. What is a neuron, and approximately how many are in the human brain? What are glia?

Clinical observation

5. Indicate the advantages and disadvantages of studying the human brain by clinical observations of patients with brain damage.

Neuropsychology

6. Describe how neuropsychology elaborates on clinical observation.

Experimental techniques

7. Describe the advantages and ethical limitations of using invasive techniques to study the human brain.
8. Describe the techniques of lesioning, transection, and transcranial magnetic stimulation and the advantages and limitations of each.

Neuroimaging techniques

9. Understand the mode of operation of the neuroimaging techniques that reveal brain anatomy: CT (CAT) scan and MRI.
10. Understand how neuroimaging instruments can measure brain activity or function by using EEG, PET scan, and fMRI.
11. Explain how neuroscientists measure relative increases in activity and how they use a subtraction technique to obtain this information.
12. Be aware of the advantages and disadvantages of each of the neuroimaging and other techniques for exploring the brain. Evaluate for each the ease of obtaining information, invasiveness, ethical concerns, and type of information (activity, structure) obtained.

Correlation and causation

13. Indicate how the use of multiple approaches helps to clarify the relation between a brain area and a particular psychological function.
14. Describe the double-dissociation technique, and indicate how it helps in the assignment of different functions to different brain areas.

THE ARCHITECTURE OF THE NERVOUS SYSTEM

The central and peripheral nervous systems

15. Be able to distinguish the peripheral and the central nervous systems, and the somatic and autonomic nervous systems.
16. What are efferent and afferent nerves?
17. What are the cranial nerves and how do they differ from the other nerves?
18. Describe the basic anatomy of the brain: What functions do the hindbrain, midbrain, and forebrain serve?
19. Indicate the location within the hindbrain and the function of the medulla, pons, and cerebellum.
20. Explain the nature and functions of the convolutions of the cortex.
21. Describe the anatomy and function of the cerebral cortex, including the major fissures and the four lobes.
22. Review the anatomy and function of subcortical structures, including the thalamus and hypothalamus.
23. What is the location and function of the limbic system? Include a discussion of the location and function of two critical parts of the limbic system, the hippocampus and amygdala.
24. Explain the meaning of lateralization.
25. What is the corpus callosum?

26. What are split-brain patients, and what is the function of the corpus callosum?

27. What do we know about the differences between the left and right hemispheres in the types of psychological processes they carry out?

28. How have these ideas been exaggerated or distorted in the popular press?

THE CORTEX

29. Know the structure of the cerebral cortex, including the four lobes.

Localization of function

30. Explain localization of function.

31. Indicate the problems of inferring that function X is localized in area Y from the observation that a destruction of area Y produces a deficit in function X.

Projection areas

32. Indicate the major projection areas of the brain.

33. Describe the function of projection areas of the brain, and indicate what determines how much space in these areas is devoted to different parts of the body.

34. What do contralateral control and contralateral projection mean?

35. Explain the principle of topographic organization in the primary motor and sensory projection areas.

36. Describe the somatosensory projection area.

37. Indicate the lobe in which each of the motor, somatosensory, and visual projection areas resides.

38. What are nonprimary (association) areas?

The results of cortical damage

39. What are apraxia, agnosia, and prosopagnosia? What brain areas are associated with each of these disorders?

40. What are the symptoms of the neglect syndrome? What part of the brain is usually damaged in such cases?

41. Distinguish fluent and nonfluent aphasias in terms of the site of brain damage and the type of symptoms. Indicate problems with this distinction.

42. Describe some of the symptoms of prefrontal lobe damage.

ORIGINS OF THE NERVOUS SYSTEM

The evolution of nervous systems

43. Distinguish between ganglia and brains.

44. Describe the tendency toward increasing centralization in the evolution of the nervous system.

Phylogeny and ontogeny: The developing nervous system

45. Explain the basic process and stages of development of the nervous system.

46. Outline how the circuitry of the nervous system is established, including the role of a protomap and neuron death.

BUILDING BLOCKS OF THE NERVOUS SYSTEM

The neuron

47. What is a neuron? What are dendrites, the axon, the myelin sheath, and the nodes of Ranvier?

48. What purposes do the sensory neurons, motoneurons, and interneurons serve?

Glia

49. Describe the nature and function of glial cells.

COMMUNICATION AMONG NEURONS

The electrical activity of the neuron: Resting potential, excitation threshold, action potential

50. Be able to describe the electrical activity of the neuron: Know the difference between resting potential and action potential.

51. Describe the events involved in the reversal of membrane polarization.

52. How is the nerve impulse propagated? What is the role of myelin?

53. What is the all-or-none law?

54. What effect does stimulus intensity have on the number of neurons stimulated and on the frequency of impulses?

The synapse

55. How did Sherrington infer the existence of the synapse?

56. Describe spatial and temporal summation and reciprocal inhibition.

The synaptic mechanism

57. Know the anatomy of the synapse (pre- and postsynaptic neurons and membranes, synaptic gaps, synaptic vesicles, and neurotransmitters) and the way that neural excitation (the nerve impulse) is transmitted across the synapse.

58. Be able to explain how inhibition and excitation occur at synapses, and how the postsynaptic neuron integrates the various inhibitory and excitatory effects on it. Describe synaptic reuptake.

59. What are the basic differences between action potentials and synaptic transmission?

60. What is a neurotransmitter? Give some examples.

61. What is the lock-and-key model?

62. Distinguish primary and secondary messengers in neural function.

63. What are the effects of some major neurotransmitters (acetylcholine, serotonin, dopamine, and norepinephrine)?

64. What are drugs called agonists and antagonists, and what are the different ways in which they can exert their effects?

INTERACTIONS THROUGH THE BLOODSTREAM

Blood circulation

65. Describe the circulation of blood to the brain, and the blood-brain barrier.

The endocrine system

66. Explain the mode of action of the endocrine system, and know the similarities and differences among the types of interactions and transmissions in the nervous and endocrine systems.

RECOVERY FROM BRAIN INJURY

67. Indicate some of the general determinants of whether and how much recovery of function occurs.

Finding alternative strategies

68. Explain cognitive rehabilitation.

Neural substitution of function

69. Give examples from aphasia and the split brain about how intact areas take over the function of damaged areas.

Replacing connections

70. Describe collateral sprouting and the role of neurotrophic factors, such as nerve growth factors.

71. Describe the nature and course of Alzheimer's disease and its potential treatment with nerve grafts.

72. Indicate the potential of neural stem-cell grafts, and recent progress in dealing with spinal cord injury.

Programmed Exercises

THE ORGANISM AS A MACHINE

1. The conception of organisms as machines can be traced to the great French philosopher __________. — Descartes

2. According to Descartes, excitation from the senses leads to muscle contraction in what we now call a __________. — reflex

3. Descartes attributed the choices made by humans, and their values, not to reflexes but to the __________. — soul

HOW THE NERVOUS SYSTEM IS STUDIED

4. The new discipline that is devoted to the study of the nervous system is called __________. — neuroscience

5. The individual nerve cells that collectively make up the nervous system are called __________. — neurons

6. The other basic cells in the nervous system, more common than neurons, are called __________. — glia

7. In the method of __________ __________, the symptoms of individual patients with brain damage are assessed. — clinical observation

8. In __________, experimental techniques and brain imaging techniques are added to clinical observation. — neuropsychology

9. __________ techniques involve stimulating or deactivating parts of the nervous system. — Invasive

10. Nervous tissue is damaged in a local area with the techniques of __________ and __________. — lesioning, transection

11. Brain tissue near the scalp can be temporarily deactivated with brief magnetic pulses, in the technique of __________ __________ __________. — transcranial magnetic stimulation (TMS)

12. The two principal ways of imaging the structure (anatomy) of the human brain are __________ __________ and __________. — CT (CAT) scan, MRI

13. Brain electrical activity is measured directly with the __________. — electroencephalogram (EEG)

14. Brain activity can be measured by rate of uptake of different brain areas of a radioactive substance using the __________ scan. — PET

15. A less invasive technique measures metabolic activity in the brain revealed by exposing the brain to a very strong magnetic field. This technique is called __________. — fMRI

16. Using a PET scan or fMRI, we can obtain a measure of what brain areas are changing in activity by __________ an image of the brain at rest from an image of the brain engaged in a particular task of interest. — subtracting

17. To clarify the functions of different brain areas, it is useful to use __________ techniques. — multiple

18. The technique of __________ __________ helps to establish that two different brain areas or circuits correspond to two different processes or functions. — double dissociation

THE ARCHITECTURE OF THE NERVOUS SYSTEM

19. The brain and spinal cord together make up the __________ __________ __________.

central nervous system

20. __________ nerves transmit information from sense organs to the central nervous system.

Afferent

21. __________ nerves transmit information from the central nervous system to the muscles and glands.

Efferent

22. __________ nerves connect the brain and the periphery.

Cranial

23. The afferent and efferent nerves and the cranial nerves are all part of the __________ nervous system.

peripheral

24. The peripheral nervous system has two parts, the __________ and the __________ nervous systems.

somatic, autonomic

25. The three basic divisions of the brain, from bottom to top, are the __________, __________, and __________.

hindbrain, midbrain forebrain

26. The portion of the hindbrain concerned with controlling some critical body processes, such as respiration and heartbeat, is called the __________.

medulla

27. The part of the hindbrain that is above the medulla and is involved in the control of attentiveness is called the __________.

pons

28. The portion of the hindbrain that controls bodily balance and motor coordination is called the __________.

cerebellum

29. The brain area that serves as a relay station between hindbrain and forebrain and carries out many functions, including some aspects of motor coordination, is called the __________.

midbrain

30. The convoluted outer surface of the forebrain is called the cerebral __________.

cortex

31. The __________ fissure divides the brain into two halves, the __________ and __________ cerebral hemispheres.

longitudinal, left right

32. Label the four major lobes of the human cerebral cortex.

A. __________ C. __________

B. __________ D. __________

A. Frontal

B. Parietal

C. Occipital

D. Temporal

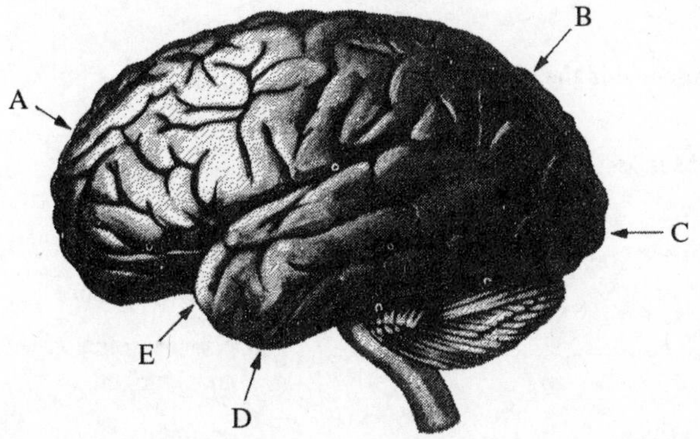

33. The separation between the frontal and temporal lobes labeled E in the figure above is called the __________ __________.

lateral fissure

34. Subcortical structures include the __________, the __________, and the __________ system.

thalamus, hypothalamus limbic

35. The __________ is a part of the forebrain involved in the control of behavior patterns that stem from basic biological urges such as hunger.

hypothalamus

36. An older portion of the cerebral hemispheres with particular importance in the mediation of emotion, learning, and memory is called the __________ system.

limbic

37. Two important parts of the limbic system that are involved in emotion, learning, and memory are the __________ and __________.

hippocampus, amygdala

38. Label the following structures on the sketch of the human brain.

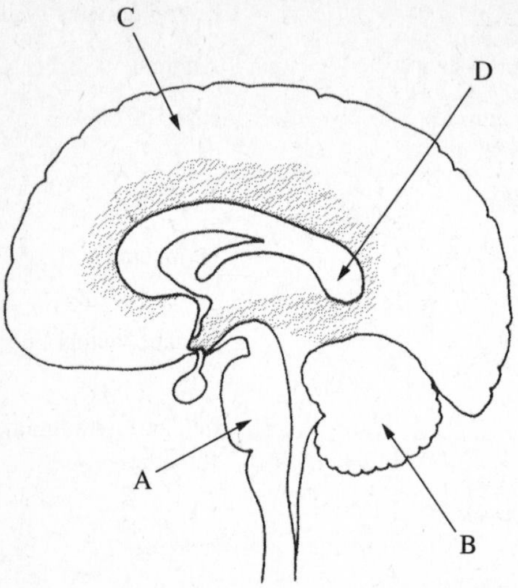

C D A B

A. __________ A. Hindbrain (medulla)

B. __________ B. Cerebellum

C. __________ __________ C. Cerebral cortex

D. __________ __________ D. Corpus callosum

39. The asymmetry of function in the human cerebral cortex is described as __________. lateralization

40. The __________ __________ is the major commissure that connects to the two cerebral hemispheres. corpus callosum

41. A right-handed split-brain patient would probably not be able to name a common object placed in his or her __________ hand. left

42. There is evidence that in most individuals, the left hemisphere specializes in __________ functions, and the right hemisphere in __________ functions. language (verbal) spatial

43. The idea and demonstration that different parts of the brain have different functions is called __________ of function. localization

44. If a function is localized in brain area A, then __________ to that area should compromise that function and __________ of that area should increase expression of that function. damage stimulation (activation)

45. Sensory information and motor control for one side of the body is on the opposite side of the brain. This is called __________ projection. contralateral

46. The control of body movement as represented in the cortex is represented in the __________ __________ area, located in the ________ lobe. primary motor, frontal

47. In humans, the greatest amount of cortical space for motor functions is assigned to the __________ and the __________. fingers, tongue

48. In the cortex, mapping of the body surface and the input from the sense organs in the head is established in the __________ __________ areas. primary sensory

49. Each portion of the body surface is represented in the __________ __________ __________, located primarily in the __________ lobe. primary somatosensory area, parietal

50. The projection of the visual area from the eyes is in the __________ lobe. occipital

51. The portions of the cerebral cortex that are part of neither the primary motor nor the primary sensory areas are described as the __________ or __________ areas. nonprimary, association

52. __________ is a serious disturbance in the organization of voluntary action. Apraxia

53. A disorganization of aspects of the sensory world, without loss of basic sensory capacities, is termed __________. When this type of disorder primarily involves a deficit in face recognition, it is called __________. agnosia prosopagnosia

54. A disorder of attention in which a patient ignores one side of his or her world and body is called the __________ __________. neglect syndrome

55. A patient with a primary disorder in the expression of speech can be described as suffering from language apraxia or a __________ __________. This disorder is commonly caused by lesions in __________ area in the __________ __________ lobe. nonfluent aphasia Broca's, left frontal

56. In right-handed persons, aphasia usually results from lesions in the __________ hemisphere.

left

57. A language defect reflected primarily by an inability to comprehend language, or a language agnosia, is described as a __________ __________. The lesions responsible for this disorder commonly occur in __________ area, located in the __________ __________ lobe.

fluent aphasia
Wernicke's, left
temporal

58. Difficulty in applying strategies, lack of spontaneity, and deficits in response inhibition characterize patients with damage in the __________ area.

prefrontal

THE ORIGINS OF THE BRAIN

59. Early in evolutionary history, the cell bodies of many interneurons began to clump together to form __________. This is an early stage in the evolution of __________.

ganglia, centralization
(the brain)

60. The production of a nervous system by processes of cellular signaling, differentiation, migration, and proliferation is called __________.

neurogenesis

57. The development of the vertebrate nervous system proceeds from neural __________ to neural __________.

plate
tube

61. Processes that help to establish the complex circuitry of the brain in development include a genetically programmed __________ and selective cell __________ following inappropriate connections.

protomap, death

BUILDING BLOCKS OF THE NERVOUS SYSTEM: NEURONS AND NERVE IMPULSES

62. The basic building block of the nervous system is the nerve cell, or __________.

neuron

63. The basic unit of nervous function is the __________ __________.

nerve impulse

64. Label the following diagram of the neuron.

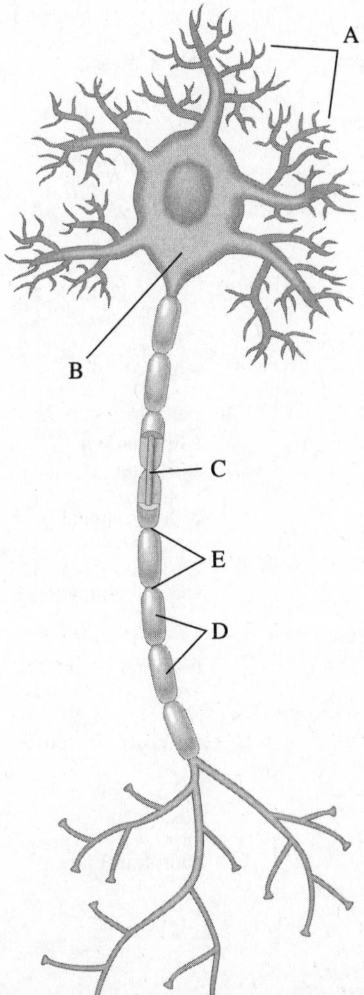

A. __________ dendrites

B. __________ cell body

C. __________ axon

D. __________ __________ myelin sheath

E. __________ __________ __________ nodes of Ranvier

65. Receptor cells __________ stimulus energy into nerve impulses. transduce

66. The axons of __________ __________ terminate in effector cells and activate the skeletal __________. motor neurons musculature (muscles)

67. In complex organisms, the vast majority of neurons are neither sensory nor motor neurons, but rather __________. Their connections form the __________ of the central nervous system. interneurons microcircuitry

68. The very numerous nervous system cells that form a scaffold for the system and constitute the __________ sheath are called __________ cells. myelin, glial

69. The parts of the brain containing many myelinated axons are called __________ matter. The rest is called __________ matter. white grey

70. The fine wire or tube that allows investigators to record electrical activity in neurons is called a(n) __________. microelectrode

71. The __________ __________ of the neuron is about –70 millivolts. resting potential

72. The reversal of polarization that passes along a nerve fiber when it is stimulated is called the __________ __________. action potential

73. When the nerve cell membrane is depolarized past its __________ __________ by a(n) __________ stimulus, a(n) __________ __________ results. excitation threshold adequate, action potential

74. Ion __________ and ion __________ maintain the resting potential. The opening of the __________ is responsible for the sharp voltage change called the action potential. pumps, channels channels

75. The __________ speed of the nerve impulse would be relatively slow, except that __________ wrapped around the neuron allows the impulse to jump from one node of __________ to another. propagation, myelin Ranvier

76. The disease __________ __________ involves the deterioration of the myelin surrounding neurons. multiple sclerosis

77. The __________ law states that the size of the action potential and its speed are independent of the intensity of the stimulus, provided the stimulus is above threshold intensity. all-or-none

78. The above-mentioned law does not apply to the stimulation of nerves since there is much variation in the __________ of the neurons in the nerve. thresholds

79. Stimulus __________ is conveyed both by increases in the number of neurons firing and by increases in individual neurons' __________ of firing. intensity frequency

INTERACTION AMONG NERVE CELLS

80. The gap between the axon terminals of one neuron and the dendritic processes of another is called the __________. synapse

81. The existence of the synapse was inferred from evidence at the level of __________ by the great English physiologist __________. behavior (Sir Charles) Sherrington

82. Sherrington studied simple __________ in the __________ animal. reflexes, spinal

83. Subthreshold stimulation at two adjacent points, when applied simultaneously, may lead to a response. This illustrates the phenomenon of __________ __________. spatial summation

84. Subthreshold stimulation, when applied a few times in rapid succession, may lead to a response. This illustrates the phenomenon of __________ __________. temporal summation

85. Sherrington observed that when a flexor muscle contracts, the corresponding extensor muscle relaxes. This is an example of __________ __________. reciprocal inhibition

86. Electrical activity is transmitted across the synapse by neurotransmitters, from the __________ neuron to the __________ neuron. presynaptic postsynaptic

87. The synaptic vesicles contain chemical substances called __________. neurotransmitters

88. Place the following labels on the diagram of a synapse below.

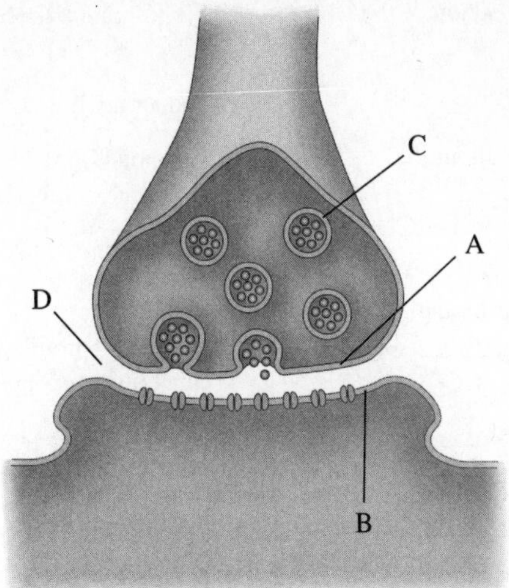

A. presynaptic membrane
B. postsynaptic membrane
C. synaptic vesicle
D. synaptic gap (or synapse)

89. According to Sherrington, temporal summation occurs because of integration at the __________, which is accomplished by the storage of excitation from previous stimulation.

synapse

90. Whether a neuron fires is determined by the net result of its integration of __________ and __________ stimulation.

excitatory
inhibitory

91. The activity of the postsynaptic neuron results from the summation of __________ and __________ postsynaptic potentials. These are produced by __________ released by the presynaptic neuron.

excitatory
inhibitory,
neurotransmitters

92. While action potentials are all-or-none, synaptic potentials are __________.

graded

93. Inhibitory neurotransmitters __________ the nerve's resting potential, whereas excitatory neurotransmitters __________ it.

increase
decrease

94. Excitatory neurotransmitters open __________ channels in the postsynaptic membrane.

ion (sodium)

95. Neurotransmitters are eventually removed from the synaptic gap by deactivation or by __________ __________.

synaptic reuptake

96. The idea that neurotransmitters affect only the postsynaptic membrane if their shape fits the shape of certain receptor sites on that membrane is called the __________-__________-__________ model.

lock-and-
key

97. Acetylcholine, dopamine, serotonin, and norepinephrine are all __________.

neurotransmitters

98. Neurotransmitters secreted by the presynaptic cell are called __________ messengers. Chemical processes in the postsynaptic cell that regulate its sensitivity are called __________ messengers.

primary
secondary

99. There is evidence that some neurons interact more directly than through neurotransmitters, by transmission across very narrow __________ synapses.

electrical

100. Drugs that enhance a transmitter's activity are called __________. Drugs that impede a transmitter's activity are called __________.

agonists
antagonists

101. Some drugs enhance synaptic function by interfering with __________ by the presynaptic cell. Some drugs act by altering the levels of substances called __________, which are required for the synthesis of particular neurotransmitters.

reuptake
precursors

102. Drugs of "abuse" may act by their involvement with brain neurotransmitter systems. Thus, heroin is an agonist for the brain __________ system, and marijuana activates __________ receptors.

endorphin
cannabinoid

INTERACTIONS THROUGH THE BLOODSTREAM

103. The brain gets special protection from potential toxins in the blood through the action of the __________-__________ __________. blood-brain barrier

104. The __________ glands secrete __________ into the bloodstream. endocrine, hormones

105. __________ are chemical messengers that are distributed indiscriminately throughout the body, whereas __________ exert their effects in a very limited area. Hormones neurotransmitters

RECOVERY FROM BRAIN INJURY

106. Recovery, within the nervous system, from loss of cerebral nerve cells can occur by the processes of __________ __________, recovery of damaged neurons, and __________ __________ __________. collateral sprouting, substitution of function

107. The brain's capacity to recover, generally greater in younger people, is called its __________. plasticity

108. Three new methods for producing repair in the damaged nervous system are __________ __________, administration of __________ factors, and injection of neural __________ cells. fetal transplants, neurotrophic, stem

109. Three modes of recovery from cerebral brain damage are __________, __________, and __________. finding alternative strategies (cognitive rehabilitation), neural substitution of functions, replacing connections (neurons)

110. A rather common disease of the elderly involving a general decline in intellectual functioning is __________ disease. One of the pathological features of brain anatomy in patients with this disease is __________ __________. Alzheimer's neurofibrillary tangles (amyloid plaques)

111. Brain __________ involving fetal brain tissue of rats have had some success and hold the promise of replacing cells lost in disease. transplants

Self-Test

1. Which of the following commonly observed characteristics of human or animal behavior goes counter to Descartes' reflex notion?
   a. The withdrawal response on touching a hot object
   b. The appearance of a behavior (e.g., running) in the absence of any obvious stimulus
   c. The existence of nerves connecting receptors and effectors to the brain
   d. The repeatability of reflexes
   e. None of the above

2. By viewing animal behavior as the result of a machine's responding to external stimuli, Descartes made the claim that
   a. animal behavior is governed by physical laws and is therefore predictable.
   b. animal behavior can be understood only in terms of the hierarchical organization of the nervous system.
   c. animals must have rich mental lives.
   d. neither humans nor animals have free will.
   e. introductory psychology is *the* fundamental science.

3. The nervous system is made up of
   a. hormones.
   b. computers.
   c. glia.
   d. neurons.
   e. c and d

4. Clinical observation has the following advantage over other techniques for investigating the human brain:
   a. It is replicable.
   b. It can measure the activity of the brain.
   c. It can control precisely the area of the brain that is damaged.
   d. It allows for detailed analysis of symptoms produced by specific brain damage in an individual.
   e. It is more invasive.

5. Which of the following brain exploration techniques can be described as destroying nervous tissue?
   a. Transection
   b. TMS
   c. MRI
   d. EEG
   e. CT (CAT) scan

6. In terms of providing information about structure versus activity, EEG is to CAT scan as
   a. PET scan is to fMRI.
   b. EEG is to PET scan.
   c. lesioning is to MRI.

d. transection is to PET scan.
e. fMRI is to MRI.

7. Which of the following procedures would you most prefer to experience, assuming your brain was normal and your aim was to keep it that way?
   a. Transection
   b. Lesioning
   c. EEG
   d. PET scan
   e. c or d

8. Assume a patient is suspected of having brain seizures (uncontrollable activity in some part of the brain). Which brain exploration technique(s) would be most likely to reveal the affected brain area?
   a. EEG
   b. CAT scan
   c. fMRI
   d. a and b
   e. a and c

9. Which of the following findings would suggest that area X of the brain performs function or process Y?
   a. When there is a lesion in X, there is a deficit in function Y.
   b. When there is a lesion in X, there is an improved function in Y.
   c. When area X is stimulated, there is a greater presence of function.
   d. An MRI shows that area X is well defined in the brain.
   e. a and c

10. Stimulation of area A in the brain is followed by an increase in behavior X but not in behavior Y, and stimulation of area B in the brain is followed by an increase in behavior Y but not in behavior X. This pattern of results
   a. suggests that areas A and B are closely connected in brain anatomy.
   b. is an example of a double dissociation.
   c. argues against a clear relation between a brain area and a psychological process or function.
   d. must have been accomplished with fMRI.
   e. c and d

11. Afferent and efferent nerves are both found in the
   a. cranial nerves.
   b. peripheral nervous system.
   c. central nervous system.
   d. b and c
   e. a and b

12. Match the structure on the left with its associated function on the right.

i. Medulla	a. Respiration and heartbeat
ii. Cerebellum	b. Basic biological urges
iii. Hypothalamus	c. Balance and motor coordination

i. ________
ii. ________
iii. ________

13. Which of the following statements is *not* true of the limbic system?
   a. It is a subcortical structure.
   b. It is anatomically associated with the hypothalamus.
   c. It is present on both sides of the brain.
   d. It is involved in the control of emotional and motivational activities.
   e. It integrates the functions of the cerebral hemispheres.

14. In which of the following sequences are the main divisions of the central nervous system arranged in ascending order?
   a. Peripheral, somatic, autonomic
   b. Cerebellum, integration centers, transmission tracts
   c. Spinal cord, autonomic system, brain
   d. Spinal cord, cortex, hypothalamus
   e. Spinal cord, brain stem, cerebral hemispheres

15. The lobes of the cerebral hemisphere are
   a. frontal, parietal, occipital, and temporal.
   b. hindbrain, midbrain, and forebrain.
   c. limbic system, corpus callosum, and cerebral cortex.
   d. Each cerebral hemisphere is a single lobe of the cerebral cortex.
   e. none of the above.

16. Areas of the brain that are involved in learning, memory, or emotion include
   a. the limbic system.
   b. the hypothalamus.
   c. the amygdale.
   d. a and c
   e. all of the above.

17. Afferent input from the right hand projects primarily to the left hemisphere whereas afferent input from the left hand projects primarily to the right hemisphere. In an average right-handed, split-brain patient (whose two cerebral hemispheres have been surgically separated), which hand would the patient have to use to handle an unseen object in order to name it?
   a. The left hand
   b. The right hand
   c. Neither hand could do it.
   d. Both hands could do it equally well.
   e. This type of patient cannot name any object.

18. In which of the following tasks would you expect superior performance from the left hemisphere of a typical person?
   a. Matching paint colors
   b. Recognizing faces
   c. Remembering the words of a poem
   d. Drawing the floor plan of a familiar house
   e. All of the above

19. Theories of lateralization hold that for most people, the left hemisphere is more involved with ________, and the right hemisphere is more involved with ________.
   a. spatial material, verbal material
   b. organization in time, organization in space
   c. PET scans, CAT scans
   d. visual perception, auditory perception
   e. a and d

20. Localization of function is established by
    a. showing a relation between damage to an area of the brain and a deficit in a particular function.
    b. showing that stimulation of an area of the brain produces increased expression of that function.
    c. showing that during the performance of that function, the area in question is more active.
    d. a and b
    e. all of the above.

21. What part of an elephant might you expect to have a particularly large representation in the motor homunculus?
    a. The ears
    b. The front legs
    c. The back legs
    d. The trunk
    e. The eyes

22. Following a stroke, a patient shows grossly diminished sensitivity to touch and other stimulation in the right hand and arm. The probable site of the lesion is the
    a. motor homunculus.
    b. left somatosensory area.
    c. right somatosensory area.
    d. left frontal area.
    e. right frontal area.

23. Motor and sensory projections in the cerebral cortex can be characterized as
    a. almost always contralateral.
    b. topographic.
    c. associative.
    d. all of the above.
    e. a and b

24. A disorder in the organization of voluntary movement is called
    a. agnosia.
    b. aphasia.
    c. apraxia.
    d. amenorrhea.
    e. none of the above.

25. A person exhibiting an inability to coordinate the separate details of the visual world into a whole suffers from
    a. visual agnosia.
    b. receptive aphasia.
    c. a lesion in Broca's area.
    d. a lesion in Wernicke's area.
    e. visual apraxia.

26. A patient with the neglect syndrome and damage to her right parietal area looks straight at the X in the figure below.

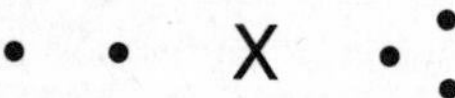

She is asked how many dots she sees. The answer we would expect is
    a. 1.
    b. 2.
    c. 3.
    d. 4.
    e. 5.

27. Just as a fluent aphasia can be described as a language agnosia, a nonfluent aphasia can be described as
    a. a fluent dyslexia.
    b. a language neglect.
    c. a language apraxia.
    d. a language deficit.
    e. none of the above.

28. Apraxia, neglect syndrome, and nonfluent and fluent aphasia have in common
    a. lesions in the same brain area.
    b. basic sensory and motor functions that are intact.
    c. some deficit in voluntary motor function.
    d. a and b
    e. a and c

29. A patient shows an inability to produce organized movements, though he can move any part of his body if asked to do so. He also has trouble inhibiting actions once he has begun them and has great difficulty making decisions. This patient probably has
    a. primarily left-side brain damage.
    b. extensive damage on both sides to the forward parts of the frontal lobe.
    c. damage to the limbic system.
    d. broad damage to most of the cerebral cortex.
    e. a neglect syndrome.

30. Neuron is to ganglion as
    a. brain is to hierarchical organization.
    b. ganglion is to brain.
    c. excitation is to inhibition.
    d. synapse is to neurotransmitter.
    e. dentist is to pain.

31. A basic theme in the evolution of nervous systems is
    a. increase in the size of neurons.
    b. increase in the number of ganglions.
    c. centralization.
    d. merging of ganglions into larger structures.
    e. c and d

32. It is extremely difficult to imagine how a structure as complex as the nervous system could develop. Which of the following are features that contribute to the assembly of the nervous system?
    a. Genetically determined protomaps
    b. Chemical signals that attract certain neurons to certain places
    c. Structures created by glia
    d. Selective death of inappropriately connected cells
    e. All of the above

33. Which of the following is *not* part of an individual neuron?
    a. Axon
    b. Myelin sheath
    c. Synapse
    d. Dendrite
    e. Cell body

34. Receptor cells
    a. are always a specialized part of sensory neurons.
    b. transduce physical stimuli into neural impulses.
    c. are responsible for the conduction of optic stimuli.

d. a and b
e. b and c

35. Which of the following properties is (are) characteristic of interneurons?
    a. They usually show much branching of dendrites.
    b. They form the microcircuitry of the central nervous system.
    c. They make up the majority of neurons.
    d. All of the above.
    e. None of the above.

36. When graphed over time, the complex electrical event known as the action potential looks something like which of the following diagrams?

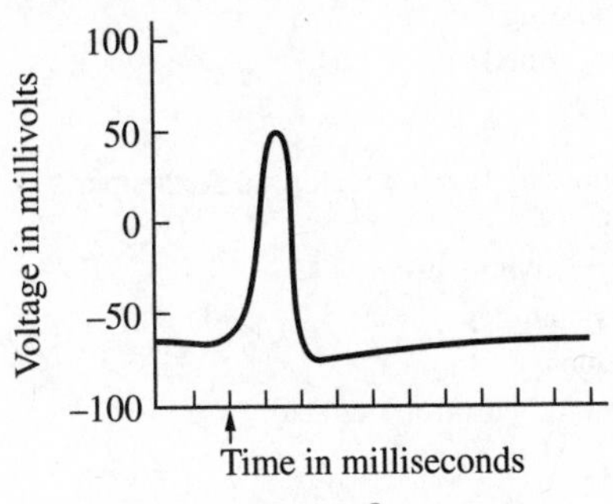

a

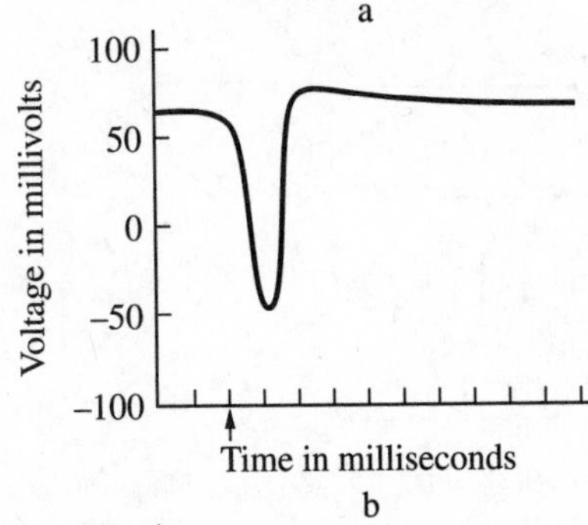

b

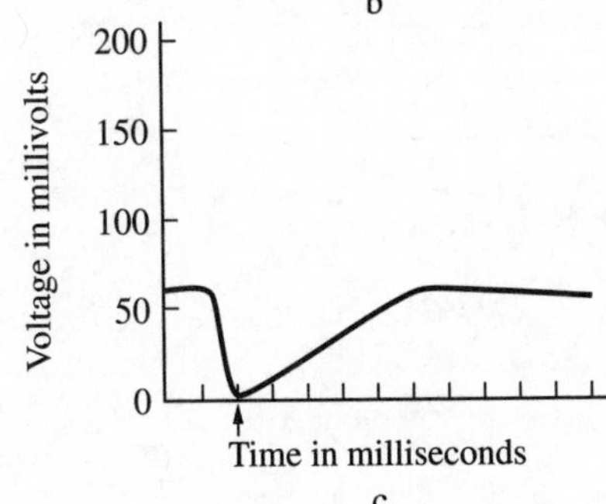

c

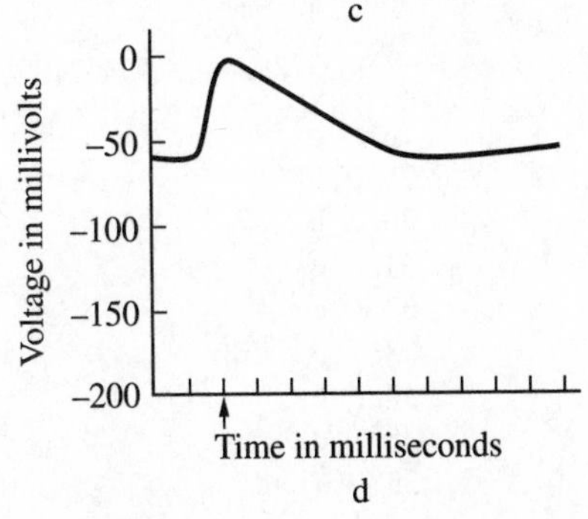

d

37. The all-or-none law states that
    a. the threshold of a single neuron is a property that alternates between two extreme values but never has any of the values in between.
    b. reflexes cannot involve just the spinal cord; the entire nervous system must respond by generating a central excitatory state.
    c. an axon terminal releases a chemical substance, called a neurotransmitter, when an action potential arrives.
    d. the frequency of spikes in an individual nerve fiber increases with the number of action potentials per unit of time.
    e. once a stimulus exceeds the threshold of an individual neuron, further increases in stimulation intensity make no difference in the height and form of the action potential generated.

38. The all-or-none action potential is
    a. accompanied by depolarization of the nerve membrane.
    b. accompanied by opening of the sodium channels in the membrane.
    c. propagated from one part of the membrane to another.
    d. all of the above.
    e. none of the above.

39. How can the nervous system represent increase in the intensity of a stimulus?
    a. By an increase in the size of the action potential in every neuron fired by the stimulus
    b. By an increase in the number of neurons being fired by the stimulus
    c. By an increase in the frequency of firing in the neurons fired by the stimulus
    d. b and c
    e. a and c

40. Sherrington used a spinal animal in order to
    a. eliminate inhibition.
    b. simplify the system he was studying.
    c. take advantage of brain modulation in neural activity in the spinal cord.
    d. study the irreversibility of conduction.
    e. cut expenses.

41. From his observations of temporal and spatial summation in reflexes, Sherrington inferred the existence of
    a. receptors.
    b. inhibition.
    c. the synapse.
    d. disinhibition.
    e. the simple reflex.

42. Brief strong stimulation of a receptor produces no movement, but a longer period of stimulation causes a particular muscle to stop contracting. These results could most easily be explained by the principles of
    a. excitation and inhibition.
    b. inhibition and spatial summation.
    c. the all-or-none law and inhibition.
    d. temporal summation, spatial summation, and the all-or-none law.
    e. inhibition and temporal summation.

43. Sherrington reported that the time (reflex latency) between stimulation of a reflex and the reflex response was much longer than the time it would take for an action potential to go from the receptor to the muscle. This "delay" could be accounted for in terms of
    a. inhibition.
    b. excitation.
    c. spatial summation.
    d. the time for depolarization of the axon membrane.
    e. the time for the neurotransmitter to cross the synaptic gap and stimulate the postsynaptic neuron.

44. Axon conduction resembles synaptic transmission in that
    a. both involve neurotransmitters.
    b. both are about the same speed.
    c. both are all-or-none.
    d. all of the above.
    e. none of the above.

45. Many neurons fire action potentials at a moderate rate even when they are not receiving synaptic excitation from presynaptic neurons. This is called spontaneous activity. Which plot indicates what would happen to the firing rate of such a neuron if it were first exposed to synaptic inhibition and then synaptic excitation?

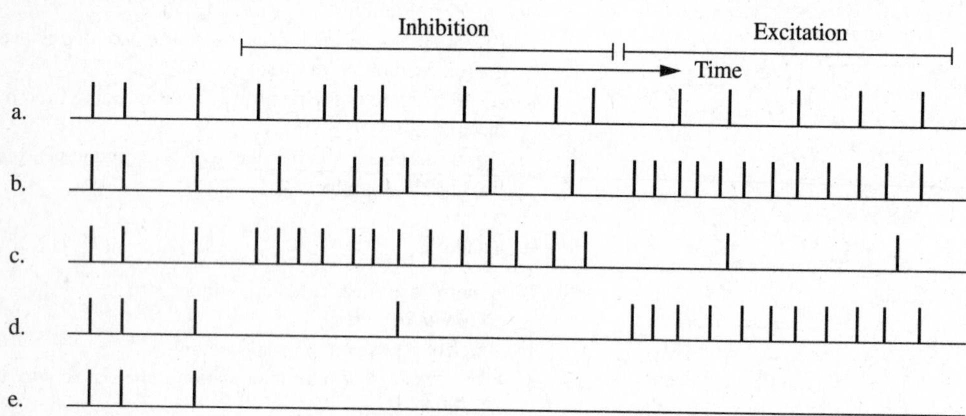

46. Both excitatory neurotransmitters and above-threshold depolarization of axons
    a. open ion channels.
    b. produce synaptic delay.
    c. explain temporal summation.
    d. all of the above.
    e. none of the above.

47. The lock-and-key model accounts for the
    a. existence of neurotransmitters.
    b. summation of excitation and inhibition in postsynaptic neurons.
    c. fact that specific neurotransmitters stimulate specific postsynaptic neurons.
    d. release of neurotransmitters from synaptic vesicles.
    e. all-or-none law.

48. A new drug is found to increase arousal. Which of the following is *not* a possible mode of action of that drug?
    a. Blocks reuptake of dopamine
    b. Increases availability of norepinephrine
    c. Blocks the enzyme that breaks down dopamine at the synapse
    d. Mimics the effect of norepinephrine
    e. Blocks the postsynaptic receptor for norepinephrine

49. Hormones and neurotransmitters are both
    a. secreted only by endocrine glands.
    b. secreted into the bloodstream.
    c. chemical messengers.
    d. all of the above.
    e. none of the above.

50. Recovery from cerebral damage occurs in a number of ways. Which of the following involves the addition of new nerve cells to the damaged brain?
    a. Transplantation of fetal nerve tissue
    b. Rehabilitation
    c. Collateral sprouting
    d. Substitution of function
    e. All of the above

51. Which of the following is *not* a feature of Alzheimer's disease?
    a. Decline in cognitive function
    b. Neurofibrillary tangles
    c. Amyloid plaques
    d. Absence of brain neurotrophic factor
    e. Onset typically after age 65

Answer Key for Self-Test

1. b
2. a
3. e
4. d
5. a
6. e
7. c
8. e
9. e
10. b
11. e
12. i. a, ii. c, iii. b
13. e
14. e
15. a
16. d
17. b
18. c
19. b
20. e
21. d
22. b
23. e
24. c
25. a
26. c
27. c
28. b
29. b
30. b
31. e
32. e
33. c
34. b
35. d
36. a
37. e
38. d
39. d
40. b

41. c
42. e
43. e
44. e
45. d
46. a
47. c
48. e
49. c
50. a
51. d

Investigating Psychological Phenomena

SPEED OF THE NERVE IMPULSE: THE USE OF REACTION TIME IN THE MEASUREMENT OF A PSYCHOLOGICAL PROCESS

Equipment: A stopwatch that indicates seconds
Number of participants: Five
Time per participant: Fifteen minutes (All participants are involved at the same time.)
Time for experimenter: Twenty-five minutes

One of the great stumbling blocks to advances in theory about psychological processes was the belief that thought, and hence nervous impulses, occurred instantaneously or nearly so. In fact, the German physiologist Johannes P. Müller (1801–1858) once estimated that the speed of the nerve impulse was 11 million miles per second. Naturally, this claim that nerve impulses travel at an immeasurably fast rate discouraged scientific research on the physiology of the nervous system and encouraged mystical or dualistic interpretations of mind. It also discouraged study of the speed of various mental activities, research that is today an important cornerstone of the field of cognitive psychology.

In 1850, Herman Ludwig Ferdinand von Helmholtz (1821–1894) succeeded in measuring the speed of the nerve impulse and found it to be much slower than previously believed, between 50 and 100 meters per second in humans. This finding was followed by intensive investigation of the nervous system within the framework of the physical and biological sciences. It also opened the door to the use of reaction time as a tool in the study of thought processes. This experiment is an attempt to familiarize you with the general logic used by a psychologist who is interested in measuring the speed of a psychological event that cannot be directly observed. To accomplish this, you must first understand the experiment that Helmholtz performed and also how his experimental technique can be applied to the measurement of the speed of the nerve impulse in humans.

Helmholtz's technique was quite simple. He first dissected out a muscle and an attached nerve fiber from a frog's leg. The experiment then consisted of stimulating the nerve at various distances from the muscle and measuring the length of time between nerve stimulation and muscle contraction. First, he electrically stimulated the nerve close to the point at which it was attached to the muscle; then he stimulated the nerve farther from this point of attachment. He found that the second reaction time (i.e., the time between stimulation and contraction) was longer than the first. To obtain an estimate of nerve impulse speed, he used a simple bit of reasoning: the difference in time between the two measurements must correspond to the time it takes the impulse to travel the distance between the two points of stimulation (**see the figure**). Hence, the distance between the points of stimulation divided by the time *difference* between the conditions of stimulating close to the muscle versus stimulating farther away should yield an estimate of nerve impulse speed. This is how he obtained his estimate of 50 to 100 meters per second. Let *A* and *B* be two points of stimulation, *M* be the point at which the nerve connects to the muscle, t_A be the time to contraction from stimulation at *A*, and t_B, the time to contraction from stimulation at *B*.

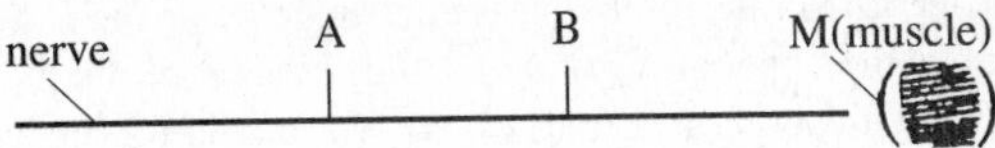

Then $\frac{(A \text{ to } M) - (B \text{ to } M)}{t_A - t_B}$ = speed of nerve impulse.

Happily, Helmholtz's estimate can be demonstrated in humans without resorting to dissection. You might suppose that the simplest way to do this would be to perform the following sort of experiment: stimulate someone on the ankle (e.g., by pinching) and have the participant respond by pushing a button as soon as he or she feels the stimulation. With a good timer, you could then measure the time between stimulation and depression of the button. To estimate nerve conduction time, you would then measure the total distance between ankle and brain and between brain and finger, add the two together, and divide this number by the participant's reaction time. But there are complications that make this procedure unsuitable. Part of the reaction time, for example, would be due to the length of time it took the participant to decide to press the button, a figure that is obviously more than simply nerve impulse time. From the point of view of processes in the nervous system, the reaction time includes the time to cross synapses as well as axon conduction time. In short, total reaction time is a confounded measure.

Thus, the experiment must be made more complicated. Using Helmholtz's logic, you could measure not only the time between ankle stimulation and response but also the time between, say, upper arm stimulation and response. The ankle stimulation should result in a longer reaction time than the upper arm stimulation. The difference between these reaction times corresponds to the time it takes for the nerve impulse to travel a distance equal to the difference between the ankle and the finger and the upper arm and the finger. Notice that this difference excludes any time due to such things as decision-making processes. So the nerve conduction time can be estimated by subtracting the distance of the upper arm to the brain from the distance of the ankle to the brain (the distance from the brain to the finger is constant) and dividing by the reaction time difference.

In practice, the reaction time for either stimulating the ankle or stimulating the upper arm is quite small, and hence a clock that measures time in hundredths of a second would be needed to measure it. This problem can be solved by adding together the reaction time of several people; after obtaining the total time, simply dividing this by the number of people would give the average individual time. This general mass reaction time technique will be used to measure the speed of the nerve impulse. Perform the nerve impulse speed experiment in the following way:

Get five people to participate. Have them form a circle with each person very loosely clasping the ankle of his or her neighbor to the right. Tell participants to squeeze the ankle they are holding when they feel their ankle squeezed. Be sure the participants' eyes are closed during all trials. You can then start the experiment by squeezing one person's ankle and simultaneously noting the time on the second hand of a watch. Now watch the ankle that you squeezed. When you see it squeezed for the fifth time (excluding your initial squeeze), note the time that elapsed. Repeat this procedure a total of five times, each time recording the time in the space provided in Part I of the answer sheet (record results to an accuracy of 0.1 second).

Have everyone in the circle release the ankle he or she is holding and grasp the upper arm *just below the shoulder* of the person to the right. Run another five trials exactly as you did for the ankle trials, each time recording the time in Part II of the answer sheet.

You will probably note that the total reaction time dropped within each set of five trials. Why? The last two to three trials probably yielded about the same values.

These ten trials serve as practice: The group of five participants and the measurer "learn" in some general way to do this task efficiently. Having completed practice, you are now ready to begin the measurement of the speed of the nerve impulse. Run four more trials as before, the first and fourth with ankle stimulation, the second and third with upper arm stimulation. This will generate two ankle and two upper arm mass reaction times (record these in Part III of the data sheet).

Each reaction time represents the sum of 25 reaction times (five participants, five times each). Obtain the average individual reaction time by dividing the total reaction times by 25. Now average the two ankle reaction times and, separately, the two upper arm reaction times. Subtract the average upper arm time from the average ankle time. This is the amount of time it takes the impulse to go the extra distance from the ankle to the level of the upper arm. To calculate the speed of the nerve impulse, you must estimate the magnitude of this distance (in meters).

Measure the distance for the third tallest person in your group of five participants. Measure the distance from the ankle to the base of the neck and from the upper arm to the base of the neck. Take the difference between the numbers and divide by the time difference, and you will have an estimate of the speed of the nerve impulse. How does it compare with Helmholtz's estimate? (Helmholtz estimated a speed of from 50 to 100 meters per second. Modern measurements range from 6 to 122 meters per second, depending on the type of nerve fiber.) (If your instructor collects the data, fill out the report sheet in Appendix 2.)

FURTHER EXPERIMENTS

Now that you have calculated an estimate of the speed of the nerve impulse, you might want to test whether some fairly common variables will affect this speed. Consider fatigue, for instance. If a person is tired, does his or her nerve impulse speed slow down? To test this, design your own experiment, using the same measurement technique you used to get your main estimate of nerve impulse speed. To test whether fatigue has an effect, measure the speed both at a time when participants are well rested and at a time when the same participants are tired (e.g., in the morning and at night, or before and after exercise). Does fatigue affect nerve impulse speed? Note that given the way the estimate is obtained, it is possible to find that fatigue may well slow down reaction time in general, yet have no effect on the speed of the nerve impulse. Can you think of other variables that might affect (speed up or slow down) nerve impulse speed? If so, design experiments to test your hypotheses.

REPORT SHEET

Practice — Time in seconds*

Part I
Trial 1 ankle = ________
Trial 2 ankle = ________
Trial 3 ankle = ________
Trial 4 ankle = ________
Trial 5 ankle = ________

Part II
Trial 1 upper arm = ________
Trial 2 upper arm = ________
Trial 3 upper arm = ________
Trial 4 upper arm = ________
Trial 5 upper arm = ________

Test Part III
a. Trial 1 ankle time = ________ ÷ 25 = ________
b. Trial 2 upper arm time = ________ ÷ 25 = ________
c. Trial 3 upper arm time ________ ÷ 25 = ________
d. Trial 4 ankle time = ________ ÷ 25 = ________

$\frac{a + d}{2}$ = ________ (average ankle time)

$\frac{b + c}{2}$ = ________ (average upper arm time)

Average ankle time – average upper arm time = ________
(difference 1)

Distance of ankle to base of neck
(for third tallest person) = ________

Distance of upper arm to base of neck
(for third tallest person) = ________

Distance 1 – distance 2 = ________ (difference 2)

$\frac{\text{difference 2}}{\text{difference 1}}$ = (speed of nerve impulse)

*Record time accurate to .1 second.

CHAPTER 4

Sensation

Learning Objectives

THE ORIGINS OF KNOWLEDGE

An early view—the empiricists

1. Be familiar with the viewpoint of the empiricists.
2. What is the distinction between proximal and distal stimuli?
3. What are sensations?
4. Understand the role of association in the empiricists' view of perception.
5. What is the relevance of visual perspective in a discussion of association?

The active perceiver

6. How does nativism differ from empiricism?
7. What is the psychophysical approach to this problem?

Measuring sensory intensity

8. Why is the just-noticeable difference (jnd) important in measuring sensory intensity?
9. What is Weber's law? How is Weber's fraction used to compare the sensitivities of different sensory modalities?
10. Does Fechner's law hold up in all situations?

Detection and decision

11. What is the role of expectations in signal detection?
12. What sorts of errors might result from setting a criterion? How do different criteria affect response bias?
13. How can an analysis of the proportions of yes and no responses measure the separate effects of sensitivity and response bias?
14. How is signal-detection theory applicable to problems other than the detection of weak stimuli?
15. Why are false alarms and misses nearly inevitable in decision situations?

Sensory coding

16. How is stimulus intensity coded?
17. Explain the doctrine of specific nerve energies as it applies both within and between sensory modalities. Explain how specificity and pattern theories account for sensory coding.

THE FUNCTIONING OF THE SENSES

18. What are the various senses that humans have?

HEARING

Sound

19. What is the stimulus for hearing? How do sound waves vary?
20. Know how the amplitude and frequency of sound stimuli are measured.
21. What is the difference between simple and complex auditory stimuli? How does the brain treat complex stimuli?

From sound waves to hearing

22. Describe the structure of the ear as it collects the auditory stimulus. How does this structure permit the perception of sounds?
23. How is the cochlea designed?
24. Describe the place and firing frequency theories of pitch perception. Why does each seem important to perception, and what triggers each?

VISION

The stimulus: Light

25. What are the characteristics of light, and what are their visual consequences?

Gathering the stimulus: The eye

26. How is the eye like a camera?

The visual receptors

27. Describe the retina.
28. Be familiar with the following terms: *rods, cones, bipolar cells, ganglion cells, optic nerve,* and *blind spot.*
29. Where is visual acuity greatest, and why?

30. Understand the duplex theory of vision. What is the evidence for two types of receptors, and why are they needed?

31. How does spectral sensitivity help to distinguish rods from cones?

32. What is a pigment and how does it result in a neural signal from a light stimulus?

The importance of change: Adaptation

33. What is sensory adaptation? What does the organism gain by sensory adaptation?

34. Explain the technique used to show that stabilization of the retinal image leads to visual adaptation.

Interaction in space: Contrast

35. Recall that brightness contrast increases with progressive intensity difference between two regions and with decreasing distance between them. How is this phenomenon important to visual perception? How do Mach bands illustrate this? What is the physiological mechanism that underlies Mach bands?

36. Be familiar with the effects of lateral inhibition. What is its effect on vision?

Color

37. What are the dimensions of color?

38. Describe the "unique" colors.

39. Are differences in brightness best observed in chromatic or in achromatic colors?

40. How can colors be varied in saturation?

The physiological basis of color vision

41. Explain the differences among the three cone types in human color vision.

42. What are complementary colors? How do their complementary characters account for simultaneous color contrast and negative afterimages?

43. It is important to understand the opponent-process theory thoroughly. Be aware of the relevance of primary colors, color antagonists, and inhibition in the perception of hue and brightness.

44. What is the physiological evidence for the opponent-process theory?

45. Describe different types of color blindness.

Perceiving shapes

46. How do electrophysiological studies of the action of single neural cells tell us about the perception of contours?

47. Define a receptive field.

48. What is the significance of studies designed to understand how frogs perceive their environment?

49. Understand how the perception of faces might be related to the use of feature detectors.

Programmed Exercises

THE ORIGINS OF KNOWLEDGE

1. John Locke postulated that all knowledge comes by way of experience. This school of thought is known as_________. — empiricism

2. Locke used the metaphor of a _________ _________ in describing the human mind at birth. — tabula rasa (blank slate)

3. An object in the real world is known as a _________ stimulus. — distal

4. When the energy from an object impinges on a sensory surface, we say that this pattern of energy has become a _________ stimulus. — proximal

5. Empiricists assumed that all knowledge comes from the _________. — senses

6. According to the empiricists, complex ideas are perceived by the linking together, or _________, of two or more sensations. — association

7. Empricists argue that _________ cues help us to navigate and understand our three-dimensional world. — distance

8. Kant believed that a number of aspects of perception are innate. This view has since been labeled _________. — nativism

9. The study of the relationship between properties of the stimulus and sensory experience is known as _________. — psychophysics

10. You find that you are unable to tell the difference between a 25-lb weight and a 28-lb weight, but you can differentiate the 25-lb weight from any other weight over 28 lb. Something slightly over 3 lb is your _________ _________. It will produce a _________-_________ _________ (_________) in this weight range. — difference threshold; just-noticeable difference (jnd)

11. A difference threshold is 2 lb when the standard is 40 lb. ________ law predicts that the difference threshold with a 20-lb standard would be ________ lb.

Weber's
1

12. The jnd divided by the standard stimulus is known as ________ ________ and, in general, seems to be constant.

Weber's fraction

13. Imagine that for a certain psychophysical task we found that sensation grew as a function of the logarithm of the physical stimulus intensity. This would be support for ________ law.

Fechner's

14. One duty of air traffic controllers is to watch a radar screen and determine what planes are in the area. There are two kinds of errors they may make in this task. First, they may not see a small dot on the screen, thus committing a ________, as it is often called in signal-detection theory. On the other hand, they may report a plane when there is none there. This is called a ________ ________. Considering the costs of these two errors, the ________ ________ error is probably more common than the ________ error.

miss

false alarm, false alarm, miss

15. Corresponding to the two types of errors, there are also two kinds of correct responses. When an event occurs in the world and we say that the event occurred, that is known as a ________. When an event hasn't occurred in the world and we say that it hasn't, we have given a ________ ________.

hit
correct negative

16. If you make a selection error during the admission of a student to medical school that results in admitting a student who cannot complete the degree requirements, you have made a ________ ________ error.

false alarm

17. The theory that accounts for performance when participants are trying to determine whether a weak stimulus was presented is called ________-________ theory.

signal-detection

18. When a weak stimulus is presented, participants must set a ________ to determine whether the level of activity within their sensory system warrants saying that the stimulus was present.

cutoff

19. There clearly are qualitative differences in sensations (e.g., smells are different from sounds). These differences are due to differences in sensory ________.

quality

20. According to the doctrine of ________ ________ ________, differences in subjective quality are caused by differences in associated nervous structures rather than by differences inherent in the stimuli.

specific nerve energies

21. There are two theoretical approaches that explain the neural processes that underlie sensations. The ________ theory states that different sensory qualities are signaled by different quality-specific neurons. The other theory, the across-fiber ________ theory, asserts that substances produce a pattern of activation across a set of fibers, and that this pattern is the neural code that gives rise to sensory quality.

specificity
pattern

THE FUNCTIONING OF THE SENSES

22. In addition to the senses of vision, hearing, touch, taste, and smell, humans also have the sense of ________ (sensitivity to body position) and the ________ sense (signaling movements of the head).

kinesthesis, vestibular

23. The sense of touch can be subdivided into the four sensations of ________, ________, ________, and ________.

pressure, warmth, cold, pain

HEARING

24. The ________ canals indicate rotation of the head. They are located in the ________ ear.

semicircular, inner

25. Light intensity is to vision as ________ is to hearing.

amplitude

26. Hue is to vision as ________ is to audition.

pitch

27. Many different ________ ________, differing in both frequency and amplitude, combine to form a ________ ________.

sine waves
complex wave

28. The purpose of the middle ear, oval window, and inner ear is to ________ sound waves.

amplify

29. The structure that contains the auditory receptors is known as the ________.

cochlea

30. The auditory receptors are the ________ ________, which are stimulated by deformation of the ________ ________. hair cells basilar membrane

31. Pitch perception seems to be based on two mechanisms. High frequencies are coded using the ________ of excitation, whereas lower frequencies are coded by the ________ firing rate. place, neural

32. For all modalities, stimulus energy must be converted into a form that can be used by the senses. The translation is termed ________. transduction

VISION

33. Light can be either ________ or ________. emitted, reflected

34. Light energy can vary in ________, thus giving rise to perceived brightness, and in ________, which determines perceived hue. intensity wavelength

35. The visible spectrum extends from roughly ________ to roughly ________ nanometers. 360, 750

36. The first place at which light energy from the world interacts with the senses (where transduction first occurs) is at the ________. retina

37. The focusing of the eye is affected by the ________ and the ________. lens, cornea

38. ________ are most densely packed in the fovea, while ________ are most frequent in the periphery. Cones, rods

39. The first cells to be stimulated by light are the ________, which activate the ________ cells, which in turn stimulate the ________ cells. receptors, bipolar ganglion

40. The axons of the ganglion cells form a bundle, which is known as the ________ ________; this exits the eyeball at the ________ ________. optic nerve blind spot

41. The fact that primarily nocturnal animals have no cones and many rods, whereas animals that operate in daylight have many cones and few rods, is evidence for a ________ theory of vision. duplex

42. The fact that sensitivity to dim light is greater in the periphery of the visual field (where rods are) than in the fovea (where cones are) supports the ________ theory of vision. duplex

43. The chemical reaction in which the visual pigment rhodopsin breaks down and then reforms into rhodopsin takes place in the ________. rods

44. A ________ ________ is an example of a color phenomenon that involves temporal relationships. negative afterimage

45. ________ ________, a phenomenon similar to brightness contrast, occur when a light region borders a dark region, causing the light region to appear ________. Mach bands lighter

46. The physical resolution of the eye is not very good. In terms of physics, we shouldn't be able to see as clearly as we do. However, the exaggeration of contrast through ________ ________ enhances the visual message. lateral inhibition

47. The three attributes used to describe color are ________, ________, and ________. hue, brightness, saturation

48. ________ colors cannot be distinguished on the basis of hue. Achromatic

49. Unique red is the red that appears to have neither any ________ nor any ________ in it. blue, yellow

50. Only ________ colors can differ in saturation. chromatic

51. A person with normal vision can detect over ________ different color shades. 7 million

52. A ________ hue is one that, when mixed with another hue in the correct proportion, will produce an achromatic color. complementary

53. A gray color, when surrounded by green, appears reddish. This is known as ________ ________ ________ and is evidence for antagonistic pairing of colors. simultaneous color contrast

54. _________ _________ have the complementary hue and the opposite brightness of the original stimulus.	Negative afterimages
55. Human vision is termed _________, since there are three cone types.	trichromatic
56. According to the opponent-process theory of color vision, it should never be possible to see a red hue with a trace of _________ in it.	green
57. Color blindness is most common in _________ and could entail the _________ of one of the opponent-process pairs.	males, absence
58. _________ have contributed significantly to the study of form perception by studying the behavior of single nerve cells in the visual system.	Electrophysiologists
59. In recording from a single nerve cell, we discover that its firing rate varies when a stimulus is presented at a certain place in the visual field. This is the cell's _________ field.	receptive
60. A nerve cell that selectively responds to some characteristics of a stimulus but not to others is often called a _________ _________.	feature detector
61. One of the characteristics that visual nerve cells respond to selectively is _________.	orientation
62. It has been shown that monkeys have feature detectors that are selectively sensitive to very complex stimuli, such as _________.	faces (hands)

Self-Test

1. John Locke, the British empiricist, would most likely agree with which of the following statements?
   a. All knowledge is determined by innate mechanisms.
   b. We are born with a fair amount of innate knowledge, with experience playing a small role in the acquisition of more knowledge.
   c. Knowledge arrives through the senses.
   d. John Locke was not an empiricist and would not have agreed with any of the above statements.

2. The metaphor that best describes the empiricists' view of the human mind at birth is a(n)
   a. camera.
   b. encyclopedia.
   c. pad and pencil.
   d. blank slate.

3. An example of a distal stimulus is
   a. the pattern of light energy hitting the retina.
   b. a Chevrolet.
   c. the sensation produced by a distant mountain.
   d. a hallucination.

4. An example of a proximal visual stimulus is
   a. the activity of the retina hit by an array of photons.
   b. an object situated very close to the retina.
   c. a distant object that appears closer than it really is.
   d. all of the above.

5. According to the empiricists, visual perspective serves as a depth cue because
   a. it produces a memory of an associated movement and an experience of depth.
   b. it mitigates the effect of convergence.
   c. its use by painters has familiarized us with its symbolic representation of depth.
   d. we are classically conditioned to accept it as such.

6. Immanuel Kant believed
   a. in innately determined categories of perception.
   b. that all knowledge came through the senses.
   c. that associations of sensations determined perception.
   d. none of the above.

7. Psychophysics studies the relationship between
   a. the distal and proximal stimulus.
   b. the distal stimulus and sensory experience.
   c. nativism and empiricism.
   d. the proximal stimulus and sensory experience.

8. It can be argued that sensations cannot be measured directly. It should be possible, though, to compare sensations. For instance, we should be able to determine whether one sensation is the same as or different from another. This viewpoint would most likely be expressed by
   a. Kant.
   b. Locke.
   c. Fechner.
   d. Berkeley.

9. You are shopping for a new car. You have test-driven a number of cars to determine which models have the best performance. You discover that you cannot tell the difference between models A and C. The difference (however measured) between cars A and C is below your
   a. difference threshold.
   b. response bias.
   c. criterion.
   d. sensitivity.

10. Which of the following agrees with Weber's law? (In each case, the first number represents the weight difference needed to produce a jnd, and the absolute stimulus energy is specified by the second number. Two pairs are provided for each possible answer.)
   a. 1, 10/2, 100
   b. 20, 50/1, 2.5
   c. 5, 100/5, 50
   d. All of the above are in agreement with Weber's law.

11. As in 10 above, each of the pairs of numbers below represents a hypothetical difference threshold with its associated stimulus energy value. Which of the Weber fractions that results from these values represents the greatest sensitivity?
   a. 1, 100
   b. 1, 10
   c. 100, 1,000
   d. 50, 1,000

12. Fechner's law states that the strength of the sensation increases __________ with stimulus intensity.
   a. inversely
   b. minimally
   c. logarithmically
   d. linearly

13. A doctor is scanning a lung X ray. She sees something that may be either the beginnings of a tumor or harmless scar tissue. It is likely that some factors will come into play when the doctor decides whether to operate. Which are some of these factors?
   a. The probability that it is a tumor
   b. The risks associated with surgery
   c. The risks associated with an untreated tumor
   d. All of the above
   e. None of the above; response bias is fixed and cannot be easily changed.

14. In the example in question 13, which type of error is worse to make?
   a. False alarm
   b. Miss
   c. a and b are equally important.
   d. It cannot be determined without knowing associated costs and benefits.

15. Still considering the example in question 13, imagine that there are five different types of tumors such that each is associated with a different death rate when left untreated. Type I has the highest death rate, and Type V has the lowest rate (with the others falling between I and V, in order). Imagine further that these five tumors can be distinguished from each other with X rays, but none of them can be distinguished from scar tissue (which is harmless). Assuming that everything else is constant from one tumor type to another, under which condition would the doctor be most likely to operate and risk putting the patient under the dangers of surgery?
   a. The patient has either scar tissue or a Type III tumor.
   b. The patient has either scar tissue or a Type V tumor.
   c. The patient has either scar tissue or a Type I tumor.
   d. If the doctor were competent, the probability of her operating would be constant, despite the type of tumor.

16. If, under certain circumstances, a participant's hit rate went up while his false alarm rate stayed the same, we could conclude that his
   a. bias to say yes went up.
   b. accuracy decreased.
   c. sensitivity increased.
   d. accuracy and bias both changed.

17. Which of the following is an example of transduction?
   a. Sound waves in the air being translated into electrical energy by a microphone
   b. Electrical waves being translated into sound waves by a loudspeaker
   c. Light energy being converted into nerve energy by the retina
   d. All of the above

18. Differences among the taste of a cold beer, the sound of a Mozart quartet, and the sight of a fireworks display are due to
   a. our past experiences with these stimuli.
   b. differences in the sense organs that respond to the stimuli.
   c. physiological differences in the conduction velocities of the neurons attached to the various sense organs.
   d. all of the above.

19. If, by some freak of nature, the optic and olfactory nerves were crossed and led to the opposite sense organ, the law of specific nerve energies would predict
   a. smelling red.
   b. normal sensations.
   c. a or b
   d. The law of specific nerve energies makes no predictions in such a case.

20. Kinesthesis is
   a. information from the muscles, tendons, and joints.
   b. a function of the ossicles in the inner ear.
   c. the movement of hair cells in the cochlea.
   d. the crystallization of the viscous liquid in the semicircular canals.

21. The physical stimulus for hearing is described in terms of amplitude and frequency. The corresponding psychological dimensions are
   a. loudness and tone.
   b. amplitude and pitch.
   c. loudness and timbre.
   d. loudness and pitch.

22. Which pair of the following representative sound waves includes both a simple and a complex wave?
    a. 1 and 3
    b. 2 and 4
    c. 2 and either 3 or 4
    d. either 1 or 2, and 3

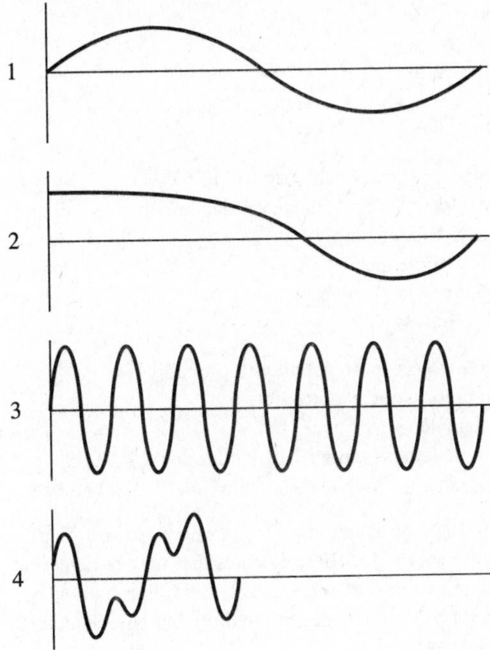

23. The correct ordering of anatomical structures in the ear (from outside in) is
    a. eardrum, middle ear, oval window, and cochlea.
    b. oval window, middle ear, eardrum, and cochlea.
    c. eardrum, oval window, middle ear, and cochlea.
    d. none of the above.

24. For low-frequency tones (below 400 hz), pitch is detected by
    a. the eardrum.
    b. localization on the basilar membrane.
    c. firing frequency of the auditory nerve.
    d. none of the above.

25. For frequencies above 5,000 hz, pitch is detected by
    a. the eardrum.
    b. localization on the basilar membrane.
    c. firing frequency of the auditory nerve.
    d. none of the above.

26. One light source appears bluish and another appears greenish. This difference in appearance is due to differences in
    a. intensity.
    b. wavelength.
    c. opponent processes.
    d. none of the above.

27. Intensity is to brightness as wavelength is to
    a. sensitivity.
    b. darkness.
    c. wattage.
    d. hue.

28. Which of the following wavelengths is *not* considered to be part of the visible spectrum?
    a. 650
    b. 400
    c. 300
    d. 575

29. Which of the following structures bends light rays so that they are projected onto a light-sensitive surface?
    a. The retina
    b. The iris
    c. The lens
    d. All of the above

30. Which of the following structures focuses incoming light in the mammalian eye?
    a. The lens
    b. The cornea
    c. a and b
    d. None of the above

31. The two types of receptors in the human eye are known as __________ and __________.
    a. bipolars, horizontals
    b. ganglions, bipolars
    c. rods, cones
    d. bipolars, cones

32. An area near the center of the retina has virtually no rods, consisting entirely of cones. It is approximately 2 degrees in diameter and is known as the
    a. periphery.
    b. optic nerve.
    c. optic chiasm.
    d. fovea.

33. Which of the following is *not* in agreement with the duplex theory of vision?
    a. The rods are the receptors for night vision, whereas the cones serve day vision.
    b. Rods respond to low light levels, cones to high levels.
    c. Rod vision provides good acuity; cones provide poor acuity.
    d. Rods result in achromatic vision; cones provide color vision.

34. In the tonotopic map on the cortex,
    a. neurons with similar preferred pitches tend to be located near each other.
    b. neurons with similar preferred pitches tend to be located far from each other.
    c. the location of neurons with specific preferred pitches is random.
    d. there are no neurons with specific preferred pitches.

35. What happens when light hits a visual receptor?
    a. Silver bromide molecules combine with light to release silver.
    b. Light strikes the retina and generates rhodopsin.
    c. Energy is converted to nervous impulses via a photochemical process that bleaches rhodopsin.
    d. The reflected light from the receptor causes a photochemical alteration leading to neural excitation.

36. Which of the following is an example of sensory adaptation?
    a. The cold ocean feels warmer after we've been in it for a while.
    b. We are able to see in a dark room after a period of adjustment.
    c. We have increasing sensitivity to salt with continued exposure.
    d. All of the above.
    e. a and b

37. The first time you see a friend's new car, it is parked against a black wall. Later you see that same car parked against a white backdrop (at the same time of day) and comment that you remember the car as being much brighter. This is an example of
    a. brightness contrast.
    b. adaptation.
    c. temporal interaction.
    d. none of the above.

38. Lateral inhibition is responsible for
    a. color vision.
    b. Mach bands.
    c. stabilized image.
    d. all of the above.

39. Which of the following is *not* used to classify colors?
    a. Brightness
    b. Hue
    c. Amplitude
    d. Saturation

40. White and black can be distinguished only on the basis of
    a. brightness.
    b. hue.
    c. wavelength.
    d. saturation.

41. Red and green must differ at least on
    a. brightness.
    b. hue.
    c. amplitude.
    d. saturation.

42. White and black *cannot* differ on
    a. hue.
    b. saturation.
    c. a and b
    d. none of the above.

43. The extent to which a color of some fixed hue is mixed with an achromatic color is represented by a value on the __________ dimension.
    a. brightness
    b. hue
    c. intensity
    d. saturation

44. Any wavelength will stimulate
    a. all three receptor types, but unequally.
    b. all three receptor types, and equally.
    c. only one or two receptor types.
    d. from one to three receptors, depending on the intensity and wavelength.

45. In the opponent-process theory, the three pairs of receptors are
    a. red-blue, green-yellow, and black-white.
    b. red-yellow, blue-green, and black-white.
    c. red-green, blue-yellow, and black-white.
    d. never specified.

46. An achromatic color results when which system(s) is(are) in balance?
    a. Red-green
    b. Blue-yellow
    c. Red-green and blue-yellow
    d. Black-white

47. The opponent-process theory would predict
    a. the dark gray appearance of black pepper placed against a gray background.
    b. chromatic contrast.
    c. negative afterimages.
    d. all of the above.

48. A person who is color-blind will probably
    a. use color names appropriately.
    b. be female.
    c. be unable to distinguish any hues at all.
    d. be unable to imagine how ultraviolet looks to a bee.

49. The presence of detectors in frogs which are specifically attuned to search for flies indicates that feature detectors
    a. can be responsive to quite complex objects.
    b. cannot be wired to detect anything but simple attributes of shapes.
    c. cannot be shaped by evolutionary pressure.
    d. are a minor part of the visual response to objects.

Answer Key for Self-Test

1. c
2. d
3. b
4. a
5. a
6. a
7. b
8. c
9. a
10. b
11. a
12. c
13. d
14. d
15. c
16. c
17. b
18. b
19. a
20. a
21. d
22. b
23. a
24. c
25. b
26. b
27. d
28. c
29. c
30. c
31. c
32. d
33. c
34. a
35. c
36. e
37. a
38. b
39. c
40. a
41. b
42. c
43. d
44. a
45. c
46. c
47. d
48. a
49. a

Investigating Psychological Phenomena

MEASURING BRIGHTNESS CONTRAST

Equipment: Stimuli included; one sheet of black construction paper needed
Number of participants: One or more
Time per participant: Ten minutes
Time for experimenter: Twenty minutes

In this "Sensation" chapter, the authors describe a phenomenon that clearly illustrates the effect of context on perception. The phenomenon is brightness contrast. Examine Figure 4.16 in the text once again. Note how sharply different in brightness the four central gray squares appear to be; yet they are identical. (You can prove this to yourself by laying a sheet of paper over the figure with holes cut out where the squares are located.) The difference in brightness is apparently a result of interaction between each central square and its surrounding light or dark border. As the text explains, the surrounding border induces a contrast effect such that a patch will appear lighter when surrounded by a dark border, and darker when surrounded by a light border. The greater the difference in lightness between the center and its surroundings, the greater the illusion.

Of course, as you have probably already suspected, brightness contrast has limits. That is, there is just so much illusion that can be produced by a surrounding context, no matter how great the difference between the center and its surroundings. The present experiment provides an opportunity to examine the extent to which the visual system can be fooled by context. More important, however, in this exercise you will have a chance to conduct a psychophysical experiment to measure quantitatively the relationship between physical stimuli and psychological experience.

The purpose of the experiment is to measure the magnitude of brightness contrast for a particular test patch of a given, fixed lightness. This test patch will be surrounded by several borders that differ in lightness, one from another. With this arrangement, you should be able to produce different degrees of brightness contrast. But how do you measure the extent of the effect? One way would be to ask a participant to assign numbers to the test patch corresponding to how bright she thought it was. But you will use a more accurate technique: each time you present a border around the test patch, you will ask the participant to match the apparent brightness of the test patch by choosing another patch that seems to match it. The matching patch that is chosen, having been carefully measured for its lightness, will then serve as an index of how light the participant perceived the test patch to be.

First, cut out the matching patches and the borders on the insert for Chapter 4. The matching patches are the 10 squares on the left. Note that there is a number on the back of each that corresponds to its lightness. (The units for these numbers have to do with how various lightnesses are actually created by printers, and it is not necessary to know them for this exercise. It is sufficient that the patches are ordered correctly.) Now cut out the six borders on the right side of the insert, and cut out the central square area of each. Note that the borders are also marked with a lightness code on the back. Be very careful with both matching patches and borders to trim away any gray from the adjoining figures so that each cutout is an even gray. On the bottom of the insert is the test patch that has already been placed on a white surrounding region. The test patch has a lightness value of 6. *Do not cut out the test figure!* Leave it on its background and place this in turn on a sheet of black construction paper.

Now you are ready to run the experiment. The procedure is to select one background, place it over the test patch, and ask your participant to select a matching patch from among her 10 choices that appears to match the test patch in brightness. (Be sure that she lays down the matching patch on the black area to the right of the background to be certain of her choice.) Be careful to tell the participant not to hesitate to select different matching patches with different backgrounds if she feels this is appropriate. Participants may think that because the test patch remains the same, they should always select the same matching patch. Do not let the participant see the test patch without a border between trials as this may also cause a bias toward a particular matching patch.

Place the matching patches at the top of the black construction paper haphazardly. Run the participant through 18 trials of the experiment, 3 trials with each background. To have the backgrounds presented in a random order in each set of six, here are three random orders that you may use to determine the sequence in which the backgrounds are presented: 5, 10, 3, 1, 4, 7; 4, 3, 10, 7, 1, 5; and 10, 4, 1, 5, 7, 3 (the numbers refer to the lightness codes on the back of each background).

After you have presented a background over the test patch and the participant has chosen her matching patch, place the value of the matching patch in the appropriate space in the table that follows. After the experiment is complete, add up the values in each column and divide by 3 to get an average matching patch value for each background.

Now you can plot these data in the graph provided. Along the *x*-axis are the six values of background that you used. Above each find the average value of the matching patch that you calculated from the table, and place a dot at the value (as determined from the *y*-axis). Now connect the dots and note the shape of the function.

Recall that the test patch has a lightness value of 6. Given this, what shape should the function have? How much of a brightness contrast were you able to obtain? How could you improve the experiment to get an even larger effect?

Reference

Heinemann, E. G. (1955). Simultaneous brightness induction as a function of inducing- and test-field luminance. *Journal of Experimental Psychology, 50,* 89–96.

Background values:	1	3	4	5	7	10
Matching value 1:	______	______	______	______	______	______
Matching value 2:	______	______	______	______	______	______
Matching value 3:	______	______	______	______	______	______
Total matching value:	______	______	______	______	______	______
Average matching value:	______	______	______	______	______	______

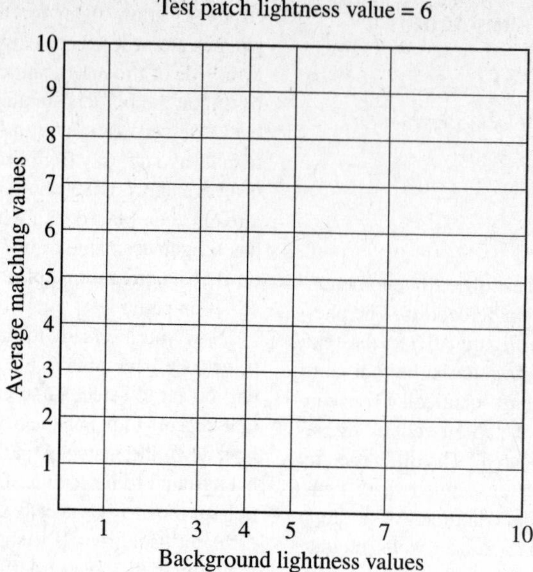
Test patch lightness value = 6
10
9
8
7
6
5
4
3
2
1
Average matching values
1
3
4
5
7
10
Background lightness values

CHAPTER 5

Perception

Learning Objectives

THE COMPLEXITY OF PERCEPTION

1. Know that the central issue of perception is not why a stimulus is recognized as an object, but why it is even seen as an object.
2. Keep in mind the characteristics of the proximal stimulus in comparison with the distal stimulus.
3. Understand that to organize the sensory world, three questions must be asked of any given stimulus: Where is it? What is it doing? What is it?

THE PERCEPTION OF DEPTH: WHERE IS IT?

Binocular cues

4. Be aware of the significance of binocular disparity in depth perception.

Monocular cues

5. What are the monocular cues to depth perception? How is texture important?

The perception of depth through motion

6. How do motion parallax and optic flow contribute to our perception of depth? How do they differ?

The role of redundancy

7. Why do we have multiple mechanisms for perceiving depth?

THE PERCEPTION OF MOVEMENT: WHAT IS IT DOING?

Retinal motion

8. Be familiar with cells known as motion detectors

Apparent movement

9. Be familiar with the phenomena of apparent movement and induced motion, and the relevance of these phenomena to the study of real movement.

Eye movements

10. How are we able to distinguish between a moving world with a stationary self (e.g., watching a car go by) and a stationary world with a moving self (e.g., looking out the window of a moving train)?
11. Understand that there is a mechanism that compensates for retinal displacement of objects when the eyes move.

Illusions of motion

12. Describe some motion illusions.

FORM PERCEPTION: WHAT IS IT?

13. Why is form perception not simply a matter of accumulating a checklist?
14. What kinds of information are we able to disregard in order to understand what we see?
15. Be aware of the central assumption of Gestalt psychology as it applies to perception.
16. Why do we need to understand both the perception of parts and the relationships among the parts to account for form perception?

The elements of form

17. Review the evidence for mechanisms in the physiology of the brain that underlie the perception of features.

19. Describe some behavioral evidence for the existence of elementary feature detectors in the visual system.
20. Be aware of the later stage of processing at which features are assumed to be conjoined. How does the study of illusory conjunctions pinpoint the stage of processing that is at work in pattern recognition?

Perceptual parsing

21. What is the role of perceptual parsing in scene perception? Why is it important?
22. Give examples of how perceptual parsing occurs in vision and audition.
23. How is the parsing of figure and ground an example of perceptual segregation?
24. Be familiar with reversible figures and how they contribute to our understanding of perceptual parsing. What proposal has been made about the perception of reversible figures?
25. What phenomena occur through perceptual parsing, and how do they relate to each other?

Pattern recognition

26. Describe the feature net model as an approach to pattern recognition. Be familiar with its systems of activation.

27. What phenomena show that context affects pattern recognition? What is priming?

28. How do top-down and bottom-up activations combine to yield pattern recognition?

29. Why is an intermediate step corresponding to the use of geons necessary in some perception? What are geons?

30. How do patients with visual agnosias inform us about the creation of structural descriptions and the interpretation of them in perception?

The processing sequence in form perception

31. Review the major steps in form perception. Be prepared to discuss how these may be arranged in sequence or in parallel in actual perception.

The perceiver's active role

32. What examples illustrate that the perceiver has an active role in perception?

33. Describe a study of apparent movement that illustrates the constructive nature of perception.

FORM PERCEPTION AND THE NERVOUS SYSTEM

Early stages of visual processing

34. Know the difference between magno and parvo cells. How do they function differently in perception?

Visual processing in the brain

35. Be able to distinguish between the "what" and "where" pathways in the brain. How are they different anatomically and in function? What evidence supports these differences?

The binding problem

36. Be aware of the binding problem and how it is created by a visual system that is based on component analyses of scenes.

37. How does firing synchrony among neurons figure into a solution to the binding problem?

PERCEPTUAL SELECTION: ATTENTION

38. What is attention?

Selection through orientation

39. How can the study of orienting movements inform us about attention?

Selective looking

40. What is visual search?

41. What are the conditions that permit parallel visual search, and what are those that require serial search?

42. Be familiar with studies showing that even in vision, attention can be moved internally without moving the eyes.

43. What role does attention play in solving the binding problem?

44. How is priming relevant to attention?

45. What happens to perception when an object is not in the focus of attention? Is it processed duly?

46. Be familiar with studies focusing on unattended stimuli.

PERCEIVING CONSTANCY

47. What is the relationship between distal objects and the proximal stimuli they cause that gives rise to the problem of constancy?

Size and shape constancy

48. Be able to describe the phenomena of size and shape constancy.

49. What is meant by higher-order invariants, and how can they be used to solve the problem of size constancy?

50. What role is played by distance cues such as motion parallax in the perception of constant size?

51. Helmholtz's principle of unconscious inference is a powerful explanation of size constancy. Describe it and give an example.

52. How important are distance cues to the perception of size constancy?

Programmed Exercises

THE COMPLEXITY OF PERCEPTION

1. The properties of a three-dimensional distal stimulus are perceived as constant despite continuing variation of the __________ stimulus. — proximal

2. To perceive an object, the observer must __________ the sensory world into a coherent, meaningful scene. — organize

THE PERCEPTION OF DEPTH: WHERE IS IT?

3. The two eyes look out on the world from slightly different positions and thus obtain a somewhat different view of any solid object on which they converge. This is called __________ __________. — binocular disparity

4. Relative size is an example of a __________ depth cue. — monocular

5. The impression of depth gained by looking at sand on a beach is an example of a __________ __________. — texture gradient

6. Far-off objects are blocked from view by other opaque objects that obstruct their optical path to the eye. This is a depth cue called __________. interposition

7. As we move our head or body from right to left, the images projected by the objects outside will move across the retina. The direction and speed of this motion is an effective monocular depth cue called __________ __________. motion parallax

8. The phenomenon that causes an apparent change in the size of objects as we move toward or away from them is known as __________ __________. optic flow

THE PERCEPTION OF MOVEMENT: WHAT IS IT DOING?

9. Suppose we briefly turn on a light in one location in the visual field, then turn it off, and after an appropriate period of time (somewhere between 30 and 200 msec), turn on a second light in a different location. The resulting phenomenon is called __________ movement. apparent

10. If the ground is moving and a figure is stationary in the visual field, the figure is seen as moving. This phenomenon of illusory movement is called __________ motion. induced

11. The perception of movement in one of two stimuli depends on which is seen as a stationary __________ of reference. frame

12. Perceived __________ seems to be a result of the brain's compensation for the retinal displacement caused by voluntary eye movements. stability

13. Induced motion of the __________ may occur when we sit in a stationary train while observing an adjacent train in motion. self

FORM PERCEPTION: WHAT IS IT?

14. One theory of form perception is that observers consult a mental __________ to see if an object has certain properties. checklist

15. __________ __________ allows us to continue processing a stimulus even when our eyes have shifted. Sensory memory

16. A form is perceived as a __________, a whole that is different from the sum of its parts. Gestalt

17. A task used frequently to study form perception requires a research participant to indicate whether a certain target appears in a briefly presented array. This is called a __________ __________ task. visual search

18. Cells that respond to specific movements on the retina are __________ __________. direction specific

19. An __________ __________ occurs when a participant mistakenly ties together two features in an object that did not occur together. illusory conjunction

20. The process known as __________ enables us to separate figure from ground. parsing

21. __________ figures are ones in which either of two figure-ground organizations is possible. Reversible (ambiguous)

22. Proximity, similarity, and good continuation are examples of the laws of __________ __________. perceptual parsing

23. Contours that continue smoothly along their original course follow the law of __________ __________, a principle that is illustrated by __________ contours (perceiving contours when they don't exist). good continuation, subjective

24. The model of feature analysis that uses activation and deactivation to recognize stimulus patterns is known as the __________ __________ model. feature net

25. A feature net model is an example of __________-__________ processing, an approach to pattern recognition that begins with component features and builds up to larger units. bottom-up

26. The __________-__________ process of pattern recognition begins with higher units, because it is often affected by higher-level knowledge and expectations. top-down

27. __________ effects demonstrate that there is some top-down processing in the perceptual process. Priming

28. Three different approaches for understanding how we combine sensory information to observe the world are the __________, __________-__________, and __________ approaches. classic, process-model, neuroscience

29. One model by Biederman uses approximately 30 geometric primitives called __________ as the basis for recognizing all objects. geons

30. Simultaneous multiple-constraint satisfaction refers to the idea that the output must be __________ with the information received. compatible

31. If a patient is able to perceive an object but not recognize it, the patient has a visual __________. agnosia

32. The processing steps that occur during the course of object recognition may occur all at once or sequentially, demonstrating __________ and __________ processing, respectively. parallel, serial

33. The stimulus information we receive is often __________. It is not sufficient to permit a clear perception of what the distal stimulus is. ambiguous

34. We rarely encounter perceptual __________ in daily life because there are multiple sources of information about each object we encounter. illusions

FORM PERCEPTION AND THE NERVOUS SYSTEM

35. There are two sorts of ganglion cells that exit the retina. One is responsible for detecting movement in the periphery and is composed of __________ cells, and the other is responsible for carrying pattern and form information from the fovea and is composed of __________ cells. magno parvo

36. The __________ system, located in the temporal cortex, codes for object identity, while the __________ system, located in the parietal cortex, is responsible for detecting object location. what where

37. The __________ problem is caused by the visual system's analysis of scenes by breaking them up into parts; the consequence is that there must be a mechanism that puts the parts back together again. binding

38. The __________-__________ oscillation refers to the 40 times-per-second rate at which neurons fire. gamma-band

PERCEPTUAL SELECTION: ATTENTION

39. The ways by which we perceive selectively are grouped under the label "__________." attention

40. On the average, our eyes move three or four times per second to fixate objects. These fixations are purposeful, not random. Our eye movements serve the purpose of __________ us to salient stimuli. orienting

41. During an internal selection process, the __________ __________ may move even though the eyes remain stationary. mind's eye

42. Visual search for __________ features can be accomplished by examining all the objects in an array at the same time; when searching for a __________ object, though, search proceeds one object at a time. simple complex

43. Injury to the __________ cortex impairs a patient on tasks with conjoined features. parietal

44. __________ can bias perceivers to process information at a particular spatial location if that location is cued in advance of the information that is presented to them. Priming

45. In the absence of __________ it is remarkable how little of a visual display is processed even if an observer is looking right at the objects he or she fails to process. attention

46. When stimuli are presented over earphones so that each ear receives a different message, the content of the __________ message is almost completely unprocessed. unattended

47. A participant's attention can be grabbed if her __________ is used in the unattended message. name

PERCEIVING CONSTANCY

48. The perceptual system responds to real objects outside regardless of variations in their proximal images. This is best illustrated by the perceptual __________: lightness, size, and shape. constancies

49. Gibson has stressed the importance of __________ relationships within a stimulus pattern in explaining perceptual organization. invariant (higher-order)

50. A Boeing 747 at a distance of 1,000 feet will look larger than a single-engine two-seater at a distance of 50 feet even though the retinal image of the latter will be greater than that of the former. This is called __________ __________. An analogous phenomenon occurs in the perception of __________.

size constancy
shape

51. According to Helmholtz, the use of distance cues to guide our perception can occur in a process known as __________ __________.

unconscious inference

52. We don't perceive changes in retinal stimulation as motion because of __________ __________.

position constancy

Self-Test

1. Which of the following is *not* true of the proximal stimulus?
   a. It is two-dimensional in vision.
   b. It can vary in size and shape.
   c. It alone enables us to perceive the constant properties of objects.
   d. It is the retinal image of the distal stimulus in vision.

2. Binocular disparity is caused by
   a. a slight difference in the size of the two eyes.
   b. small imperfections in the lens or cornea.
   c. the slightly different position of each eye.
   d. the favoring of one eye over the other.

3. Binocular disparity
   a. is an effective cue to depth for long distances.
   b. occurs because our eyes receive virtually the same image.
   c. is not by itself a sufficient cue to depth.
   d. can be simulated by viewing specially designed two-dimensional drawings.
   e. is effective only for familiar objects.

4. The figure below illustrates all of the following monocular cues to depth *except*
   a. linear perspective.
   b. relative size.
   c. binocular disparity.
   d. texture gradients.
   e. interposition.

5. Looking at cobblestones on the street gives us an example of
   a. linear perspective.
   b. relative size.
   c. texture gradients.
   d. interposition.

6. Which of the following is *not* true of motion parallax?
   a. Nearby objects move in a direction opposite to our own as we move through space.
   b. Objects farther away move in a direction similar to our own as we move through space.
   c. Objects farther away move at a lesser velocity than objects closer.
   d. Objects closer to us move at a greater velocity than objects farther away.

7. The change in the size of objects as we move closer or farther away from them is known as
   a. optic flow.
   b. motion parallax.
   c. linear perspective.
   d. apparent movement.

8. One of the most effective monocular depth cues is __________, which is absent in pictorial representations but present in real life.
   a. linear perspective
   b. relative size
   c. interposition
   d. motion parallax

9. The View-Master was able to create the illusion of depth using
   a. binocular disparity.
   b. monocular cues.
   c. motion parallax.
   d. none of the above.

10. Apparent movement refers to
    a. the perception of movement when two stimuli are presented in alternation at the proper temporal and spatial intervals.
    b. the perception of movement of a target when in fact it is stationary but the background is moving.
    c. the perception of self-movement when we are stationary but the scene that we are watching is moving.
    d. none of the above.

11. Induced motion differs from apparent movement in that
    a. in the former case it is the figure that moves, whereas in the latter case it is the ground that moves.
    b. the former is a physical phenomenon and the latter is a retinal phenomenon.
    c. induced motion is based on relative displacement, whereas apparent movement is based on absolute displacement.
    d. none of the above.

12. Which two of the following are examples of induced movement?
    a. The moon moving through the clouds
    b. Perceiving movement of a stationary spot of light in darkness
    c. Perceiving movement of a stationary spot of light when the rectangular frame around it moves
    d. Perceiving that the moon moves when we move with respect to it
    e. Perceiving movement in the successive frames of a movie

13. When several investigators temporarily paralyzed their eye muscles and then tried to move their eyes, they saw objects move in their visual field even though their eyes did not move (nor did the objects). This suggests that
    a. paralyzing the eye muscles doesn't affect motion perception.
    b. perceived stability is produced by compensating for motor movement.
    c. perceived motion is produced by compensating for motor movement.
    d. none of the above.

14. One of the most interesting features of form recognition is that forms are recognized in spite of
    a. transpositions of pattern.
    b. the fact that their apparent lightnesses change with changes in illumination.
    c. the change in perceived shape that occurs when the angle of regard of an object is changed.
    d. none of the above.

15. According to the Gestalt point of view, the perception of an object depends on the
    a. perception of the relations among parts of the object.
    b. perception of the elementary features of the object.
    c. perception of the object's geons.
    d. flow of information as an object is transformed with successive process steps.

16. Object recognition begins with
    a. recognition of Gestalt properties.
    b. visual search.
    c. selective attention.
    d. conjunction of features.
    e. feature detection.

17. If a target in a visual search task differs from the background items on a feature such as color or curvature, participants will
    a. struggle to detect the target.
    b. engage in a conjunctive search for the target.
    c. perceive the target quickly with little search required.
    d. none of the above.

18. If a participant were presented with a display of letters printed in colored inks that included a blue G, a red M, and a yellow B, and if this display were presented briefly, he or she might see
    a. a blue D.
    b. a red T.
    c. a yellow R.
    d. a blue M.

19. Which of the following statements about perceptual parsing is *not* true?
    a. It is contributed by the individual and is not a part of the stimulus.
    b. It is the first stage of perceptual organization and separates the stimuli into various subcomponents.
    c. It occurs only in the realm of visual perception.
    d. All of the above.

20. Segregating figure from ground (as in a reversible figure)
    a. is a high-level perceptual process that requires a good deal of preliminary analysis.
    b. can be done only with reversible figures.
    c. is accomplished by perceiving the contour separating two regions as belonging to the ground.
    d. is too elementary a perceptual process to be used effectively by artists.
    e. none of the above.

Reversible figure that can be perceived either as two faces in profile or as a white vase.

21. For reversible figures such as the one above, which of the following is *false?*
    a. The figure is generally seen in front of the ground.
    b. A reversible figure-ground display is characterized by two adjoining regions alternately acting as figures.
    c. A contour can be seen as simultaneously belonging to figure and to ground.
    d. None of the above.

22. All of the following are parsing cues *except*
    a. proximity.
    b. similarity.
    c. good continuation.
    d. simplicity.

23. The law of proximity states that
    a. the closer an object is to an observer, the easier it is to identify it.
    b. the closer two objects are to each other, the greater the chance that they will be grouped together perceptually.
    c. given any two objects, one is always nearer (perceptually) to an arbitrary third object than the other.
    d. none of the above.

24. Feature net and other similar theories of pattern recognition are based on the principle that
    a. feature detectors can be in competition and the correct one can win out.
    b. feature detectors are all independent of one another in their analysis of a pattern.
    c. feature detectors work on an object only after the relationships among the parts have been determined.
    d. top-down and bottom-up processes cannot work together in object recognition.

25. Pattern recognition is a
    a. top-down process.
    b. horizontal process.
    c. bottom-up process.
    d. a and c
    e. a and b

26. A professor is giving a lecture on the state of the U.S. economy. His lecture is suddenly broken up when he coughs several times so his speech stream is interrupted but not stopped. Although the coughs produce physical gaps in his speaking, the students hear and understand the presentation. This is an example of
    a. feature analysis.
    b. context effect.
    c. bottom-up processing.
    d. attention.

27. Which of the following statements about geons is *not* true?
    a. About 70 geons serve as the geometric primitives of the perceptual system.
    b. Geons can be combined with other geons to make up many different objects.
    c. The recognition of geons is accomplished by an early stage of pattern recognition.
    d. The relationships among geons are an important part of perceptual recognition.

28. A person with an agnosia would be
    a. able to recognize an object but not perceive its parts.
    b. unable to recognize an object even though he or she could perceive its shape.
    c. unable to recognize the color or shape of an object.
    d. able to write a structural description of an object but unable to copy the object.

29. Which of the following does *not* illustrate the active role that perceivers play in perception?
    a. The separation of figure from ground
    b. The perception of an ambiguous figure
    c. Priming
    d. Visual search for a single feature that can proceed by simultaneous examination of several objects in a display

30. Given the properties of magno and parvo cells, and given the two flows of information in the visual system into the "what" and "where" streams, it seems likely that
    a. magno cells feed into the "where" system.
    b. parvo cells feed into the "what" system.
    c. magno cells feed into the "what" system.
    d. parvo cells feed into the "where" system.
    e. magno and parvo cells feed into both systems.
    f. a and b
    g. c and d

31. The binding problem is caused by the visual system's breaking up of
    a. proximity and similarity information.
    b. form and location information.
    c. size and shape information.
    d. location and movement information.
    e. information about large and small objects.

32. Orienting movements, like turning of the head, are external manifestations of
    a. differentiation.
    b. attention.
    c. recalibration.
    d. adaptation.

33. During a visual search procedure
    a. a participant is asked to pick out the most relevant component of a stimulus pattern as quickly as possible.
    b. participants may employ methods of physical orientation and central selection to locate the target.
    c. the orienting movements that a participant makes show little relation to the features of objects that are attended to during scanning.
    d. the internal selection process often hinders accurate scanning and location of the correct target.

34. In a visual search task, if the target is a blue T that is embedded among green Rs, blue Gs, and red Ts, participants would have to engage in
    a. a serial search for the target.
    b. a parallel search for the target.
    c. either a serial or a parallel search for the target, depending on their choice.
    d. none of the above.

35. In a study, subjects are presented with a sequence of visual displays each of which is composed of a line drawing of one object superimposed on a line drawing of another object. One of the drawings is in red, and the other in blue. We ask subjects to monitor the red line drawing and respond when they see any object that is human-made (e.g., a wrench). Suppose we surprise the subjects after they see the entire sequence by asking them about the blue objects. On the basis of what we know about the effect of attention on perception, they should be able to
    a. name quite a number of objects.
    b. accurately judge whether there were many human-made objects drawn in blue.
    c. a and b
    d. none of the above.

36. Which of the following is *not* true of the effects of selective attention?
    a. Some information gets in from an unattended message.
    b. It primes certain feature analyzers.
    c. It helps prepare us for an upcoming stimulus.
    d. It is restricted to vision only.
    e. All of the above.

37. Two proposals have been made about the perception of constancies. One is based on the idea that there
    a. are invariant relationships among elements of the distal stimulus.
    b. are invariant relationships among elements of the proximal stimulus.
    c. is an unconscious inference made about the relationships between elements of a proximal stimulus.
    d. is an unconscious inference made about the relationships between invariant features of a distal stimulus.

38. The other proposal about the perception of constancy is based on the idea that
    a. we perceive constancy in shape by making an unconscious inference about the orientation of a retinal image and texture elements from the background.
    b. we perceive size constancy by making an unconscious inference about the size of a retinal image and the distance we are from an object.
    c. we perceive lightness constancy by making an unconscious inference about the size of a retinal image and the reflectance of that image.
    d. none of the above.

39. Size constancy appears to depend on
    a. the fact that although the retinal image of an object changes as we move away from it, its size relative to other objects in a display does not.
    b. the perceived distance that an object is from an observer.
    c. various cues such as linear perspective, binocular disparity, and motion parallax.
    d. all of the above.

40. Sensory memory
    a. allows us to continue processing even when a stimulus vanishes from view.
    b. accounts for the phenomenon where we ask "What did you say?" only to realize that we did in fact hear what was said.
    c. is created by the decaying activity in each step of perceptual processing.
    d. all of the above.

Answer Key for Self-Test

1. c
2. c
3. d
4. c
5. c
6. b
7. a
8. d
9. a
10. a
11. c
12. a, c
13. b
14. a
15. a
16. e
17. c
18. d
19. c
20. e
21. c
22. d
23. b
24. a
25. d
26. b
27. a
28. b
29. c
30. f
31. b
32. b
33. b
34. a
35. d
36. d
37. a
38. b
39. d
40. d

Investigating Psychological Phenomena

THE EFFECT OF MENTAL SET

Equipment: Stimuli included
Number of participants: One
Time per participant: Twenty minutes
Time for experimenter: Twenty minutes

The issue of how past experience influences perception (an example of top-down processing) is an important one in psychology and has generated quite a bit of research. This is a difficult issue to resolve because there are many ways in which past experience might influence perceptual processes. In this problem you are asked to consider a series of hypothetical experiments (modeled after a study by Epstein and Rock, 1960) and to provide alternative interpretations of the hypothetical results. As you move through the experiments, try to develop one hypothesis that will account for all of the results described. The stimuli for all the experiments are the ambiguous and unambiguous versions of Leeper's old woman–young woman figure shown below.

A

Y

O

Notice that the first picture (A) can be seen either as a young woman or as an old woman; that is, it is ambiguous. The second picture (Y) is quite similar to the first (A) except that some detail has been changed so that it has become a fairly unambiguous picture of a young woman. Likewise, the third picture (O) is a fairly unambiguous version of an old woman. The purpose of all the experiments is to determine how prior exposure to the unambiguous versions of the figure influences whether participants call the ambiguous version an old woman or a young woman. Imagine that 20 participants are run in each hypothetical experiment.

EXPERIMENT 1

Each participant is shown the following series of slides (at a rate of one slide every eight seconds) and asked to identify each picture as "young" or "old" as it is presented: YYOOOOOOOOA (Y refers to a presentation of the unambiguous young woman, O refers to a presentation of the unambiguous old woman, and A refers to the presentation of the ambiguous image). All participants name the Y and O versions of the figure correctly. On the critical trial, the ambiguous picture A, the results are as follows: Twenty participants call it "old"; no participants call it "young." One interpretation of this result is that the more-frequently presented unambiguous version determined the perception of the ambiguous picture. This is listed as Hypothesis 1 on the answer sheet. What alternative explanations can you propose to explain the responses of participants in this hypothetical experiment? Write them on the answer sheet. There are at least three other plausible possibilities.

Before you go on to Experiments 2 through 4, check to see whether the hypotheses you have developed coincide with those given in the answers to the problem. If not, use the given hypotheses as the basis for your answers to the questions posed in Experiments 2 through 4.

EXPERIMENT 2

A new set of 20 participants receives the following series of slides: YYYYYOOOOOA. Again the responses to all the Y and O stimuli are correct, and the responses to the A stimulus are as follows: Twenty participants respond "old woman"; none respond "young woman." Consider each of the four hypotheses raised to account for the results of Experiment 1 and evaluate how each fares with the results of the experiment. Record your responses under Experiment 2 on the answer sheet.

EXPERIMENT 3

Twenty participants each receive the series of slides OOOOOOOYYYA. All respond correctly to the Y and O stimuli. The responses to A are these: 20 participants call it "young woman"; none call it "old woman." Again evaluate the success of each of the four hypotheses at accounting for these results.*

EXPERIMENT 4

Twenty new participants are shown the series of slides YYOYY-OYYOA. All Os and Ys are identified correctly. The data on the A presentations are these: 18 participants respond "old woman"; 2 participants respond "young woman" (a reliable difference). Which of the four hypotheses can explain these results? Is one of the four hypotheses confirmed by the results of all four experiments?

*We continue to consider Hypothesis 1 even though Experiment 2 cannot be explained by it; scientists do not typically discard a hypothesis because of a single contradictory finding.

ANSWER SHEET

Experiment 1

Hypothesis 1 Frequency of presentation determines the response to the ambiguous figure.

Hypothesis 2 ____________________

Hypothesis 3 ____________________

Hypothesis 4 ____________________

Experiment 2

Hypothesis 1 ____________________

Hypothesis 2 ____________________

Hypothesis 3 ____________________

Hypothesis 4 ____________________

Experiment 3

Hypothesis 1 ____________________

Hypothesis 2 ____________________

Hypothesis 3 ____________________

Hypothesis 4 ____________________

Experiment 4

Which of the four hypotheses can account for these results? ____________________

Which hypotheses can account for the results of all four experiments? ____________________

Answers to Problem

EXPERIMENT 1

Hypothesis 2: It is possible that the interpretation of the ambiguous picture was entirely influenced by the perception of the immediately preceding picture of the old woman. If so, this would be called a recency effect, because the most recently presented picture would have had the strongest influence on perception of the ambiguous picture.

Hypothesis 3: An alternative possibility has to do with what the participant might be expecting to be presented on the last trial. He or she has just seen eight consecutive pictures of the old woman and so might reasonably expect that the next picture will also be that of an old woman. Thus, if this were the case, the participant's cognitive expectations would be guiding his or her perceptions.

Hypothesis 4: A final possibility is that participants in general have a bias to respond with the name "old woman." One might suppose that such a bias exists (for some reason) even independently of what the participant actually sees. That is, participants are biased to call the ambiguous version an "old woman" regardless of what precedes it.

EXPERIMENT 2

This experiment rules out Hypothesis 1, the frequency hypothesis. Both unambiguous versions were presented equally frequently before the ambiguous version was presented. Thus, a participant's perception of the ambiguous version could not have been influenced by the more frequently presented unambiguous version. None of the alternative hypotheses is ruled out by these results:

1. The response to the ambiguous version was the same as that to the most recently presented unambiguous version. Thus, recency is a viable interpretation of these results.
2. Because the responses to the sixth through tenth stimuli were "old woman," the participants may have built up an expectation that the eleventh stimulus would be an old woman as well. So cognitive expectations may well have guided their response to the ambiguous item.
3. The fact that most participants identified the ambiguous picture as an old woman is consistent with the possibility that they have a bias to call it that regardless of their immediately prior perceptual experience.

EXPERIMENT 3

Once again this experiment disconfirms the frequency hypothesis. This time participants responded to the test picture with the name of the *least* frequently presented unambiguous picture. Also, the experiment rules out Hypothesis 4, which states that participants have a predisposing bias to call the ambiguous version an old woman. Both the recency and the cognitive expectation hypotheses can account for the results.

EXPERIMENT 4

The cognitive expectation hypothesis probably is ruled out. In responding to the unambiguous versions, participants were following a regular pattern of two "young woman" responses followed by one "old woman" response. The last unambiguous picture was that of the old woman; thus participants should have been expecting a young woman next. Instead, most responded "old woman," a result that can be explained only by noting that the most recently presented unambiguous picture was that of the old woman. Thus, the recency explanation is compatible with these results. Once again the frequency hypothesis is disconfirmed because the most frequently presented unambiguous picture was the young woman. The response bias explanation might be brought up to explain the results of this experiment except that it was ruled out by Experiment 3. Thus, the only explanation that can explain the results of all four experiments satisfactorily is Hypothesis 2, which claims that the picture a participant sees most recently will affect his or her current perception.

This exercise demonstrates how it is sometimes possible to start with several potential explanations of a phenomenon and successfully rule out the incorrect ones with further experimentation. Initially there were four plausible interpretations of the results of hypothetical Experiment 1. The results of hypothetical Experiments 2 through 4, however, rule out all but one of the alternatives.

Even though the experiments described above are only hypothetical, they illustrate this process of narrowing down alternative interpretations. You may want to try out any of these experiments to determine the actual results. On page 57 you will find sets of pictures of both the unambiguous versions and the ambiguous version of the figure. Cut them out and return to the previous pages of this section. Perform the experiments as described there and record the results. Do your results correspond to the hypothetical data? Do the same hypotheses apply?

Reference

Epstein, W., & Rock, I. (1960). Perceptual set as an artifact of recency. *American Journal of Psychology, 73,* 214–228.

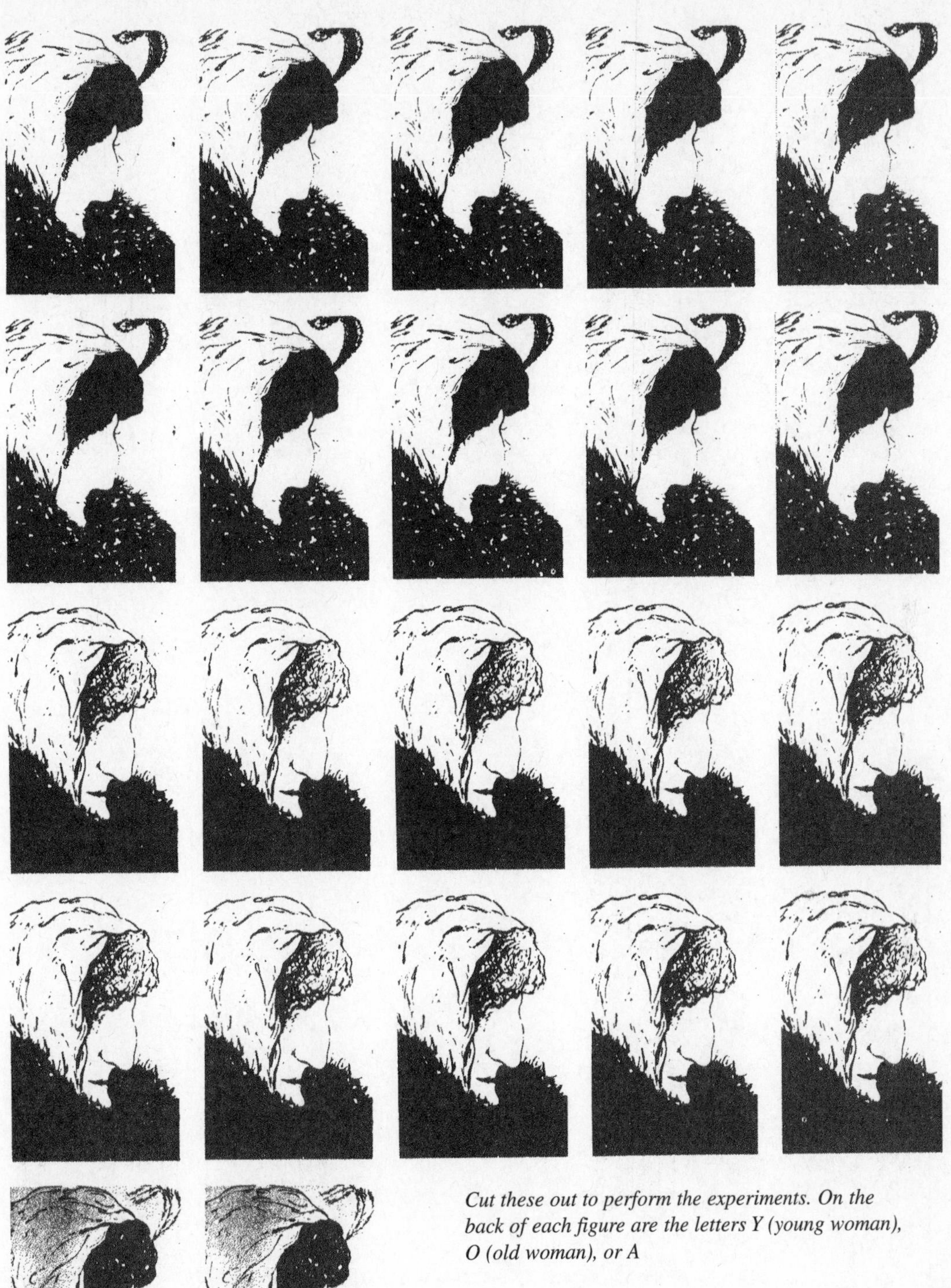

Cut these out to perform the experiments. On the back of each figure are the letters Y (young woman), O (old woman), or A

Y	Y	Y	Y	Y
Y	Y	Y	Y	Y
O	O	O	O	O
O	O	O	O	O
			A	A

CHAPTER 6

Learning

Learning Objectives

THE PERSPECTIVE OF LEARNING THEORY

1. Describe the point of view of learning theorists, the role of the process of association in their thinking, and the reason that most of their work focused on nonhuman animals.

HABITUATION

2. Define habituation and discuss its adaptive significance. Do the same for dishabituation.

CLASSICAL CONDITIONING

3. Distinguish habituation from association

Pavlov and the conditioned response

4. Explain the basic procedure (paradigm) of classical conditioning, and define conditioned and unconditioned stimuli and responses.
5. Distinguish between classical conditioning and habituation.

The major phenomena of classical conditioning

6. Draw a curve to represent the acquisition of a conditioned response.
7. Define and indicate the significance of second-order (or higher-order) conditioning.
8. Be able to define extinction, spontaneous recovery, and reconditioning and to indicate why they are adaptive.

Generalization

9. Describe generalization.
10. Describe discrimination and contrast it with generalization.
11. Discuss the effects of different times of onset of the conditioned and unconditioned stimulus. What is the most effective CS-US interval, and why is this adaptive?
12. Distinguish contiguity and contingency, and explain the studies that indicate that contingency is a critical factor in the formation of conditioned responses.
13. Evaluate the idea that informativeness is critical in conditioning.
14. What are the consequences of absence of contingency, even in the presence of contiguity, between a potential CS and US? Distinguish between fear and anxiety.
15. Explain the role of surprise in learning, and show how blocking demonstrates this.

Extensions of classical conditioning

16. Indicate how classical conditioning can account for acquired fears and phobias, and describe how conditioned fear is measured. Describe the conditioned emotional response.
17. Show that the conditioned response often functions to prepare the organism for the unconditioned stimulus, and hence that the CR and UR often differ.
18. Give an example of how a conditioned response can compensate for the effect of an unconditioned stimulus. Why are conditioned compensatory responses adaptive?

INSTRUMENTAL CONDITIONING

19. Review the major similarities and differences between classical conditioning and instrumental conditioning.

Thorndike and the law of effect

20. Explain the law of effect and indicate the evidence that supports it.
21. What is the relation between the law of effect and the evolutionary principle of survival of the fittest?

Skinner and operant behavior

22. What modifications in conceptions and methods did Skinner propose to Thorndike's approach to instrumental conditioning?

The major phenomena of instrumental conditioning

23. How do the phenomena of instrumental conditioning parallel those of classical conditioning?
24. Describe the processes of generalization and discrimination in instrumental conditioning. Indicate how discrimination training can be used with complex stimuli, such as in training pigeons to peck at pictures of water.
25. What is shaping? Give an example of how it is used to create complex behaviors.

26. Give examples of conditioned and primary reinforcers, and describe how a conditioned reinforcer can be produced or eliminated.

27. Evaluate the importance of information, behavioral contrast, and intrinsic motivation as extensions or modifiers of the concept of reinforcement.

28. Describe the study that shows that adding a primary reinforcer to an intrinsically reinforcing activity can cause it to eventually decrease. Give some explanations for this effect.

29. Define and describe schedules of reinforcement and their properties, and indicate the effect of the schedules on resistance to extinction.

30. Define punishment, and indicate how it is used to influence learning. Compare the effect of gradually increasing punishment to the effect of introducting a strong punishment at the outset of training.

Changing behaviors or acquiring knowledge

31. Describe Tolman's experiments on latent learning and cognitive maps, and indicate how they provide an alternative account of instrumental learning, in terms of acquiring knowledge.

32. Define act-outcome representations and describe a study that provides evidence for their existence.

33. Describe evidence for the existence of the joy of mastery and of learned helplessness. How do both demonstrate the importance of contingency in instrumental learning?

VARIETIES OF LEARNING

34. Explain what is meant by predispositions to learn or biological constraints on learning.

Biological influences on learning: Belongingness

35. Describe the phenomenon of taste-aversion learning, and indicate why it illustrates biological constraints.

36. Explain the link between belongingness or preparedness and the acquisition of phobias.

37. Discuss belongingness in response-outcome representations in instrumental conditioning.

Different types of learning

38. Describe the specialized learning associated with memory for sites of nuts hidden in many different places or the acquisition of the species-specific song in birds.

39. Account for the impressive learning feats shown in memory for sites and acquisition of song in birds and for their limitation to a particular domain of life. Relate this to the idea of adaptation to a particular niche.

40. Discuss observational learning and imitation as special features of human learning, and language as an area of specialized learning in humans.

41. Indicate some more or less universal properties of learning, and suggest why there should be such similarities.

THE NEURAL BASIS FOR LEARNING

42. Review the evidence for diversity in learning in terms of the neural basis for learning; include a discussion of both different areas of the brain mediating different types of learning, and differences in mechanisms at the level of the synapse.

43. Briefly describe each of the three ways that neural plasticity can occur at synapses.

44. In more detail, describe presynaptic facilitation, in terms of neurotransmitter changes as demonstrated in *Aplysia.*

45. What is long-term potentiation, and how might it account for learning and, in particular, contingency detection?

46. How can the structure of synapses change, involving dendritic spines in the postsynaptic neuron?

47. Review the evidence for widespread (across many species) mechanisms of neural plasticity, and also for at least one mechanism that may be limited to mammals.

SOME FINAL THOUGHTS: LEARNING THEORY AND BEYOND

48. Evaluate the strengths and shortcomings of accounts of all learning based on habituation, classical conditioning, and instrumental conditioning.

49. In what sense is key pecking by pigeons not an arbitrary operant? In what sense is key pecking classically conditioned?

Adaptive specializations of learning

50. Summarize the argument that there are specialized types of learning in particular species and ecological niches. Provide an illustration.

Similarities in what different species learn

51. Indicate some similarities across situations and species in properties of learning. How do these relate to environmental universals?

Programmed Exercises

THE PERSPECTIVE OF LEARNING THEORY

1. _________ _________ believe that a few simple laws of learning can account for most of human and animal behavior.	Learning theorists
2. Historically, the basic concept in learning theory is that of _________.	association

HABITUATION

3. __________ is a decline in the tendency to respond to stimuli that have become familiar through repeated exposure. Habituation

4. __________ is an increase in responsiveness caused by the perception of something novel. Dishabituation

CLASSICAL CONDITIONING

5. Unlike habituation, classical conditioning involves the formation of __________ between events. associations

6. __________ __________ was first demonstrated in the laboratory by Ivan Pavlov. Classical conditioning

7. After classical conditioning, the salivation of a dog on presentation of a previously neutral bell would be called a(n) __________ __________. The previously neutral bell is now called a(n) __________ __________. conditioned response conditioned stimulus

8. In Pavlov's laboratory, food in the mouth was a(n) __________ __________, and the salivation it produced was a(n) __________ __________. unconditioned stimulus unconditioned response

9. Salivation to meat powder in the mouth is a(n) __________ __________. Salivation to a tone paired with meat powder in the mouth is a(n) __________ __________. unconditioned response conditioned response

Strength of CR

Reinforced trials

10. The graph above is an example of an idealized __________ __________. learning curve

11. A light is paired with shock. Subsequently, a tone paired with the light comes to elicit fear. This is an example of __________-__________ __________. second(higher)-order conditioning

12. If after a CR has been established, the CS is presented but is not followed by the US, the result will be __________ of the CR. extinction

13. If time is allowed to pass, the CR will reappear when the CS is presented. This is the phenomenon of __________ __________. spontaneous recovery

14. If, after extinction, the pairings of the CS and US are resumed, the result will be __________. reconditioning

15. Horizontal stripes on a card (CS) are paired with a puff of air to the eye (US), resulting in a conditioned eye blink response. Now, the first time vertical stripes are presented, a conditioned eye blink is observed. This is an example of __________ __________. stimulus generalization

16. The greater the difference between a CS and another test stimulus, the weaker the CR to this test stimulus. This relationship is described as a __________ __________. generalization gradient

17. Reinforcement (US presentation) after CS^{+}, and nonreinforcement (no US) after CS^{-}, leads to __________. discrimination

18. Learning a conditioned response (CR) occurs most efficiently when the __________ precedes the __________ by a small time interval. This is called __________ pairing. CS US, forward

19. Pavlov and others claimed that togetherness in time, pairing, or __________ forms the basis for classical conditioning.
(temporal) contiguity

20. Later research suggests that what is critical for conditioning is that the CS predicts the US, so that there is a __________ between the CS and US.
contingency

21. The importance of contingency as opposed to contiguity suggests that the CS must be __________.
informative

22. The __________ of contingency prevents conditioning, and if a negative event like shock is the US, may increase __________.
absence
anxiety

23. Learning seems to occur when there is some __________ in the ongoing events.
surprise

24. In the presence of an informative stimulus, there is little conditioning to a new stimulus that is always added to (co-occurs with) the previously conditioned stimulus. This is because the new stimulus is not __________; this is called the __________ effect.
informative, blocking

25. Animals show __________ __________ when a stimulus-paired shock is presented to them. This is called the __________ __________ __________.
response suppression
conditioned emotional response

26. According to a classical conditioning analysis, the object of a phobia or fetish can be considered a __________ __________.
conditioned stimulus

27. In many instances, the CR does not duplicate the UR, but rather __________ the animal to deal with the UR.
prepares

28. Sometimes the CR has the opposite effect from the UR. This type of CR is called a __________ __________.
compensatory response

INSTRUMENTAL CONDITIONING

29. Another name for instrumental conditioning is __________ conditioning.
operant

30. In contrast to classical conditioning, the response in instrumental conditioning is __________.
voluntary

31. The experimental study of instrumental learning was begun by __________ in the context of a debate over the mental continuity of humans and animals, which was stimulated by the evolutionary theories of __________.
Thorndike
Darwin

32. Thorndike's __________ __________ __________ states that the consequences of a response determine whether it becomes strengthened or weakened.
law of effect

33. The most prominent figure in modern learning theory was __________.
(B. F.) Skinner

34. Skinner emphasized distinctions between classical conditioning and instrumental learning. In classical conditioning responses are __________, while in instrumental learning they are __________.
elicited
emitted

35. Skinner used the term __________ to describe the voluntary or emitted responses that are studied in instrumental learning. He preferred to use the __________ __________ as a measure of learning.
operant
response rate

36. Although operants are not elicited by external stimuli, the stimuli can control behavior as __________ __________.
discriminative stimuli

37. In classical conditioning, a(n) __________ tells an organism about events in the world: "No matter what you do, the US is coming." In instrumental learning, a(n) __________ tells the animal about the impact of its own behavior: "If you respond now, you'll get rewarded."
CS^+
S^+

38. Through discrimination training, pigeons have learned to peck a key only when presented with a picture of __________.
water

39. Animals can be trained to perform difficult responses by the process of __________, using the method of __________ __________.
shaping
successive approximation

40. After a neutral stimulus is paired with a __________ reinforcer such as food, the neutral stimulus acquires reinforcement properties. This is called __________ __________.	primary conditioned reinforcement
41. Animals and humans can be reinforced not only by events that reduce biological needs but also by __________ from the environment.	information
42. The effectiveness of a reinforcement depends on the context of reinforcement; whether prior reinforcements were larger or smaller than the current one. This is called __________ __________.	behavioral contrast
43. Behaviors performed for their own sake, providing their own reward, are described as cases of __________ motivation.	intrinsic
44. The rule set up by the experimenter (or society) that determines the occasions on which a response is reinforced is called a __________ __________ __________.	schedule of reinforcement
45. An animal that is reinforced for every five responses is on a __________-__________ schedule.	fixed-ratio
46. In __________ training, an aversive stimulus follows a particular response.	punishment

CHANGING BEHAVIORS OR ACQUIRING KNOWLEDGE

47. Edward Tolman's studies showing that rats learn about a maze by exploring it without explicit reinforcement demonstrate __________ learning and the creation of __________ maps by rats.	latent, cognitive
48. Animals seem able to learn about the specific relationships between their actions and the outcomes of those actions. They can acquire __________-__________ __________.	act-outcome representations
49. Dogs given inescapable shocks are then placed in an avoidance situation shuttlebox where they could learn a jumping response to escape and avoid shock. Instead, they lie quietly and take the shocks. Their behavior has been interpreted as learning that the presence or absence of shocks is not contingent on their behavior, a state called __________ __________.	learned helplessness
50. The symptoms shown by helpless dogs resemble those seen in the human disorder of __________.	depression

VARIETIES OF LEARNING

51. One criticism of traditional learning theory holds that there are certain built-in limitations called __________ __________ that determine what a given animal can easily learn.	biological constraints
52. Learned taste aversions are an example of __________, and their rapid acquisition makes them an example of __________-__________ learning.	belongingness (preparedness) one-trial
53. Belongingness in animal learning, as illustrated by taste-aversion learning, seems to fit well with the survival needs of animals. Thus, rats, who rely heavily on __________ in feeding, tend to associate that with the aftereffects of eating, while birds, who rely on __________ in feeding, tend to associate this type of stimulus with the aftereffects of eating.	taste vision (sight)
54. A predisposition to learn a connection between a picture of a snake and a shock suggests that belongingness, or preparedness, may be involved in the acquisition of __________.	phobias
55. The fact that it is easier to train a pigeon to flap its wings to escape shock than to receive food is an instance of __________ in __________-__________ representations of instrumental learning.	belongingness, act-outcome
56. The acquisition of bird song and memories for sites where food has been stored all represent __________ of learning.	specializations (varieties)

57. Similarities in properties of learning across species and situations suggest __________ features of the world across environments. common (similar)

THE NEURAL BASIS FOR LEARNING

58. The capacity for neurons to change the way they function as a consequence of experience is called __________ __________. neural plasticity

59. The study of the marine mollusk *Aplysia* is advantageous for research on the neural basis of learning because the nervous system of *Aplysia* is a relatively __________ system. simple (small)

60. One form of neural plasticity, called presynaptic facilitation, as demonstrated in *Aplysia* involves the increase in release of __________ by the presynaptic neuron. a neurotransmitter

61. In the process of __________-__________ __________, activation of a synapse makes that synapse more sensitive for periods lasting for days or weeks. long-term potentation

62. Long-term potentiation occurs only when different inputs to a postsynaptic neuron occur at about the same time. Thus, the spread of potentiation is __________ __________, and this helps to explain the principle of __________ in conditioning. activity dependent contingency

63. Learning in mammals produces structural changes, such as the growth of __________ spines. dendritic

SOME FINAL THOUGHTS: LEARNING THEORY AND BEYOND

64. There is evidence for both the existence and value of a set of __________ learning processes, such as habituation and classical and instrumental conditioning, but there is also evidence for __________ in learning mechanisms depending on the species and the demands of the learning situation. common (basic) diversity

Self-Test

1. Learning theorists share with Descartes and Locke the conviction that
   a. one must study the nervous system to understand behavior.
   b. learning is the most important aspect of animal behavior.
   c. complex behavior can be analyzed into simpler, more elementary processes.
   d. almost all behavior can be described as hardwired (innate).
   e. c and d

2. An animal startles when it is exposed to the sound of either a door slamming or a gong ringing. It is then exposed, about 10 times, to the gong ringing followed by the door slamming. Now, when the gong rings, the animal does not startle. This is an example of
   a. habituation.
   b. classical conditioning.
   c. extinction.
   d. associations.
   e. a learning curve.

3. Classical conditioning and habituation have in common the fact that both
   a. involve associations.
   b. require a conditioned stimulus.
   c. are built-in responses that animals show in laboratory situations.
   d. involve a change in response to a stimulus.
   e. occur primarily in dogs, though they may occur in some other species.

4. In a classical conditioning experiment in which a tone is paired with meat in the mouth, a dog comes to salivate to the sound of the tone. The tone is called the
   a. conditioned stimulus.
   b. unconditioned stimulus.
   c. unconditioned response.
   d. stimulus generalization.
   e. reinforcer.

5. Ivan Pilaff developed a fear of German shepherds because, on a few occasions, he was bitten by them. Some weeks later, he became friendly with someone who had a German shepherd as a pet. After a few visits to this friend plus German shepherd, he became fearful of the friend, even though this particular German shepherd never bit him. This is an example of
   a. discrimination.
   b. extinction.
   c. reinforcement.
   d. learning with a long delay.
   e. second-order conditioning.

6. A dog is first classically conditioned to seven stimuli (A–G) until he responds equally to all. He then gets some further training. At the end he produces the unusual generalization curve shown below. What was the further training the dog received?

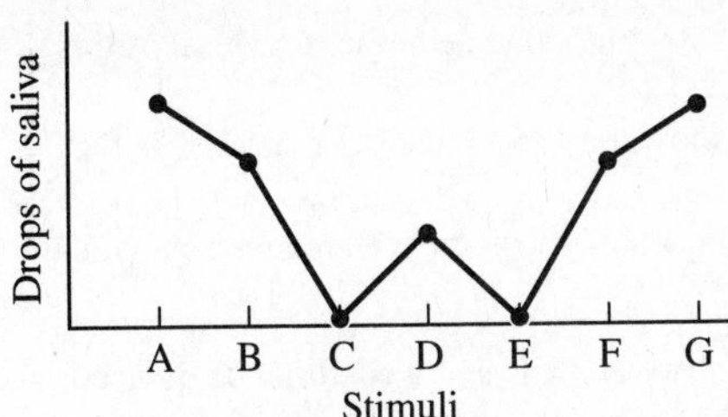

a. Extinguishing stimuli A, B, D, F, and G
b. Extinguishing stimuli B, D, and F and further conditioning A and G
c. Extinguishing stimuli C and E
d. Extinguishing stimuli C, D, and E
e. Further conditioning stimuli A and G

7. This figure illustrates the phenomenon of

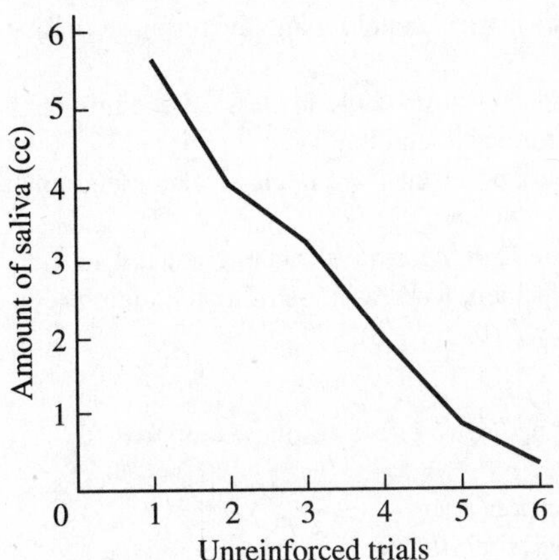

a. conditioning.
b. generalization.
c. extinction.
d. reconditioning.
e. spontaneous recovery.

8. This figure demonstrates that it is very difficult to produce conditioning with

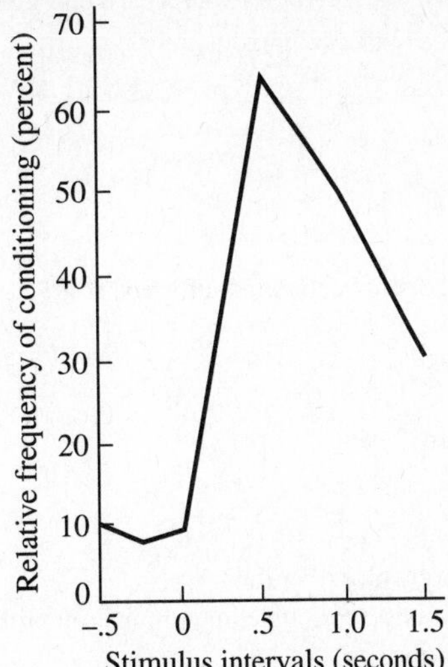

a. forward pairing.
b. second-order conditioning.
c. extinction.
d. simultaneous pairing.
e. all of the above.

9. Consider the following table of occurrences of CS and US. What predictions would the contiguity and contingency accounts make of whether conditioning would occur in this case?

	US	No US
CS	9	1
No CS	9	1

a. Both predict conditioning.
b. Both predict no conditioning.
c. Only contingency predicts conditioning.
d. Only contiguity predicts conditioning.
e. Neither predicts conditioning.

10. Consider the following table of occurrences of CS and US. What predictions would the contiguity and contingency accounts make of whether conditioning would occur in this case?

	US	No US
CS	7	3
No CS	3	7

a. Both predict conditioning.
b. Both predict no conditioning.
c. Only contingency predicts conditioning.
d. Only contiguity predicts conditioning.
e. Neither predicts conditioning.

11. In the case of unsignaled shock (a random relation between a signal and shock), the relation between a signal and the shock is one of

a. anxiety.
b. absence of contingency.
c. contingency.
d. contiguity.
e. blocking.

12. Some properties of classical conditioning suggest that it functions to make predictions about events in the world, somewhat as a scientist does. Which feature(s) of classical conditioning suggests(s) this property?
    a. Sensitivity to contingency
    b. Forward pairing
    c. Blocking
    d. All of the above
    e. b and c

13. A stimulus is more likely to become conditioned if it is
    a. not contiguous.
    b. blocked.
    c. surprising.
    d. likely to produce anxiety.
    e. b and d

14. Classical conditioning has been
    a. shown to occur only with salivation.
    b. used to explain responses to music, in conjunction with Romantic conditioning.
    c. demonstrated only in vertebrates.
    d. suggested as an explanation for phobias.
    e. a and c

15. During World War II, air raid sirens preceded bombing raids. A person who, as a result of fear, stopped her ongoing activity (e.g., eating or working) when sirens sounded showed
    a. response suppression.
    b. a siren phobia.
    c. extinction.
    d. spontaneous recovery.
    e. a generalization gradient.

16. Harriet gets very excited whenever she approaches the house of her boyfriend, Milton. She notices that her heart starts beating when she turns his corner and sees the name of his street on the corner sign. But she is surprised one day to note that the sign is down, and that she does not get excited on turning the corner or on passing Milton's street mailbox, just 20 feet from the corner. Why doesn't the mailbox cause her heart to increase beating?
    a. Blocking
    b. Backward pairing
    c. Extinction
    d. No contingent relation of the mailbox with Milton
    e. Fear, which suppresses her response

17. The CR is often quite different from the UR. This can be explained on the grounds that
    a. the CR is not fully conditioned to the UR.
    b. there is no contingency between the CR and UR.
    c. the CR is adaptively a preparation for the arrival of the UR.
    d. the CS is often different from the US.
    e. none of the above.

18. An experienced skydiver does not show nearly as much arousal on entering the plane from which he will jump as a novice skydiver does. Consider an experienced skydiver who is just about to enter the plane, but is called back at the last minute. If he shows a conditioned compensatory response, we would expect that
    a. his arousal would be about the same as that of the novice.
    b. he would show a bigger increase in arousal than the novice.
    c. he would show the same decrease in arousal as the novice.
    d. he would show the same increase in arousal as the novice.
    e. he would become less aroused than he normally is in daily life.

19. The relation between a UR and a conditioned compensatory response is like the relation between excitation and
    a. conditioning.
    b. reconditioning.
    c. extinction.
    d. response suppression.
    e. inhibition.

20. Instrumental learning differs from classical conditioning in that
    a. in instrumental learning, the response is voluntary, whereas in classical conditioning, the response is elicited by the US.
    b. associations are formed only in classical conditioning, not in instrumental learning.
    c. responses are never involved in classical conditioning as in instrumental learning.
    d. instrumental learning always occurs gradually, in trial-and-error fashion, whereas classical conditioning occurs very rapidly.
    e. a and c

21. According to the law of effect, responses followed by reward
    a. decrease in frequency.
    b. are not always reinforced.
    c. become trials or errors.
    d. are strengthened.
    e. all of the above.

22. The parallel between Darwin's theory of evolution and instrumental conditioning is between
    a. mental continuity and trial-and-error learning.
    b. learning and extinction.
    c. survival of the fittest and the law of effect.
    d. all of the above.
    e. a and b

23. As described by Thorndike, instrumental learning
    a. is gradual.
    b. involves no complex, uniquely human processes.
    c. is accomplished on a trial-and-error basis.
    d. is a means of strengthening particular responses.
    e. all of the above.

24. Skinner added to Thorndike's conception the idea that the responses conditioned in instrumental learning are
    a. emitted or voluntary, as opposed to elicited as in classical conditioning.

b. increased in strength by the process of reinforcement.
c. selected from all responses emitted on the basis of the law of effect.
d. all of the above.
e. a and c

25. Skinner and Thorndike share in common a belief in
a. the importance of schedules of reinforcement.
b. the law of effect.
c. the idea that instrumental behavior is emitted.
d. the superiority of instrumental training with discrete trials.
e. all of the above.

26. A rat is placed in a chamber and given a number of pellets of food, each preceded by a clicking sound. It is later trained to lever-press, with the reinforcement of only the sounding of the click, but no food. Every other day the rat receives pairings of click and food, and on the alternate days, it presses only for the click. Eventually, it stops pressing the lever on the click days. This cessation could be explained as
a. generalization.
b. loss of conditioned reinforcement properties by the click.
c. discrimination between clicks in two different situations.
d. an illustration of the importance of extinction.
e. spontaneous recovery.

27. In order to shape an animal to perform a difficult response, all but one of the following procedures should be followed. Which procedure is *not* appropriate?
a. Provide a clear signal for the arrival of reinforcement.
b. Present the reinforcement immediately after the response is performed.
c. Initially reinforce approximations to the desired response.
d. At first, reinforce those parts of the desired response sequence that come at the end of the sequence.
e. Work with the most difficult component in the response sequence first.

28. The desire for good grades illustrates the phenomenon of
a. stimulus generalization.
b. simultaneous discrimination.
c. conditioned reinforcement.
d. successive approximation.
e. a and d

29. Which of the following can function as reinforcers?
a. Food or sex
b. Stimuli paired with primary reinforcers
c. Information
d. All of the above
e. a and c

30. Offering a primary reinforcer to a child who is already engaged in an intrinsically motivated activity can, after the primary reinforcer is removed, decrease the frequency of the behavior. This can be explained in terms of
a. conditioned reinforcement.
b. behavioral contrast.
c. information.
d. reducing or eliminating the intrinsic value of an activity.
e. b and d

31. The idea that reinforcement can be understood completely as the reduction of biological need is challenged by
a. intrinsic motivation.
b. behavioral contrast.
c. schedules of reinforcement.
d. b and c.
e. a and b

32. Consider each swing by a baseball player as an operant response and every successful hit (single, double, etc.) as a reinforced swing. Which schedule of reinforcement is a baseball batter on?
a. Continuous reinforcement (fixed ratio)
b. Fixed ratio
c. Variable ratio
d. Extinction
e. Variable interval

33. A behavior being followed by an aversive event is an example of
a. extinction.
b. a schedule of reinforcement.
c. punishment.
d. discrimination.
e. none of the above.

34. Evidence for learning as acquiring knowledge rather than just changing behavior comes from the demonstration of
a. latent learning.
b. punishment.
c. act-outcome representations.
d. a and c
e. a and b

35. In a classic experiment on classical conditioning, it was shown that classical conditioning could occur when animals were temporarily paralyzed with a drug, so that they could not respond. (Of course, when testing for conditioning with a CS, the animals were no longer paralyzed.) Which position does this result support?
a. The acquiring knowledge view
b. The learning theory view
c. Pavlov's position
d. The changing response view
e. b and c

36. A rat learns to run down a runway when reinforced with a sugar solution in a box at the end of the runway. After learning this, it is then fed a bitter (negatively reinforcing) solution in this same box. When put back in the start box of the runway, it runs to the end box less quickly than before. This illustrates
a. second-order conditioning.
b. blocking.
c. learned helplessness.
d. the law of effect.
e. acquiring knowledge.

37. Studies on learned helplessness in dogs' and infants' responses to mobiles that they could or could not control are evidence for the importance of
   a. the law of effect.
   b. contiguity.
   c. contingency.
   d. belongingness.
   e. none of the above.

38. Animals exposed to lights randomly paired with shock (hence, unsignaled shock) sometimes develop pathologies related to stress. The relation of this finding to learned helplessness is the same as the relationship of
   a. conditioning to extinction.
   b. the optimum CS-US interval to contingency.
   c. generalization in classical conditioning to generalization in instrumental conditioning.
   d. extinction to partial reinforcement.
   e. extinction of instrumental conditioning to establishment of classical conditioning.

39. A simplified version of John Garcia's belongingness experiment would present bright-noisy tasty water to rats, followed by X-ray produced illness. The rats would show an aversion only to the taste (one of the groups in the experiment described in the text). However, without the use of a second group in which shock is the US, this experiment could be criticized by a learning theorist, because
   a. bright-noisy types of stimuli do not associate well with USs, like those induced by X rays.
   b. the bright-noisy stimuli might have been generally less effective as CSs than the taste stimulus.
   c. this result would contradict the bird studies, showing selective association of visual stimuli and gastrointestinal effects.
   d. the selective association could have been previously learned by the rats.
   e. all of the above.

40. Rats have a special ability to associate tastes with illness. Pigeons learn to peck a key for food, but have difficulty learning to peck a key to avoid shock. Both of these phenomena demonstrate belongingness. However, they differ in that the belongingness in the case of learned taste aversions occurs between __________ while in the pigeon example it occurs between __________.
   a. species-specific stimuli, general stimuli
   b. stimuli, responses
   c. responses, stimuli
   d. stimuli, responses and outcomes
   e. stimulus and response, responses

41. Which of the following instances of human learning most clearly represents arbitrary, as opposed to biologically specialized or prepared, learning?
   a. Learning grammar
   b. Learning to catch a ball
   c. Learning the rules of chess
   d. Learning to judge distance
   e. a and b

42. Which of the following summary statements about learning in humans and animals is probably *false?*
   a. There are some important specializations of learning in areas of particular importance for a particular species.
   b. There seem to be some general principles of learning, probably resulting from certain universal properties of environments.
   c. Specializations seem to occur in both instrumental and classical conditioning.
   d. There is no evidence for specializations in learning in humans.
   e. There is evidence that humans and animals can learn without explicit reinforcement.

43. There are three known mechanisms for neural plasticity. These are
   a. different brain areas involved, long-term potentiation, and diversity.
   b. presynaptic facilitation, long-term potentiation, and structural changes at the synapse.
   c. *Aplysia,* neurotransmitters, and dendritic spines.
   d. a and b
   e. none of the above.

44. What is the property of long-term potentiation (and perhaps other types of neural plasticity) that helps to explain the phenomenon of contingency in learning?
   a. Activity dependence
   b. Modulation of neurotransmitter release
   c. Growth of dendritic spines
   d. All of the above
   e. b and c

45. Which of the following phenomena presents a serious problem to traditional learning theory?
   a. Learning without performing a response or without getting a reward
   b. Taste-aversion learning
   c. Acquisition of bird song
   d. Acquisition of cognitive maps
   e. All of the above

46. Which of the following statements describes a fundamental difference between traditional learning theorists and the later, more cognitive theorists?
   a. Traditional learning theorists think a response is necessary for learning, while more cognitive theorists think responses may be merely an index of learning.
   b. Traditional learning theorists believe in learning as a change in behavior, whereas more cognitive theorists think of learning as the acquisition of knowledge.
   c. Traditional learning theorists believe that contingency is critical for associative learning, and more cognitive theorists do not believe this.
   d. All of the above.
   e. a and b

Answer Key for Self-Test

1. c
2. a
3. d
4. a
5. e
6. c
7. c
8. d
9. d
10. a
11. b
12. d
13. c
14. d
15. a
16. a
17. c
18. e
19. e
20. a
21. d
22. c
23. e
24. a
25. b
26. c
27. e
28. c
29. d
30. e
31. e
32. c
33. c
34. d
35. a
36. e
37. c
38. c
39. b
40. d
41. c
42. d
43. b
44. a
45. e
46. e

Investigating Psychological Phenomena

MAZE LEARNING

Equipment: Stopwatch or watch with second indicator
Number of participants: One (yourself)
Time per participant: Twenty to 35 minutes
Time for experimenter: Twenty to 35 minutes

This experiment illustrates a basic feature of learning: the acquisition curve, or the gradual acquisition of a skill or task. It employs a technique that was commonly used with animals in the earlier part of this century. The task is to find a way through a maze, presumably through learning a series of correct choices at the various choice points. In the experiment you will proceed through the same maze four times: each time, a record will be kept of both your total time to completion and the number of errors (false entries). Learning will be demonstrated by a drop in either time to completion or the number of errors as the number of trials increases.

Beginning on page 72, a maze is reprinted four times. In each case, using the second indicator on a wrist watch or a stopwatch, time yourself from the moment you begin with a pencil at the starting point to the moment you leave the maze. You should never pick your pencil off the paper until the maze is completed. If you make an error, simply retrace your steps with the pencil. On completion of the maze, record the total time taken at the bottom of the page. Do not record the number of errors until you have finished all the mazes, since the calculation of errors would be like another trial (you would have to work through the maze again).

Finish all four trials and then calculate the errors for each trial. An error is defined as the crossing of the imaginary line at the mouth of a blind alley, an alley that leads to a dead end. One such entry into a blind alley can only count for one error, no matter how far you go up the alley before realizing that it is blind. In other words, once you have entered an alley that will ultimately be blind, you can only score one error, even if there is another choice point farther along this path (both of these choices would of course have to be blind alleys). The only way you can score two errors for the same blind alley is if you enter the same alley twice.

Plot the time/trial and errors/trial on the two graphs provided below. Do you show evidence for gradual mastery of the maze? Compare your results with those from a group of undergraduate students that we have plotted on the same graph. We have plotted the mean (the average) scores. Individuals vary a lot; not all individuals show smooth curves like these averaged curves. In the graph, •——• represents the mean for eight participants. H and L represent the range. H is the highest score of eight participants; L is the lowest score of eight participants.

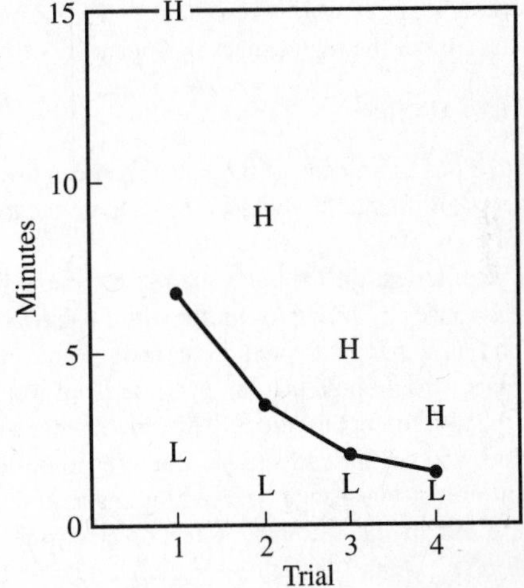

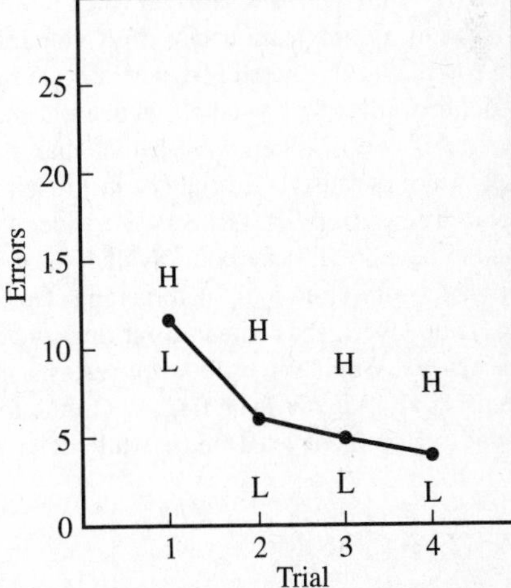

In the earlier part of this century, psychologists speculated about what exactly is learned when a rat or human learns a maze. Some, like John B. Watson, took a "molecular" position and claimed that a sequence of responses is learned. The most critical responses would be those at the choice points: In this view, the learning would be represented as a series of turning instructions (e.g., left, right, right), one for each successive choice point. Others, such as Edward Chace Tolman, argued that the participant, rat or human, developed a spatial representation of the maze in his or her head, a cognitive map, rather than a sequence of responses. What do you think you actually learned in this task?

You should realize that this type of maze differs markedly from the mazes used for rats or the life-size mazes for humans. In these cases, the participant does not get a direct picture of the whole layout; rather, the participant can only see the part of the maze in the immediate vicinity of the choice point. This, of course, makes it much harder for the participant to build up a map of the maze. To get a feeling for the difference, cut out a hole about 1/2-inch square from the center of a full-size piece of paper. Place it at the beginning of the fifth duplication of the maze, and attempt to move through the maze with the pencil again, moving the hole along as you move the pencil. If you had learned a series of turns or choices, this procedure should not seriously affect your performance. On the other hand, insofar as you used a "map," or some sort of larger view of the shape of the maze and your path through it, this procedure would seriously affect your performance. (If your instructor collects the data, fill out the report sheet in Appendix 2.)

FURTHER ACTIVITIES

We have included one extra copy of the maze. You can use this copy for further experiments: If you need more than one maze, you can make a copy of this unused maze.

You might wish to test the idea of a map of the maze versus a set of turning responses by trying to run the maze backward (start at finish and end at start). What predictions would you make? A cognitive map view would hold that the backward run would be a lot easier than the first run in the "proper" direction, since the same maze map would work in both directions. But a response-learning view would not predict that having learned the maze in the original order would aid in the learning of the reversed maze. The sequence of turns (e.g., left, left, right, left, etc.) would be entirely different when running the maze backward.

Of course, there is a problem here. How do you know how long it would have taken to run the maze backward if you did that on your first trial? You don't. One possibility would be to run a few people on one trial forward and a few others on one trial backward. You could then see if one direction were harder than the other. Another possibility, not as satisfying, would be just to assume that it should be about as easy forward as backward, since the maze was not designed to be more difficult one way than the other.

Another activity would be to look at forgetting. Do the final maze in a few days or a week and compare your time and errors to your performance today. Would you expect you performance to be about the same as Trial 4? Better than Trial 1? On the following three pages, cover the top (completed) maze while doing the bottom one.

LEARNED TASTE AVERSIONS

Equipment: None
Number of participants: Five to eight
Time per participant: Five minutes
Time for experimenter: Sixty minutes

One of the basic assumptions of behavior theory is that any conditioned stimulus (CS) could become associated with any unconditioned stimulus (US). That is, it is assumed that the relation of the CS to the US is arbitrary. This assumption has been seriously challenged by the discovery of the phenomenon of learned taste aversions in rats. As first documented by John Garcia and his colleagues, rats can learn in one trial to associate a taste (CS) with illness (US). They will subsequently avoid the taste. This learned taste aversion was of particular importance because Garcia and his colleagues showed that this rapid learning would only occur with tastes as the CS and certain types of illnesses as the US. This specificity of association between tastes and illnesses is an illustration of belongingness, the nonarbitrariness of associations.

Because learned taste aversions differ from most of the frequently studied types of learning, they were investigated in some detail. We now know that:

1. The specificity (belongingness) is between tastes and specific types of illness: symptoms from the upper gastrointestinal system, especially nausea, seem by far the most effective.
2. The learning typically occurs in one trial (thus allowing rats to avoid poisons without too many life-threatening trials).
3. The rat can accomplish this learning even if the illness follows the taste by more than one hour. This challenges the view that two stimuli must occur close together in time in order to be associated. CS-US intervals of more than an hour rarely, if ever, support conditioning in traditional classical conditioning, using salivation or startle responses, and tones, bells, and lights.
4. Novel tastes show much more conditioning than familiar ones. This makes sense: If eating of the familiar food has not been followed by illness, it is reasonable to associate the illness with the new food. This is true in other types of classical conditioning as well: There is generally more conditioning to novel stimuli.

It often happens that after a new phenomenon is described, it is found to be common, and one wonders how it could have escaped notice before. So it was with learned taste aversions. A phenomenon similar to that described by Garcia in the rat seems to occur in humans. Most commonly, someone eats a (usually new) food and gets ill within a few hours. Nausea and vomiting are particularly common symptoms. After this one experience, a person finds the food distasteful. Garb and Stunkard (1974) distributed a questionnaire about such experiences to about 700 people. They found that somewhat over one-third of people have had at least one such experience. The analysis of the results of their questionnaire confirmed the presence of the basic properties of learned taste aversions in humans:

1. Belongingness: Aversions were almost always limited to the food and its taste. Rarely were there reports of aversion to the restaurant, tablecloth, accompanying people, or other stimuli that were also associated, in time, with the illness. Furthermore, the illness in question almost always (87 percent of the time) involved the gastrointestinal system.
2. One-trial learning: The aversions usually occurred after one food-illness pairing.
3. Long CS-US intervals: There was often an interval measured in hours between food ingestion and illness.
4. Novelty: Novel foods (tastes) seem more effective. In spite of the fact that almost everything eaten on any given day would be familiar, 45 percent of the aversions involved foods that had been eaten no more than twice before the pairing with illness.

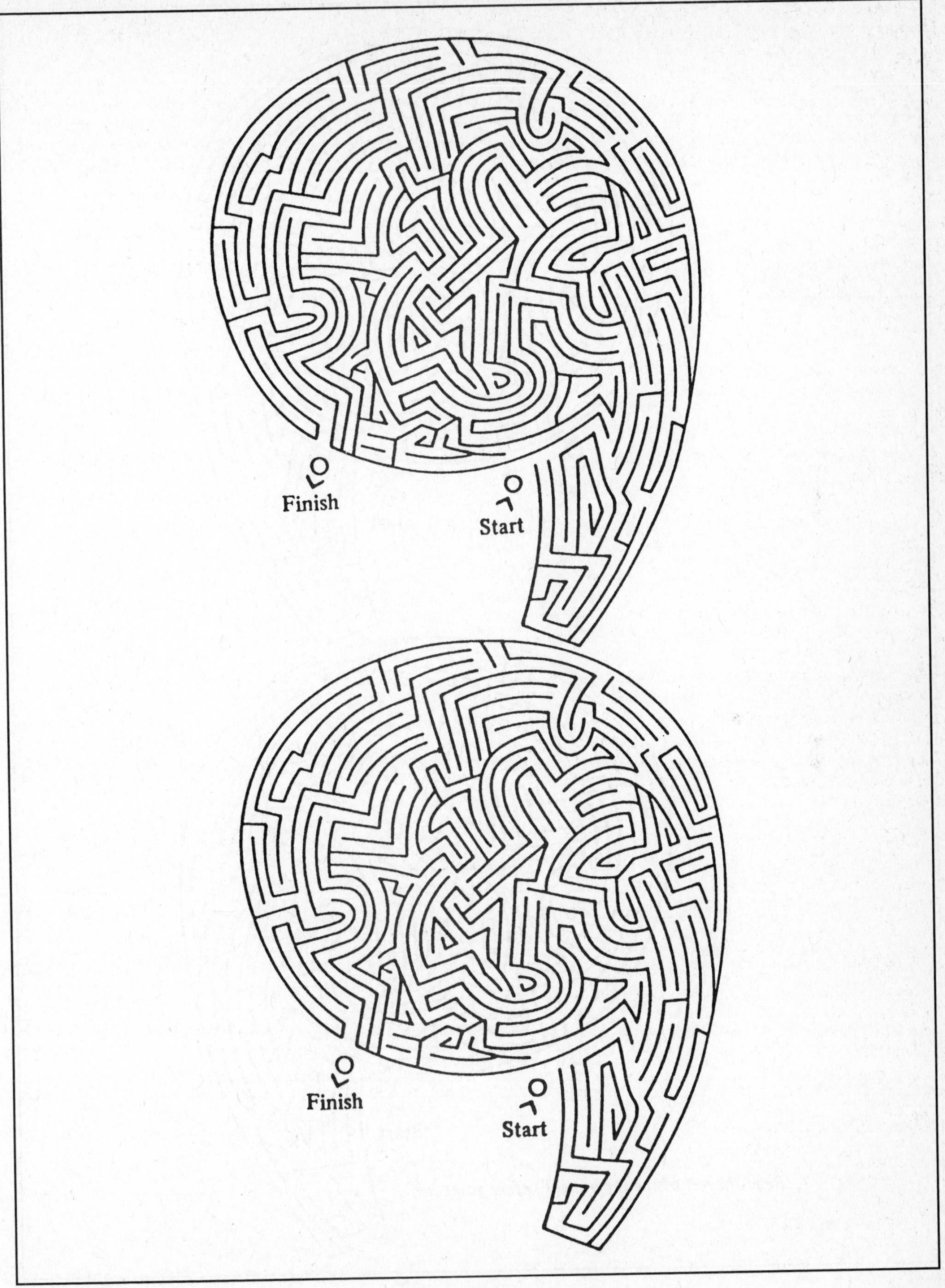
Finish
Start
Finish
Start

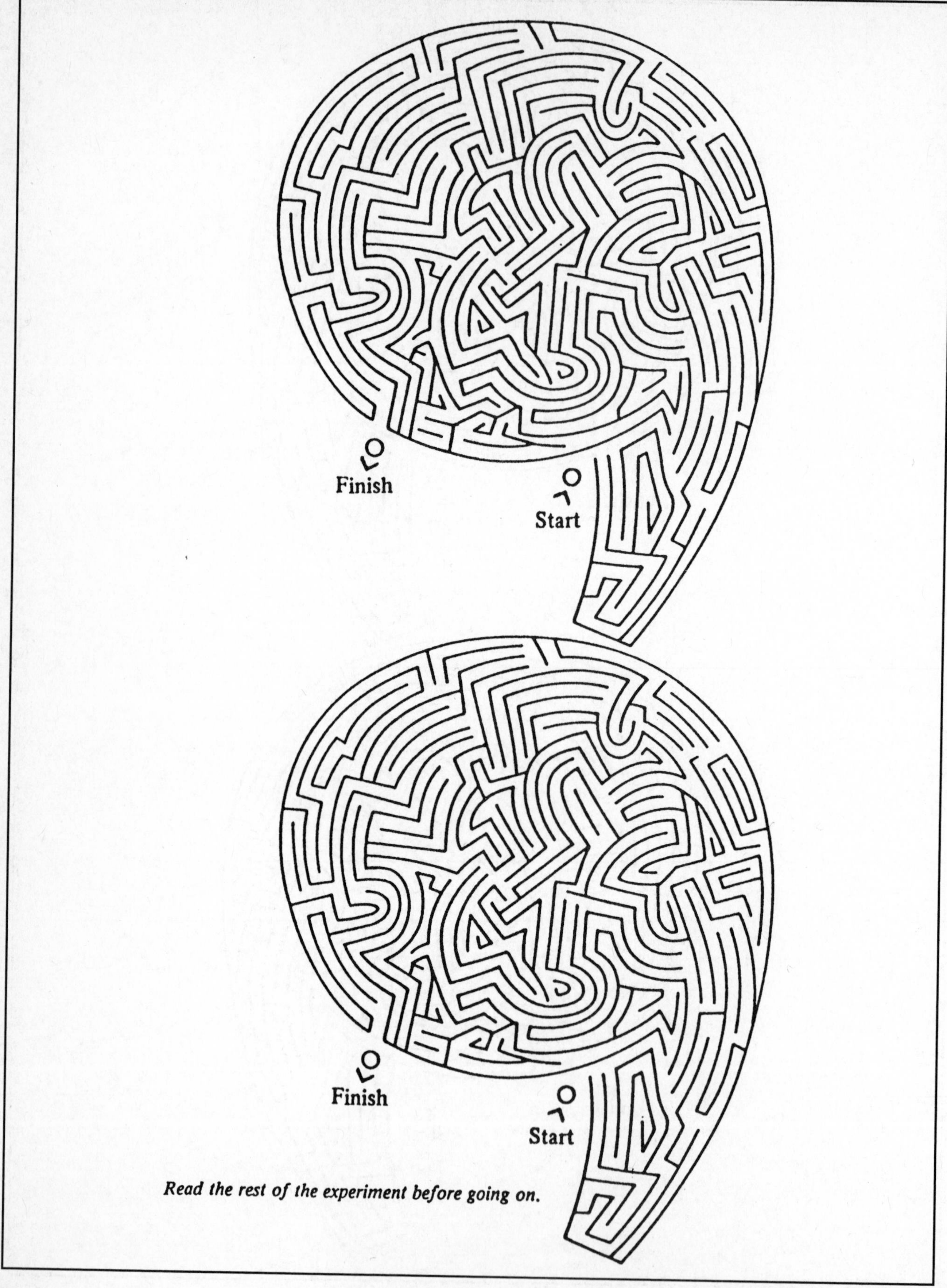

Read the rest of the experiment before going on.

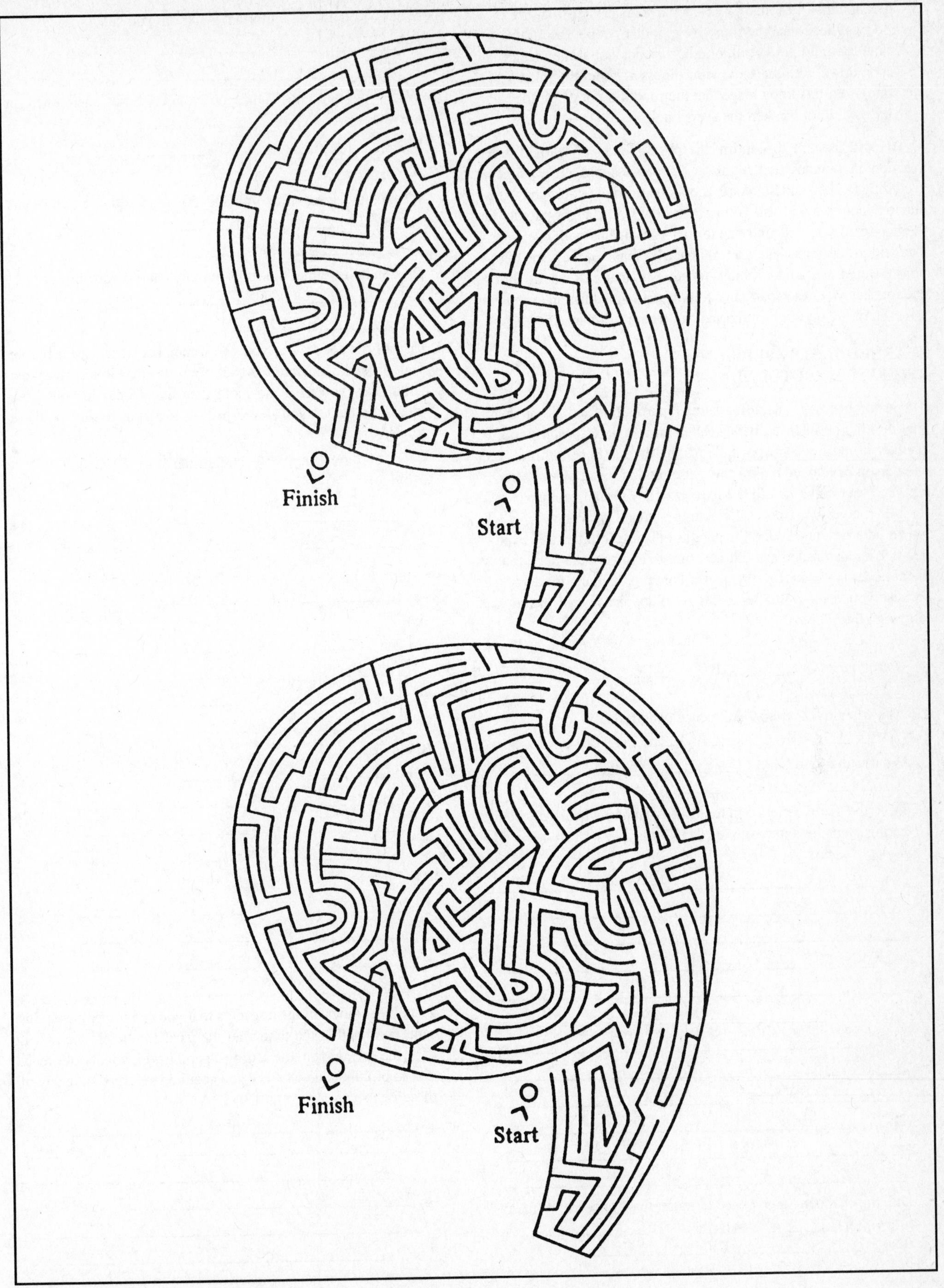
Finish
Start
Finish
Start

5. "Irrationality": In many cases, a participant knew that the food did not cause the illness (e.g., other people eating the same food did not get ill, or other friends not at the meal came down with the same viral illness at about the same time). Yet, this knowledge that the food did not cause the illness did not weaken the aversion.

We will attempt to confirm the phenomenon of learned taste aversion in humans and highlight its unusual properties. Since, according to Garb and Stunkard, about one-third of people show this phenomenon, we will ask you to interview five to eight people, in the hope that you will find one to four participants with aversions. You will use an interview protocol that asks many of the same questions covered in Garb and Stunkard's questionnaire. Read the introduction, below, to each participant. If the participant has an aversion, ask each of the questions indicated and record the answers.

LEARNED TASTE AVERSIONS: INTERVIEW PROTOCOL

If a person becomes sick after eating a particular food, he or she may develop an intense dislike, called an aversion, for that food, whether or not it was responsible for the illness. For example, one person developed a high fever after eating pizza in a restaurant, and found that he did not like pizza any more. Another person became very nauseous after eating a breakfast with hash brown potatoes, and found the potatoes distasteful after this experience. She also found she did not want to eat from the plate that the potatoes were on. Have you ever come to dislike a food because you became ill after eating it? If so, please answer the following questions:

1. Your current age.
   (Participant A) ________ (B) ________
   (C) ________ (D) ________
2. Age when the aversion experience occurred.
   (A) ________ (B) ________ (C) ________ (D) ________
3. What is the food? (A) ________ (B) ________
   (C) ________ (D) ________
4. Describe the experience in terms of what and where you were eating, and the symptoms of the illness. *(Use extra sheet of paper if necessary.)*
   (A) ________
   (B) ________
   (C) ________
   (D) ________
5. Did this happen only once? If more than once, how many times? (A) ________, ________ (B) ________, ________
   (C) ________, ________ (D) ________, ________
6. What was the most important symptom you had?
   (A) ________ (B) ________
   (C) ________ (D) ________
7. Were you nauseous? Did you vomit (if not mentioned in answer above)? (A) ________, ________
   (B) ________, ________ (C) ________, ________
   (D) ________, ________
8. About how long after you ate the food did the symptoms appear? (A) ________ (B) ________
   (C) ________ (D) ________
9. Do you believe that the food actually caused your illness?
   (A) ________ (B) ________
   (C) ________ (D) ________
10. List all the foods that you can remember at the meal before you got sick. Indicate for each food whether it was relatively unfamiliar (you ate it no more than three times in your life). Indicate whether you developed an aversion to any of these foods:

	Food	Unfamiliar	Aversion
(A)			
	________	________	________
	________	________	________
	________	________	________
	________	________	________
(B)			
	________	________	________
	________	________	________
	________	________	________
	________	________	________
(C)			
	________	________	________
	________	________	________
	________	________	________
	________	________	________
(D)			
	________	________	________
	________	________	________
	________	________	________
	________	________	________

11. List all the other things or events that you can remember at this same meal and in the time after the meal and before the illness (e.g., the restaurant, table settings, people with you, books read, and so on). Indicate whether you acquired an aversion to any of these items.
    (A) ________
    (B) ________
    (C) ________

(D) ______________________________

____

____

12. Do you still have this aversion? (A) ________ (B) ________
(C) ________ (D) ________

13. Was (Is) the aversion to the taste, smell, and/or sight of the food?

Taste	Smell	Sight
(A) ________	(A) ________	(A) ________
(B) ________	(B) ________	(B) ________
(C) ________	(C) ________	(C) ________
(D) ________	(D) ________	(D) ________

Summarize the results from all of your participants below. You decide which questions are relevant to each feature of learned taste aversion and summarize your results with respect to each of the features listed below.

BELONGINGNESS Relevant questions (Nos.)

____

____

____

ONE-TRIAL LEARNING Relevant questions (Nos.)

____

____

____

LONG CS-US INTERVAL Relevant questions (Nos.)

____

____

____

NOVELTY EFFECT Relevant questions (Nos.)

____

____

____

"IRRATIONALITY" Relevant questions (Nos.)

____

____

____

OTHER INTERESTING RESULTS

____

____

____

Do your data confirm the basic properties of learned taste aversion?

Comment: Interview protocols like this are quite common in psychological research. They are essentially questionnaires, but they are administered by a researcher or someone on his or her staff. In a way they are more subjective than questionnaires because the interviewer could influence the answers of the participant, especially if there is embarrassing material in the protocol. On the other hand, the interview allows for an interaction between the researcher and the participant: If a participant misunderstands a question, she can be corrected. If the participant says something that is ambiguous, it can be expanded. Similarly, if the participant says something of unusual interest, it can be followed up.

The introductory statement in the interview is critical. We tried to write it so as not to guarantee that participants would only describe specific food aversions based on gastrointestinal illness. Note that we gave one example of another sort of illness and also suggested the possibility of an aversion to items other than tastes. This certainly does not guarantee an unbiased sample of aversions, but it allows for exceptions to the phenomena as described by Garcia and, later, by Garb and Stunkard. Garb and Stunkard's introductory paragraph was more suggestive of gastrointestinal illness than is the paragraph we used here. (If your instructor collects the data, fill out the report sheet in Appendix 3.)

PROBLEMS AND FURTHER ACTIVITIES

Garb and Stunkard's questionnaire and our interview are not experiments. They can demonstrate that one-trial taste-illness aversions occur in humans. But by themselves they cannot demonstrate belongingness. Remember that Garcia's experiments with rats showed that although lights and tastes were equally paired with both illness and electric shock, the taste was much more strongly associated with illness and the lights with shock. Our introduction for the participants (and more so Garb and Stunkard's) pointed the participant toward taste-illness associations. We did not ask the participants if they ever got to dislike a restaurant or a person because they were "followed by" illness or whether they ever got to dislike a food because it was followed by pain or a variety of other unpleasant events. On the contrary, we could ask whether, as a consequence of a very unpleasant event such as a death in the family or painful injury, a participant developed an aversion to any object, event, or food. Such questions have not been asked systematically. Do you have any such aversion? Do any of your friends? If there are many aversions linking food with unpleasant events "outside of the body" or outside of the gastrointestinal system, or if there are aversions to visual or other objects paired with illness, then there is little evidence for the belongingness effects in humans. We don't think there are many such effects, but we are not sure at this time.

We have suggested that nausea and vomiting are especially important in generating taste aversion. See if you can get evidence for this. If you know anyone (including yourself) with a food allergy, interview that person, using a protocol like the one we have used for aversions. (You will have to make a few modifications.) The critical question is whether people with food allergies develop aversions to those foods. In particular, if the allergy produces no symptoms in the gastrointestinal system, is there an aversion? There is some data (Pelchat & Rozin, 1982) that suggest that people with food allergies outside of the gastrointestinal system do not have aversions to these foods; that is, they do not dislike these allergenic foods.

References

Garb, F., & Stunkard, A. (1974). Taste aversions in man. *American Journal of Psychiatry, 131,* 1204–1207.

Logue, A. W., Ophir, I., & Strauss, K. E. (1981). The acquisition of taste aversion in humans. *Behavior Research and Therapy, 19,* 319–333.

Pelchat, M. L., & Rozin, P. (1982). The special role of nausea in the acquisition of food dislikes by humans. *Appetite, 3,* 341–351.

CHAPTER 7

Memory

Learning Objectives

1. Be sure you see the parallel between perception and memory in the active role that the perceiver or memorizer plays.
2. Understand the central role that memory plays in life.

ACQUISITION, STORAGE, AND RETRIEVAL

3. What is meant by the terms *acquisition, storage,* and *retrieval*? How do these processes differ from one another?
4. Know that both recall and recognition are used to measure retrieval. How do these two methods differ from one another?
5. What are causes of failures to retrieve?

ENCODING

The stage theory of memory

6. What motivates a stage theory of memory, both historically and introspectively?
7. How is the relationship between desktop and bookshelves relevant to working and long-term memory?
8. What is the capacity of working memory? How is it measured?
9. There are two mechanisms that account for forgetting from working memory. What are they, and how do they work?
10. Rehearsal is a process important to working memory. Describe its function in relation to both working and long-term memory.
11. One of the most robust phenomena in the study of memory is the appearance of primacy and recency effects in free recall. Describe these, and indicate what causes them. Be sure you can cite evidence that supports the presumed causes.
12. What is a chunk, and how does this concept apply to the capacity of working memory? How do chunks get created?

A changed emphasis: Active memory and organization

13. How do findings about rehearsal challenge the stage theory of memory?
14. What is maintenance rehearsal? Does the amount of maintenance rehearsal affect the probability of information's entering long-term memory? Cite the relevant evidence.
15. What is the concept of working memory, and how does it differ from the concept of short-term memory?
16. Understand the concept of depth of processing and how it affects memory. Give examples of processing at different depths.
17. What role does meaning play in remembering?
18. Mnemonics are tools to increase the capacity of memory. Describe some mnemonics, and understand how they work to affect memory capacity. What are the practical limitations of mnemonics? How do mnemonics create retrieval paths?

RETRIEVAL

19. Understand the role of retrieval cues in increasing the accessibility of memory traces.

The relation between original encoding and retrieval

20. What is the concept of encoding specificity, and how does it influence successful retrieval? Understand the range of contexts in which this principle operates.
21. The importance of matching encoding and retrieval contexts has to do with mental, not physical, contexts. Explain.

Elaborative rehearsal

22. Contrast maintenance and elaborative rehearsal. Give examples of elaborative rehearsal.

Implicit memory

23. Be aware of the difference between implicit and explicit memory retrieval. What is the essence of an implicit measure, and what are some examples?
24. Describe how repetition priming and fragment completion show implicit retrieval effects.
25. Describe evidence showing that implicit memory can influence whether you believe something is true.

26. Be aware of how variations in depth of processing and in peripheral aspects of the stimulus produce differential effects on explicit and implicit tests of memory.

27. What are some theoretical accounts of the difference between implicit and explicit memory?

WHEN MEMORY FAILS

Forgetting

28. What is the shape of the forgetting curve?

29. Recount the evidence both for and against a decay theory of forgetting.

30. What is an interference theory of forgetting, and how does it differ from a decay theory?

31. Give some accounts of the forgetting of childhood memories and why there may be individual differences in this forgetting.

32. Be sure you understand the effect that emotion and trauma can have on memory.

Disordered memories

33. What are some of the characteristics of having a word on the tip of your tongue?

34. Some memories seem to last quite a long time. Give examples. What factors affect this?

35. How are flashbulb memories claimed to be different from other memories? Are these memories really treated differently by the memory system? Discuss the evidence.

Conceptual frameworks and remembering

36. What effects did Bartlett document in his studies of recollection?

37. Describe some effects that schemas have on memory.

38. Memory is an important issue in the courtroom. What does research tell us about the fallibility of eyewitness testimony? Why is it difficult to distinguish between the declarative/procedural versus explicit/implicit accounts of amnesia?

39. Describe how eyewitness memory may be a reconstruction of earlier events.

40. What is source confusion, and when does it occur?

41. Can the fallibility of eyewitness testimony be overcome?

42. Is hypnosis a reliable way of helping a witness remember an event? What is the evidence on whether hypnosis improves retrieval?

43. What is the verdict on the videorecorder theory of memory?

44. Why is there reason to be cautious about the concept of repressed memories? What issues should we be concerned about in examining cases of this alleged phenomenon?

45. Discuss the limits to which our memories are distorted. How do top-down and bottom-up processes play a role in enhancing and limiting distortion?

What amnesia teaches us

46. What are the symptoms of anterograde amnesia, and what are some of its causes?

47. How does retrograde amnesia differ from anterograde amnesia? What mechanism has been proposed to account for retrograde amnesia?

48. What sorts of learning are not affected by anterograde amnesia? How is the distinction between declarative and procedural knowledge relevant to this issue?

49. The distinction between implicit and explicit memory has also played a prominent role in accounting for anterograde amnesia. Explain why.

50. Be prepared to give examples of amnesias that selectively disrupt either episodic or generic memory.

51. How does evidence from brain imaging help us distinguish among different types of memories?

Programmed Exercises

AQUISITION, STORAGE, AND RETRIEVAL

1. The first stage of memory is __________, in which information is acquired and brought into the system. — encoding

2. The records of experience made on the nervous system are called memory __________. — traces

ENCODING

3. The second stage of memory is __________, during which information is filed away. The final stage is __________, the point at which one tries to remember. — storage, retrieval

4. A __________ test is a test of retrieval in which a participant is asked to produce an item from memory. — recall

5. A __________ test is a test of retrieval in which several items are presented and the participant must decide which ones were presented earlier as part of a studied list. recognition

6. Learning that takes place without intention is called __________ learning. incidental

7. Translating raw input to memory into an intellectual record of the input is called __________ encoding. memory

8. The theory of memory that argues for separate memory systems working together is called the __________ theory. stage

9. __________ memory holds information for a brief interval. __________-__________ memory stores information for longer periods of time. Working, Long-term

10. The __________ capacity of working memory has been estimated as about seven items. storage

11. The __________ __________ is the number of items an individual can recall after just one presentation. memory span

12. __________ is one way of either keeping an item in working memory or allowing it to pass into long-term memory. Rehearsal

13. The method of __________ __________ allows a participant who is presented with a list of unrelated items to report them in any order desired. free recall

14. Of a long list of presented items, a participant is most apt to remember the first few (known as the __________ effect) and the last few (known as the __________ effect). primacy, recency

15. The process that allows the contents of working memory to expand is called __________. Using this process results in the creation of __________ of information. organization, chunks

16. __________ rehearsal consists of repeating items over and over to keep them in memory for a short time, as in repeating a telephone number. Maintenance

17. __________ memory holds information for short intervals, while we are processing it. Working

18. One theory of memory asserts that the extent to which information is subject to semantic analysis, as opposed to analysis of its surface features, will determine how firmly the information will be held in memory. This theory attributes permanence in memory to __________ of __________. depth, processing

19. The various devices designed to improve memory are collectively called __________. mnemonics

20. When it comes time to recall something from memory, connections linking one memory to another become retrieval __________. paths

21. The method of __________ requires learners to visualize each of the items they want to remember in a different spatial location. loci

22. The most effective kind of image for remembering is one in which the elements of the image are __________. interacting

RETRIEVAL

23. When you know a piece of information (i.e., you have stored it), but you cannot retrieve it at the moment, the trace is said to be __________. inaccessible

24. A stimulus that provides a trigger to get an item out of memory is called a(n) __________ __________. retrieval cue

25. The principle of __________ __________ states that retrieval success is most likely if the context at the time of retrieval approximates that during original encoding. encoding specificity

26. __________ rehearsal consists of the organization of information in working memory so that it can be transferred to long-term memory. Elaborative

27. Instances in which we tap our memory quite consciously to retrieve something are called __________ memory. By contrast, when our memory is used in an indirect way in the service of some other task, this is termed __________ memory. explicit implicit

28. Recall and recognition are both __________ measures of memory, whereas word fragment completion is a(n) __________ measure. explicit implicit

29. __________ priming is a technique used to study implicit memory; words that appear on a study list are identified more readily than words that do not. Repetition

WHEN MEMORY FAILS

30. The __________ curve was first plotted by Ebbinghaus who tested himself on the relearning of lists of nonsense syllables. forgetting

31. If it was found that items faded from working memory even though no new information entered, this would support a __________ theory of forgetting. decay

32. Animals forget when their internal temperatures are higher; this is evidence for a __________ theory of forgetting. decay

33. One cause of forgetting is __________, in which some items in memory cause the forgetting of others. interference

34. Misinformation presented as new ideas can often __________ old, correct memories with new, false ones, resulting in __________ errors. overwrite intrusion

35. The __________-__________-__________-__________ phenomenon is an example of unsuccessful retrieval in which the participant comes close to the searched-for item in his memory but cannot quite find the right memory location. tip-of-the-tongue

36. Certain salient and emotional events produce what are called __________ memories, which are quite vivid. flashbulb

37. The conceptual framework that a person builds on the basis of her knowledge of the world is called a __________. schema

38. Eyewitnesses to crimes seem to reconstruct the past from their partial knowledge of it in the process of trying to remember it. This leaves them open to memory __________. errors

39. Getting a witness into the mind-set that she was in at the time of an incident is called context __________. reinstatement

40. Eyewitness __________ of a culprit from a police lineup are subject to mistakenly identifying someone who is innocent. identifications

41. Sometimes an observer can recall an event but not the origin of that event. This is called __________ confusion. source

42. __________ seems to make people overly willing to cooperate with their questioner, not to substantially improve retrieval of information from memory. Hypnosis

43. The __________ theory of memory asserts that everything we have heard or seen is stored in memory. videorecorder

44. __________ memories are alleged to occur when an emotionally traumatic event happens in early childhood and cannot be easily retrieved. Repressed

45. Lesions in the temporal cortex result in __________ amnesia, in which the patient has difficulty learning new material. anterograde

46. __________ syndrome occurs after extended bouts of alcohol abuse. Korsakoff's

47. A patient has suffered an accident involving trauma to the head. Following this, his ability to learn things is unimpaired, but he seems to have forgotten some things that happened prior to the accident. This is an example of __________ __________. retrograde amnesia

48. The fact that more recent memories are more likely to have been impaired in cases of retrograde amnesia is known as __________ __________. Ribot's law

49. An amnesiac's memory is relatively unaffected when the memory task involves __________ knowledge, but is drastically impaired when it involves __________ knowledge. procedural declarative

50. __________ tests of memory show great performance declines in amnesic patients, whereas __________ tests show little difference from the performance of people with normal memory capacity. Explicit implicit

51. There are amnesic patients who lose __________ memory while preserving episodic memory. generic

52. __________ refers to a general sense that a stimulus has been encountered before, while __________ refers to a direct recall of the context in which the stimulus occurred. Familiarity recollection

53. The __________ plays a role in memory of emotional events. amygdala

Self-Test

1. For us to remember something, we must first engage in the process of
   a. storage.
   b. rehearsal.
   c. encoding.
   d. recall.

2. An enduring physical record of a memory is called
   a. a memory trace.
   b. a chunk.
   c. short-term memory.
   d. none of the above.

3. Suppose you are given a choice between a multiple-choice test and a short-answer test for the final exam in this course. You want to maximize your chance of doing well. On the basis of what you know about recall and recognition, all other things being equal, which test should you choose?
   a. Short answer
   b. Multiple choice
   c. Either, there is no difference.
   d. It depends on the nature of the material.

4. Multiple-choice questions are to fill-in-the-blank questions as
   a. recognition is to recall.
   b. recall is to retention.
   c. recognition is to retention.
   d. learning is to memory.

5. In principle, the stages of memory processes must be arranged in which of the following orders?
   a. Memory trace—encoding—storage—retrieval
   b. Encoding—memory trace—storage—retrieval
   c. Encoding—storage—memory trace—retrieval
   d. Encoding—memory trace—retrieval—storage

6. The following are all characteristics of working memory *except*
   a. limited capacity.
   b. contents lost without rehearsal.
   c. that displacement causes forgetting.
   d. none of the above.

7. It has been found that people can hold about seven items in working memory. When more items are presented, complete recall is generally not possible. This demonstrates the __________ of working memory.
   a. retention interval
   b. memory trace
   c. displacement
   d. memory span

8. What is true about forgetting from working memory?
   a. It can be caused by erosion of the memory trace with time.
   b. The memory trace can be knocked out of short-term memory by another trace.
   c. It can be inhibited by rehearsal of the material stored there.
   d. All of the above.

9. Suppose we are given driving directions by a gas station attendant and we repeat them over and over to ourselves, "First left, second right, left at the first light, third right." Now suppose that our repetition of the directions is interrupted by an emergency driving maneuver. This would likely cause us to forget the directions, thereby demonstrating the importance of __________ in preserving working memory.
   a. storage capacity
   b. retrieval
   c. accessibility
   d. rehearsal

10. Suppose cryogenics (freezing patients and awakening them at some future time) were possible. If we were to discover that after being awakened, the patients had retained very accurate memories of what they had experienced immediately before freezing, this would be evidence for which hypothesis of forgetting in working memory?
    a. Interference
    b. Decay
    c. a or b
    d. None of the above

11. At a party we are taken around the room by the host and introduced to the other guests. Some time after the introductions are finished, one of these people comes up to talk to us. All other things being equal, we have the best chance of remembering her name if she was one of the __________ people we met. This phenomenon is called __________.
    a. first, primacy
    b. middle, inhibition
    c. last, recency
    d. first or last, the opposition effect

12. Now imagine the same situation (as in question 11) except that the person comes up to us immediately after we have been very quickly introduced to everyone. Again, other things being equal, we would have the worst chance of remembering her name if she was one of the __________ people we met and the best chance if she was one of the __________.
    a. first, last
    b. middle, last
    c. first, middle
    d. last, first

13. Suppose a participant is asked to memorize the following list of words: *apple, horse, desk, carpet, mug, milk, parrot, disk, street, tree*. Which of the following will occur?
    a. The word *street* will be rehearsed more than the word *horse,* causing *tree* to be stored in long-term memory.
    b. The word *parrot* will be rehearsed more than the word *mug*, causing *parrot* to be stored in working memory.
    c. The word *apple* will be rehearsed more than the word *carpet,* causing *apple* to be stored in long-term memory.
    d. The word *desk* will be rehearsed more than the word *parrot,* causing *desk* to be stored in working memory.

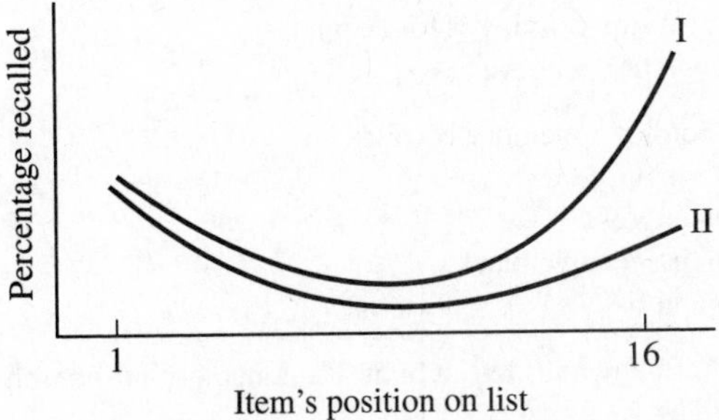

14. The figure above depicts recall curves for a list of 16 items. Two conditions were employed, I and II. What was the difference between the conditions?
    a. The interval between items was longer for II than I.
    b. The interval between items was longer for I than II.
    c. The interval between the last item and the recall test was longer for I than II.
    d. The interval between the last item and the recall test was longer for II than I.

15. Increasing the capacity of working memory is a misnomer because
    a. all we do is rehearse the material already there, keeping it fresh while new material is added.
    b. the number of items stored is the same, about seven; just the content of each item has changed.
    c. it is the number of chunks that has changed, not the capacity of working memory.
    d. it is not possible to increase the capacity of working memory.

16. Suppose we run an experiment in which we present one word, say *rabbit,* and the participant has to repeat it. Then we present another word, say *pear,* and the participant has to repeat *rabbit, pear*. Then we present a third word, and the participant has to repeat all three, and so on. At the end of our list, we test the participant's memory for all words on the list. On the basis of what we know about the effect of maintenance rehearsal on long-term memory, we predict
    a. that *rabbit* should be entered into long-term memory with higher probability than the last word on the list.
    b. that *rabbit* should be entered into long-term memory with lower probability than the last word on the list.
    c. that *rabbit* should be entered into long-term memory with the same probability as the last word on the list.
    d. none of the above.

17. Working memory is to long-term memory as
    a. storage is to processing.
    b. processing is to storage.
    c. recall is to recognition.
    d. recognition is to recall.

18. The concept of depth of processing is intended to account for the fact that
    a. deeper structures in the brain are involved in memory in contrast to the more surface cortical structures that are involved in other aspects of cognition.
    b. deeper levels of analysis of material yield better memory of the material.
    c. deeper organization of material into hierarchically organized chunks produces a better long-term memory for that material.
    d. none of the above.

19. Which of the following processes will *not* result in the effective storage of memory traces in long-term memory?
    a. Maintenance rehearsal
    b. Clustering
    c. Elaborative rehearsal
    d. Organization by phrases

20. A follow-up to the experiment in which participants recalled the passage about washing clothes found that telling them the title of the paragraph after they had read it did not improve recall compared to not telling them the title at all. This result, taken together with the effect of telling participants the title of the paragraph before it is presented, suggests that
    a. chunking is not an effective strategy to memorize material.
    b. chunking is effective if it can be accomplished at the time of encoding.
    c. chunking is effective if it can be accomplished at the time of retrieval.
    d. chunking is effective if it can be accomplished during storage.

21. Mnemonic devices (memorizing aids) use the principle of
    a. consolidation of retrieval.
    b. recoding.
    c. retrieval of consolidation.
    d. all of the above.

22. Which of the following images would produce the greatest increase in recall performance for the pair of items horse-rock?
    a. A horse standing next to a rock
    b. A horse dragging a rock
    c. A horse and a rock pictured separately
    d. All of the above would be equivalent.

23. You have been trying to remember the name of a street that a friend lives on. Despite all of your efforts, you are unable to recall it. While in the kitchen looking for a snack (to console yourself), you reach for a can of nuts and suddenly the street name comes to you—Walnut. This is an example of the role of
    a. anterograde amnesia.
    b. retrograde amnesia.
    c. mnemonics.
    d. retrieval cues.

24. Retrieval cues are most effective if they
    a. coincide with the way in which a trace was originally encoded.
    b. are presented at the time of recall, not at encoding.
    c. are quite concrete.
    d. elicit visual images.

25. The kind of rehearsal that establishes long-term memories is __________. The type of rehearsal that holds material in working memory temporarily is __________.
    a. mnemonics, chunking
    b. maintenance rehearsal, elaborative rehearsal
    c. elaborative rehearsal, maintenance rehearsal
    d. method of loci, mnemonics

26. The major role that elaborative rehearsal plays in improving memory, as opposed to maintenance rehearsal, is to
    a. increase the number of retrieval cues.
    b. increase the number of times an item is rehearsed.
    c. speed up the encoding time.
    d. all of the above.

27. Repeating word pairs aloud and forming images of words in a pair are respectively examples of
    a. maintenance rehearsal and maintenance rehearsal.
    b. maintenance rehearsal and elaborative rehearsal.
    c. elaborative rehearsal and elaborative rehearsal.
    d. elaborative rehearsal and maintenance rehearsal.

28. The tip-of-the-tongue phenomenon provides us with evidence concerning
    a. the hierarchical organization of long-term memory.
    b. accessibility in working memory.
    c. the search process in long-term memory.
    d. the use of retrieval cues in working memory.

29. Having something "on the tip of the tongue" indicates a problem
    a. in the way the item was chunked.
    b. with reconstruction.
    c. with proactive inhibition.
    d. with retrieval.

30. What is the relationship between implicit and explicit memory tests?
    a. They must be correlated because they both measure memory.
    b. They can be uncorrelated as shown by demonstrations of implicit memory without explicit memory.
    c. They must be correlated because the tests measure different aspects of memory.
    d. Available evidence does not permit an answer.

31. Evidence that implicit and explicit memory tests may tap at least some different aspects of the memory trace comes from studies showing that
    a. implicit tests lead to better retrieval.
    b. forgetting as indicated by implicit tests is slower than forgetting indexed by explicit tests.
    c. learning instructions affect tests of explicit but not implicit memory.
    d. all of the above.

32. The following are tests of explicit retrieval *except*
    a. fragment completion.
    b. repetition priming.
    c. free recall.
    d. memory span.
    e. more than one of the above.

33. According to one view, explicit retrieval is to implicit retrieval as
    a. conscious is to unconscious.
    b. bottom-up processing is to top-down processing.
    c. repetition priming is to recognition.
    d. none of the above.

34. A record of a memory is called
    a. a memory trace.
    b. an engram.
    c. an associative block.
    d. a and b

35. When Ebbinghaus tested himself on memory for nonsense syllables, he found that
    a. forgetting was fastest immediately after learning.
    b. his episodic and generic memory were equivalent.
    c. his implicit memory was better than his explicit memory.
    d. none of the above.

36. According to a decay theory of forgetting, if a participant learning a list of words was then subjected to one of the following procedures, he would forget the greatest number of words if he
    a. slept for four versus two hours.
    b. learned other lists for four versus two hours.
    c. performed arithmetic problems for four versus two hours.
    d. All of the above would be comparable.

37. One hypothesis about forgetting is that it is due to a change in retrieval cues. Which of the following would be *counterevidence* for this hypothesis?
   a. A demonstration that decay caused forgetting of explicit memories
   b. A demonstration that decay caused forgetting of implicit memories
   c. a and b
   d. None of the above

38. When misinformation is used to insert new ideas into memory, the resulting errors are called
   a. intrusion errors.
   b. source confusion.
   c. childhood amnesia.
   d. none of the above.

39. When misinformation is used, it can __________ other memories, so that the original memory is replaced by the new false memory.
   a. join
   b. overwrite
   c. a and b
   d. none of the above

40. The compelling nature of flashbulb memories has caused some to argue that they are caused by a special memory mechanism. Contrary to this hypothesis, though,
   a. the accuracy of these memories may not be all that impressive.
   b. some of the good memory may come from conversations about the event after it has occurred.
   c. a and b
   d. none of the above.

41. Distortions of memory seem to be accentuated as a function of time between original acquisition of the information and testing. Such distortions could be due to effects of
   a. encoding.
   b. storage.
   c. retrieval.
   d. b and c

42. Bartlett's experiments and evidence about the fallibility of eyewitness testimony highlight the importance of the recall factor of
   a. reconstruction.
   b. proactive inhibition.
   c. retrieval cues.
   d. retroactive inhibition.

43. Suppose two groups of participants watched a videotape of a minor theft, in which someone in a room full of people reached into a drawer and took a $20 bill. After the videotape, Group 1 was asked, "Did you see the custodian reach into the drawer?" while Group 2 was asked, "Did you see a custodian reach into the drawer?" (Actually, there was no custodian in the room.) Which group is more likely to accuse the custodian of the theft?
   a. Group 1
   b. Group 2
   c. Group 1 and Group 2 will be equally likely to accuse the custodian.
   d. It is not possible to tell from the available information.

44. Suppose an eyewitness to a crime was hypnotized and asked to recall as much as she could of the events of the crime. She would most likely
   a. recall more of what she had seen.
   b. recall less of what she had seen.
   c. recall about the same as if she had not been hypnotized, but report more.
   d. resist recalling more about the crime because of its emotional impact.

45. There are reasons to believe that some of the recent reports of repressed memories of childhood sexual abuse are not correct. Several factors may be exaggerating the number of such reports:
   a. Some of the therapists involved in eliciting them are using hypnosis, which is known to cause the patient to report more things that may be confabulations in the hopes of pleasing the therapist.
   b. Some of the therapists who work on this problem have a bias to find childhood causes of adult problems even when there may be no such causes.
   c. Highly charged memories such as those of childhood abuse are not likely to be repressed for such a long time without having come out before.
   d. All of the above.

46. Retrograde amnesia may be caused by
   a. a disruption in the mechanism that causes new material to be placed into long-term memory, thus preventing any new learning.
   b. a disruption of trace consolidation at the time of the trauma.
   c. a difficulty in retrieving events that occurred just prior to the trauma.
   d. more than one of the above.

47. One experiment has shown that while amnesic patients get better at reading mirror-reversed text, they cannot recognize the words they have read later on, whereas people with normal memories can. This indicates that
   a. amnesiacs lose the ability to learn new information.
   b. amnesiacs lose the ability to learn declarative information, but not procedural information.
   c. amnesiacs can learn procedural skills, but only if the very same stimuli are repeated over and over.
   d. anterograde amnesiacs are different from retrograde amnesiacs.

48. Three major symptoms characterize anterograde amnesia. They are
   a. accurate memory for pretrauma events, normal working memory, and inaccurate memory for most posttrauma events.
   b. inaccurate memory for pretrauma events, normal working memory, and inaccurate memory for most posttrauma events.
   c. accurate memory for pretrauma events, abnormal working memory, and accurate memory for most posttrauma events.
   d. inaccurate memory for pretrauma events, normal working memory, and accurate memory for most posttrauma events.

49. Milner's patient H. M. (an anterograde amnesiac) was tested for his memory span for unrelated nouns. What is your best guess about his span?
   a. 0
   b. 4
   c. 7
   d. 10

50. A theory of memory that says that memory needs time to be fixed into a permanent form is called
   a. rehearsal.
   b. spreading activation.
   c. memory consolidation.
   d. memory priming.

51. You witness an automobile accident in which one of the drivers hits his head on the windshield. He appears uninjured, but when a police officer asks him what happened just prior to the accident, the man seems confused and is unable to answer. The police officer is about to haul the man off to jail (assuming that he must be drunk) when you step forward and (having studied your psychology text) say, "This man is suffering from __________!"
   a. trace consolidation
   b. anterograde amnesia
   c. retrograde amnesia
   d. Korsakoff's syndrome

52. Patients with anterograde amnesia may experience impaired
   a. explicit memory but normal implicit memory.
   b. declarative learning but normal procedural learning.
   c. long-term memory processes but normal working memory processes.
   d. all of the above.
   e. none of the above.

53. Familiarity refers to
   a. a general sense that a stimulus has been previously encountered, but without direct knowledge of the context.
   b. a memory of a certain context, but a lack of knowledge of the stimulus now associated with that context.
   c. a solid memory for both a stimulus and its context.
   d. none of the above.

54. Studies of patients with brain lesions and studies of control patients using brain-imaging techniques has revealed a number of regions of the brain that seem to be critical for memory. These include
   a. the prefrontal cortex for working memory.
   b. the amygdala for emotional memory.
   c. the occipital lobes for visual memory.
   d. the temporal lobes for episodic memory.
   e. all of the above.

Answer Key for Self-Test

1. c
2. a
3. d
4. a
5. c
6. d
7. d
8. b
9. d
10. a
11. a
12. b
13. c
14. d
15. b
16. a
17. b
18. b
19. a
20. b
21. b
22. b
23. d
24. a
25. c
26. a
27. b
28. c
29. d
30. b
31. c
32. e
33. a
34. d
35. a
36. d
37. d
38. a
39. b
40. c
41. d
42. a
43. a
44. c
45. d
46. d
47. b
48. a
49. c
50. c
51. c
52. d
53. a
54. e

Investigating Psychological Phenomena

THE EFFECT OF IMAGERY INSTRUCTIONS ON MEMORY

Equipment: None
Number of participants: One
Time per participant: Fifteen minutes
Time for experimenter: Twenty minutes

As the text discusses, there are several mnemonic techniques that will improve memory performance. One of these is the use of images. By now there is a good deal of research that demonstrates the memorial effectiveness of asking participants to create images of the objects or events that they are trying to commit to memory. In the present experiment, which involves learning paired-associate lists, you will have an opportunity to demonstrate the effectiveness of imagery instructions for yourself.

The procedure is quite simple. Below you will find two lists of 20 noun pairs each that you can use as stimuli for the experiment. You will need just one person to participate in the experiment. The procedure is as follows:

First, read the following instructions to the participant:

> This is a memory experiment in which you will be required to memorize and recall two lists of words, each of which is composed of 20 pairs of fairly common nouns. First I will

> read aloud the 20 noun pairs from List 1 at the rate of one pair every seven seconds or so. While I am reading the pairs, just sit quietly and listen to them, trying as well as you can to memorize the words in each pair. After I have presented all the pairs, I shall go through the list again, this time reading only the first noun in each pair. As I read each of these nouns, I would like you to recall the second noun that was paired with it when I originally presented the list. You will have seven seconds or so to recall the second noun for each pair and to write it in the space provided on your answer sheet. Do you have any questions?

After you have read these instructions to the participant, give him or her the report sheet for this chapter from Appendix 2. Then follow the testing procedure outlined in the instructions. After you have completed the procedure for List 1, read the following instructions to the participant:

> Now I shall present you with another list of 20 noun pairs that I would like you to memorize. The procedure for this list will be identical to that for the first list except for one change: This time, when you are presented with each pair, try to form a mental image of the words in which there is some sort of interaction. For example, if you were presented with the pair *horse-rock,* you might form an image of a horse who is harnessed to a large boulder, dragging the boulder along the ground. Such images should help you memorize the words. Do you have any questions?

Now give the participant another answer sheet for List 2 and present List 2 exactly as List 1 was presented.

To score the participant's performance, count up the number of items that were answered correctly on each list. If all went well, the participant should have scored better on List 2 (unless the participant was already forming mental images for the nouns in List 1).

At this point you may raise a question. Was the participant's performance on List 2 better because of the influence of the imagery instructions, or could it have been better for some other reason? For example, it may already have occurred to you that performance on List 2 may have been better than List 1 because List 2 was presented *after* List 1, and therefore the participant may simply have been better practiced at memorizing words. Before reading on, try to think of a way that you might have run this experiment that would have avoided this problem.

One way to have avoided a practice effect would have been to use two different participants. This first participant would have received only List 1 with its instructions; the second would have received only List 2 with its imagery instructions. If performance on List 2 was still better than on List 1, you might feel more confident in attributing this difference to the effect of the instructions (assuming that your two participants were fairly comparable in their overall memory ability). At least practice could not account for the difference.

But, you might object, there might *still* be an explanation for the difference between lists that has nothing to do with the effect of imagery instructions. Suppose, for instance, List 2 were composed of words that were more common or concrete than the words on List 1 (e.g., *horse* versus *liberty*). This alone might make List 2 more memorable. There are two ways that you might control for this possibility. The first would be to choose words for the two lists that were equated for frequency of usage and concreteness (and, for that matter, whatever else you might think of that would affect the memorability of words). The second method would be to balance experimentally which word lists were paired with which instructions. The following table shows one arrangement that should work in which you would have to run at least four participants:

	Neutral instructions	Imagery instructions
List 1	Participant 1	Participant 2
List 2	Participant 3	Participant 4

If you were to run this experiment, then you could tell whether the word lists differed from one another in memorability or whether there were an effect of instructions. If List 2 were more memorable than List 1, then Participants 3 and 4 should perform better than Participants 1 and 2. If imagery instructions produced better performance than neutral instructions, then Participants 2 and 4 should perform better than Participants 1 and 3. If List 2 were more memorable than List 1 *and* imagery instructions produced better performance than neutral instructions, then Participant 4 should perform best of all.

If you want to check on the possible influence of practice in the experiment that you ran, and if you want to be sure that the lists of words are comparable (they have been balanced for meaningfulness and commonness of the words), then you should try this last experiment. Whether you try it or not, however, you should realize that one of the points of this exercise is to show that even a fairly simple experiment such as the one that you ran with the lists of words is sometimes open to several interpretations. To find the right one requires careful experimentation.

Noun pairs for List 1	Noun pairs for List 2
1. *building-letter*	1. *sail-bowl*
2. *grass-meat*	2. *coffee-lake*
3. *animal-village*	3. *girl-flood*
4. *house-lip*	4. *corn-river*
5. *sky-seat*	5. *stone-bottle*
6. *dress-apple*	6. *paper-shore*
7. *fur-mountain*	7. *dust-army*
8. *flag-coast*	8. *ocean-fire*
9. *sugar-ship*	9. *clothing-board*
10. *mother-city*	10. *door-king*
11. *market-church*	11. *butler-tree*
12. *plant-baby*	12. *gold-chair*
13. *sea-iron*	13. *flower-car*
14. *woods-engine*	14. *bird-skin*
15. *arm-boulder*	15. *hall-child*
16. *woman-forest*	16. *garden-book*
17. *table-wood*	17. *money-shoes*
18. *queen-college*	18. *cat-camp*
19. *bar-diamond*	19. *wife-storm*
20. *cotton-street*	20. *dollar-machine*

CHAPTER 8

Thinking

Learning Objectives

1. What is directed thinking, and how does it differ from other senses of the word *thinking?*

ANALOGICAL REPRESENTATIONS

2. Be able to define a mental representation and to distinguish it from an external representation.

3. Understand the difference between analogical and symbolic representations. Be able to give examples of each.

Mental images

4. Why is introspection not completely trustworthy as evidence about imagery?

5. What does evidence about mental rotation and mental scanning tell us about imagery?

6. What does neuroimaging evidence contribute to our understanding of the relationship between imagery and perception? How does this evidence blend with evidence from transcranial magnetic stimulation?

Spatial thinking

7. Be familiar with the evidence showing that some spatial knowledge is imagelike in quality; but also be familiar with the evidence showing that some spatial knowledge is more symbolic and conceptual.

SYMBOLIC REPRESENTATIONS

Symbolic elements

8. Be able to describe the definition of a concept and to give examples.

9. Be familiar with the term *proposition* and with its elements (the subject and predicate).

Knowledge and memory

10. Describe the differences between episodic and generic memory. What is semantic memory, and how is it related to episodic and generic memory?

11. Understand the role that nodes and associative links play in network models.

12. Understand how network models of generic memory work.

THE PROCESS OF THINKING: SOLVING PROBLEMS

Organization in problem solving

13. How is problem solving best conceived as a search? How is means-end analysis relevant to this search?

14. How is thinking goal directed?

15. How is thinking hierarchical? How are the concepts of subgoal and subroutine related to the hierarchical nature of thought?

16. Be able to describe how chunking ability differentiates novices from experts. What is the role of automaticity in skill development?

17. Describe the Stroop effect and discuss its relevance to automaticity.

18. What are the major differences between masters and beginners in problem solving? What skills do masters have that novices don't?

Obstacles to problem solving

19. Be aware of the effects of set on problem solving. How does set influence solution strategies?

Overcoming obstacles to solutions

20. How can the strategy of working backward help in problem solving? What is the role of analogy in problem solving? What factors govern whether people will retrieve analogies from memory and use them?

Restructuring

21. What is restructuring? How is it related to creative thinking?

22. How is incubation related to the effects of set? Understand how it is related to creative thinking.

23. How is restructuring in problem solving similar to the process required to appreciate certain kinds of humor?

24. Understand local representation models and distributed representation models. How do they differ?

THE PROCESS OF THINKING: REASONING AND DECISION MAKING

25. Are the laws of logic the laws of thought?

26. Be able to explain the difference between deductive and inductive reasoning and give examples of each.

Deductive reasoning

27. What is a syllogism? What causes many participants to do poorly in solving syllogisms?

28. What sorts of strategies do people use to solve syllogisms?

29. Describe the selection task and the errors people make on it.

30. When is performance on the selection task improved? What are two accounts of this?

Inductive reasoning

31. What are frequency estimates?

32. What is the availability heuristic and how do people use it to make judgments?

33. How is the representative heuristic used to make judgments about instances?

34. What is the confirmation bias? Why are disconfirmations more helpful in testing hypotheses than confirmations? Can you give an example of the confirmation bias?

35. How does formal training in statistics help people to reason inductively? What else can be done to improve reasoning?

Decision making

36. Give examples of errors in reasoning that are due to the way a problem is framed. How do people feel about gains and losses in their willingness to take on risk?

37. What is the dual-process theory of thinking? What types of situations call for the use of system 1? What types of situations call for the use of system 2?

THE THINKING BRAIN

38. Be aware of the approach used by the field of cognitive science.

Localization of thought

39. Give some examples of regions of the cortex used in different thinking tasks.

40. Be able to describe some of the deficits of patients with damage to the prefrontal cortex.

41. What is the role of the prefrontal cortex in working memory? What are some theories about the organization of the prefrontal cortex?

Cognition and consciousness

42. Why is the study of consciousness so difficult?

43. Be able to distinguish between Freud's unconscious and the unconscious processes discussed at the end of the chapter.

44. Be familiar with the phenomenon of blindsight and what its implications are for consciousness in perception.

45. What does it mean to use memory unconsciously? Give examples of the use of memory in comprehension that show its influence even when we are not conscious of it.

46. Describe how actions may be taken without conscious awareness.

47. Understand what it means to be aware of the products of processing without being aware of the processing itself.

48. How might consciousness be useful in situations requiring flexibility?

49. What are some views about the neural correlates of consciousness?

Programmed Exercises

1. The word __________ may be used as a synonym for remembering, attention, or belief. — *thinking*

2. If we are talking about __________ thinking, we are referring to reasoning or reflecting on some problem, with some goal in mind. — directed

ANALOGICAL REPRESENTATIONS

3. Mental __________ refer to internal codes that stand for external __________. — representations, representations

4. A(n) __________ representation is one that captures some of the characteristics of what it represents; a(n) __________ representation stands for what it represents, but does not resemble it in any simple way. — analogical, symbolic

5. Mental __________ seems to be analog in that the time it takes to effect a transformation is related to the number of degrees of transformation. — rotation

6. We can show that people can __________ images by showing that the time it takes them to traverse from one part of an image to another is linearly related to the distance that must be traversed, as if they were looking over an actual map of the space. — scan

7. __________ thinking is sometimes picturelike and sometimes requires conceptual representations. This is illustrated by examining several phenomena of mental maps. — Spatial

8. __________ __________ stimulation is a technique used to disrupt normal brain activity at some site by applying magnetic pulses to the scalp. — Transcranial magnetic

9. Mental images are just like __________, the representations of the world around us. — percepts

SYMBOLIC REPRESENTATIONS

10. A __________ is an internal representation of a class or category for which some instances can be enumerated. — concept

11. A __________ asserts a relationship between concepts such that it relates a __________ and a __________, the former of which is what the __________ is about and the latter of which is what it asserts. — proposition, subject predicate, proposition

12. It is generally believed that there are two kinds of memory representations: ones that tag an event with its time or place of occurrence (called __________ memory), and ones that constitute memory for items of knowledge (called __________ memory). — episodic generic

13. One type of generic memory is __________ memory, which concerns the meanings of concepts. — semantic

14. One popular type of model for semantic memory involves a representation called a __________, in which various __________ are linked together by lines and arrows in a complex system of relationships to show how they are interrelated. — network nodes

15. A network in which one concept was stored under others that subsumed it throughout would be called __________. — hierarchical

16. Semantic __________ occurs when a word activates mental representations of related words. — priming

17. In semantic priming experiments, __________ trials are often necessary to ensure that the participant is paying attention. — catch

THE PROCESS OF THINKING: SOLVING PROBLEMS

18. One conceptualization of problem solving has solvers beginning in an __________ state and traversing a path to a __________ state. — initial goal

19. How to fall in love is an example of an __________-__________ problem; solving a crossword puzzle is an example of a __________-__________ problem. — ill-defined well-defined

20. The use of master plans to organize subsidiary actions suggests that thought is organized into __________. — hierarchies

21. __________-__________ analysis is a method of problem solving that involves minimizing the distance between a current state and a goal state. — Means-ends

22. The ability to organize many details into larger __________ is one of the crucial features of directed activity, including thinking. — chunks

23. As Adrian de Groot demonstrated with chess, master problem solvers use __________ that contain more information than those used by beginners do. — chunks

24. Much of the difference between a master and an apprentice is in the degree to which subcomponents of an activity have been chunked hierarchically; to the master, the substeps have become __________. — automatic

25. The __________ effect is an example of how reading letter strings has become an automatized activity for adults. Reading incompatible color names interferes with naming colors in which the color words are printed. — Stroop

26. When a person becomes __________ on one approach to a task, it is hard for him to approach it any other way. — fixated

27. A person who attempts to solve a problem by thinking along a line of thought created by previous thinking is operating under a __________ __________. — mental set

28. In general, the greater the motivation toward reaching a solution, the greater the __________ __________ with which the problem is approached. — mental set

29. __________ __________ is a problem-solving strategy that frequently helps because we can work from the solution. — Working backward

30. When two problems have a similar structure, using one as a(n) __________ to the other can be an effective problem-solving strategy. — analogy

31. Solutions of difficult problems often involve a perceptual __________ of the problem in order to break a false perceptual set. — restructuring

32. The phenomenon whereby we arrive at an insightful solution to a problem after intense preparation followed by rest is called __________. — incubation

33. It has been suggested that both __________ and __________ involve a dramatic shift from one cognitive organization to another. — humor, insight

THE PROCESS OF THINKING: REASONING AND DECISION MAKING

34. A __________ contains two premises and a conclusion. — syllogism

35. In __________ reasoning, we apply a general rule to a particular case. — deductive

36. In __________ reasoning, we consider different cases and try to find the rule that covers them all. — inductive

37. In the __________ task, subjects are given cards and they must turn over some to determine whether a rule they have been given is violated. — selection

38. __________ statements are of the "if-then" sort. — Conditional

39. A(n) __________ perspective on psychology attributes failure at the selection task to its inability to make contact with adaptively significant problems. — evolutionary

40. Reasoning __________ allow us to reason about problems that involve the concepts of obligation, permission, and cause and effect. — schemas

41. When we use the __________ heuristic to make frequency judgments, we rely on ease of retrieval from memory. — availability

42. The __________ heuristic may lead to error if we are making a judgment about an atypical case. — representativeness

43. The fact that we primarily seek evidence that will confirm our hypotheses suggests that we have a strong __________ __________. — confirmation bias

44. One __________ shows that a hypothesis is false, but countless __________ cannot prove that it is true. — disconfirmation, confirmations

45. The way a problem is __________ can influence the way we will solve it. — framed

46. We are more prone to take risks to limit __________ than to achieve __________. — losses, gains

47. There is a good deal of evidence that throws a poor light on human __________; we make all sorts of reasoning errors. But many important intellectual judgments are rational because they come about by __________ effort. — rationality, collective

48. __________ __________ tasks are used to determine how well we can coordinate two interrelated activities. — Operation span

THE THINKING BRAIN

49. Patients with frontal lobe damage have a difficult time in __________ situations that require some new plan, and they also show distinct patterns of __________, in which they continue the same action repeatedly. — novel, perseveration

50. One important role of the frontal lobes has to do with __________ memory, the memory that is used in problem solving and planning situations. — working

51. The study of __________ has proven very difficult in psychology because mental events are private and not subject to external observation. — consciousness

52. Major advances in the study of consciousness have come about through the study of patients with __________ __________. — brain damage

53. Freud's conception of the __________ included the notion that memories were actively kept out of our awareness. — unconscious

54. There are patients with damage to the occipital lobe of the brain who experience __________, the ability to make judgments about visual objects with no conscious experience of those objects. — blindsight

55. The __________ __________ of consciousness refer to changes in our brain state when we are engaged in conscious thought. — neural correlates

54. By and large, we seem to be unaware of mental __________; but, by contrast, we are sometimes aware of the __________ of mental operations. — processes, products

55. In relying on automatic routines, we give up __________. — flexibility

Self-Test

1. All of the following are examples of directed thinking *except*
   a. discovering a geometric proof.
   b. deciding on the next move in a chess game.
   c. daydreaming about last night's meal.
   d. trying to figure out why a car will not start.

2. A hand drawing of a tractor is what kind of representation, as compared to an actual tractor?
   a. Analogical
   b. Symbolic
   c. a and b
   d. None of the above

3. The relationship between the quality of mental images and the ability to perform tasks that require imagery is
   a. positive.
   b. negative.
   c. sometimes positive, sometimes negative.
   d. unstudied.

4. You have probably seen standardized tests in which you are given a picture of a flat piece of paper in which folds are drawn in. You have to mentally fold the paper and compare it to several objects shown to determine which of the objects will be formed after the folding is completed. Studies of this skill show that the more folds that have to be executed, the longer it takes to perform the task. The task thus produces performance analogous to mental
   a. search of a hierarchical network.
   b. solution of a water jug problem.
   c. solution of a syllogism.
   d. rotation.

5. It appears that the relationship between scanning mental images and scanning actual pictures is
   a. symbolic.
   b. representational.
   c. haphazard.
   d. analog.

6. Studies of mental images for ambiguous figures show that participants
   a. can "see" either form of the figure.
   b. cannot reverse the figure in their mind's eye.
   c. can see both versions of the figure simultaneously, in contrast to what they see when they are viewing such a figure.
   d. none of the above.

7. Brain lesions that disrupt vision often disrupt
   a. hearing.
   b. touch.
   c. smell.
   d. imagery.

8. Studies of the time it takes to estimate distance in a familiar environment result in data very much like studies of
   a. mental rotation.
   b. deductive reasoning.
   c. mental scanning.
   d. functional fixedness.

9. A concept
   a. may designate a quality.
   b. must have a finite number of instances.
   c. must not refer to a relationship.
   d. all of the above.

10. Various theories argue that concepts should be represented by
    a. an image that is abstract.
    b. features that characterize them.
    c. memories of the individuals within the category.
    d. all of the above.

11. A proposition
    a. can be simply a mental image.
    b. must be a full sentence.
    c. has a truth value.
    d. none of the above.

12. A proposition must have
    a. a subject and a predicate.
    b. a product and a process.
    c. a node and a relation.
    d. none of the above.

13. Remembering that Paris is the capital of France is a(n)
    a. semantic memory.
    b. generic memory.
    c. hierarchical memory.
    d. episodic memory.

14. The neuronal workspace hypothesis
    a. states that workspace neurons connect one area of the brain to another.
    b. may be a biological explanation for consciousness.
    c. a and b
    d. none of the above.

15. Behavior and thought patterns that are specific to situations we encounter in everyday life are called
    a. reasoning schemas.
    b. mental sets.
    c. network associations.
    d. none of the above.

16. Organization in problem solving is often
    a. lacking.
    b. ill defined.
    c. determined working backward.
    d. goal determined.

17. The Stroop effect clearly shows that
    a. certain mental activities become automatized.
    b. colors are named faster than words.
    c. words are named faster than colors.
    d. none of the above.

18. Research has shown that master chess players are better than novices in
    a. solving algorithms.
    b. chunking chess moves.
    c. memorizing in general.
    d. memorizing random patterns of chess pieces.

19. A person is asked to solve a series of math problems. The first five problems can be solved only one way, each the same. The sixth problem can also be solved using this method, but there is also a much simpler solution. The participant solves this problem in the way he solved the first five. This person's problem-solving ability has been hampered by
    a. working backward.
    b. a lack of motivation.
    c. mental set.
    d. an improper heuristic.

20. The use of analogy in problem solving
    a. seems to be a habitual characteristic of the human problem solver.
    b. seems to work only when the analogy is somehow pointed out to the problem solver by someone else.
    c. requires that there be several potential analogues in memory for a single problem.
    d. depends on the problem solver's noticing a structural similarity between two problems.

21. All of the following often contribute to insights *except*
    a. a period of intense preparation.
    b. a period of retreat.
    c. a different environment.
    d. working backward.

22. One likely reason that incubation helps in reaching a problem solution is that it
    a. allows for perceptual restructuring.
    b. helps break mental set.
    c. gives time to set up subgoals.
    d. none of the above.

23. The concept of an incubation period (in the explanation of insight) is unsatisfactory because
    a. it tells us nothing of the underlying processes.
    b. the term *unconscious thought* is too vague.
    c. it has been demonstrated to be false.
    d. a and b

24. Insight and humor are similar in that
    a. both involve heuristics.
    b. both can be based on cognitive restructuring.
    c. neither will work if the participant is mentally set.
    d. none of the above.

25. Restructuring seems to be an important component in humor and in problem solving. In both cases
    a. the person is caught off guard by the unexpected.
    b. some cognitive reorganization is required.
    c. there is usually some incongruity between the way things seem to be initially and the way they resolve themselves.
    d. all of the above.

26. Ill-defined problems differ from well-defined problems in that
    a. ill-defined problems have more difficult and complex solutions.
    b. well-defined problems always have solutions; ill-defined problems are unsolvable.
    c. it is hard to define what changes are needed to reach the goal stated in ill-defined problems.
    d. all of the above.

27. All A are B.
    Some B are C.
    Therefore, some A are C. This is a(n)
    a. invalid syllogism.
    b. valid syllogism.
    c. invalid algorithm.
    d. valid algorithm.

28. Results from the selection task tell us that
    a. we are poor in reasoning about abstract problems that are not set in a concrete context.
    b. our reasoning may be governed by whether the problem masks contact with some evolutionarily important problem that our ancestors faced.
    c. our reasoning is improved if a problem is couched in terms of some social schema that is relevant, such as a schema having to do with obligation.
    d. all of the above.

29. Which of the following statements is true?
    a. We often attempt to see whether our hypotheses are false.
    b. We rarely attempt to see whether our hypotheses are false.
    c. We do not seek evidence that will confirm our hypotheses.
    d. None of the above.

30. In making predictions about the outcome of situations, we seem to make too little use of
    a. salient information that is presented in the form of a memorable scenario.
    b. base-rate information that tells us the past history of a situation.
    c. deductive reasoning.
    d. none of the above; we appropriately balance these sources of information.

31. In an experiment (similar to one that was actually performed), participants were shown a series of slides on each of which there was a male or female name. The females were relatively famous people; the males were not. Unknown to the participants, 20 males and 20 females were included in the list. At the end of the presentation, participants were asked to judge whether there had been more male names on the list or more female names. According to the availability heuristic, the results should have been that
    a. female names were judged more frequent because they were more retrievable.
    b. male names were judged more frequent because they were more retrievable.
    c. female names were judged more frequent because they were more representative of famous people.
    d. female and male names were judged equally frequent because they were equally retrievable.
    e. none of the above.

32. According to the representativeness heuristic, if we are told that Sam L. is hard working, conservative, meticulous, and exact in his behavior, we will most likely judge him to be
    a. a poet.
    b. an engineer.
    c. a high school teacher.
    d. a creative writer for an advertising firm.
    e. any of the above.

33. Participants are involved in an experiment in which they have to test whether the following rule is true: If a box contains red, black, or green balls, then it also contains yellow balls. To test out the rule, the participants are given a choice of a number of boxes from which to select. The fact that people are subject to the confirmation bias suggests that they will not select a box that they are told contains
    a. red balls.
    b. green balls.
    c. yellow balls.
    d. black balls.

34. One thing that improves reasoning ability is stating a problem in terms of
    a. probability.
    b. frequency.
    c. heuristics.
    d. representativeness.

35. Statistical training does seem to improve our inductive reasoning. This is probably due to its
    a. providing us with formal training on such issues as sample size effects.
    b. allowing us to apply more appropriately our own intuitions about such things as chance to situations.
    c. showing us links between our intuitions and formal statistical effects.
    d. all of the above.

36. When a decision is affected by events that come readily to mind, this is a manifestation of
    a. inductive reasoning.
    b. framing.
    c. the representativeness heuristic.
    d. the availability heuristic.

37. Problem framing has an effect on decision making because we are
    a. very risk-averse when we face losses.
    b. not very risk-averse when we face losses.
    c. risk-seeking when we face gains.
    d. none of the above.

38. One common marketing technique by consumer electronics stores is to advertise frequent sales (some as frequent as every week!). With sales this frequent, we could think of pricing as not involving discounts on the weeks of the sale but as price markups on the weeks when no sale was advertised. But marketing would not be as successful this way because people
    a. are more willing to accept losses than to forgo gains.
    b. are more willing to forgo gains than to accept losses.
    c. are generally irrational and will not see the symmetry in these two modes of marketing.
    d. will use the marked-up price as the reference point in the alternative scenario.

39. All of the following are shortcomings of human rationality *except* we
    a. cannot perform the operations of addition, subtraction, multiplication, and division adequately.
    b. make errors in deductive reasoning.
    c. make errors in inductive reasoning.
    d. are not concerned with demonstrating that our hypotheses are wrong.

40. Studies of patients with frontal lobe damage have implicated these structures in
    a. planning novel actions.
    b. working memory.
    c. forming strategies.
    d. all of the above.

41. The study of consciousness has been aided by the study of
    a. blindsight.
    b. incubation.
    c. functional fixedness.
    d. mental set.

42. Which of the following phenomena has been instrumental in the study of consciousness?
    a. Perception without awareness
    b. Memory without awareness
    c. Action without awareness
    d. All of the above

43. It has been suggested that consciousness is needed for
    a. flexibility in processing.
    b. automaticity in processing.
    c. avoiding the deleterious effects of mental set.
    d. promoting the use of analogy in reasoning.

Answer Key for Self-Test

1. c
2. a
3. a
4. d
5. d
6. b
7. d
8. c
9. a
10. d
11. c
12. a
13. b
14. c
15. a
16. d
17. a
18. b
19. c
20. d
21. d
22. b
23. d
24. b
25. d
26. c
27. a
28. d
29. b
30. b
31. a
32. b
33. c
34. b
35. d
36. d
37. b
38. b
39. a
40. e
41. a
42. d
43. a

Investigating Psychological Phenomena

THE STROOP EFFECT

Equipment: Included (see insert)
Number of participants: One
Time per participant: Thirty minutes
Time for experimenter: Forty minutes

It is frequently observed that as we are given more experience at the task of reading, the skill becomes more and more automatic. One symptom of this increasing automatization is that it is difficult to prevent a skilled reader from reading material that he is exposed to. This appears to be a general characteristic of skills that become automated. Given the proper conditions for the occurrence of such a skill, it is difficult to inhibit it.

Since automatization is a prominent characteristic of skilled activities ranging from reading to motor behavior to problem-solving routines, it is useful to investigate it to determine its characteristics. One task that has been studied extensively in this regard is the Stroop task (turn to p. 282 in the text for a full description of the task; Stroop, 1935). The following three experiments are designed to demonstrate the basic Stroop effect and to extend it somewhat so that you can develop some intuitions about why it occurs.

EXPERIMENT 1

First, before performing Stroop's actual demonstration, you should conduct a simple version of it that will provide some baseline data on the effectiveness of our ability to ignore irrelevant information (see Chapter 6, "Perception," for a full discussion of this ability). In this experiment participants are required to name colors. In the control condition of the experiment, the colors are simply displayed in patches. In the experimental condition, the colors are presented by having randomly ordered letter strings, each string of a different color. The question is whether having the letters present interferes with a participant's ability to name the colors. In principle, if the participant is capable of selectively attending to color, having the letters present should not interfere with his or her color-naming performance. Thus, naming the colors of the letter strings should be as easy as naming the colors of the color patches. On the other hand, the extent to which the participant cannot ignore the letter information is the extent to which his or her performance in color naming will decline.

Your measure of ease of color naming will be the amount of time it takes a participant to name a string of 15 colors. To obtain reliable data, you should have the participant name the colors in five lists of color patches and in five lists of letter strings, alternating between the two kinds of lists (see the number below each list).* The procedure is as follows: cut out the 10 lists of stimuli for Experiment 1. On each trial have the appropriate list in front of the participant turned over so that he or she cannot see the stimuli (**see book insert for these lists**). Then read the following instructions:

> When I say go, turn over the list in front of you and name the colors in the list from top to bottom. There will be 15 colors total. Name these colors as fast but as accurately as possible. After you have named the last color, say Stop. We will do this with 10 different lists. Five have the colors printed in patches of ink; the other five have the colors printed in strings of randomly arranged letters. You should *ignore* how the colors are presented and simply name them. Any questions?

You should keep time from when you say Go until when the participant says Stop. Make sure to present the 10 lists in the order indicated by the number under the list. Record the time elapsed for each list and the number of errors for each list in the spaces provided on the report sheet.

*Notice that the two types of lists are matched for the length of the stimulus. That is, the color patches of Lists 1, 3, 5, 7, and 9 are matched in length to the letter strings of length 2, 4, 6, 8, and 10. Why is this an important control? How have the lists of Experiments 2 and 3 been matched? Why?

Average the times for each type of list and total the errors. Does it appear that there is a difference between the average naming time or the total number of errors comparing the two types of lists? How would you interpret the data?

EXPERIMENT 2

In this experiment you are going to duplicate Stroop's demonstration. In the previous experiment you probably found either no effect or a very small effect of list type. The question we now ask is: Are there any conditions under which the participant cannot selectively attend well? In this experiment we have constructed such a condition by having the letters in the experimental condition spell color words themselves. Participants are still required to name the color of the word, not what it spells, but now the name of what it spells is itself going to be a color name. If selective attention is not very effective, these names should interfere with the participant's response and slow him or her down relative to a control condition that has neutral (noncolor) words printed in color.

Use the same procedure as before, but read the following set of instructions:

> In this experiment you are going to perform the same task as in the previous experiment. This time, however, the ink colors will be printed in the form of words. For half the lists, the words will be randomly chosen. For the other half, they will be color words. In both lists, however, you are to ignore the meaning of the words themselves and simply name the colors in which they are printed from the top to the bottom of each list. Remember that you should be as fast and as accurate as possible. Don't turn over each list until I say Go, and when you have finished be sure to say Stop.

When you record the data, keep track of both the time to read the list and the number of errors made. Average the time and errors for each type of list. Is the difference in average time and total errors between list types greater than the difference found in Experiment 1? How would you interpret this?

EXPERIMENT 3

Now you will try a somewhat more subtle version of the Stroop experiment to get a better idea of the extent to which the participant can selectively attend. In the experimental condition, the words printed in color represent nouns whose referents themselves have a characteristic color. This color is never the same as the color in which the word is written. If the word suggests the characteristic color of its referent to the participant, this color might interfere with naming the color in which the word is printed (Majeres, 1974).

Use the same procedure as in Experiments 1 and 2, but read the following instructions to the participant:

> In this experiment you are going to perform the same task as in the previous experiment; that is, you will be naming colors. This time the ink colors will be printed in the form of words that themselves are not colors. For example, one of the lists might contain the word *stove* printed in green ink. Disregard the word that is present and simply name the ink color of each word in the list. Remember that you should not turn over the list until I say Go, you should name the colors as quickly as possible, and you should say Stop when you have finished.

Conduct this experiment as you did the others. Is there a difference in performance between the lists? Is it larger or smaller than in Experiment 2? What does this suggest about selective attention? What does it suggest about the automaticity of the reading process? (If your instructor collects the data, fill out the report sheet in Appendix 2.)

References

Majeres, R. L. (1974). The combined effects of stimulus and response conditions on the delay in identifying the print color of words. *Journal of Experimental Psychology, 102,* 868–874.

Stroop, J. R. (1935). Studies of interference in serial verbal reactions. *Journal of Experimental Psychology, 18,* 643–662.

REPORT SHEET

Experiment 1

Color patch list

List 1 ________ sec. ________ errors

List 3 ________ sec. ________ errors

List 5 ________ sec. ________ errors

List 7 ________ sec. ________ errors

List 9 ________ sec. ________ errors

Average = ________ sec.

Total errors = ________

Letter string list

List 2 ________ sec. ________ errors

List 4 ________ sec. ________ errors

List 6 ________ sec. ________ errors

List 8 ________ sec. ________ errors

List 10 ________ sec. ________ errors

Average = ________ sec.

Total errors = ________

Experiment 2

Neutral words

List 1 ________ sec. ________ errors

List 3 ________ sec. ________ errors

List 5 ________ sec. ________ errors

List 7 ________ sec. ________ errors

List 9 ________ sec. ________ errors

Average = ________ sec.

Total errors = ________

Color words

List 2 ________ sec. ________ errors

List 4 ________ sec. ________ errors

List 6 ________ sec. ________ errors

List 8 ________ sec. ________ errors

List 10 ________ sec. ________ errors

Average = ________ sec.

Total errors = ________

Experiment 3

Neutral words

List 1 ________ sec. ________ errors

List 3 ________ sec. ________ errors

List 5 ________ sec. ________ errors

List 7 ________ sec. ________ errors

List 9 ________ sec. ________ errors

Average = ________ sec.

Total errors = ________

Color referent words

List 2 ________ sec. ________ errors

List 4 ________ sec. ________ errors

List 6 ________ sec. ________ errors

List 8 ________ sec. ________ errors

List 10 ________ sec. ________ errors

Average = ________ sec.

Total errors = ________

CHAPTER 9

Language

Learning Objectives

THE BASIC UNITS OF LANGUAGE

The sound units

1. What are the major hierarchical levels of linguistic structure?
2. What is a phoneme? Give examples of phonemes.
3. Given what we know about phonemes, why is it difficult for humans to understand speech in a language that is not very familiar to them?
4. Are phonemes combined haphazardly? Give examples to support your answer.
5. How do phonemes vary among languages?

Morphemes and words

6. What is a morpheme? Give examples of morphemes.
7. How are morphemes combined?
8. What are content and function morphemes? How do the two kinds of morphemes differ from each other?

Phrases and sentences

9. How is the organization of words into phrases related to meaning?
10. How do the rules of syntax help convey meaning?
11. What is syntax, and how is it related to the acceptability of sentences?
12. What is phrase structure and how is it related to meaning?
13. How are phrases governed by rules?
14. What role do function morphemes play in organizing phrase structure?
15. Understand how the great complexity that is possible in sentence structure relies on the hierarchical structure of morphemes, words, and phrases.
16. Notice how the organization of some phrases leaves the meaning of a sentence ambiguous. Can you devise other ambiguities?

HOW LANGUAGE CONVEYS MEANING

The meanings of words

17. Describe the different kinds of word classes and how some aspects of the meaning of a word are conveyed by the class to which it belongs.
18. According to a definitional theory of word meaning, how are words stored in memory? What is the role of semantic features?
19. What is the relationship between a definitional theory and a dictionary definition?
20. Name two observations about a definitional theory of meaning that suggest it is incomplete. How does the concept of a prototype deal with these observations?
21. How does a prototype theory differ from a definitional theory? What is the role of features? What is a family resemblance structure?
22. How does a prototype view of meaning deal with the problem that many words do not seem to have necessary and sufficient features?
23. What evidence compels us to believe that we store both definitional representations of words as well as prototype representations? Describe the concept of a grandmother to illustrate this.
24. How is it that our understanding of word meanings confers constraints on our beliefs about the properties of objects?

Word meanings in folk theories of the world

25. Explain how we can have nonconscious theories of language that are not necessarily based on experience.

The meanings of sentences

26. What is the significance of calling sentence meanings propositions? How can two propositions differ even if they contain the very same words?
27. How do sentence diagrams help convey the meaning of a sentence?

28. English uses word order heavily to signal meaning, but how do other languages signal meaning without being as reliant on word order?

29. Be able to give examples of how different verbs require different sentence structures to convey their meaning.

30. Explain the role of function morphemes in helping to encode meaning in complex sentences.

Ambiguity in words and sentences

31. How might ambiguity arise in sentences? What types of sentences or phrases can create ambiguity?

How we understand

32. Why is it that we are sometimes led down a garden path in interpreting the meaning of a sentence? What causes such an effect, and how can it be reduced by changing grammatical construction?

33. Explain how often the conversational setting prescribes which sort of sentence should be constructed, giving just the information that is needed for comprehension.

34. Note that speakers do not speak in linear form, filling in all the details of an utterance that they are trading with a partner. They often leave large blanks that have to be inferred. What is the consequence of this? What savings does it produce?

How comprehension works

35. Describe the various cues to word meaning, and give two views of how these cues are amassed in the service of sentence comprehension.

THE GROWTH OF LANGUAGE IN THE CHILD

36. Describe the course of word and syntax acquisition in children starting around age two.

The social origins of language learning

37. Give an example showing how children use social context as a guide to word learning.

Discovering the building blocks of language

38. Describe evidence about the brains of newborns suggesting that they already have a propensity to listen to human speech.

39. Beyond recognizing speech, within a short time, infants can discriminate the speech of one language from that of another. What is the evidence to support this claim?

40. Every baby eventually learns its native language, but at the outset, there is nothing to tell the baby which language this will be. How does the baby's innate capacity compensate for this in the first year of life?

41. Parsing out the words of a language is difficult because speech is continuous. How do babies solve this problem by paying attention to the relative frequencies of syllables and their combinations?

The growth of word meaning

42. What words do children learn first and what parts of speech are not learned at all early on?

43. What is the difficulty in explaining how young children come to understand what words mean? Do they not simply associate a word with an object?

44. Describe evidence that words are tied to the context in which they are spoken for children learning language. They seem to understand that words refer to things in the world.

45. What is a basic level of word understanding? Describe evidence that children focus on the basic level as they learn new words.

46. To what properties of an object will a child generalize a new word—color, shape, size?

47. Apparently, one of the powerful principles of word learning is that children assume that each new word applies to a new thing. Describe evidence to support this claim.

48. Discuss evidence supporting the claim that children have primitive theories of the essence of objects, allowing them to discriminate human-made things from living things.

49. There is evidence that children also use grammatical class to differentiate what objects are; be able to describe this evidence.

50. Describe evidence showing that even children as young as 18 months have some sensitivity to the function morphemes even though they do not produce them.

51. Even children who utter only single words seem to have some evidence of the importance of word order; what evidence supports this?

The progression to adult language

52. What is the evidence that children do not learn to utter sentences by memorizing ones they have heard?

53. Describe the course of learning the past tense and why children at one point revert to incorrect forms (e.g., saying *runned* rather than *ran*).

LANGUAGE LEARNING IN CHANGED ENVIRONMENTS

54. What is the value of studying language learning in very different environments from the ones children normally experience?

Wild children

55. How does early wild rearing affect language learning in the children who have been reared this way?

Isolated children

56. What does the study of isolated children tell us about language acquisition? How does the study of these children reveal the importance of early language learning?

Language without sound

57. Describe the characteristics of American Sign Language (ASL). Why is ASL an important example of language from a theoretical point of view?

Language without a model

58. Describe the language-learning studies with deaf children of hearing parents. What do the results imply?

59. What happens to children who are in a language-impoverished environment? Do they develop any language at all?

Children deprived of access to some of the meanings

60. Theoretically, blind children should learn sentence meanings more slowly than sighted children because blind children are cut off from opportunities to observe word referents. Nevertheless, evidence shows that the rate of language acquisition is not significantly different. Explain this finding.

LANGUAGE LEARNING WITH CHANGED ENDOWMENTS

61. What do cases of children with specific language impairment and Williams syndrome reveal about the relationship between language and other cognitive functions?

The critical period hypothesis

62. Summarize the evidence that points out the importance of critical periods in language learning.

63. Describe the initial difference between young learners of a second language and older learners. How does this difference change over time?

64. How does age relate to achieving native-level fluency in a language?

Second language learning

65. Explain the relationship between the stage of life in which a language is learned and the localization of that language in the brain.

Late exposure to a first language

66. How does the age at which ASL is learned affect a user's fluency?

Language in nonhumans

67. Compare vocabulary learning in chimpanzees and humans. Which method works best to teach chimpanzees vocabulary?

68. What evidence has suggested early syntax acquisition in chimpanzees? Be able to evaluate the quality of this evidence.

69. If we say that trained chimpanzees use language, what does our definition of language exclude?

Animal communication

70. How does animal communication differ from human communication?

LANGUAGE AND THOUGHT

71. Give some examples of how languages differ from one another and how this might influence differences in thought among the linguistic groups.

72. Explain the Whorfian hypothesis and the evidence against it.

How language connects to thought

73. Name some obvious ways in which language influences thought.

Do people who talk differently come to understand the world differently?

74. Realize that the connection between language and thought may be one that is mutually influenced by a common environment.

How can we study language and thought?

75. Is there universal agreement about the perception of colors regardless of the terms used to refer to individual colors? Give an example.

76. Is there universal agreement about the perception of space regardless of the terms used to refer to spatial relations? Give an example.

77. Understand the logic behind the tests of spatial priming to test for effects of mental representations of time.

Programmed Exercises

THE BASIC UNITS OF LANGUAGE

1. We can think of language as existing at a number of levels, from sounds to ideas. The structure of language is therefore ________.	hierarchical
2. The spoken words *bed* and *dead* differ only in the *b* and *d* sounds at the beginning. This is a difference in one ________.	phoneme
3. English uses about ________ speech sounds.	40
4. Some of the facts about how phonemes combine in words are accidental choices. Others are ________ choices.	systematic
5. Morphemes are the smallest language units that carry ________.	meaning
6. *Strange, er,* and *s* are all ________.	morphemes
7. An organized grouping of words is known as a ________, the unit from which sentences are composed.	phrase

8. A tree structure of phrases and words is referred to as a __________ __________ __________ of a sentence. — phrase structure description

9. In the sentence, "The boy saw the ice cream truck," the phrase "the boy" is called the __________ phrase. — noun

10. A __________ __________ is a useful way of partitioning a sentence to show its hierarchical structure. — tree diagram

11. Very often a single use of language can be interpreted in more than one way. That is, language is often __________. — ambiguous

HOW LANGUAGE CONVEYS MEANING

12. The theory that argues that words are organized in our minds much as they are in a dictionary is the __________ theory of word meaning. — definitional

13. According to the theory described in question 12, the meaning of a word is a set of __________ that are essential for something to be a member of the class specified by a word. — features

14. The __________ theory of meaning argues that words are defined by features, but the features are not necessary and sufficient. — prototype

15. Many times members of a category share features that overlap but none of which is necessary or sufficient for membership in that category. Rather, the features share a __________ __________ structure. — family resemblance

16. Sentences introduce a topic, the __________ of the sentence, and they offer a comment about that topic, the __________ of the sentence. — subject, predicate

17. In English and many other languages, word __________ is important to convey the semantic role of the words. — order

18. Sometimes, case __________ provide important grammatical information, and they are usually function morphemes. — markers

19. Sentences in which we are led to one interpretation but that switch to another interpretation are called __________ __________ sentences. — garden path

20. One technique for understanding the processes used by readers is to record with an __________ __________ the motion of their eyes as they read sentences. — eye tracker

21. Language comprehension is influenced by syntax, semantics, __________ context, and __________ that speakers and listeners make about what each of them knows and intends to communicate. — extralinguistic, inferences

THE GROWTH OF LANGUAGE IN THE CHILD

22. Language appears to be __________ and interpersonal at its very outset; even the tone of voice of a speaker of a language that is not a child's will elicit a response in the child. — social

23. Recording __________ flow in two-day-old babies' brains reveals that the babies are sensitive to natural language input. — blood

24. One technique that has proven valuable in detecting what language sensitivity infants have is to record the rate of their __________ when they hear novel or familiar language sounds. — sucking

25. By the age of two months, infants are sensitive to distinctions among __________. — phonemes

26. The way infants are prepared to learn the sounds of any language when they are born is that during the first year of life, they can distinguish all the __________ of any language. — phonemes

27. One way that infants learn the words of a language is that they keep a record of the frequency with which __________ co-occur in speech that they hear. — syllables

28. Young children acquire _______-_______ words for whole objects before learning the superordinates or subordinates. — basic-level

29. Preschoolers apparently believe that no word can have a _______; that is, they act as if any one concept has only one word that refers to it. — synonym

30. Toddlers as young as 15 months seem to know how __________ words are used in English even though they do not use any themselves yet. function

31. Children at about 18 months seem to have some grasp of the part of __________ that involves word order; they can tell the difference between a sentence in which X is doing something to Y versus one in which Y is doing something to X. syntax

32. Learning of past tense in English is subject to __________ errors in young children; they learn that *-ed* added to a word makes it refer to the past, but they then apply this rule to irregular forms of the past as well, such as *ranned*. overgeneralization

LANGUAGE LEARNING IN CHANGED ENVIRONMENTS

33. Cases of wild children raised by animals show that a proper environment is important for normal __________ development. language

34. One thing is clear about language learning: Children do not produce sentences by simply __________ ones they have heard and then simply uttering them. memorizing

35. Evidence that language can develop without sound comes from studies of __________ children. deaf

36. A widely used manual communication system among deaf people is __________ __________ __________. American Sign Language (ASL)

37. A biological __________ enables children to learn language, whether they invent the basics themselves (if there is no language model) or follow the model that they are exposed to. predisposition

38. It is remarkable that __________ children come to use words such as *look* and *see* as early as __________ children. blind, sighted

LANGUAGE LEARNING WITH CHANGED ENDOWMENTS

39. When language capacities are lost or diminished because of damage to a cerebral hemisphere (usually the left), this state is termed __________. aphasia

40. Patients who have a deficit in language only may have a __________ language impairment; by contrast, patients with __________ syndrome have other cognitive deficits, but their language is normal. specific, Williams

41. One hypothesis of language learning postulates an ideal time to learn languages, after which the learning process is significantly more difficult. This time is known as the __________ __________. critical period

42. In comparing adults with children, it is clear that __________ pick up a second language more efficiently than __________ do. children, adults

43. There is evidence that the brain loci of __________-learned languages is different from that of __________-learned languages. late, first

44. After four years of training, the chimpanzee Washoe had learned 130 __________ for objects, actions, and action modifiers. signs

45. Even if chimpanzees were shown to have some sense of sequence this would not be sufficient evidence to claim that they have knowledge of __________. syntax

LANGUAGE AND THOUGHT

46. Studies of the perception of __________, facial __________, or __________ position suggest that perception is universal, and all that differs among cultures is the words that are assigned to perceptions. color, expression, spatial

47. There are cases, such as the phenomenon of framing discussed in Chapter 8, in which __________ guides thought. In this case, describing an outcome in positive or negative terms influences how people choose among alternatives. language

48. Experiments have shown that __________ can facilitate thinking, but that a small bit of training on them can change which ones a thinker uses. metaphors

Self-Test

1. When we say that language is hierarchical, we mean that
   a. different language uses demonstrate social class differences.
   b. language structure exists at many levels.
   c. language has developed from other cognitive functions.
   d. modern languages are descended from other languages.

2. Which of the following represents the hierarchy of language structures from the smallest to the largest unit?
   a. Phrase, word, phoneme, morpheme
   b. Word, morpheme, phrase, phoneme
   c. Phoneme, morpheme, word, phrase
   d. Morpheme, phoneme, word, phrase

3. The smallest units of speech that contain meaning are
   a. phonemes.
   b. morphemes.
   c. syllables.
   d. words.

4. One reason that foreign languages sound strange is that
   a. the same phonemes are pronounced differently.
   b. other languages are spoken more rapidly.
   c. there are fewer gaps in foreign languages than in English.
   d. some of the phonemes are different from those of English.

5. New words are being coined every day. Some sound combinations are not used, though. This is due to __________ rules.
   a. syntactic
   b. semantic
   c. pragmatic
   d. none of the above

6. A morpheme is a
   a. word.
   b. single sound.
   c. perceptual unit.
   d. unit of meaning.

7. A phrase is
   a. several sentences put together.
   b. unrelated to the meaning of a sentence that contains it.
   c. an organized group of words.
   d. always delineated by grammatical markings.

8. What are two kinds of morphemes that represent the kinds of information that is in a sentence?
   a. Content and function
   b. Sound and content
   c. Semantic and sound
   d. Pragmatic and semantic

9. At its most detailed level of specification, the phrase structure description of the sentence "A boy lost his ball" would contain
   a. a noun phrase and a verb phrase.
   b. a noun phrase, a verb, and a noun phrase.
   c. a noun phrase and two verb phrases.
   d. two noun phrases and two verb phrases.

10. A two-branch tree diagram of a sentence structure would include
    a. principle rules and prescriptive rules.
    b. verb phrase and noun phrase.
    c. morphemes and phonemes.
    d. pragmatic rules and verb phrases.

11. Almost every child learns to speak grammatically, yet when a teacher tries to teach the grammatic structure of a language, this is difficult for a child to learn. The lesson from this is that grammar
    a. does not exist psychologically.
    b. may be an implicit but not an explicit skill.
    c. is not the same as syntax.
    d. is unnatural for humans to understand and use.

12. The sentence "Flying planes can be dangerous" is ambiguous because there are
    a. three possible phrase structure descriptions.
    b. alternative possible phoneme descriptions.
    c. alternative ways of grouping the phrases.
    d. ambiguities of word meaning contained in the sentence.

13. The definitional theory of word meaning attempts to define the __________ attributes that are included in a given concept.
    a. necessary
    b. sufficient
    c. a and b
    d. none of the above

14. One problem with the definitional theory of word meaning is that some
    a. words are used to describe more than one attribute.
    b. concepts involve more than one attribute.
    c. concepts have no attributes.
    d. members of a category seem to be better examples of that category than other members.

15. The major characteristic of a prototype theory of meaning is that
    a. no feature is individually necessary.
    b. no feature is individually sufficient.
    c. a whole set of features describes word meaning.
    d. all of the above.

16. A family resemblance structure is an analogy to support which theory?
    a. Prototype
    b. Definitional
    c. Interpersonal
    d. Language attribution

17. According to a definitional theory of word meaning, the concept of a semantic feature is similar to the concept of a(n)
    a. attribute of a concept.
    b. function morpheme.
    c. content morpheme.
    d. all of the above.

18. Some words such as *grandmother, bachelor,* and *six*
    a. have only prototype representation.
    b. are function morphemes.
    c. have no pragmatic value.
    d. do have necessary and sufficient semantic features.

19. Sentences contain topics or comments about some subject which are called
    a. prototypes.
    b. predicates.
    c. paraphrases.
    d. phonemes.

20. If we utter the sentence "Mary bought John a ball," we intend to convey that a ball was purchased for John by Mary. This meaning is called a
    a. prototype.
    b. predicate.
    c. proposition.
    d. phoneme.

21. Which sentence has a different proposition from the others?
    a. The girl kissed the boy.
    b. The boy was kissed by the girl.
    c. The boy kissed the girl.
    d. All of the above include the same proposition.

22. Case markers allow a language to have flexibility in
    a. morphemes.
    b. phonemes.
    c. word order.
    d. all of the above.

23. Complex sentence meanings are often made easier to understand by adding
    a. function morphemes to guide understanding.
    b. content morphemes to guide understanding.
    c. pragmatics to guide understanding.
    d. none of the above.

24. One of the factors that make it easier for us to comprehend complex sentences is that we take into account
    a. the number of content morphemes in a sentence.
    b. the frequency with which events happen.
    c. the number of function morphemes in a sentence.
    d. all of the above.

25. Which of the following are contributors to sentence understanding?
    a. The context in which a sentence is uttered
    b. The likelihood that an event might happen
    c. The placement of function morphemes in a sentence
    d. All of the above

26. Garden path sentences are defined by
    a. ambiguous words in a sentence that can be interpreted in either of two ways.
    b. an initial semantic interpretation based on the first few words that is then changed by the remaining words.
    c. descriptions of flowers growing along a path.
    d. none of the above.

27. Language comprehension is influenced by more than syntax and semantics. In addition, listeners make heavy use of
    a. the order of words in a sentence.
    b. the meanings of individual words in a sentence.
    c. the context in which a conversation occurs.
    d. a and b

28. Speakers and listeners appear to honor a set of unwritten rules when they converse. For example,
    a. a speaker would normally specify which of several possible objects in a room is the topic of an utterance.
    b. a listener would normally honor a request that was given indirectly rather than answering yes or no to a question such as "Can you pass the butter?"
    c. a speaker would normally not utter a comment that is not relevant to an interchange that is currently occurring.
    d. all of the above.

29. Language comprehension is guided by
    a. syntax.
    b. semantics.
    c. extralinguistic context.
    d. inferential activity by the listener.
    e. all of the above.
    f. a and b
    g. a, b, and c
    h. c and d

30. The number of words in an average adult vocabulary is
    a. 10,000.
    b. 40,000.
    c. 80,000.
    d. 150,000.

31. If French infants are playing and are scolded by an English speaker, they will
    a. not understand the scolding because of the language difference and therefore not change their behavior.
    b. begin laughing.
    c. stop their play because of the intonation of the speaker regardless of the fact that they cannot understand the words.
    d. speak back in English to the speaker because they imitate everything they hear.

32. One indication that language is not mere imitation, but that young children pay attention to the social context in which utterances occur is that
    a. when children hear a new word, they will try to figure out what object was being referred to.
    b. young children will talk with each other using a different language from the one they use to adults.
    c. children emit utterances that have nothing to do with the social situation in which they occur.
    d. none of the above.

33. In sound discrimination in early language learning, initially infants
    a. respond to all sounds in all languages.
    b. respond only to the sounds of their own language.
    c. cannot respond to sound distinctions at all.
    d. respond only to the most common sound distinctions in their own language and ignore other sounds.

34. An indication of the interest level that an infant has is
   a. a decrease in the rate at which he sucks a nipple.
   b. an increase in the rate at which he sucks a nipple.
   c. the amount of habituation he shows toward a familiar stimulus.
   d. the amount of dishabituation he shows when given a novel stimulus.
   e. all of the above.

35. A way to show that infants can discriminate phonemes is to show that their rate of sucking when they hear
   a. *ba* repeatedly goes down but then rebounds when they hear *pa*.
   b. *go* repeatedly goes down but then rebounds when they hear *mo*.
   c. *fi* repeatedly goes down but then rebounds when they hear *ti*.
   d. *du* repeatedly goes down but then rebounds when they hear *lu*.
   e. all of the above.
   f. none of the above.

36. The reason children will often say "Carry you" when they mean "Carry me" is that they
   a. hear their parents say the former to them.
   b. want to carry their parents.
   c. do not understand the pronoun *me* but only understand the pronoun *you*.
   d. none of the above.

37. Which of the following is most likely to be among a child's first words?
   a. *Push*
   b. *And*
   c. *The*
   d. *Pain*

38. Children learn new words at about the rate of
   a. 1 word per day.
   b. 10 words per day.
   c. 100 words per day.
   d. 1,000 words per day.

39. If a two-year-old child is asked where the kitty is when no cat is present, she will
   a. do nothing because she will respond only to objects that are present in the environment.
   b. stare blankly at the person asking the question.
   c. stare at an object that is most similar to a kitten in the environment.
   d. search for a kitty by shifting her eyes around.

40. Which of the following is a basic-level word?
   a. *Beagle*
   b. *Animal*
   c. *Poodle*
   d. *Dog*

41. Suppose a child has a fish tank in her house in which there is a goldfish named Max that is often called by his name by the child's parents. The child will likely learn the word
   a. *fish* before the word *Max*.
   b. *Max* and apply it to any animal.
   c. *Max* and apply it to any fish.
   d. *fish* and apply it to any animal whose name is Max.

42. Suppose a child knows the word for dog and you point to a Dalmatian dog and say "This is my rif." If you then ask the child to show you more rifs, she will
   a. point to more dogs.
   b. point to other spotted things.
   c. point to nothing because the word *rif* is not a word in English.
   d. point aimlessly to lots of things in the environment.

43. Linguistic activity in the brain occurs largely
   a. in the left hemisphere.
   b. in the right hemisphere.
   c. across both hemispheres.
   d. in the cerebellum.

44. People with specific language impairment
   a. also have trouble with spatial tasks.
   b. also have trouble with mathematics.
   c. usually have otherwise normal intelligence.
   d. a and b

45. Which of the following aspects do *not* differ between languages?
   a. Rhythm
   b. Tone
   c. Stress
   d. None of the above

46. The use of a word form such as *sitted* by a child is known as
   a. telegraphic.
   b. undergeneralization.
   c. overgeneralization.
   d. syntactics.

47. Evidence from wild children who have been found reveals that
   a. some can be rehabilitated to use language without problems.
   b. some can learn to speak a few words.
   c. all can learn to speak a few words.
   d. none of the above.

48. Language development does *not* depend on hearing language, as evidenced by
   a. wild children learning language.
   b. children learning ASL.
   c. isolated children learning language.
   d. learning challenged children learning language.

49. Deaf children whose parents did not teach them sign language demonstrated language development similar to that of hearing children in that they
   a. went through one-word production, two-word production, and so on.
   b. invented a communication system of their own.
   c. eventually put signs together in predictable serial order.
   d. all of the above.

50. As compared to sighted children, blind children will
   a. not learn language as quickly.
   b. not be able to learn words related to sight such as *look*.
   c. learn language later in life.
   d. all of the above.
   e. none of the above.

51. The loss of language function is known as
   a. aphasia.
   b. anorexia.
   c. asphyxia.
   d. aphaeresis.

52. The following individuals were deprived of exposure to language since birth. Which one has the best chance of learning to speak?
   a. An 8-year-old boy
   b. A 14-year-old boy
   c. A 20-year-old man
   d. A 30-year-old woman
   e. All are equivalent in their language learning ability.

53. First-language learning, second-language learning, and recovery from aphasia may all depend on
   a. intelligence.
   b. the particular language involved.
   c. generalization.
   d. the critical period.

54. In bilinguals, there is evidence that when they learn their languages
   a. at the same time, the languages are represented in different areas of the brain.
   b. one after another, the languages are represented in the same area of the brain.
   c. one after another, the languages are represented in different areas of the brain.
   d. none of the above.

55. People who learn American Sign Language late in life will
   a. have all the same facility with the language as those who learned it early in life.
   b. not have all the elaborations of the language as those who learned it early in life.
   c. have difficulty learning much of the language.
   d. only be able to learn the language if they have not learned another sign language beforehand.

56. Studies in which experimenters have attempted to teach chimpanzees language have led us to the conclusion that chimpanzees can learn
   a. words.
   b. to express propositions.
   c. to use syntax to express thoughts.
   d. all of the above.
   e. a and b
   f. b and c
   g. a and c

57. Some have argued that the many words Eskimos have for snow have shaped their perception of snow. However, this argument is flawed because Eskimos do not
   a. perceive snow any differently than residents of the southern United States do.
   b. have more than one word for snow.
   c. have as many words for snow as English has.
   d. all of the above.

58. Various experimental studies have been conducted that cast doubt on Whorf's claim about the relation of language to thought. For example, studies have shown that people of different
   a. cultures perceive colors the same regardless of the words they use to name colors.
   b. languages have similar perceptions of spatial position even if their languages are inconsistent in assigning names to particular spatial relationships.
   c. cultures perceive time differently but that this perception can be changed with minimal training.
   d. all of the above.
   e. a and b
   f. a and c

Answer Key for Self-Test

1. b
2. c
3. b
4. d
5. d
6. d
7. c
8. a
9. b
10. b
11. b
12. c
13. c
14. d
15. d
16. a
17. a
18. d
19. b
20. c
21. c
22. c
23. a
24. d
25. d
26. b
27. c
28. d
29. e
30. c
31. c
32. a
33. a
34. e
35. e
36. a
37. a
38. b
39. d
40. d
41. c
42. b
43. a
44. c
45. d
46. c
47. b
48. b
49. d
50. e
51. a
52. a
53. d
54. c
55. b
56. e
57. c
58. d

Investigating Psychological Phenomena

IMPLICIT LEARNING

Equipment: A stopwatch or a watch that indicates seconds, index cards
Number of participants: One
Time per participant: Thirty minutes
Time for experimenter: Forty minutes

One of the most impressive aspects of language is its acquisition: children learn an enormous amount about their language without ever being explicitly taught. Consider syntax, for instance. Not until children have already learned a substantial number of syntactic rules do parents correct syntactic constructions that their children use. Somehow the growing child manages to induce the syntactic rules of language from the variety of utterances that he or she happens to encounter. This ability to induce complex rules from examples is one that we use all the time, but its use without intention, or even awareness, and with complex linguistic construction is what makes it impressive as a characteristic of language acquisition. Having just learned about language acquisition, you can now begin to appreciate how complex the language-learning process must be, especially since it is largely mediated by implicit induction.

You can demonstrate this implicit induction process using the following experiment modeled after one by Arthur Reber (1967). There are two phases to the experiment. In the first phase, your participant will memorize a series of strings of letters after being told only that he or she is a participant in a memory experiment. In the second phase, the participant will be told that the letter strings from the first phase were constructed using a rule. Then the participant will be shown 24 new strings that he or she has never seen before and asked to judge which 12 of these were constructed from the same rule used in Phase 1. If the participant correctly categorizes more of these 24 strings than you would expect by chance alone (12 by chance, since there are only two responses the participant can make), then you can conclude that the participant has learned something about the rule even though he or she was not trying to in Phase 1.

PHASE 1

Instruct your participant as follows:

> This experiment concerns memory for unmeaningful material. You will be presented with 20 strings of letters that you must memorize and recall. These strings of letters will be presented in groups of four that you can study for 15 seconds. Then the groups will be taken away, and you will be asked to recall all four strings (in any order). Following this you will be presented with the same strings again for another 15-second study period. This will be followed by another recall attempt. In all, the five groups of strings will be presented five times each for study and recall.

The stimulus materials for this first phase are at the end of this section. Write each of the five lists of strings on index cards and present them to the participant individually. Provide the participant with 20 slips of paper on each of which he or she can recall one quadruplet of strings. Be sure to remove each recall attempt before showing the next repetition of a set of strings or before going on to a new set of strings.

PHASE 2

Instruct your participant for Phase 2 as follows:

> The strings of letters were constructed according to a rule. The rule dictated the orders in which letters were allowed to follow one another. In the second phase you will be shown 24 new strings of letters, and you must decide for each one whether it was constructed according to the same rule for the letter strings in Phase 1. When you decide, place your answer in the appropriate place on the answer sheet.

Score the participant's answers after he or she has completed Phase 2, using the answer key provided. Did the participant do better than chance? Ask whether he or she has any guesses about what the rule is. You will probably be surprised to discover how little the participant appears to be aware of the rule even though he or she can use it (in some sense) to make judgments about individual instances.

A diagrammatic representation of the rule is shown below. It works as follows: If you begin at Start and trace through the diagram along any path in the direction of the arrows, you can get to End. By noting the order of the letters that you pass along the way, you can construct a string. Notice that because of loops, some strings may be quite long but still permissible according to the rule.

Think about some of the following issues: In what way does this experiment mimic language learning? In what way is language learning different? As a model of language learning, why was it important not to tell the participants about the existence of a rule until after Phase 1? What do the results suggest about language learning?

Reference

Reber, A. S. (1967). Implicit learning of artificial grammars. *Journal of Verbal Learning and Verbal Behavior, 6*, 855–863.

PHASE 1: STIMULUS LISTS

(Write these on index cards or pieces of paper for presentation to the participant.)

List 1	List 2	List 3	List 4	List 5
VVTRXRR	VVRXRR	VTRRR	VVTRXR	XMVTRX
XMVTTRX	XXRR	XMVRXRR	VTRR	XMTRRRR
XMVRXR	VVRMVRX	VVTTRMT	VVRMTRR	XMVRX
VVTRX	XMVRMT	VVRMTR	XMVTRMT	XXRRR

PHASE 2: LIST OF ALTERNATIVES FOR RECOGNITION TEST

(Write these on index cards as well.)

1.	RXTTVMXR	13.	VVTTRX
2.	XMTR	14.	VVRX
3.	MXXR	15.	VVRRRTX
4.	XMVRXRRR	16.	MT
5.	VVRXR	17.	VVTRMVRX
6.	VTTX	18.	VM
7.	MVTTXVR	19.	XXR
8.	XX	20.	XMT
9.	VRT	21.	RXTMV
10.	VVTTTRX	22.	XXM
11.	TTV	23.	TTRXXM
12.	VT	24.	VTR

ANSWERS

1. no
2. yes
3. no
4. yes
5. yes
6. no
7. no
8. yes
9. no
10. yes
11. no
12. yes
13. yes
14. yes
15. no
16. no
17. yes
18. no
19. yes
20. yes
21. no
22. no
23. no
24. yes

RECOGNITION TEST REPORT SHEET

(You can find this report sheet in Appendix 2; cut it out and give it to the participant.)

RULE FOR LETTER-STRING CONSTRUCTION

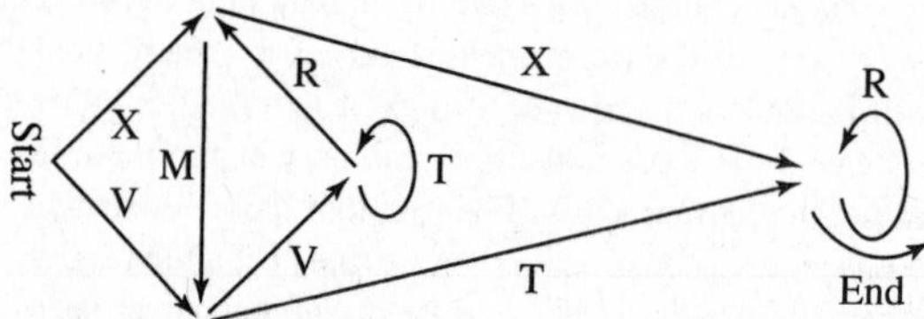

CHAPTER 10

Cognitive Development

Learning Objectives

WHAT IS DEVELOPMENT?

Development as growth

1. Review the major events in physical growth of humans from conception to adulthood.
2. How does humans' physical growth compare with that of other animals? What is the effect of the difference?
3. Review the basic sensory and response capacities of the human infant.

THE PHYSICAL BASIS OF DEVELOPMENT

The mechanism of genetic transmission

4. Indicate how gender is determined by chromosomes.

Environments at different points in development

5. Review gene-environment interactions in the embryo, including the role of both the cellular and hormonal environments in development.
6. Define and describe critical periods and sensitive periods.
7. Describe how development depends on a complex interaction of genes and environment.
8. How do studies of adopted children underscore the importance of genes in cognitive development?

COGNITIVE DEVELOPMENT

9. What are the major philosophical positions on development? How does Piaget's theory relate to these? What are the four developmental stages, according to Piaget?

Sensorimotor intelligence

10. Describe the hallmarks of this stage. How do children see themselves and objects around them? What distinctions develop during this period?
11. Why is object permanence seen as an end to this stage of development?
12. What do the terms *assimilation* and *accommodation* mean according to Piaget? How do children's schemas progress?

The preoperational period

13. What does Piaget mean by the term *mental representation?* What are some examples of mental representations?
14. How is the name of this period derived?
15. Be familiar with various tests of conservation. How does the child's conservation ability develop during this period? Why do children fail to conserve at the beginning of this period? What operations are crucial for conservation?
16. Describe egocentrism.

Concrete and formal operations

17. What is the difference between these stages? How does Piaget describe formal operations?

WHAT IS THE COGNITIVE STARTING POINT?

21. What are the two principal challenges to Piaget's views?

Space and objects in infancy

22. What is occlusion? How does it affect adult object perception?
23. What is the habituation procedure, and how has it been used to study infant perception?
24. What evidence suggests that infants have some notions of the principles that govern objects in space?
25. How do studies of the effects of removing supports from objects reveal a developmental progression in object learning?
26. Cite the evidence that indicates that infants do have a notion of object permanence, but that they have incomplete control over their motor responses.

Number in infancy

27. What is Piaget's position on the conception of number? What do studies of "threeness" in infancy say about this position?
28. Describe an experiment showing that primitive ideas of addition and subtraction are also present in infancy.

Social cognition in infancy: The existence of other minds

29. Describe the evidence that very young infants are capable of discriminating a face from other stimuli, a skill that is fundamental to early social interaction.

30. What is the evidence regarding facial imitation in young infants? What is the significance of this evidence?

31. A next important step in social interaction is sharing attention with another person. Be familiar with the data showing that this skill develops early as well.

32. What is the evidence that infants can separate an object from a physical movement toward that object?

COGNITIVE DEVELOPMENT IN PRESCHOOLERS

The meaning of mental stage

33. What are the characteristics of a developmental *stage* as Piaget uses the term? How is this contradicted by modern evidence?

Numerical skills in preschoolers

34. Even though preschoolers may use idiosyncratic counting terms, how does evidence show that they may nonetheless have a rudimentary understanding of counting principles?

35. How do modern studies of number cast doubt on the Piagetian concept of a stage? Why do these studies differ in their results from Piaget's work?

Social cognition in preschoolers: Developing a theory of mind

36. What are some basic assumptions of a theory of mind?

37. How has it been shown that young children have the rudiments of an understanding of some of these assumptions?

38. What is the course of development of a theory of beliefs about what others know?

39. In what sense can one claim that young children have a theory of mind?

40. Describe some evidence about the idea that humans have a brain module concerned with reasoning in social situations.

Sequence or stages?

41. Understand the argument that Piaget's fundamental conception of stages as transitions still has plausibility even in spite of modern evidence about his tasks.

THE CAUSES OF COGNITIVE GROWTH

The role of biological inheritance

42. What are three sources of evidence on the importance of biological factors in understanding cognitive development?

The cultural context of development

43. Realize that the culture in which a child develops can have a substantial influence on the course of development.

Differences in competence

44. What is the evidence regarding the development of formal operations in different cultures? Do tests of formal operations tell us about the sophisticated reasoning skills of people?

The cultural context of testing

45. How can the kinds of questions that are asked in cognitive testing influence what one infers about development of cognitive skills?

Social and cultural influences on development

46. How do the surrounding cultural influences help determine what a child will learn?

The child's role in shaping the impact of culture

47. How do changes in parental questioning about past events help shape the child's memory of those events?

48. Understand how questioning by adults can shape a child's memory so much that it can distort it if the adults are not careful.

49. What are examples of cultural influences of adult questioning on children's memory?

The information-processing approach

50. What are the memory skills of young children? Can they sometimes remember as much as adults?

51. Describe some strategies for remembering that adults and children use. How do young children approach a memory task, and how does their approach change as they mature?

52. What is meant by the term *metacognition?* How is metacognition manifested in memory, perception, language, thinking, and problem solving?

Dynamic systems theory

53. Define dynamic systems theory. How does it differ from other development theories?

54. What is meant by a system of self-organizing?

COGNITIVE DEVELOPMENT IN OLD AGE

Aging and intelligence

55. What is the study of life-span development?

56. Distinguish between fluid and crystallized intelligence.

57. What are some possible causes of a decline in fluid intelligence?

58. How does bodily health influence mental status and its change with age?

Aging and memory

59. What are some possible causes of memory decline with age?

Programmed Exercises

WHAT IS DEVELOPMENT?

1. Physical growth continues until approximately the end of the _________ decade of life. — second

2. The part of the human body that grows at a disproportionately high rate before birth is the _________. — head (brain)

3. Because of extensive growth of the brain after birth, humans have a longer period of _________ than most other species. — dependency

4. Human growth does not occur smoothly, but in _________. — spurts

5. The _________ reflex is elicited in an infant by a touch to the cheek, which makes the infant turn his head toward the stimulating object. — rooting

6. The _________ reflex is elicited by a touch of the palm. — grasp

7. In general, the infant's sensory capacities are _________ advanced at birth than are her _________ capacities. — more; response (motor)

THE PHYSICAL BASIS OF DEVELOPMENT

8. The genetic material of humans is arranged in pairs of structures called _________. — chromosomes

9. In contrast to a female, who has two X chromosomes, a male has a(n) _________ and a(n) _________ chromosome in each body cell. — X; Y (in either order)

10. During _________ periods in development, certain important events will have an impact that they would not have (or would have to a much lesser extent) at earlier or later times. — critical (sensitive)

11. Adopted children are more similar to their _________ parent than to their _________ parent in language use. — biological, adoptive

COGNITIVE DEVELOPMENT

12. Piaget regards cognitive development as a dynamic process in which the child progresses through several _________. — stages

13. A child has begun to learn that he lives in a stable world that can be distinguished from his sensory impressions. This child is most likely in the _________ stage. — sensorimotor

14. Children develop the notion of _________ _________ near the end of the sensorimotor stage as they become aware that objects exist independently of their sensory experience and motor manipulations. — object permanence

15. Perhaps the most significant accomplishment of children in the last phase of the sensorimotor stage is their ability to _________ objects or events in their absence, rather than merely reacting to their presence. — represent

16. Recurrent action patterns (such as sucking, swallowing, and head and eye movement) are the first mental elements, or _________. It is in terms of these that the infant organizes the world. — schemas

17. According to Piaget, development proceeds by infants' _________ new objects to existing schemas and by changing those schemas appropriately, a process called _________. — assimilating; accommodation

18. Representations may be internalized actions, images, or words; in all cases they function as _________, which stand for whatever they may signify. — symbols

19. According to Piaget, a conceptual system of thought can be constructed only by means of higher-order schemas. These _________ allow the internal manipulation of ideas according to a stable set of rules and emerge at age seven or so; the period from two to seven is therefore termed _________. — operations; preoperational

20. A characteristic of children in the preoperational stage is their inability to _________ quantity, as shown by their lack of knowledge about relative quantities of liquids in two glasses. — conserve

21. According to Piaget, children also have trouble with conservation of __________ at the preoperational stage of development. number

22. A preoperational child believes her point of view is the only one. Such a belief is known as __________. egocentrism

23. A child can determine whether a given number is odd or even and can also add 1 to any number. The child finds that 3 + 1 is even and 5 + 1 is even, but doesn't understand that any odd number added to 1 results in an even number. This child would be categorized as being in the __________ __________ stage. concrete operations

24. The ability to entertain hypothetical possibilities and deal with potential relationships is characteristic only of the stage of __________ __________. formal operations

WHAT IS THE COGNITIVE STARTING POINT?

25. The fact that an infant can perceive an object that is partially blocked by another object gives evidence that infants are capable of reacting appropriately to the perceptual effect of __________. occlusion

26. The procedure in which a perceptual display is kept in view until an infant becomes bored is called __________. habituation

27. It appears that young infants have some knowledge of the fact that two objects cannot occupy the same __________ at the same time. space (place)

28. Young infants believe that any contact with an object will provide __________ for it, keeping it from falling. support

29. Modern investigators believe that although infants may believe that objects exist, they do not actively search for them. Much of the proof for this theory comes from studies on the __________-__________-__________ effect. A-not-B

30. Studies show that infants have a primitive notion of __________: they can distinguish two items from three items. number

31. Studies of the knowledge of number in infants have relied on the __________ method, which depends on showing a stimulus repeatedly and then testing with it and a novel stimulus. habituation

32. Studies of numerical reasoning show that infants as young as five months had a primitive understanding of __________ operations: they could distinguish when a stimulus had been added to an array. arithmetic

33. Investigations of infants minutes after birth have demonstrated that they have a preference for looking at normal rather than scrambled __________. faces

34. Infants will turn their __________ in the direction in which the mother is looking. attention

COGNITIVE DEVELOPMENT IN PRESCHOOLERS

35. According to Piaget, cognitive development is characterized by a series of __________, each qualitatively different from the others. stages

36. Even though children may use idiosyncratic symbols to denote given numbers of objects, they may still have the basic principle of __________. counting

37. Piaget demonstrated the failure of young children to __________ number, in that if a number of items was stretched out, the children thought there were more items present. conserve

38. Recent studies of cognitive development suggest that stages are not __________ or __________ in nature. The demarcations between stages are not sharp. all, none

39. The fact that young children will turn a photograph in the proper orientation when showing it to another person suggests that they have a rudimentary theory of __________. mind

40. At about two-and-a-half years of age, children can predict what another child will want.

They understand something about the mental state of __________. | motive (desire)

41. There are two crucial components to the notion of a __________. One is that they can be true or false; the other is that different people can have different ones. | belief

42. The __________ __________ test asks a child to predict what another being will know in a certain situation. This test compares the child's own knowledge with what the child knows about another's knowledge. | false belief

43. Some have argued that natural selection would favor people with the ability to predict the actions of others. So, evolution may have promoted the development of a __________ __________ module. | social cognition

44. Most developmental psychologists would say that Piaget's cognitive milestones are not a succession of mental stages, similar to those found in embryological development, but rather a __________ of mental steps. | sequence

THE CAUSES OF COGNITIVE GROWTH

45. Piaget was probably wrong in thinking that all development stemmed from a few reflexes. The role of biological __________ appears to be much more extensive than that. | inheritance

46. People from different __________ appear to differ on tests of formal operations even though those who fail these tests still show sophisticated reasoning skills. | cultures

47. __________ differ in the activities to which children are exposed, so it is hardly surprising that children who live near the water will be good swimmers. | Cultures

48. The zone of __________ __________ refers to the tasks that are just out of reach of children but that they are capable of attaining with guidance. | proximal development

49. A more current approach to cognitive development asserts that it results from a change in __________ __________. | information processing

50. According to this approach, mental growth is partly based on the acquisition of various __________ for thinking and remembering. | strategies

51. The fact that adults can reflect on the cognitive operations whereby they gain knowledge shows that they are capable of __________. | metacognition

52. The idea that many factors can influence a child's performance at any stage of development is known as __________ __________ theory. | dynamic systems

53. In dynamic systems theory, ideas can be translated into precise __________ terms, allowing prediction of the child's behavior. | mathematic

54. Dynamic systems theory attempts to explain fine-grained __________ often dismissed by other theories. | variations

COGNITION DEVELOPMENT IN OLD AGE

55. The study of development at all ages, not just in children, is called __________-__________ __________. | life-span development

56. __________ intelligence refers to the ability to reason quickly and efficiently about novel problems. | Fluid

57. __________ intelligence refers to a person's accumulated knowledge. | Crystallized

58. Both __________ and __________ memory show little change with age. | implicit, semantic

59. Both __________ and __________ memory show declines with age. | working, episodic

Self-Test

1. Which of the following is (are) *not* a distinctive feature (features) of human development, in comparison with most other mammals?
   a. A long period of dependency on the parent
   b. Being born at a very immature stage
   c. The presence of reflex at birth
   d. The continuation of growth until about 20 years of age
   e. All of the above

2. The sex of a child is determined by chromosomes from the
   a. mother.
   b. father.
   c. mother and father.
   d. neither mother nor father.

3. Development is influenced by
   a. genetics.
   b. environment.
   c. a and b
   d. none of the above.

4. The fact that at different ages organisms perceive their environment differently and the existence of critical periods together argue for the view that
   a. it is not possible to describe the meaningful environment for an animal by just listing all the physical and social events that are occurring.
   b. initially behavior is controlled by genes, and later by environment.
   c. it is not possible to evaluate the role of environment in determining behavior.
   d. all of the above.
   e. b and c

5. Adopted children are an important source of information about the interplay of heredity and environment in the development of cognition. Study of these children shows that
   a. they are more similar to their adoptive than their biological parents.
   b. their similarity to their adoptive parents increases the longer they live with those parents.
   c. their similarity to their biological parents decreases as they grow older.
   d. none of the above.

6. A child has learned that whether a toy box is open or closed, there are toys inside. It could be said that the child has attained the concept of
   a. object permanence.
   b. representations.
   c. directed action.
   d. solipsism.

7. When a child just becomes aware that objects exist independent of her own sensory experience, she would most likely have completed which Piagetian stage?
   a. Sensorimotor
   b. Preoperational
   c. Concrete operations
   d. Formal operations

8. Recurring action patterns, such as sucking and swallowing, are
   a. simple reflexes that have little developmental interest.
   b. the first mental elements with which the infant organizes the world.
   c. examples of intentional acts.
   d. none of the above.

9. The two processes that Piaget sees as being responsible for cognitive development are
   a. deferred imitation and assimilation.
   b. schemas and representations.
   c. assimilation and accommodation.
   d. none of the above.

10. A toy is hidden under a box in the presence of a child. The child is prevented from reaching the box for a few seconds. When he is released, he immediately lifts the box off the toy. The earliest stage that this child could be in is
    a. sensorimotor.
    b. preoperational.
    c. concrete operations.
    d. formal operations.

11. When a child searches for an object in a location where it was previously present, but from which she saw it moved, she demonstrates
    a. the A-not-B effect.
    b. deferred imitation.
    c. object permanence.
    d. all of the above.

12. Demonstrations of the child's understanding that symbols (i.e., internalized actions, images, or words) may stand for objects but are not equivalent to them include all of the following *except*
    a. object permanence.
    b. deferred imitation.
    c. make-believe play.
    d. metacognitions.

13. A child who is not able to realize that two equal amounts of liquid are still equal after one is poured into a differently shaped glass is not able to display an understanding of
    a. conservation.
    b. assimilation.
    c. accommodation.
    d. none of the above.

14. Children who do not conserve are
    a. unable to attend to all of the relevant dimensions of a stimulus.
    b. usually in the concrete operations stage.
    c. usually in the formal operations stage.
    d. none of the above.

15. One of the features of the world for which children fail to show conservation is number. They apparently believe that
    a. the number 4 is the same as the number 5.

b. the number of items is equivalent to its length when laid out.
c. number and quantity are the same thing.
d. the number of items that are present is the same as the number that were present a few minutes ago.
e. all of the above.

16. The social counterpart of an inability to attend to more than one dimension in a conservation task is
a. aggressive behavior.
b. having only one friend during a particular time interval.
c. egocentrism.
d. none of the above.

17. The major difference between a child in the concrete operations stage and one in the formal operations stage is that as opposed to the child in the formal operations stage, the child in the concrete operations stage
a. is incapable of following the rules.
b. cannot deal with numbers.
c. cannot deal with abstract concepts.
d. all of the above.

18. The idea behind using habituation to study knowledge of occlusion is to have an infant
a. habituate to an occluded stimulus and then see whether the infant sees the whole unoccluded stimulus as novel.
b. habituate to an unoccluded stimulus and then see whether the infant sees the whole occluded stimulus as novel.
c. see a stimulus and then see whether the infant habituates to that stimulus faster when it is occluded.
d. none of the above.

19. The experiment showing that infants have knowledge about objects and the fact that two objects cannot occupy the same place at the same time made use of a procedure in which a screen moved over an object and either stopped when it reached the object or seemed to pass through it. This procedure indicated that the infants had a sense of objects because they
a. habituated to the moving screen.
b. spent more time looking at the screen when it stopped at the object behind it.
c. moved their hands and arms more while the screen was moving, indicating that they anticipated its stopping when it hit the object.
d. spent less time looking at the screen when it stopped at the object behind it.

20. One problem in interpreting results from the A-not-B effect is that
a. it gives an infant too many places to search for a hidden object.
b. it does not allow habituation sufficient time to develop.
c. the results may simply depend on an infant's preference to avoid a place where it has just searched for an object.
d. none of the above.

21. A major claim of Piaget's theory that has been challenged is
a. development proceeds by transitions.
b. the boundaries between developmental stages are sharp.
c. infants have a wealth of built-in capacities.
d. all of the above.

22. Some developmental psychologists have challenged Piaget's view on what is given to the infant at the start of life. With which of the following would these critics agree?
a. Four-month-old infants can perceive partially hidden objects similar to the way adults do.
b. Young infants have a primitive notion of number, at least for small numbers.
c. Young infants have a primitive notion of arithmetic operations.
d. All of the above.

23. What do three-month-old infants understand about what supports objects so they will not fall?
a. Nothing
b. That any physical contact with an object provides support
c. That contact with an object from below it provides support
d. That contact with an object has to come from two sources to provide support

24. Studies of number and addition knowledge in young children
a. confirm Piaget's view of the young child's cognitive competence.
b. raise the possibility that young children are endowed with more cognitive sense than Piaget supposed.
c. indicate that concrete operations can precede the preoperational period.
d. none of the above.

25. Piaget's demonstration of the failure of young children to conserve number
a. has been called into question by more recent work on children's ability to focus attention where the mother is focusing attention.
b. has stood the test of time in that more recent investigations have also found the preoperational child to be unable to conserve number or any other quantity.
c. is inconsistent with his demonstrations of other skills in conservation tasks at the same age.
d. needs to be modified on the basis of more recent evidence of number conservation by young children of small numbers of items.

26. Evidence that infants have primitive social abilities that will later develop more fully includes the fact that infants are
a. more responsive to faces than to other stimuli with the same features scrambled.
b. capable of taking another person's perspective in Piaget's problem where he asks children to predict what another person's perspective will be.
c. sensitive to where another person is concentrating attention.
d. all of the above.
e. a and b
f. a and c

27. What are two characteristics of a *developmental stage* as Piaget uses the term?
   a. Consistent and continuous
   b. Continuous and discrete
   c. Consistent and concrete
   d. Consistent and discrete

28. The fact that children younger than five count with unusually ordered numbers (e.g., one, two, eight, five) but assign a unique label to each item counted
   a. casts doubt on Piaget's discrete-stage view of development in which these children should be in a preoperational stage.
   b. suggests that the preoperational and concrete operational stages are one and the same.
   c. forces one to abandon the notion of sequentially ordered stages altogether.
   d. is inconsistent with the ability of even younger children to have a primitive notion of number and addition.

29. Evidence that young children have a primitive theory of mind is that they have an early sense of another person's
   a. beliefs.
   b. perceptual capacities.
   c. motives.
   d. all of the above.

30. A rudimentary theory of mind has been demonstrated in young children by the result that they
   a. will appropriately orient a picture they are showing to an adult so that it faces the adult.
   b. will be egocentric in trying to take the perspective of another person of how that person views a scene.
   c. can recognize faces only minutes after birth.
   d. none of the above.

31. Some have argued that a social cognition module may have evolved in human brains because
   a. brain damage sometimes causes impairments to a patient's theory of mind.
   b. different cultures make very similar assumptions about the mind and people's motives.
   c. adaptively it would make sense to be able to predict the actions of others.
   d. all of the above.
   e. a and b
   f. a and c

32. The Piagetian theory of stages faces difficulty because
   a. children often display cognitive competence earlier than they should according to the theory.
   b. development is sometimes continuous rather than stagelike.
   c. a and b
   d. none of the above.

33. Evidence that biological factors have a heavy influence on development includes the fact that
   a. adopted children are more similar to their biological than to their adoptive parents.
   b. certain cognitive capacities are tightly tied to particular neural structures.
   c. some cognitive skills are evident so early in life that it is implausible for the environment to have had much influence.
   d. all of the above.

34. Cultures in which there is no formal schooling raise children
   a. with no object permanence.
   b. who fail tests of formal operations.
   c. who cannot count.
   d. all of the above.

35. One way of reconciling modern evidence with Piaget's view of stages of development is to say that
   a. young children begin with very few cognitive capacities and need to learn them all.
   b. young children have some cognitive skills but cannot apply them to very many situations.
   c. Piaget was essentially correct in all of his assertions about stages, but he was wrong in when the stages begin.
   d. none of the above.

36. An approach to cognitive development asserts that mental growth is based partly on the acquisition of better strategies for handling information. This approach explains cognitive development as a change in
   a. accommodation.
   b. information processing.
   c. phenotype.
   d. assimilation.

37. Which of the following is *not* an example of metacognition?
   a. Being realistic about how many numbers you can recall at one time
   b. Recognizing the difference between reality and illusion
   c. Using strategies for reaching solutions
   d. Reading and following directions for a recipe

38. Dynamic systems theory
   a. claims that many factors influence a child's behavior.
   b. attempts to explain differences in behavior that other theories dismiss as "noise" in the data.
   c. uses mathematics to attempt to predict behavior.
   d. all of the above.
   e. a and b

39. The A-not-B error was eliminated in infants by having
   a. the infants change position (stand up) after the location of the object was changed.
   b. the new position of the object be much farther away from the infant than the original position.
   c. a and b
   d. none of the above.

40. Which of the following is true?
   a. Unschooled people are incapable of abstract thought.
   b. Schooled and unschooled people think alike.
   c. Schooled people cannot apply their knowledge to a variety of contexts or situations.
   d. None of the above.

41. When parents are trying to elicit recalled memories in children, they often tailor their questioning to the age of the child by
   a. asking more specific questions the older the child.
   b. never asking young children to recall from memory because they know that young children do not have the appropriate strategies to answer.
   c. giving very explicit clues to young children about what to recall and more general cues to older children.
   d. changing their speech to older children to make clear that the child should only recall what she is confident about.

42. Fluid intelligence is to crystallized intelligence as
   a. genotype is to phenotype.
   b. assimilation is to accommodation.
   c. problem solving is to word retrieval.
   d. heredity is to environment.

43. What might be a cause of the individual differences in people in fluid intelligence and the decline in fluid intelligence with age?
   a. Differences in neuroanatomy with age and among individuals
   b. Increased blood flow with age
   c. Increases in working memory capacity with age
   d. All of the above

44. Many insults to bodily organs can have an important spillover effect on brain function because
   a. if overall health declines, then there will likely be a decline in brain function.
   b. the brain is an unusually large consumer of metabolic energy and so any compromise to the body's ability to metabolize oxygen and glucose will have a large effect on brain function.
   c. a and b
   d. none of the above.

45. What sorts of memory performance will show declines with age?
   a. Priming and other implicit measures of memory
   b. Retrieving facts about the world that are the province of semantic memory
   c. Retrieving episodic memories
   d. Retrieving information from working memory
   e. All of the above
   f. a and b
   g. c and d

Answer Key for Self-Test

1. c
2. b
3. c
4. d
5. d
6. a
7. b
8. a
9. c
10. b
11. a
12. c
13. a
14. a
15. b
16. c
17. c
18. a
19. d
20. d
21. b
22. d
23. b
24. b
25. d
26. f
27. d
28. a
29. d
30. a
31. d
32. c
33. d
34. b
35. b
36. b
37. d
38. d
39. a
40. d
41. c
42. c
43. a
44. c
45. g

Investigating Psychological Phenomena

CONSERVATION OF NUMBER

Equipment: Thirty-three red poker chips and 34 blue ones
Number of participants: One, age four or five (preoperational stage, according to Piaget)
Time per participant: Fifteen minutes
Time for experimenter: Thirty minutes

In Chapter 10, we consider the development of conservation ability as children move into what Piaget calls the stage of concrete operations. The characteristic of this ability is that children come to use a set of mental rules, or operations, to govern their thought about objects in the world. For example, they learn that a certain volume of water is unchanged by the characteristics of the container that happens to contain it. Thus, pouring a certain amount of water from a low and wide container into one that is tall and thin does not change its volume even though the water achieves a greater height in the tall container.

There is also research suggesting that Piaget may have underestimated the ability of children to conserve. Apparently, when faced with somewhat less demanding tasks, which nevertheless are formal tests of conservation ability, young children who should be in a preoperational stage show some signs of conservation. This has been shown most impressively with the conservation of number. The problem that preoperational children face in conserving number is that they confuse number with the physical length of the series that contains the items whose number must be judged. That is, they frequently judge that a row of items contains more items if it is simply longer than another row of items.

The present exercise allows you to take an empirical look at this issue. One of the variables that may influence whether children show evidence of conservation is the number of items that are included in a test. Common sense suggests that the more objects in a set whose number must be judged, the more difficult will be the judgment. We shall test this hypothesis in the context of a number conservation test in which the number of objects whose number must be judged will vary. In both conditions of the experiment, your participants will be asked to judge which of two rows contains more objects. In one condition, the number of objects in each row will be less than in the other condition.

In order to conduct this experiment most efficiently, and with the greatest chance of keeping the attention of your participant, prearrange the stimulus arrays before you begin. The accompanying figure shows you the five stimulus arrangements for each of the two number conditions. Each letter in the figure represents a chip of the appropriate color (B = blue, R = red). On the left are the arrangements for the lower number condition. The first arrangement is the control condition in which each row contains the same number of chips, and in which the two rows are of equal length. In the second figure, the two rows contain the same number of chips, but the lengths of the rows differ. In the third figure, the lengths of the rows are equal, but one row contains more chips than the other. The fourth arrangement pits the two variables against one another: the row that is longest also contains fewer chips than the shorter row. On the right are comparable arrangements for the condition in which more chips are used. The four arrangements are in the same order as the ones on the left of the figure.

Make each of the eight arrangements on a separate piece of cardboard, and place them out of sight. Then seat your child participant comfortably and explain to him or her that you are going to play a game in which the child has to say which row of chips has more chips. Take out Arrangement 1 first and ask the child, "Which row has more, the one with red or the one with blue? Or are they the same?" If the child answers that they are not the same, then lengthen or shorten one of the rows so that the child agrees that they are equal. Be sure that the red and blue chips are equal. Be sure that the red and blue chips line up above one another, so there is a one-to-one correspondence.

Now move on to Arrangement 2. Again ask which row contains more, the red one or the blue one. After getting an answer, which you should record on the answer form that is given on page 117, ask your participant to explain his or her response. That is, ask why the participant judged one of the rows as having more (or fewer, or equal, depending on the answer) chips, and record the substance of this answer on the answer form. Continue with Arrangements 3 and 4, after which you should move on to Arrangements 5 through 8. In each case, record the data in the spaces provided on the answer sheet. For each arrangement decide whether your participant was paying attention to the number or the length of the series in making his or her judgment. Which condition shows better number conservation overall?

The critical comparison that is of interest in this experiment is whether your participant shows evidence of competence in number conservation with fewer chips, but falters with a greater number of chips. If this is so, how does it fit in with the discussion in the text about the development of conservation? What does it imply about a stage theory of development?

Some other questions that might be raised by this exercise are the following: Would your results have been any different if the two conditions had been run in the opposite order, from the more to the less difficult? Is there something inherent in the questioning of the participant that may bias him or her to attend to length rather than number? Why might number conservation be better with fewer chips in the stimuli? What kinds of operations did your participant seem to be using as the basis for his or her judgment? What kinds of tests could be constructed to discover whether other conservation skills might also develop earlier than previously thought?

STIMULI FOR NUMBER CONSERVATION EXPERIMENT

Small Numbers

```
1. B   B   B
   R   R   R

2.    B   B   B
   R      R     R

3. B       B
   R   R   R

4. B              B
    R     R     R
```

Large Numbers

```
5. B  B  B  B  B  B
   R  R  R  R  R  R

6.     B  B  B  B  B  B
   R   R   R   R   R   R

7. B     B     B    B    B
   R  R     R     R  R  R

8. B    B    B    B      B
    R  R   R  R   R  R
```

ANSWER SHEET FOR A NUMBER CONSERVATION EXPERIMENT

1. More blue ______________________
   More red ______________________
   Both equal ______________________

   Explanation:

2. More blue ______________________
   More red ______________________
   Both equal ______________________

   Explanation:

3. More blue ______________________
   More red ______________________
   Both equal ______________________

   Explanation:

4. More blue ______________________
   More red ______________________
   Both equal ______________________

   Explanation:

5. More blue ______________________
   More red ______________________
   Both equal ______________________

   Explanation:

6. More blue ______________________
   More red ______________________
   Both equal ______________________

   Explanation:

7. More blue ______________________
   More red ______________________
   Both equal ______________________

   Explanation:

8. More blue ______________________
   More red ______________________
   Both equal ______________________

   Explanation:

CHAPTER 11

Social Development

Learning Objectives

THE PATH TO ATTACHMENT

1. Describe differences in infants' responses to still versus active faces.
2. Discuss the infant's use of social referencing in evaluating unfamiliar situations.

ATTACHMENT

Contact comfort

3. How do Harlow's experiments on monkeys provide support for the assumption that the caregiver is primarily important as a source of psychological comfort, not food?

Bowlby's theory of attachment

4. Explain Bowlby's theory of attachment.
5. Describe the process of imprinting in animals. Is there imprinting in humans?
6. Discuss the importance of the caregiver as a secure base for the infant's exploration of unfamiliar environments.

THE DIFFERENCES AMONG CHILDREN

Differences in temperament

7. Describe the two categorization schemes used to describe differences in infants' temperament.
8. Discuss how twin studies are used to determine the contributions of genes to temperament.

Differences in experience

9. How do infant temperament and caregiver behavior interact in early learning experiences?

Differences in attachment

10. Describe Ainsworth's procedure for measuring attachment. What characterizes the securely attached child?

Stability of attachment

11. To what extent are attachment styles stable across childhood? What kinds of events are likely to cause changes in attachment styles?

Attachment and later adjustment

12. What is the evidence that the early parent-child relationship, as assessed in the Strange Situation, is a major determinant of later social and emotional adjustment? What are some counterarguments?
13. Discuss Bowlby's idea of an internal working model as a template for relationships later on in life.

Attachment to the father

14. What is the evidence of attachment to the father? What is the difference between paternal and maternal attachment, and what are possible causes of this difference?
15. How have changes in modern Western societies affected father and mother relations with their children?

Early maternal separation and day care

16. What are the effects of early maternal separation and the effects of career mothers and day care on later social adjustment?

Disrupted attachment: Domestic conflict and divorce

17. Summarize the effects of divorce on child adjustment, and indicate the possible role of domestic conflict as a causal agent.

When there is no attachment at all

18. Summarize the effects of maternal deprivation on young monkeys and humans. To what extent are the effects similar in monkeys and humans?

Culture, biology, and attachment

19. Discuss how far cultural differences can influence the results of the Strange Situation and our interpretation of these results.

PARENTING

Socialization

20. What are some values that are socialized in all cultures? How do the characteristics of a culture or social class influence the values that are socialized?

Parenting styles

21. Describe the authoritarian, permissive, authoritative, and uninvolved parenting styles. What are the characteristic behaviors of children raised under each of these approaches?

The child's effect on the parents

22. Explain the interaction between the child's temperament and the parent's pattern of child rearing, and indicate how this interaction complicates the task of relating patterns of child rearing to the child's personality.

PEER RELATIONSHIPS

Friendships

23. Discuss the multiple ways in which friendships are important to the child's development.

The effects of friendship

24. How are rejected children different from neglected children?

25. How do temperament and attachment contribute to children ending up being popular, neglected, or rejected?

EMOTIONAL DEVELOPMENT

Understanding others' feelings

26. What are some of the earliest feelings infants express through facial displays?

27. Discuss how language development facilitates a child's understanding of others' emotions.

Emotion regulation

28. What are some cultural differences in display rules?

29. Discuss how emotion regulation develops over time.

30. What factors contribute to the child's capacity for emotion regulation?

MORAL DEVELOPMENT

Moral judgment

31. Describe Kohlberg's stages of moral reasoning.

32. According to Gilligan, what is the fundamental sex difference in moral attitudes or reasoning? What is the evidence on this potential sex difference?

33. Discuss cultural differences in moral reasoning and moral behavior.

34. What is the relation between moral reasoning and moral behavior? To what extent do Kohlberg's stages represent the ability to describe principles, rather than guidance of behavior by these principles?

Learning to be moral

35. Discuss the idea that children learn to be moral through mechanisms of reward and punishment. Does the evidence support this idea?

Prosocial behaviors and empathy

36. What is empathy, and how does it support altruistic behavior? Is it sufficient?

Individual differences in prosocial behavior

37. Discuss how far biological predisposition and early childhood experiences interact in creating individual differences in prosocial behavior.

SEXUAL DEVELOPMENT

Gender roles

38. Discuss the direct and indirect ways in which parents and other adults shape children's understanding of gender roles.

Sources of gender-role differences

39. What do studies of androgenized females tell us about biological influences on gender differences?

Gender differences in ability

40. Compare biological and sociocultural perspectives on gender differences in ability.

Gender identity

41. Define the concept of gender constancy.

Sexual orientation

42. Distinguish among gender roles, sexual orientation, and gender identity.

43. Discuss the incidence of homosexuality at different historical times and in different cultures.

Origins of homosexuality

44. Discuss how the interpretation of data on differences between straight and gay men is one example of how we have to carefully distinguish between correlation and causation.

DEVELOPMENT AFTER CHILDHOOD

45. Describe Erik Erikson's conception of human growth. What are his "eight ages of man"?

Adolescence

46. Discuss the particular problems of adolescence as a transition to adulthood. Is adolescence always turbulent?

47. In what sense is there an adolescent identity crisis?

Adulthood

48. Describe the midlife transition.

49. Indicate how changes in American society have markedly altered the experience of old age.

Programmed Exercises

THE PATH TO ATTACHMENT

1. Infants' interest in __________ as opposed to __________ faces provides evidence that an interest in social interaction develops early in life.

moving (active), still

ATTACHMENT

2. According to Bowlby's theory of attachment, fear of the _________ forms one basis of attachment. Another basis is a tendency to engage in _________ _________ _________ _________.	unknown (unfamiliar), exploration of the environment
3. According to Bowlby, proximity to an attachment figure provides _________ and _________, and separation from it leads to _________.	comfort, security distress
4. Harlow's experiments with terry-cloth mothers suggest that in monkeys, the nutrient provided by the mother is less important for attachment than the _________ _________ that she provides.	contact comfort
5. The formation of strong attachments by the young of a species to objects (typically the parent) encountered early in life is called _________.	imprinting
6. This type of attachment (imprinting) can occur in response to any salient _________ _________, not just the mother.	moving object

THE DIFFERENCES AMONG CHILDREN

7. Babies who display a playful temperament and adapt quickly to new situations are sometimes referred to as _________ _________.	easy babies
8. In Ainsworth's Strange Situation measurements, a child who explores freely when the mother is present, shows some distress at her leaving, and greets her return with enthusiasm is called _________ _________.	securely attached
9. In Ainsworth's Strange Situation measurements, a child who doesn't explore even in the mother's presence becomes intensely upset when she leaves and shows ambivalence during reunion is called _________/_________.	anxious/resistant
10. In Ainsworth's Strange Situation measurements, a child who is distant and aloof toward his mother, shows little distress when she leaves, and ignores her when she returns is called _________/_________.	anxious/avoidant
11. While attachment style is moderately consistent across childhood, it can be changed by events such as _________ or _________ _________.	divorce, marital problems, serious illness, unemployment (any two)
12. A child's attachment status is a reflection of his/her beliefs and expectations about the social world and is directly influenced by _________.	experience
13. In the Strange Situation, the disappearance of the father also produces some _________.	distress
14. While mothers are preferred sources of care and comfort for most children, fathers are often the preferred _________.	playmate
15. The consequences of early separation from the mother, such as placement in _________ _________, have not been clearly established.	day care
16. Attachment may be disrupted by_________. This may have a causal effect, or the effect may be explained by _________ conflict.	divorce domestic
17. Evidence indicates that the effects of early social isolation may not be _________ and can leave the child with permanent deficits in _________ processes and _________ development.	reversible learning, brain
18. Motherless monkeys and humans reared in some _________ show marked deficits in social performance.	institutions
19. Maternal deprivation has severe long-term effects in both monkeys and humans, but not if it occurs for no more than a few _________.	months
20. Studies of children put in nurturant environments after being in institutions indicate that many of the effects of maternal deprivation are _________ to some degree.	reversible

21. In general, early deprivation of parental contact, or poor parental contact, produces poorly adjusted children. But later interventions can partially _________ these effects, and high-_________ substitutes for parental contact, as in some day care, can reduce or eliminate the effects.	reverse quality

PARENTING

22. _________ is the process by which the child learns how to be a member of a social group, including the acquisition of the patterns of thought and behavior that are characteristic of the society in which she was born.	Socialization
23. The child-rearing style in which the parent controls the child strictly, and does not explain the justification for the governing rules to the child, is called the _________ pattern.	authoritarian
24. The opposite extreme is called the _________ pattern.	permissive
25. An intermediate approach, in which the parents exercise power, but also recognize the child's point of view, is called the _________ pattern.	authoritative
26. The parenting style that is characterized by few rules and demands, and a relative insensitivity to the child's needs is referred to as _________.	uninvolved
27. Of these four patterns referred to above, the one that leads to the best-adjusted children is the _________ pattern.	authoritative
28. Some differences in the pattern of child rearing may result from differences in the _________ of the child, some of which differences are present at birth.	temperament

PEER RELATIONSHIPS

29. Friendships provide the child with an opportunity to engage in shared _________, to obtain _______ in times of stress, and to try out and master _________ _________.	activity support, social skills
30. The _________-rejected child is more likely to grow up to be chronically hostile in adolescence and adulthood.	aggressive
31. The _________-rejected child is more susceptible to anxiety and depression.	withdrawn

EMOTIONAL DEVELOPMENT

32. Emotion-related discussion with parents can help further the child's understanding of the causes and consequences of emotions and contribute to her development of a _________ _________ _________.	theory of mind
33. Culture-specific sets of _________ _______ govern the expression of emotions.	display rules
34. The ability to control, diminish, or change emotions is referred to as the capacity for _________ _________.	emotion regulation
35. Common emotion regulation strategies include _________, _________, and _________.	distraction compensation reinterpretation

MORAL DEVELOPMENT

36. Kohlberg interviewed both adults and children in an attempt to describe the development of _________ _________.	moral reasoning
37. Kohlberg describes this development in a series of successive _________.	stages
38. According to Kohlberg, moral reasoning develops along a course in which right and wrong are defined by first _________ _________/_________ _________, second _________ _________, and third _________ /_________ _________.	getting rewards/ avoiding punishment social convention ideals/moral principles
39. According to Gilligan, in making moral decisions, men tend to emphasize _________, while women tend to be more influenced by _________.	justice compassion

40. A criticism of Kohlberg's cognitive approach to moral behavior is that although it may be able to __________ moral rules, these rules may not actually guide __________. describe, behavior

41. Kohlberg's results may measure our __________ to describe moral rules rather than our tendency to believe them. ability

SEXUAL DEVELOPMENT

42. One aspect of our sexuality is our inner sense of being male or female, called __________ __________. gender identity

43. Another aspect of our sexuality is a group of behavior patterns that our culture deems appropriate for each sex, called __________ __________. gender roles

44. Yet another aspect of our sexuality is our choice of sexual partner, which is called __________ __________. sexual orientation

45. The expectation that someone labeled as male will be more aggressive and more interested in things than people is an example of __________ __________. gender typing

46. The idea that girl babies should be dressed in pink and boy babies should be dressed in blue is an example of a gender role __________. stereotype

47. Characteristics of the female gender role stereotype in American society include __________, __________ __________ __________, and __________. submissiveness feeling toward others, emotionality

48. Women born with the genetic condition congenital adrenal hyperplasia illustrate the effects of the male hormone __________ on development. androgen

49. It is important to remember that most sex differences are differences in __________. averages

50. There may be a biological predisposition for male superiority in __________ ability. spatial (spatial mathematical)

51. There is evidence that higher __________ levels lead to better spatial abilities. testosterone

52. By age five or six, children have a basic understanding of fundamental sex differences and their permanence, or __________ __________. gender constancy

53. A boy who is born with cloacal exstrophy is lacking normal __________ __________. male genitals

54. People who are genetically male but raised as female from infancy usually show normal female gender __________, but a tendency toward a masculine gender __________. identity, role

55. A female who sees herself as female and is sexually attracted to males but is aggressive and athletic could be said to have some characteristics of the male __________ __________. gender role

56. The majority of men and women are __________ in that they seek sexual partners of the opposite sex. The minority who seek partners of the same sex are called __________. heterosexual homosexual

57. The 1948 Kinsey study found the incidence of exclusive male homosexuality in the United States to be about __________ percent of all adult males. 4

58. __________ experience erotic or romantic feelings toward both sexes. Bisexuals

59. Studies in which testosterone was administered to gay men illustrated that hormones play a role in sexual __________, not __________. activation, orientation

60. There are some anatomical differences between heterosexual and homosexual men, including structures in the __________ that are on average larger in heterosexual men. hypothalamus

61. __________ studies suggest a genetic influence on homosexuality. Twin

62. Evidence does not support the __________ hypothesis, which claims that children of gay and lesbian couples are more likely to grow up to be homosexual themselves. imitation

63. The process by which people develop into sexual beings involves __________ as well as __________ factors. biological social

DEVELOPMENT AFTER CHILDHOOD

64. Erikson's "eight ages" are defined by __________ and their __________. crises, resolution

65. In adolescence, the major conflict, which involves discovering who and what one is, is described as a(n) __________ __________. identity crisis

66. In the __________ __________, people of middle age reappraise what they have done with their lives, and may reevaluate their marriage and career. midlife transition (crisis)

Self-Test

1. Bowlby's theory of attachment
   a. focuses on contact comfort.
   b. assumes that infants use the caregiver as a secure base.
   c. claims that the basis of attachment is rooted in our evolutionary past.
   d. all of the above.
   e. none of the above.

2. Harlow's results, showing a preference by infant monkeys for the terry-cloth mother over the a wire mother that provides food, argue
   a. against the importance of comfort contact.
   b. in favor of Bowlby's view of attachment.
   c. that nutrition has little or no effect in producing attachment between infant and mother.
   d. all of the above.
   e. a and b

3. Which of the following statements about imprinting is *false?*
   a. Imprinting is a kind of learning that provides a basis for attachment.
   b. Animals have been shown to imprint to moving objects other than the mother.
   c. Animals may lose the capacity to imprint after a certain age.
   d. One would not expect to find imprinting in a parasitic species that is typically raised by adults of another species.
   e. None of the above.

4. Proximity is to comfort as separation is to
   a. imprinting.
   b. critical periods.
   c. providing nutrients.
   d. distress.
   e. satisfaction.

5. Attachment theorists suggest that a good parent-child relationship at an early age, as assessed in the Strange Situation, is a major determinant of later social emotional adjustment. However,
   a. later adjustment may result from the current relation between parent and child.
   b. the father also plays a major role in adjustment.
   c. adjustment involves the parent-child relation, not just the child.
   d. imprinting may be the cause of later adjustment.
   e. b and c

6. In Ainsworth's Strange Situation, infants show less distress at their father's than their mother's departure. Which of the following would be most likely to increase the infant's distress response to the father's disappearance?
   a. Dress the father as a woman
   b. Dress the father as a strange man
   c. Find a father who had much more contact with his child
   d. Find a child who had been severely punished by her mother
   e. Feed the child bananas

7. The effects of maternal deprivation for more than a few months on the subsequent behavior of monkeys and humans are
   a. severe and similar.
   b. severe for humans, but mild for monkeys.
   c. severe for monkeys, but mild for humans.
   d. minimal.
   e. irreversible.

8. A conclusion that can be drawn from monkey and human maternal deprivation studies is that
   a. adequate nutrition is not sufficient to produce normal social behavior.
   b. behavior to peers is unaffected by maternal deprivation.
   c. imprinting does not have anything to do with later sexual or maternal behavior.
   d. the effects of maternal deprivation are very different in humans and monkeys.
   e. maternal deprivation effects are especially severe if the deprivation occurs in the first few months of life.

9. Monkeys deprived of mothers in about the first six months of life
   a. show a temporary depression in social behavior.
   b. are abnormal in social behavior, but will usually be successful parents.
   c. are permanently deficient in all domains of social behavior.
   d. show severe deficits in social behavior that are completely irreversible.
   e. show severe deficits in social behavior that can be at least partly cured by carefully designed therapy.

10. Institutionalized human children and motherless monkeys show social abnormalities characterized by
    a. a critical period beginning at the time of birth and ending at about three months.
    b. an inability to form good relationships with their peers.
    c. long-term effects that are irreversible.
    d. all of the above.
    e. a and b

11. The assessment of attachment using the Strange Situation yields different results in different cultures. This suggests that
    a. the processes that lead to attachment are the same in all cultures.
    b. the nature of attachment differs from culture to culture.
    c. similar patterns of caregiving yield different patters of attachment in different cultures.
    d. all of the above.
    e. none of the above; the data cannot be interpreted without further research.

12. Permissive parents and uninvolved parents
    a. both provide few rules and demands.
    b. differ in their degree of sensitivity to a child's needs.
    c. encourage a child's independence.
    d. a and b
    e. a and c

13. Imagine that a study reports that most cranky five-year-olds had parents who closed the door to their bedrooms at night when they were infants so they wouldn't wake them. What might be possible explanations of this finding?
    a. Isolating infants causes them to be cranky later in life.
    b. Cranky infants are more likely to be isolated by their parents.
    c. Parents who isolate their children in this way also do other things in child rearing that cause crankiness.
    d. Crankiness is inherited; cranky parents are more likely to be irritated by a crying child, and so are more likely to isolate it.
    e. All of the above.

14. Parenting styles are influenced by
    a. the child's temperament.
    b. the parents' socioeconomic status.
    c. emotional display rules.
    d. a and b
    e. b and c

15. Conflict in the context of the child's friendships
    a. has negative consequences on social development.
    b. is an opportunity for the child to practice skills for solving social problems.
    c. is indicative of poor attachment.
    d. is indicative of poor emotion regulation.
    e. none of the above.

16. Having close friends as a child is associated with
    a. more social success.
    b. decreased risk for mental illness.
    c. increased feelings of self-worth.
    d. all of the above.
    e. none of the above.

17. Early maturity
    a. promotes popularity in boys.
    b. promotes rejection in boys.
    c. has no effect on popularity.
    d. is associated with higher levels of aggression in boys.
    e. none of the above.

18. The development of theory of mind
    a. is linked to language acquisition.
    b. is facilitated by emotion-related discussions with parents.
    c. involves an understanding of what feelings and beliefs are and how they are linked to actions.
    d. all of the above.
    e. none of the above.

19. Emotion regulation is
    a. linked to biological maturation.
    b. based to a large extent on the child's experience observing others.
    c. seen in very young infants.
    d. a and b
    e. b and c

20. The occurrence of unselfish helping behavior by A suggests that A
    a. experiences empathic distress.
    b. is at a high stage of moral reasoning.
    c. knows how to be helpful in the particular situation.
    d. a and b
    e. a and c

21. Consider the following three objections to making three reservations on different airlines at the same time for one person: A. It is against the unwritten rules of the airlines. B. It interferes with the access of others with no tangible gain to the party in question. C. It can be detected, and penalties can be assessed. According to Kohlberg, how would these three reasons be arranged in terms of the development of moral reasoning; indicate the earliest stage first.
    a. A, B, C
    b. B, C, A
    c. C, B, A
    d. B, A, C
    e. C, A, B

22. A person says that we shouldn't double park because it is against the law. This reason is an example of
    a. fear of punishment.
    b. conventional morality.
    c. abstract principle.
    d. empathy.
    e. none of the above.

23. According to Gilligan, moral reasoning in men is relatively more influenced by justice, while in women it is relatively more influenced by compassion. But men and women don't differ on scores on Kohlberg's tests of moral reasoning. Why?
    a. Kohlberg's tests value compassion as much as abstract principles.
    b. Compassion is more abstract than justice.
    c. The male-female difference has more to do with emphases than abilities.
    d. a and b
    e. a and c

24. Seymour speaks eloquently on the issue of equal rights for all races and religions but is actually quite racially prejudiced when he hires workers at his business. This illustrates
   a. the effects of reinforcement.
   b. the influence of the Freudian unconscious.
   c. the distinction between moral reasoning and moral conduct.
   d. the conflict between the social learning view and more traditional reinforcement explanations of moral behavior.
   e. egocentrism.

25. Which of the following is illustrative of gender roles?
   a. Thinking of oneself as a female
   b. Attraction to the opposite sex
   c. Submissiveness and emotionality in a female
   d. Homosexual tendencies
   e. None of the above

26. From the clear demonstration of a biological (genetic) component to a gender difference, we can conclude that
   a. all of one gender is superior on this characteristic to all of the other gender.
   b. the gender difference cannot be eliminated.
   c. the gender difference is irreversible.
   d. b and c
   e. none of the above.

27. In American culture, females have been shown to express emotion more readily than males do. This finding should be interpreted to mean that
   a. females are biologically more inclined to express emotions.
   b. our society teaches females to be more expressive.
   c. the average female is more emotionally expressive than the average male, but that there is a great deal of overlap.
   d. gender typing is not a sufficient explanation of sex difference, and one must also consider gender identity.
   e. a and d

28. The idea that there is a biological factor contributing to sex differences in aggression is (or would be) supported by all the following *except*
   a. in early humans, the stronger male was responsible for almost all hunting and fighting.
   b. these differences are seen in many cultures.
   c. some of these differences are also seen in animals.
   d. male hormone increases aggression.
   e. all of the above.

29. Studies of early sex reassignment indicate that
   a. gender identity and role are completely shifted to the new sex.
   b. sexual orientation is usually not changed.
   c. gender identity fails to shift, but there are some effects of the original gender role.
   d. all three aspects of sex (role, gender, and orientation) show significant resistance to change.
   e. none of the above.

30. The presence of hormones of the opposite "sex" in young children is most likely to influence their
   a. gender identity.
   b. gender role.
   c. sexual orientation.
   d. all of the above.
   e. none of the above.

31. Male homosexuality
   a. is not stigmatized in all cultures.
   b. was quite acceptable in ancient Greece.
   c. seems to be more common than female homosexuality.
   d. is almost always associated with male gender identity.
   e. all of the above.

32. The psychoanalytic view suggests that male homosexuality may result when the child resolves fears aroused during the Oedipal conflict by identifying with the mother instead of the father. This theory would have difficulty explaining
   a. the absence of evidence for differences in the early experience of homosexuals and heterosexuals.
   b. the occurrence of a normal homosexual phase in adolescents in some cultures.
   c. the fact that, typically, male homosexuals have traditional male gender identity and roles.
   d. all of the above.
   e. a and b

33. The data from sex reassignment and the fact that in most cases homosexuals report homosexual tendencies early in life both argue for
   a. imitation of homosexual parents as the basis for homosexuality.
   b. the presence of a weak father figure as the basis for homosexuality.
   c. a genetic basis for important aspects of sexual orientation and gender identity.
   d. all of the above.
   e. none of the above.

34. Evidence for a biological predisposition to homosexuality comes from all of the following *except*
   a. twin studies.
   b. male hormone level differences between male homosexual and heterosexual adults.
   c. male hormone level differences between male homosexuals and heterosexuals prenatally.
   d. differences in brain structure between male homosexuals and heterosexuals.
   e. a and b

35. The transition from childhood to adolescence
   a. is characterized by the child seeking more emotional support from the parents.
   b. is always a turbulent period.
   c. usually occurs at the onset of sexual maturity.
   d. all of the above.
   e. none of the above.

36. In going through what Erikson referred to as an identity crisis, adolescents
    a. try out new roles.
    b. establish clearer distinctions between themselves and their parents.
    c. discover who they are.
    d. are tempted to act in ways that differ from their parents' typical behaviors.
    e. all of the above.

37. During Erikson's midlife transition, adults
    a. experience a midlife crisis.
    b. evaluate what they have accomplished in life so far.
    c. undergo a shift in the way they think about time.
    d. a and b
    e. b and c

Answer Key for Self-Test

1. d	20. e
2. b	21. e
3. d	22. b
4. d	23. c
5. a	24. c
6. c	25. c
7. a	26. e
8. a	27. c
9. e	28. e
10. b	29. e
11. e	30. b
12. d	31. e
13. e	32. d
14. d	33. e
15. b	34. b
16. d	35. c
17. a	36. e
18. d	37. e
19. d	

Investigating Psychological Phenomena

SEX DIFFERENCES

Equipment: None
Number of participants: Twelve
Time per participant: Five minutes
Time for experimenter: Sixty minutes

Sex differences can be analyzed into three different categories:

1. Gender identity—thinking of oneself as male or female
2. Sexual orientation—sex of desired sexual partners, leading to the heterosexual-homosexual distinction
3. Gender role—behavior patterns or attitudes associated with one or the other sex

The relative role of experience (nurture) and genes (nature) has been debated for each of these aspects of sex. But before such studies can be done definitively, we must be clear on the nature of the differences to be explained. This is more or less clear for gender identity and sexual orientation. But the major behavioral and attitudinal differences between the sexes are not obvious and surely differ across cultures.

This study is an attempt to define some reliable sex differences among American college students. We have developed 17 questions that promise to reveal sex differences (we will use as a criterion a question that discriminates between the sexes with a response pattern in which there is at least a 25 percentage point difference between males and females).

First: Answer the questionnaire. *Do not read on until you finish it.*

Questionnaire on Sex Differences

Sex: Male Female (Circle one)

1. Would you be willing to kill a cockroach by slapping it with your hands?
   a) yes b) no
2. What is Queen Anne's lace?
   a) flower d) doily
   b) embroidery e) spice
   c) perfume
3. How many times in the last twenty-four hours have you used the word "shit"?
   a) fewer than 5 times b) 5 or more times
4. Can you sew well enough to make clothes?
   a) yes b) no
5. Do you believe in sexual intercourse only after a spiritual love exists between you and your partner?
   a) yes b) no
6. Do you walk around freely in the nude in a locker room?
   a) yes b) no
7. How often do you cry?
   a) very often d) very infrequently
   b) often e) never
   c) only with good reason
8. At times I feel like smashing things.
   a) true b) false
9. Do you know your chest measurement?
   a) yes b) no
10. Can you change a tire easily?
    a) yes b) no
11. I spend no more than one hour during an average school day playing the radio or listening to records.
    a) true b) false
12. Would you prefer to be the dominant one in a relationship?
    a) yes b) no
13. Do you think that you are overweight?
    a) yes b) no
14. When you get depressed, does washing your hair make you feel better?
    a) yes b) no
15. Do you sleep in the nude?
    a) yes b) no
16. Which parent are you closest to?
    a) mother b) father
17. I try to keep my room as neat as possible.
    a) true b) false

These questions have been made up by faculty and students in introductory psychology courses. Each question has been "tested" with at least 100 undergraduate students in psychology courses. Therefore, we know how well these questions discriminate between college-age males and females (at least in 1971–1973, when the questions were tested). Of the seventeen questions, we know from past testing that five do not discriminate males from females. Try to guess, in advance, which questions would not discriminate. Then, check your guesses against the data presented on the final page of this study. *Guess before you read on.*

List questions that would not discriminate.

Note the type of successful questions in this questionnaire. Some relate to traditional male-female differences. Thus, males are more aggressive (Item 12 on dominance, but note no difference on Item 8—smashing things). Similarly males are less squeamish (Item 1, cockroach) and more restrained emotionally (Item 7, crying).

Other questions refer to knowledge or abilities that tend to go with gender in our society. This would include information about flowers (Item 2, Queen Anne's lace), sewing ability (Item 4), ability to change a tire (Item 10), and knowledge of body measurements (Item 9).

There are in addition some "miscellaneous" questions that tap into reliable differences (Item 5, attitudes to intercourse; Item 6, attitude to walking around nude in a locker room; Item 13, perception of fatness in self; Item 14, washing of hair as a response to depression; and Item 17, neatness).

Second, collaborate with at least one or two other students in the class so that you can collect enough data. Give the twelve copies of this questionnaire, located on pp. 131–41, to twelve undergraduates, six males and six females. (Try to get them to fill out the questionnaire when you give it to them; otherwise, you will find that you don't get a very high return rate.) Aim for a minimum of five completed questionnaires for each sex. Combine your results with the results of as many classmates as you can: it would be desirable to end up with at least fifteen students of each sex.

Third, tabulate your results (see p. 128) in the following way. For the "yes" or "no" questions (e.g., Item 1), add up the number of participants who answered "yes." Then calculate what percentage answered "yes." For the "true" or "false" questions (e.g., Item 8), record those who answer "true." For other items (e.g., Item 2), add up the number of participants whose answers are the same as those indicated in parentheses under "Item" (e.g., Item 1—flower).

Fourth, we have devised a "femaleness" score, by indicating the more common female response to each of the questions that discriminates sex. Compute such a score for each of your participants by counting one point for each of the following answers:

1.	no	9.	yes
2.	flower	10.	no
4.	yes	12.	no
5.	yes	13.	yes
6.	no	14.	yes
7.	very often, often, or with good reason	17.	yes

Indicate here the total number of participants of each sex from whom you have collected data:

Male ______________ Female ______________

	Your data (combined with classmates' data)				U. of Pa. Students**	
	Male		Female		Male	Female
Item	#	%	#	%	%	%
1. Killing cockroach	____	____	____	____	37	* 7
2. Queen Anne's lace (correct answer: flower)	____	____	____	____	50	*82
3. Using word "shit" (less than 5 times)	____	____	____	____	49	50
4. Sew clothes	____	____	____	____	4	*59
5. Intercourse only after spiritual love	____	____	____	____	30	*75
6. Nude in locker room	____	____	____	____	72	*31
7. Crying frequently (very often, often, or only with good reason)	____	____	____	____	22	*78
8. Feel like smashing things	____	____	____	____	75	70
9. Chest measurement	____	____	____	____	28	*78
10. Change tire	____	____	____	____	76	*13
11. Playing radio	____	____	____	____	41	42
12. Prefer dominance in relationship	____	____	____	____	72	*10
13. Overweight	____	____	____	____	17	*60
14. Washing hair when depressed	____	____	____	____	19	*53
15. Sleep in nude	____	____	____	____	39	44
16. Closest parent (mother)	____	____	____	____	61	72
17. Keep room neat	____	____	____	____	51	*77

* A male-female difference of a least 25 percentage points.

** Responses to items in the sex difference questionnaire by undergraduate introductory psychology students at the University of Pennsylvania (1971–1973). Percentages are based on responses from 70 to 270 males and from 88 to 292 females, depending on the item.

SCORES OF MALES AND FEMALES ON "FEMALENESS" SCORE

Plot the number of males and females with each score. Use solid lines for the males and broken lines for the females. The graph at the left contains data gathered from fifteen undergraduate males and seventeen undergraduate females in 1980. Plot your data on the blank graph on the right. How well does this score separate biological females from biological males? What percentage of females scores less than the highest male? How would you go about making a better behavioral discriminator of the sexes? (Note: We have avoided asking questions that might trivially distinguish males from females, such as Do you wash the hair on your chest? or Do you ever wear dresses?)

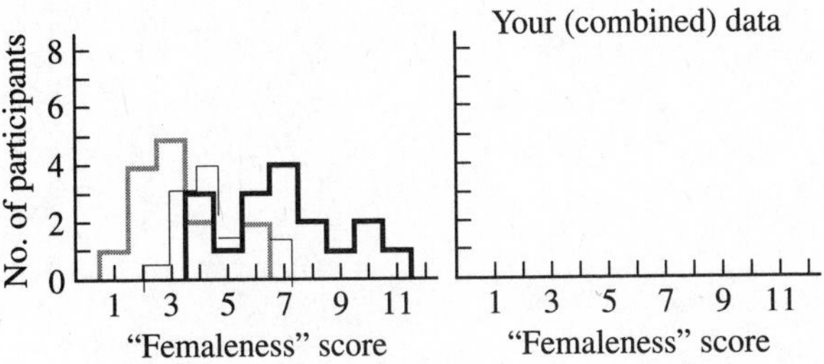

You may note some major differences between your data and the data we reported in 1971–1973. In fact, we tried the questionnaire on fifteen male and seventeen female undergraduate students in 1980 (the participants used in the femaleness ratings), and found some differences from our 1971–1973 study. The biggest effects were that male-female differences disappeared for Queen Anne's lace (Question 2), overweight (Question 13: Over half of the men as well as women thought they were overweight), and washing hair when depressed (Question 14: Practically no one in our recent sample answered "Yes" to that).

There are basically three ways to explain discrepancies (our recent data or your data) from the original large sample of 1971–1973.

1. A general change in society over the last decades. It would seem fair to say that female gender roles have become more like male gender roles in this period. Do your data show this trend for any items? (Note that this would mean that female scores could move closer to male scores, and *not* that male scores would move closer to female scores. Of course, it is also possible to argue that the roles are becoming less distinct, but not necessarily moving toward the traditional male role.)
2. A difference in the populations sampled. Students from different parts of the country or from institutions with different styles or emphases might differ markedly in gender roles. Do you think your student sample would be likely to be very different from University of Pennsylvania students? In what ways? Is this reflected in differences on any scores? (Note that the differences might not just appear as male-female differences, but as generally higher or lower levels of response. For example, one might expect a generally higher positive response on sewing or changing a tire in people from rural backgrounds.)
3. Sampling error. Some observed differences may simply result from the fact that all samples from the same population don't have precisely the same scores (see the statistical appendix to the textbook). With a small sample such as you have collected (as opposed to the large sample that we originally used), a wider variation from sample to sample would be expected. We would ordinarily use statistical methods to indicate how confident we would be that a difference between samples was not due to chance.

FURTHER ACTIVITIES

You might wish to try out some other questions that would relate gender identity to gender role. You could get a suggestion as to whether your questions were good discriminators with samples as low as twenty.

You can also try to use behavior rather than verbal responses to questionnaires. Can you think of obvious differences in such activities as manner of walking or eating, facial expressions, behavior in front of mirrors, motorcycle riding, and so on. Test your hypothesis by direct observation.

(If your instructor collects the data, fill out the report sheet in Appendix 2.)

Questionnaire on Sex Differences

Sex: Male Female
(Circle one)

1. Would you be willing to kill a cockroach by slapping it with your hands?
   a) yes b) no
2. What is Queen Anne's lace?
   a) flower d) doily
   b) embroidery e) spice
   c) perfume
3. How many times in the last twenty-four hours have you used the word "shit"?
   a) fewer than 5 times b) 5 or more times
4. Can you sew well enough to make clothes?
   a) yes b) no
5. Do you believe in sexual intercourse only after a spiritual love exists between you and your partner?
   a) yes b) no
6. Do you walk around freely in the nude in a locker room?
   a) yes b) no
7. How often do you cry?
   a) very often d) very infrequently
   b) often e) never
   c) only with good reason
8. At times I feel like smashing things.
   a) true b) false
9. Do you know your chest measurement?
   a) yes b) no
10. Can you change a tire easily?
    a) yes b) no
11. I spend no more than one hour during an average school day playing the radio or listening to records.
    a) true b) false
12. Would you prefer to be the dominant one in a relationship?
    a) yes b) no
13. Do you think that you are overweight?
    a) yes b) no
14. When you get depressed, does washing your hair make you feel better?
    a) yes b) no
15. Do you sleep in the nude?
    a) yes b) no
16. Which parent are you closest to?
    a) mother b) father
17. I try to keep my room as neat as possible.
    a) true b) false

Questionnaire on Sex Differences

Sex: Male Female
(Circle one)

1. Would you be willing to kill a cockroach by slapping it with your hands?
   a) yes b) no
2. What is Queen Anne's lace?
   a) flower d) doily
   b) embroidery e) spice
   c) perfume
3. How many times in the last twenty-four hours have you used the word "shit"?
   a) fewer than 5 times b) 5 or more times
4. Can you sew well enough to make clothes?
   a) yes b) no
5. Do you believe in sexual intercourse only after a spiritual love exists between you and your partner?
   a) yes b) no
6. Do you walk around freely in the nude in a locker room?
   a) yes b) no
7. How often do you cry?
   a) very often d) very infrequently
   b) often e) never
   c) only with good reason
8. At times I feel like smashing things.
   a) true b) false
9. Do you know your chest measurement?
   a) yes b) no
10. Can you change a tire easily?
    a) yes b) no
11. I spend no more than one hour during an average school day playing the radio or listening to records.
    a) true b) false
12. Would you prefer to be the dominant one in a relationship?
    a) yes b) no
13. Do you think that you are overweight?
    a) yes b) no
14. When you get depressed, does washing your hair make you feel better?
    a) yes b) no
15. Do you sleep in the nude?
    a) yes b) no
16. Which parent are you closest to?
    a) mother b) father
17. I try to keep my room as neat as possible.
    a) true b) false

Questionnaire on Sex Differences

Sex: Male Female
(Circle one)

1. Would you be willing to kill a cockroach by slapping it with your hands?
   a) yes b) no
2. What is Queen Anne's lace?
   a) flower d) doily
   b) embroidery e) spice
   c) perfume
3. How many times in the last twenty-four hours have you used the word "shit"?
   a) fewer than 5 times b) 5 or more times
4. Can you sew well enough to make clothes?
   a) yes b) no
5. Do you believe in sexual intercourse only after a spiritual love exists between you and your partner?
   a) yes b) no
6. Do you walk around freely in the nude in a locker room?
   a) yes b) no
7. How often do you cry?
   a) very often d) very infrequently
   b) often e) never
   c) only with good reason
8. At times I feel like smashing things.
   a) true b) false
9. Do you know your chest measurement?
   a) yes b) no
10. Can you change a tire easily?
    a) yes b) no
11. I spend no more than one hour during an average school day playing the radio or listening to records.
    a) true b) false
12. Would you prefer to be the dominant one in a relationship?
    a) yes b) no
13. Do you think that you are overweight?
    a) yes b) no
14. When you get depressed, does washing your hair make you feel better?
    a) yes b) no
15. Do you sleep in the nude?
    a) yes b) no
16. Which parent are you closest to?
    a) mother b) father
17. I try to keep my room as neat as possible.
    a) true b) false

Questionnaire on Sex Differences

Sex: Male Female
(Circle one)

1. Would you be willing to kill a cockroach by slapping it with your hands?
   a) yes b) no
2. What is Queen Anne's lace?
   a) flower d) doily
   b) embroidery e) spice
   c) perfume
3. How many times in the last twenty-four hours have you used the word "shit"?
   a) fewer than 5 times b) 5 or more times
4. Can you sew well enough to make clothes?
   a) yes b) no
5. Do you believe in sexual intercourse only after a spiritual love exists between you and your partner?
   a) yes b) no
6. Do you walk around freely in the nude in a locker room?
   a) yes b) no
7. How often do you cry?
   a) very often d) very infrequently
   b) often e) never
   c) only with good reason
8. At times I feel like smashing things.
   a) true b) false
9. Do you know your chest measurement?
   a) yes b) no
10. Can you change a tire easily?
    a) yes b) no
11. I spend no more than one hour during an average school day playing the radio or listening to records.
    a) true b) false
12. Would you prefer to be the dominant one in a relationship?
    a) yes b) no
13. Do you think that you are overweight?
    a) yes b) no
14. When you get depressed, does washing your hair make you feel better?
    a) yes b) no
15. Do you sleep in the nude?
    a) yes b) no
16. Which parent are you closest to?
    a) mother b) father
17. I try to keep my room as neat as possible.
    a) true b) false

Questionnaire on Sex Differences

Sex: Male Female
(Circle one)

1. Would you be willing to kill a cockroach by slapping it with your hands?
   a) yes b) no
2. What is Queen Anne's lace?
   a) flower d) doily
   b) embroidery e) spice
   c) perfume
3. How many times in the last twenty-four hours have you used the word "shit"?
   a) fewer than 5 times b) 5 or more times
4. Can you sew well enough to make clothes?
   a) yes b) no
5. Do you believe in sexual intercourse only after a spiritual love exists between you and your partner?
   a) yes b) no
6. Do you walk around freely in the nude in a locker room?
   a) yes b) no
7. How often do you cry?
   a) very often d) very infrequently
   b) often e) never
   c) only with good reason
8. At times I feel like smashing things.
   a) true b) false
9. Do you know your chest measurement?
   a) yes b) no
10. Can you change a tire easily?
    a) yes b) no
11. I spend no more than one hour during an average school day playing the radio or listening to records.
    a) true b) false
12. Would you prefer to be the dominant one in a relationship?
    a) yes b) no
13. Do you think that you are overweight?
    a) yes b) no
14. When you get depressed, does washing your hair make you feel better?
    a) yes b) no
15. Do you sleep in the nude?
    a) yes b) no
16. Which parent are you closest to?
    a) mother b) father
17. I try to keep my room as neat as possible.
    a) true b) false

Questionnaire on Sex Differences

Sex: Male Female
(Circle one)

1. Would you be willing to kill a cockroach by slapping it with your hands?
   a) yes b) no
2. What is Queen Anne's lace?
   a) flower d) doily
   b) embroidery e) spice
   c) perfume
3. How many times in the last twenty-four hours have you used the word "shit"?
   a) fewer than 5 times b) 5 or more times
4. Can you sew well enough to make clothes?
   a) yes b) no
5. Do you believe in sexual intercourse only after a spiritual love exists between you and your partner?
   a) yes b) no
6. Do you walk around freely in the nude in a locker room?
   a) yes b) no
7. How often do you cry?
   a) very often d) very infrequently
   b) often e) never
   c) only with good reason
8. At times I feel like smashing things.
   a) true b) false
9. Do you know your chest measurement?
   a) yes b) no
10. Can you change a tire easily?
    a) yes b) no
11. I spend no more than one hour during an average school day playing the radio or listening to records.
    a) true b) false
12. Would you prefer to be the dominant one in a relationship?
    a) yes b) no
13. Do you think that you are overweight?
    a) yes b) no
14. When you get depressed, does washing your hair make you feel better?
    a) yes b) no
15. Do you sleep in the nude?
    a) yes b) no
16. Which parent are you closest to?
    a) mother b) father
17. I try to keep my room as neat as possible.
    a) true b) false

Questionnaire on Sex Differences

Sex: Male Female
(Circle one)

1. Would you be willing to kill a cockroach by slapping it with your hands?
   a) yes b) no
2. What is Queen Anne's lace?
   a) flower d) doily
   b) embroidery e) spice
   c) perfume
3. How many times in the last twenty-four hours have you used the word "shit"?
   a) fewer than 5 times b) 5 or more times
4. Can you sew well enough to make clothes?
   a) yes b) no
5. Do you believe in sexual intercourse only after a spiritual love exists between you and your partner?
   a) yes b) no
6. Do you walk around freely in the nude in a locker room?
   a) yes b) no
7. How often do you cry?
   a) very often d) very infrequently
   b) often e) never
   c) only with good reason
8. At times I feel like smashing things.
   a) true b) false
9. Do you know your chest measurement?
   a) yes b) no
10. Can you change a tire easily?
    a) yes b) no
11. I spend no more than one hour during an average school day playing the radio or listening to records.
    a) true b) false
12. Would you prefer to be the dominant one in a relationship?
    a) yes b) no
13. Do you think that you are overweight?
    a) yes b) no
14. When you get depressed, does washing your hair make you feel better?
    a) yes b) no
15. Do you sleep in the nude?
    a) yes b) no
16. Which parent are you closest to?
    a) mother b) father
17. I try to keep my room as neat as possible.
    a) true b) false

Questionnaire on Sex Differences

Sex: Male Female
(Circle one)

1. Would you be willing to kill a cockroach by slapping it with your hands?
   a) yes b) no
2. What is Queen Anne's lace?
   a) flower d) doily
   b) embroidery e) spice
   c) perfume
3. How many times in the last twenty-four hours have you used the word "shit"?
   a) fewer than 5 times b) 5 or more times
4. Can you sew well enough to make clothes?
   a) yes b) no
5. Do you believe in sexual intercourse only after a spiritual love exists between you and your partner?
   a) yes b) no
6. Do you walk around freely in the nude in a locker room?
   a) yes b) no
7. How often do you cry?
   a) very often d) very infrequently
   b) often e) never
   c) only with good reason
8. At times I feel like smashing things.
   a) true b) false
9. Do you know your chest measurement?
   a) yes b) no
10. Can you change a tire easily?
    a) yes b) no
11. I spend no more than one hour during an average school day playing the radio or listening to records.
    a) true b) false
12. Would you prefer to be the dominant one in a relationship?
    a) yes b) no
13. Do you think that you are overweight?
    a) yes b) no
14. When you get depressed, does washing your hair make you feel better?
    a) yes b) no
15. Do you sleep in the nude?
    a) yes b) no
16. Which parent are you closest to?
    a) mother b) father
17. I try to keep my room as neat as possible.
    a) true b) false

Questionnaire on Sex Differences

Sex: Male Female
(Circle one)

1. Would you be willing to kill a cockroach by slapping it with your hands?
   a) yes b) no
2. What is Queen Anne's lace?
   a) flower d) doily
   b) embroidery e) spice
   c) perfume
3. How many times in the last twenty-four hours have you used the word "shit"?
   a) fewer than 5 times b) 5 or more times
4. Can you sew well enough to make clothes?
   a) yes b) no
5. Do you believe in sexual intercourse only after a spiritual love exists between you and your partner?
   a) yes b) no
6. Do you walk around freely in the nude in a locker room?
   a) yes b) no
7. How often do you cry?
   a) very often d) very infrequently
   b) often e) never
   c) only with good reason
8. At times I feel like smashing things.
   a) true b) false
9. Do you know your chest measurement?
   a) yes b) no
10. Can you change a tire easily?
    a) yes b) no
11. I spend no more than one hour during an average school day playing the radio or listening to records.
    a) true b) false
12. Would you prefer to be the dominant one in a relationship?
    a) yes b) no
13. Do you think that you are overweight?
    a) yes b) no
14. When you get depressed, does washing your hair make you feel better?
    a) yes b) no
15. Do you sleep in the nude?
    a) yes b) no
16. Which parent are you closest to?
    a) mother b) father
17. I try to keep my room as neat as possible.
    a) true b) false

Questionnaire on Sex Differences

Sex: Male Female
(Circle one)

1. Would you be willing to kill a cockroach by slapping it with your hands?
   a) yes b) no
2. What is Queen Anne's lace?
   a) flower d) doily
   b) embroidery e) spice
   c) perfume
3. How many times in the last twenty-four hours have you used the word "shit"?
   a) fewer than 5 times b) 5 or more times
4. Can you sew well enough to make clothes?
   a) yes b) no
5. Do you believe in sexual intercourse only after a spiritual love exists between you and your partner?
   a) yes b) no
6. Do you walk around freely in the nude in a locker room?
   a) yes b) no
7. How often do you cry?
   a) very often d) very infrequently
   b) often e) never
   c) only with good reason
8. At times I feel like smashing things.
   a) true b) false
9. Do you know your chest measurement?
   a) yes b) no
10. Can you change a tire easily?
    a) yes b) no
11. I spend no more than one hour during an average school day playing the radio or listening to records.
    a) true b) false
12. Would you prefer to be the dominant one in a relationship?
    a) yes b) no
13. Do you think that you are overweight?
    a) yes b) no
14. When you get depressed, does washing your hair make you feel better?
    a) yes b) no
15. Do you sleep in the nude?
    a) yes b) no
16. Which parent are you closest to?
    a) mother b) father
17. I try to keep my room as neat as possible.
    a) true b) false

Questionnaire on Sex Differences

Sex: Male Female
(Circle one)

1. Would you be willing to kill a cockroach by slapping it with your hands?
   a) yes b) no
2. What is Queen Anne's lace?
   a) flower d) doily
   b) embroidery e) spice
   c) perfume
3. How many times in the last twenty-four hours have you used the word "shit"?
   a) fewer than 5 times b) 5 or more times
4. Can you sew well enough to make clothes?
   a) yes b) no
5. Do you believe in sexual intercourse only after a spiritual love exists between you and your partner?
   a) yes b) no
6. Do you walk around freely in the nude in a locker room?
   a) yes b) no
7. How often do you cry?
   a) very often d) very infrequently
   b) often e) never
   c) only with good reason
8. At times I feel like smashing things.
   a) true b) false
9. Do you know your chest measurement?
   a) yes b) no
10. Can you change a tire easily?
    a) yes b) no
11. I spend no more than one hour during an average school day playing the radio or listening to records.
    a) true b) false
12. Would you prefer to be the dominant one in a relationship?
    a) yes b) no
13. Do you think that you are overweight?
    a) yes b) no
14. When you get depressed, does washing your hair make you feel better?
    a) yes b) no
15. Do you sleep in the nude?
    a) yes b) no
16. Which parent are you closest to?
    a) mother b) father
17. I try to keep my room as neat as possible.
    a) true b) false

Questionnaire on Sex Differences

Sex: Male Female
(Circle one)

1. Would you be willing to kill a cockroach by slapping it with your hands?
   a) yes b) no
2. What is Queen Anne's lace?
   a) flower d) doily
   b) embroidery e) spice
   c) perfume
3. How many times in the last twenty-four hours have you used the word "shit"?
   a) fewer than 5 times b) 5 or more times
4. Can you sew well enough to make clothes?
   a) yes b) no
5. Do you believe in sexual intercourse only after a spiritual love exists between you and your partner?
   a) yes b) no
6. Do you walk around freely in the nude in a locker room?
   a) yes b) no
7. How often do you cry?
   a) very often d) very infrequently
   b) often e) never
   c) only with good reason
8. At times I feel like smashing things.
   a) true b) false
9. Do you know your chest measurement?
   a) yes b) no
10. Can you change a tire easily?
    a) yes b) no
11. I spend no more than one hour during an average school day playing the radio or listening to records.
    a) true b) false
12. Would you prefer to be the dominant one in a relationship?
    a) yes b) no
13. Do you think that you are overweight?
    a) yes b) no
14. When you get depressed, does washing your hair make you feel better?
    a) yes b) no
15. Do you sleep in the nude?
    a) yes b) no
16. Which parent are you closest to?
    a) mother b) father
17. I try to keep my room as neat as possible.
    a) true b) false

CHAPTER 12

Social Cognition and Emotion

Learning Objectives

1. Describe the focus and study of social psychology.

PERCEIVING AND UNDERSTANDING OTHERS

2. Describe what is meant by processes of social cognition.

Attribution

3. Explain what is known as causal attribution. How do people arrive at causal attributions?
4. Compare situational and dispositional attributions.
5. Compare individualistic and collectivistic cultures. How do the differences in values between the two cultures influence attributions made by people living within them?
6. Explain what is known as the fundamental attribution error.
7. What is known as the actor-observer difference in attribution, and how does it relate to the fundamental attribution error?

Person perception and cognitive schemas

8. What are schemas or implicit theories of personality? How do they influence the way we perceive, interpret, and remember other people's actions?
9. What are the advantages of relying on schematic knowledge? What are some of the disadvantages of this strategy?
10. Compare entity and incremental theorists' views of personality. Which view is reflected more in individualistic cultures?

Stereotypes

11. What is the "ABC of prejudice"? How do the three components of stereotypes combine into a powerful phenomenon?
12. How do phenomena such as the out-group homogeneity effect and the confirmation bias contribute to the perpetuation of stereotypes?
13. What is the difference between explicit and implicit stereotypes? What kind of experimental evidence suggests that implicit stereotypes can exert powerful influences on our behavior, even when we are not aware of them?
14. Describe ways in which self-fulfilling prophecies and stereotype threat can influence our behavior.

PERCEIVING AND UNDERSTANDING OURSELVES

Self-schema

15. Describe some of the ways in which the self is rooted in the social world, that is, the extent to which our view of ourselves is influenced by our social interactions.
16. How do self-schemas help us organize our knowledge about ourselves? How are they similar to or different from the implicit theories of personality we form about others?
17. Describe some of the experimental evidence that suggests that culture influences our self-schema.
18. Explain the notion of possible selves and how it relates to the idea of self-schemas. What are the ideal and ought selves?
19. Compare promotion and prevention focus. How do these two concepts relate to the idea of actual, ideal, and ought selves?
20. What is meant by hot and cold cognition? How are schemas aspects of hot cognition?

Self-esteem and self-enhancement

21. What is self-esteem? How do trait and state self-esteem differ?
22. How does culture influence self-esteem? Describe differences in self-esteem in people from collectivistic versus individualistic cultures.
23. How is self-handicapping related to the self-serving attributional bias?

Social identities and group enhancement

24. What are in-groups and out-groups? How does identification with one's in-group influence self-esteem?
25. How is in-group favoritism related to discrimination?

ATTITUDES

Measuring attitudes

26. How are attitudes measured? What are some of the problems with traditional measures of attitudes and how have these

problems been addressed in more recent experimental designs?

27. Describe the rationale underlying the implicit attitude test (IAT).

Do attitudes predict behavior?

28. Discuss the nature of the relationship between attitudes and behavior. To what extent can attitudes help us predict future behavior?

Attitude formation

29. Discuss the different kinds of learning mechanisms underlying attitude formation.

Attitude change: Being persuaded by others

30. Compare central and peripheral routes to persuasion.

Attitude change: Being persuaded by ourselves

31. What are the claims of cognitive dissonance theory? How does cognitive dissonance induce attitude change?

32. Discuss cultural differences in how people handle dissonance.

33. Compare Festinger's theory of cognitive dissonance and Bem's self-perception theory. How do these theories differ in their view of what motivates attitude change in the face of dissonance? What is the evidence in support of each of the two theories?

Attitude stability

34. What factors contribute to attitude stability?

EMOTION

Theories of emotion

35. What distinguishes emotions from moods?

36. Compare the James-Lange's, Cannon-Bard's, and Schachter-Singer's theories of emotion. How do these theories differ in their proposed sequence of events, linking emotions to cognition and behavior?

Antecedents of emotion

37. What are appraisals? What is the experimental evidence that suggests that appraisals precede emotional responses?

Emotional responses

38. How may facial expressions of emotions be evolutionarily adaptive?

39. What are some of the cultural differences in the display of emotions?

40. Discuss the advantages and disadvantages of categorical versus dimensional classifications of emotions.

Functions of emotions

41. Discuss some of the possible functions served by emotions, including their role in memory consolidation and interpersonal interactions.

Emotion regulation

42. Discuss two examples of emotion regulation. Which is more effective and why?

Programmed Exercises

PERCEIVING AND UNDERSTANDING OTHERS

1. Processes underlying the way we think about ourselves and others are known as __________ __________. — social cognition

2. Processes through which we interpret other people's behaviors and their underlying causes are known as __________ __________. — causal attribution

3. __________ __________ involve factors external to a person, while __________ __________ focus on factors that are internal to a person. — Situational attributions; dispositional attributions

4. In assigning attributions to others' behaviors people are often strongly __________ by factors such as the culture they live in. — biased (influenced)

5. __________ cultures emphasize the rights, needs, and preferences of the individual, while __________ cultures focus on maintaining the norms, standards, and traditions of families and other social groups. — Individualistic; collectivistic

6. The tendency to ascribe others' behaviors to dispositional rather than situational forces is known as the __________ __________ __________. — fundamental attribution error

7. The fundamental attribution error is common in __________ cultures, but virtually absent in __________ cultures. — individualistic; collectivistic

8. The fact that we attribute many of our own behaviors to situational forces, whereas we see others as being influenced primarily by dispositional forces illustrates the __________-__________ difference in attribution. — actor-observer

9. In making causal attributions, we combine available information and our own __________. — experience

10. Schemas—also known as __________ __________ __________ __________—help us fill in the blanks about who a person is, on the basis of the information available to us, as well as existing beliefs and expectations. — implicit theories of personality

11. Individualistic cultures tend to see personality as __________ over time. — stable

12. __________ theorists tend to make global judgments about people's personality, whereas __________ theorists make more specific statements. — Entity incremental

13. Schemas about the characteristics of whole social groups are known as __________. — stereotypes

14. The "ABC of prejudice" refers to the __________, __________, and __________ components of stereotypes. — affective, behavioral cognitive

15. The __________-__________ __________ __________ leads us to perceive members of other groups as more similar to one another than they actually are. — out-group homogeneity effect

16. The __________ __________ refers to our heightened sensitivity to information that is consistent with our existing assumptions. — confirmation bias

17. Confirmation biases may lead us to see __________ correlations, where in fact there are none. — illusory

18. Activating or __________ stereotypes can result in people acting in a manner that is consistent with the stereotype, even if they are unaware of it. — priming

19. Stereotypes can serve as __________-__________ __________, getting people to act in ways that confirm stereotypes others have of them. — self-fulfilling prophecies

PERCEIVING AND UNDERSTANDING OURSELVES

20. __________-__________ help us organize our knowledge about ourselves. — Self-schemas

21. Schemas of how we think we may be in the future are referred to as __________ __________. — possible selves

22. Possible selves include an __________ self–the self one would ideally like to be–and a(n) __________ self–the self one thinks one should be. — ideal, ought

23. Comparing the actual and ideal selves helps us develop a __________ __________ and motivates us to actively pursue valued goals. — promotion focus

24. Comparing the actual and ought selves helps us develop a __________ __________ and motivates us to avoid doing harm. — prevention focus

25. Schemas are often emotionally and motivationally charged; this is why they are considered to be an aspect of __________ __________. — "hot" cognition

26. __________ self-esteem is thought to be typical of a person and relatively stable over time, whereas __________ self-esteem varies depending on external events and a person's focus of attention. — Trait state

27. Self-esteem is thought to be a(n) __________ of good things, rather than a(n) __________. — effect, cause

28. Individuals from __________ cultures tend to have lower self-esteem than people from __________ cultures, primarily because the latter afford more opportunities for self-promotion. — interdependent independent (collectivistic, individualistic)

29. Individuals with an independent notion of self-esteem tend to engage in self-enhancement and see themselves as superior to others, an effect known as the __________-__________ __________. — above-average effect

30. The __________-__________ attributional bias refers to our tendency to offer __________ attributions for our successes, and __________ attributions for our failure. — self-serving, dispositional situational

31. __________-__________ theory is concerned with ways in which we derive self-concepts and self-esteem from the groups to which we belong. — Social-identity

32. __________ __________ paradigms demonstrate experimentally that we will favor our __________-__________, even if it was formed on the basis of arbitrary criteria. — Minimal groups; in-group

33. In-group __________ can give rise to unfair treatment of the out-group and may be an underlying cause of __________. — favoritism; discrimination

ATTITUDES

34. Attitudes are a combination of __________ and __________, as well as a predisposition to act in accordance with these __________ and __________. — beliefs, feelings; beliefs, feelings

35. __________ measures of attitudes can help reveal attitudes people do not want to reveal or are unaware of. — Implicit

36. __________ __________ __________ assess attitudes in terms of latency to respond when faced with associations that are consistent or inconsistent with existing stereotypes. — Implicit attitude tests

37. Knowing someone's attitudes can help predict his __________ with some degree of accuracy. The __________ and the more __________ attitudes are, the more accurate the predictions made based on them. — behavior; stronger, specific

38. Attitude formation proceeds via three different kinds of mechanisms, namely __________ and __________ conditioning and __________ __________. — classical; operant, observational learning

39. The __________ route to persuasion involves mental elaboration on issues that matter to us, whereas the __________ route to persuasion is linked to issues of less relevance to us and situations in which we are distracted. — central; peripheral

40. In the central route to persuasion, the __________ and __________ of the message's source matter to us. — credibility; trustworthiness

41. In the central route to persuasion, the __________ of the message matters, while the __________ of the message is more important in the peripheral route to persuasion. — content; context

42. __________ __________ theory claims that inconsistencies between beliefs and behavior can get people to change their attitudes. — Cognitive dissonance

43. __________-__________ theory claims that distress caused by cognitive dissonance is not necessary for attitude change. Instead, we adjust our attitudes in the process of trying to make sense of our own behavior. — Self-perception

EMOTION

44. Emotions induce loosely linked changes in __________, __________, and __________. — actions, feelings, physiology

45. The James-Lange theory of emotion claims that our perception of __________ __________ is necessary in transforming mere cognitions into emotions. — physical (physiological, biological, bodily) changes

46. The __________ __________ hypothesis states that changes in our facial expressions inform changes in our emotional state. — facial feedback

47. According to the Cannon-Bard theory of emotion, a stimulus elicits an emotional response by activating a specific brain area, which then produces both __________ __________ and __________ __________. — physiological changes; emotional experiences

48. The Schachter-Singer theory of emotion claims that in addition to the perception of bodily changes, there must be a __________ as to why there have been such changes in order to produce emotions. — judgment (or interpretation)

49. Our interpretations of the situations we are in are known as __________. — appraisals

50. Evidence suggests that there are cultural differences in the __________ and not in the __________ of emotions. — display; perception

51. __________ __________ are culturally determined conventions about the appropriateness of emotional expression. Display rules

52. Some brain regions, such as the __________ __________ __________, respond to all emotions. Other brain regions respond only to specific emotions, such as the __________, which is implicated in fear responses, and the __________ __________, which is activated in response to sadness. medial prefrontal cortex amygdala cingulate cortex

53. Influencing which emotions are experienced and expressed when and how is referred to as __________ __________. emotion regulation

54. One form of emotion regulation, known as __________ __________, refers to attempts to change the meaning of a situation. cognitive reappraisal

55. Another form of emotion regulation, __________, refers to a decrease in behavioral displays of emotion. suppression

Self-Test

1. We observe Anne yelling at her sister and conclude that she must be an aggressive person. This is an example of a(n)
   a. situational attribution.
   b. dispositional attribution.
   c. illusory correlation.
   d. stereotype.
   e. prejudice.

2. We observe Anne yelling at her sister and conclude that her sister must have done something to make her angry. This is an example of a(n)
   a. situational attribution.
   b. dispositional attribution.
   c. illusory correlation.
   d. stereotype.
   e. prejudice.

3. The decision by a person that another person's behavior was internally caused (e.g., as a result of her aggressive nature) is an example of
   a. impression management.
   b. illusory correlation.
   c. stereotypes.
   d. attribution.
   e. situational factors.

4. We have a tendency to believe that actors in the theater are really like the roles that they play. This is an example of the
   a. resolution of cognitive dissonance.
   b. dominance of dispositional over situational factors in attribution.
   c. primacy effect in impressions.
   d. distinction between the bodily self and the social self.
   e. interaction of social and biological factors in the determination of behavior.

5. The actor-observer difference describes the fact that we are less likely to make ____________ attributions about ourselves than others.
   a. dispositional
   b. correct
   c. cognitively consistent
   d. situational
   e. c and d

6. Individualism is to collectivism as
   a. in-group is to out-group.
   b. society is to culture.
   c. independence is to interdependence.
   d. autonomy is to community.
   e. c and d

7. Collectivistic cultures tend to emphasize the preferences of
   a. the individual
   b. cultural norms.
   c. traditions of families.
   d. a and b
   e. b and c

8. Schemas
   a. are implicit theories of personality.
   b. cluster beliefs together.
   c. link traits to behaviors.
   d. all of the above.
   e. none of the above.

9. Collectivist cultures
   a. do not typically show the fundamental attribution error.
   b. view personality as malleable.
   c. tend to make specific statements about other people's personality.
   d. all of the above.
   e. none of the above.

10. Theorists who believe personality to be fixed are known as
    a. personality theorists.
    b. implicit theorists.
    c. entity theorists.
    d. incremental theorists.
    e. none of the above.

11. The disadvantage of relying on schemas is that they
    a. leave us vulnerable to error.
    b. force us to scrutinize every aspect of a situation.
    c. do not allow us to rely on past experience.
    d. provide us with a broad summary of people and situations.
    e. none of the above.

12. All of the following are components of stereotypes *except*
    a. behavior.
    b. physiology.
    c. cognition.
    d. affect.
    e. All of the above are components of stereotypes.

13. Stereotypes
    a. are always innaccurate.
    b. may be distorted because of illusory correlations.
    c. are always implicit.
    d. are a part of the normal construction of the person.
    e. b and d

14. Which of the following could explain the out-group homogeneity effect?
    a. We have more information about our in-group.
    b. Out-groups actually are more homogeneous.
    c. We usually value consistency.
    d. a and c
    e. b and c

15. Stereotypes
    a. create self-fulfilling prophecies.
    b. are sustained by the confirmation bias.
    c. are schemas about the characteristics of whole groups.
    d. all of the above.
    e. none of the above.

16. Jane believes that all graduate students are boring. According to the confirmation bias, when Jane meets a group of graduate students she is likely to
    a. act in a boring way herself.
    b. look for evidence to suggests that graduate students are boring.
    c. experience cognitive dissonance.
    d. learn that not all graduate students are boring and adjust her stereotype.
    e. none of the above.

17. Stereotype threat refers to
    a. expectations about a group influencing the performance of members of that group.
    b. in-groups making active threats against out-groups.
    c. a decrease in self-esteem in victims of stereotypes.
    d. all of the above.
    e. none of the above.

18. Self-schemas
    a. are implicit theories about ourselves.
    b. are similar across individuals and cultures.
    c. organize our responses to the world.
    d. all of the above.
    e. a and c

19. A promotion focus develops as the result of a comparison between
    a. actual self and ideal self.
    b. actual self and ought self.
    c. ideal self and ought self.
    d. possible selves and ideal self.
    e. possible selves and ought self.

20. A prevention focus develops as the result of a comparison between
    a. actual self and ideal self.
    b. actual self and ought self.
    c. ideal self and ought self.
    d. possible selves and ideal self.
    e. possible selves and ought self.

21. Schemas are thought of as an aspect of "hot" cognition because they involve
    a. emotions.
    b. motivation.
    c. rational decision making.
    d. a and b
    e. b and c

22. Self-esteem
    a. consists of trait and state self-esteems.
    b. is the effect and not the cause of good things.
    c. can be the cause of bad things.
    d. all of the above.
    e. a and c

23. The self-serving bias and above-average effect have in common that both
    a. reduce cognitive dissonance.
    b. enhance self.
    c. are forms of self-offense.
    d. depend on implicit attitudes.
    e. b and d

24. We can explain both self-serving bias and the above-average effect in terms of
    a. a general motive to enhance the self.
    b. the interpretation of the meaning of abilities and characteristics in a way that is favorable to the self.
    c. a biased search of memory for examples on which to base a judgment.
    d. all of the above.
    e. a and c

25. The phenomenon of self-handicapping is closely related to
    a. the fundamental attribution error.
    b. the above-average effect.
    c. the self-serving bias.
    d. cognitive dissonance.
    e. in-group homogeneity.

26. In-group favoritism could result from
    a. the out-group homogeneity effect.
    b. selective memory for positive experiences with the in-group.
    c. general self-enhancing tendencies.
    d. a and b
    e. b and c

27. Attitudes are
    a. usually measured by questionnaire.
    b. almost unrelated to behavior.
    c. an unstable set of mental views.
    d. usually almost identical to platitudes.
    e. a and b

28. An attitude is more likely to predict behavior if
    a. the attitude is strong.
    b. situational forces are not very strong.
    c. the attitude is implicit.
    d. all of the above.
    e. a and b

29. A group of people report that they think the two sexes (genders) are equally "good." In an implicit attitude test (IAT), they must categorize words as either good or bad, or male or female. The male or female words are male or female names. The people take longer to respond to the female names when they are paired with the "good" key than when paired with the "bad" key, and the opposite is true for male names. These results suggest that
    a. most of these people have racial prejudices.
    b. most of these people do not have an implicit attitude to gender.
    c. implicit attitudes to gender conflict with explicit attitudes.
    d. cognitive dissonance is operating.
    e. the implicit attitude to gender is not strong.

30. Attitudes are formed through mechanisms of
    a. classical conditioning.
    b. operant conditioning.
    c. observational learning.
    d. all of the above.
    e. none of the above.

31. In the central route to persuasion,
    a. we carefully track information.
    b. we mentally elaborate on the contents of the message.
    c. we care about the credibility of the message's source.
    d. strong arguments can cause us to change our minds.
    e. all of the above.

32. According to cognitive dissonance theory, the best way to cause people to change attitudes is to
    a. pay them a lot to make them believe they hold the new attitude.
    b. force them to behave as if they support the new attitude for at least a few weeks.
    c. tell them that they will be prejudiced if they continue with their current attitude.
    d. show them that their current attitude is inconsistent with their actual behavior.
    e. urge them to consult with an appropriate social comparison group.

33. Individuals living in collectivistic cultures
    a. do not experience dissonance.
    b. experience dissonance in the same way as people living in individualistic cultures and are driven to reduce that dissonance.
    c. experience dissonance in the same way as people living in individualistic cultures but are not driven to reduce that dissonance.
    d. experience dissonance only when evaluating their actions in light of others' opinions.
    e. none of the above.

34. Bem's self-perception theory differs from cognitive dissonance theory in that it
    a. sees emotional distress as accompanying dissonance.
    b. does not see emotional distress as accompanying dissonance.
    c. claims that individuals are trying to make sense of their behaviors in situations of dissonance.
    d. a and c
    e. b and c

35. Emotions differ from mood in that they
    a. have a specific target.
    b. last for shorter periods of time.
    c. are influenced by dispositional attributions.
    d. all of the above.
    e. a and b

36. After running for a quarter mile, a person shows increased heart rate and various other signs of arousal but may not feel any strong emotion. This fact is particularly damaging to
    a. the attribution-of-arousal theory.
    b. the James-Lange theory.
    c. Cannon's idea that subjective emotion leads to physiological responses.
    d. all of the above.
    e. a and b

37. An experiment has shown that participants alter their ratings of the attractiveness of nude photos in response to feedback about the increase or decrease of their heart rate. This result can be taken to support
    a. the attribution-of-arousal theory of emotion.
    b. the James-Lange theory.
    c. Cannon's theory (subjective emotion leads to the physiological responses, but the latter do not cause the former).
    d. all of the above.
    e. a and b

38. Appraisals
    a. often precede emotions.
    b. are necessary and sufficient for emotions.
    c. can be reached without conscious awareness.
    d. all of the above.
    e. none of the above.

39. Displays of emotions are thought to be evolutionarily adaptive because they
    a. make us appear more attractive to potential mates.
    b. can signal readiness to attack to an enemy.
    c. indicate disgust on consuming poisonous foods.
    d. a and b
    e. b and c

40. The perception of emotions is
    a. unrelated to emotion displays.
    b. governed by rules similar to display rules.
    c. similar in all cultures.
    d. all of the above.
    e. none of the above.

41. Rather unique emotion words, such as *amae* in Japanese or *Schadenfreude* in German, show that
   a. there are different emotions in different cultures.
   b. cultures have different emotion vocabularies.
   c. only basic emotions are constant across cultures.
   d. there cannot be basic emotions.
   e. b and d

42. The emotion of fear is specifically associated with activation in the
   a. amygdala.
   b. corpus callosum.
   c. cingulate cortex.
   d. medial prefrontal cortex.
   e. all of the above.

43. Emotions can
   a. increase cognitive flexibility.
   b. promote memory consolidation.
   c. facilitate social interactions.
   d. all of the above.
   e. b and c

44. Emotion regulation by changing the meaning of a situation is referred to as
   a. suppression.
   b. discrimination.
   c. cognitive reappraisal.
   d. self-enhancement.
   e. none of the above.

Answer Key for Self-Test

1.	b	23.	b
2.	a	24.	d
3.	d	25.	c
4.	b	26.	e
5.	a	27.	a
6.	c	28.	e
7.	e	29.	c
8.	d	30.	d
9.	d	31.	e
10.	c	32.	d
11.	a	33.	d
12.	b	34.	e
13.	e	35.	e
14.	d	36.	b
15.	d	37.	e
16.	b	38.	d
17.	a	39.	e
18.	e	40.	c
19.	a	41.	b
20.	b	42.	a
21.	d	43.	d
22.	d	44.	c

Investigating Psychological Phenomena

PERSON PERCEPTION: THE EFFECT OF CONTEXT OR SET ON FIRST IMPRESSIONS

Equipment: Paper and pencil, a stopwatch or a watch that indicates seconds
Number of participants: At least eight
Time per participant: Five minutes
Time for experimenter: Forty minutes

Social perception bears many analogies to more traditional areas of perception. In both cases, information is taken in selectively and put together into some organized percept. This aspect of person perception was illustrated in the text with special reference to the classic studies of Solomon Asch. Asch's work argued for an organizational basis for impression formation. This approach is in keeping with the position of Gestalt psychology. In Asch's view, impressions were not formed by summing different items of information about a particular person. One particular aspect of the active process of impression formation is the effect of set. We are constantly forming impressions of people. New information on any person is integrated with an already existing impression: the new information will be interpreted to be as consistent as possible with the existing impression. Under the circumstances, we would expect that the first information we get about a person would be especially important, since it might color what comes in later. Therefore, an organizational view would predict that the *order* of items of information about a person would affect the resulting impression, whereas for a simple *summation* hypothesis it would not matter.

Asch tested his hypothesis in a very simple manner: he gave college students a list of six adjectives that ostensibly described someone and recorded the impressions that they subsequently formed of this imaginary person. By manipulating the types of adjectives used and the order of their presentation, Asch attempted to produce systematic changes in the elicited impression formations. We will repeat his experiment on word order in precisely the same way that he performed it.

Try to get at least eight (student) participants. It might be useful for you to team up with a few friends from the course and run up to 20 participants so that your results might be more meaningful. Participants must be divided into two groups. You can run as many participants as you want at the same time, so long as they are all from the same group. Since this experiment will compare the results of participants from one group with the results from another group, it is important that the two groups be similar in general characteristics. For example, keep the percentage of females the same in both groups, and try not to run a group of friends together, since they may share many similar characteristics. If you run one participant at a time, simply assign the first participant to Group A, the second to Group B, and so on. This should give you a random and unbiased sample.

The list for Group A	The list for Group B
intelligent	envious
industrious	stubborn
impulsive	critical
critical	impulsive
stubborn	industrious
envious	intelligent

Note that the adjectives in Group B are in the reverse order of those in Group A. This arrangement is designed to enhance any effect of order, by putting adjectives that would lead to quite different impressions on opposite ends of the adjective list.

Participants should be seated comfortably and should have a blank piece of paper and a pencil in front of them. Make sure to put the group letter (A or B) on the paper and on the checklist. You read the following instructions:

> I shall read you a number of characteristics that belong to a particular person. Please listen to them carefully and try to form an impression of the kind of person described. You will later be asked to give a brief characterization of the person in just a few sentences. I will read the list slowly and will repeat it once.

Read the list of six adjectives out loud in a steady voice, with an interval of five seconds between terms. Then say:

> I will now read the list again.

Repeat the reading of the list.

> Now please write a brief characterization of this person.

Participant writes.

Finally, tell the participants while handing them the checklist (see pp. 153 and 155):

> Here is a list of pairs of adjectives. For each pair, please circle the adjectives that better characterize the person you have been describing.

After the participant has completed this task, he or she is finished.

NOTES ON PROCEDURE

In setting up any experiment, many decisions must be made. Here, these include selecting the adjectives for the list and for the checklist, deciding on the number of adjectives in the list, and so on. In most cases there are specific reasons for making these decisions. In this experiment, for example, ask yourself:

1. Why does the experimenter read the list instead of allowing the participant to read the list?
2. Why is the participant asked to write an impression before seeing the checklist rather than after filling out the checklist?

RESULTS

You should end up with eight or more written sketches and eight or more marked checklists. About half should be in each group. There is no simple way to score the written impressions. Read them over and try to summarize the impressions written by the two groups (the procedure used by Asch). You could also give the written impressions to another person and ask that person to sort them into piles, about equal in size. One pile would be for the more desirable impressions (persons) and the other for the less desirable ones. See if the impressions based on the adjective list with more desirable traits first are usually classified as more desirable. (It would be a good idea to fold back the part of the impression paper with the group letter on it before reading and analyzing the character summaries.)

It is easier to analyze the data from the checklists. Simply record the percentage of participants who selected the more favorable adjective of each pair for each group. This is the procedure used by Asch. His results, based on 24 student participants in Group A and 34 in Group B, are presented in the accompanying table. Record your data in the columns next to his data. Compare your results with his. If we take a difference of 20 percentage points as worthy of note, he reported big differences, in favor of Group A, on happy, humorous, sociable, popular, good-looking, and restrained.

(You can increase the significance of your data by combining it with data from a few friends in the class, so that you would have 20 or more participants in each group.)

On the basis of your results, what is the conclusion about the validity of the organization (set, Gestalt) versus simple summation explanations of impression formation?

Try to explain why some particular adjectives show clear effects and others do not. Obviously, in real life, people form impressions from interactions with other people or by hearing about them from other people. To what extent do you think that Asch's procedure gives an indication of how people actually form impressions? The hallmark of a good experiment is that it simplifies a situation but still preserves its essential features. Is that true of this experiment?

FURTHER STUDY

You can use Asch's technique to address other questions. You can change specific adjectives on the list. You can use brief statements about a person's *behavior* (e.g., John consistently drives over the speed limit; John is always on time) rather than general characteristics. You can see which types of adjectives cause a participant to guess that a person is male or female. There are many possibilities, should this problem interest you. Some of the possibilities that you will come up with may never have been investigated.

Reference

Asch, S. E. (1946). Forming impressions of personality. *Journal of Abnormal and Social Psychology, 41,* 258–290.

Percentage of participants checking favorable adjective at left

Adjective pair	Asch's data: Group A (24 students)	Asch's data: Group B (34 students)	Your data: Group A (__ students)	Your data: Group B (__ students)
generous	24	10		
wise	18	17		
happy	32	5		
good-natured	18	0		
humorous	52	21		
sociable	56	27		
popular	35	14		
reliable	84	91		
good-looking	74	35		
serious	97	100		
restrained	64	9		
honest	80	79		

Circle the most relevant adjective:

generous–ungenerous
shrewd–wise
unhappy–happy
irritable–good-natured
humorous–humorless
sociable–unsociable
popular–unpopular
unreliable–reliable
good-looking–unattractive
frivolous–serious
restrained–talkative
dishonest–honest
Group ____________________

Circle the most relevant adjective:

generous–ungenerous
shrewd–wise
unhappy–happy
irritable–good-natured
humorous–humorless
sociable–unsociable
popular–unpopular
unreliable–reliable
good-looking–unattractive
frivolous–serious
restrained–talkative
dishonest–honest
Group ____________________

Cut here

Circle the most relevant adjective:

generous–ungenerous
shrewd–wise
unhappy–happy
irritable–good-natured
humorous–humorless
sociable–unsociable
popular–unpopular
unreliable–reliable
good-looking–unattractive
frivolous–serious
restrained–talkative
dishonest–honest
Group ____________________

Circle the most relevant adjective:

generous–ungenerous
shrewd–wise
unhappy–happy
irritable–good-natured
humorous–humorless
sociable–unsociable
popular–unpopular
unreliable–reliable
good-looking–unattractive
frivolous–serious
restrained–talkative
dishonest–honest
Group ____________________

Circle the most relevant adjective:

generous–ungenerous
shrewd–wise
unhappy–happy
irritable–good-natured
humorous–humorless
sociable–unsociable
popular–unpopular
unreliable–reliable
good-looking–unattractive
frivolous–serious
restrained–talkative
dishonest–honest
Group ____________________

Circle the most relevant adjective:

generous–ungenerous
shrewd–wise
unhappy–happy
irritable–good-natured
humorous–humorless
sociable–unsociable
popular–unpopular
unreliable–reliable
good-looking–unattractive
frivolous–serious
restrained–talkative
dishonest–honest
Group ____________________

Cut here

Circle the most relevant adjective:

generous–ungenerous
shrewd–wise
unhappy–happy
irritable–good-natured
humorous–humorless
sociable–unsociable
popular–unpopular
unreliable–reliable
good-looking–unattractive
frivolous–serious
restrained–talkative
dishonest–honest
Group ____________________

Circle the most relevant adjective:

generous–ungenerous
shrewd–wise
unhappy–happy
irritable–good-natured
humorous–humorless
sociable–unsociable
popular–unpopular
unreliable–reliable
good-looking–unattractive
frivolous–serious
restrained–talkative
dishonest–honest
Group ____________________

CHAPTER 13

Social Influence and Relationships

Learning Objectives

SOCIAL INFLUENCE

1. What are different forms of social influence studied by psychologists? How are these influences treated in individualistic cultures?

Conformity

2. Describe experiments conducted by Muzafer Sherif and Solomon Asch that illustrate the influence of conformity. How are results of the Asch study different when the experiment is conducted in collectivistic as opposed to individualistic cultures?
3. What do studies of conformity tell us about the effects of dissent in totalitarian regimes?

Obedience

4. Why is a certain degree of obedience a necessity when living in a social group?
5. What characteristics were people with authoritarian personalities thought to have? How has the notion of the authoritarian personality changed over time?
6. Describe the design and findings of Stanley Milgram's study of obedience. What does this experiment tell us about the situational influences on our behavior in general, and specifically our willingness to obey orders?
7. What factors increased obedience in Milgram's subjects?

Compliance

8. What is meant by the door-in-the-face and that's-not-all techniques? How are these techniques used to increase our compliance?

Leadership

9. What characterizes the laissez-faire, autocratic, and democratic leadership styles? What are the effects of these different styles?
10. What types of situations can make leaders more effective?

GROUP DYNAMICS

Behaving in groups

11. What is social facilitation? Explain the mere-presence effect as one example of social facilitation.
12. Explain how divergent findings about social facilitation and social inhibition were eventually reconciled.
13. Describe experimental evidence for the phenomenon of social loafing.
14. Discuss the Stanford Prison Experiment as one example of deindividuation in a group setting.

Thinking in groups

15. How do groups affect the way individuals think and make decisions? Discuss the phenomena of group polarization and groupthink. What factors contribute to these phenomena?

Helping and altruism

16. Under what circumstances can decisions made by groups be superior to decisions made by individuals?
17. What is the bystander effect? How does the case of Kitty Genovese illustrate the notions of pluralistic ignorance and diffusion of responsibility?
18. What factors increase helping behavior? How does culture influence helping behavior?

RELATIONSHIPS

The social animal

19. What observations made Aristotle refer to human beings as "social animals"?

Types of relationships

20. What are the four types of relationships proposed by relational models theory?
21. Are these types of relationships mutually exclusive or can they co-occur? If so, what are some examples?

Fairness

22. Explain the rationale behind the ultimatum task. How does this task demonstrate the emphasis we place on fairness in relationships?

Attraction

23. Explain how proximity and similarity contribute to attraction.

Love

24. What are the different ways love has been categorized?

25. Describe the different types of love, including romantic and companionate love. What is the role played by physiological arousal in romantic love?

26. Compare the different conceptions of love in different cultures.

Programmed Exercises

SOCIAL INFLUENCE

1. __________ refers to changes in behavior due to implicit or explicit social pressure.	Conformity
2. __________ influence refers to our desire to be right, while __________ influence refers to our desire to be liked.	Informational normative
3. We are known to look for validation of our reactions by looking at the behavior of others, a process known as __________ __________.	social referencing
4. __________ refers to changes in behavior due to being told to make these changes.	Obedience
5. The __________ __________ __________ perspective holds that individuals respond to threat and uncertainty by expressing beliefs that help them manage their concerns.	Motivated social cognition
6. Hannah Arendt coined the term __________ __________ __________ during her observation of the trial of Adolf Eichmann, one of the main perpetrators of the Holocaust.	*banality of evil*
7. The series of successive steps that led participants in Milgram's study of obedience to administer progressively increasing levels of electric shock is an example of the __________ __________.	slippery slope
8. __________ refers to changes in behavior due to being asked to do so.	Compliance
9. The norm of __________ dictates that we comply with the request of someone who has done something for us in the past.	reciprocity
10. A leader who makes all the decisions is said to have adopted a(n) __________ leadership style.	autocratic
11. A leader who shows little or no involvement is said to have adopted a __________-__________ leadership style.	laissez-faire

GROUP DYNAMICS

12. The study of mutual influences among people in a group is known as the study of __________ __________.	group dynamics
13. Improvement in performance in the company of others is known as the __________ __________ __________.	mere presence effect
14. The fact that we work less hard when performing tasks in a group is referred to as __________ __________.	social loafing
15. __________ refers to a state in which we lose our sense of ourselves as an individual when in the context of a group.	Deindividuation
16. The tendency for group decisions to be more extreme than any decision an individual member of that group would have made on his own is known as __________ __________.	group polarization
17. The __________ __________, an example of group polarization, refers to the increased willingness of groups to take risks that individual members would not take on their own.	risky shift

18. The __________ __________ __________ leads us to exaggerate support for our opinion and as a result increases our commitment to that opinion. — false consensus effect

19. The groupthink phenomenon is more likely to occur in groups that are __________, closed to outside influences, and facing some external __________. — cohesive, threat

20. Groups are able to make decisions that are superior to those of individuals when there is __________ and ______________ of judgment. — diversity, independence

21. The story of Kitty Genovese, who was murdered in front of numerous witnesses, is an example of the __________ __________. — bystander effect

22. This effect predicts that the more witnesses, the higher the degree of __________ __________ and the lower the likelihood that someone will attempt to help the victim. — diffusion of responsibility

23. In helping behavior, the higher the __________ (in terms of physical danger, time, etc.), the lower the likelihood that someone will help. — cost

24. Acts of __________ suggest that human behavior is not always selfish. — altruism

RELATIONSHIPS

25. A relationship in which each partner gives something and expects something in return is referred to as a(n) __________ __________ __________. — equality matching relationship

26. __________ __________ __________ are centered around fair exchanges, where what one person puts in is proportional to what s/he gets out of the relationship. — Market pricing relationships

27. Unlike most exchange relationships, __________ __________ __________ are long term and expand the notion of the self to include the other. — communal sharing relationships

28. __________ __________ __________ are based on power and hierarchy. — Authority ranking relationships

29. The __________ __________ __________ is most susceptible to cheaters, though evolution has made us adept at identifying those who refuse to reciprocate. — equality matching relationship

30. __________ rather than fairness governs market pricing relationships. — Utility

31. Landlord-tenant relationships are an example of __________ __________ __________. — market pricing relationships

32. The ultimatum task illustrates that in certain situations people value __________ over self-interest. — fairness

33. When guided by a sense of fairness, we tend to make decisions based more on __________ responses than intellectual reasoning. — emotional

34. Increased __________ leads to increased familiarity and liking. — proximity

35. Evidence suggests that __________ on many dimensions is related to attraction and to the longevity of relationships. — similarity (homogamy)

36. Love is thought to consist of three components, namely __________, __________, and __________. An alternative classification of love identifies two types of love, __________ and __________. — intimacy, passion commitment, romantic (passionate), companionate

37. Parental opposition tends to intensify a couple's romantic passion, a phenomenon known as the __________-__________-__________ effect. — Romeo-and-Juliet

Self-Test

1. A change in behavior due to social pressure is referred to as
   a. obedience.
   b. conformity.
   c. compliance.
   d. reciprocity.
   e. none of the above.

2. A change in behavior due to being asked to do so is referred to as
   a. obedience.
   b. conformity.
   c. compliance.
   d. reciprocity.
   e. none of the above.

3. In Muzafer Sherif's study on the autokinetic effect, judgments made
   a. when the participants were alone differed greatly from one subject to the next.
   b. when the participants were alone differed greatly from one trial to the next.
   c. in a group of participants tended to converge.
   d. all of the above.
   e. none of the above.

4. In Asch's experiment on the effect of social pressure on judgments of noticeably different line lengths, he found that
   a. many participants yielded to social pressure, but their perception of line length did not necessarily change.
   b. the actual perceptions of line length were changed in the participant.
   c. the perceptions of line length were changed in the confederates.
   d. the shared sense of physical reality can affect perception.
   e. a and b

5. When Asch's experiment on the effect of social pressure on judgments of noticeably different line lengths was carried out in collectivistic cultures, it was found that subjects
   a. paid no attention to the majority opinion.
   b. refused to conform to the majority opinion.
   c. experienced more discomfort on conforming.
   d. experienced less discomfort on conforming.
   e. none of the above.

6. In Asch's experiment on the effect of social pressure on judgments of noticeably different line lengths the presence of an ally who gave an incorrect answer led subjects to
   a. conform to the majority less often if the ally's response was closer to the actual length of the line.
   b. conform to the majority less often if the ally's response was even further than the majority's response from the actual length of the line.
   c. be able to speak up without fear of embarrassment.
   d. all of the above.
   e. a and c

7. Normative influence refers to our desire to be
   a. right.
   b. liked.
   c. consistent.
   d. obedient.
   e. none of the above.

8. The process of validating our reactions by checking on others' behaviors is known as
   a. obedience.
   b. conformity.
   c. compliance.
   d. social referencing.
   e. social facilitation.

9. Uniqueness is
   a. the opposite of conformity.
   b. more valued in individualistic cultures than in collectivistic cultures.
   c. considered to be deviant in some cultures.
   d. all of the above.
   e. none of the above.

10. Which of the following factors would increase the likelihood that someone would conform?
    a. A desire to avoid being embarrassed
    b. A feeling that others in the group are more expert than oneself
    c. All others in the group taking the same position
    d. All of the above
    e. b and c

11. Obedience
    a. is necessary to a certain extent in social life.
    b. has been implicated in some of the worst atrocities of the past century.
    c. has been linked to individual character traits.
    d. all of the above.
    e. a and b

12. An explanation of obedience that emphasizes the authoritarian personality of the person in question relies on
    a. situational factors.
    b. dispositional factors.
    c. cognitive dissonance.
    d. cognitive consistency.
    e. the attribution of emotional experience.

13. Both Milgram's obedience experiment and Asch's line judgment studies show the importance of __________ in determining behavior.
    a. attribution
    b. cognitive dissonance
    c. compliance
    d. dispositional factors
    e. none of the above

14. Which of the following would tend to *prevent* obedience in a situation of the type that Milgram studied?
    a. Making a person feel like the agent of another
    b. Dehumanizing the person being punished
    c. Describing the experiment as a scientific enterprise
    d. Decreasing the psychological distance between the participant and the person being punished
    e. None of the above

15. It is probably easier for a bombardier to drop bombs on an inhabited building than for the same person to kill someone standing in front of him. This presumed fact can be accounted for in terms of
    a. anonymity.
    b. psychological distance.

c. dehumanization.
d. all of the above.
e. none of the above.

16. The terms *final solution, ethnic cleansing,* and *body count* are examples of the use of euphemisms to
a. dehumanize victims.
b. create psychological distance.
c. maintain anonymity.
d. all of the above.
e. none of the above.

17. The slippery slope refers to
a the pattern of successive steps taken by participants in Milgram's study.
b. programs of progressive escalation used by the Nazis.
c. basic training strategies used by the military.
d. all of the above.
e. none of the above.

18. Experts predicted that __________ percent of all participants in Milgram's study would go all the way in administering shocks; in reality __________ percent did.
a. 25, 50
b. 10, 90
c. 2, 65
d. 20, 8
e. none of the above

19. The door-in-the-face technique refers to
a. making a small request, followed by a larger request.
b. making a large request, followed by a smaller request.
c. presenting a series of successively increasing requests.
d. presenting a series of successively decreasing requests.
e. none of the above.

20. The leadership style in which the leader makes all the decisions is known as
a. laissez-faire.
b. autocratic.
c. authoritarian.
d. democratic.
e. dispositional.

21. The leadership style in which the leader has the group decide together about what action to take is known as
a. laissez-faire.
b. autocratic.
c. authoritarian.
d. democratic.
e. dispositional.

22. The observation that athletes perform better in groups is an illustration of
a. group dynamics.
b. social facilitation.
c. compliance.
d. normative influence.
e. none of the above.

23. The mere presence effect is an example of
a. social facilitation.
b. social inhibition.
c. obedience.
d. compliance.
e. conformity.

24. Social loafing refers to the finding that individuals
a. work less hard when in a group than when alone.
b. working in groups tend to cheat more on tasks.
c. tend to mimic the behaviors of others in a group.
d. all of the above.
e. none of the above.

25. Deindividuation
a. refers to a state in which a person loses her sense of self as an individual.
b. is associated with high levels of arousal.
c. releases impulsive actions.
d. all of the above.
e. none of the above.

26. Zimbardo's prison experiment
a. proves that the Milgram study is correct.
b. extends the range under which situational factors can cause cruelty.
c. casts doubt on the situational interpretation of Milgram's studies.
d. creates a situation in which college students behave in a cruel manner to other students.
e. b and d

27. Zimbardo's prison experiment used a variety of methods to create
a. deindividuation.
b. groupthink.
c. altruism.
d. social loafing.
e. none of the above.

28. An investigator has reported that most individuals in extremist groups are, in private, less extreme in views than their group. This disparity could be accounted for by
a. groupthink.
b. social loafing.
c. group polarization.
d. a and c
e. b and c

29. Sometimes, in making group decisions, the decision errs on the side of being too conservative, and more conservative than the views of the individuals in the group. This can be explained by:
a. the risky shift.
b. the false consensus effect.
c. group polarization.
d. a and b
e. none of the above.

30. The bystander effect is accounted for by
a. reciprocity.
b. diffusion of responsibility.
c. altruistic tendencies.
d. all of the above.
e. a and c

31. Diffusion of responsibility is
    a. an example of social exchange.
    b. decreased by increasing cost of intervention.
    c. less if there are fewer observers.
    d. b and c
    e. a and c

32. The Kitty Genovese case illustrates
    a. diffusion of responsibility.
    b. pluralistic ignorance.
    c. groupthink.
    d. a and b
    e. b and c

33. Which of the following type(s) of relationship is (are) based on social exchange?
    a. Communal sharing
    b. Market pricing
    c. Equality matching
    d. a and b
    e. b and c

34. Reciprocal exchange can become the basis of
    a. fairness.
    b. communal relationships.
    c. ultimatums.
    d. ambiguity.
    e. b and c

35. In communal relationships,
    a. the ultimatum game operates efficiently.
    b. principles of reciprocal exchange may be suspended.
    c. altruism does not occur.
    d. the self is extended beyond an individual.
    e. b and d

36. The ultimatum task illustrates that we care about
    a. fairness.
    b. our self-interest.
    c. altruism.
    d. conformity.
    e. proximity.

37. Proximity is an important factor in attraction. There is evidence that this relation results from the fact that
    a. we must ordinarily meet someone in order to be attracted to him.
    b. familiarity promotes attraction, and familiarity is increased by proximity.
    c. proximity explains the matching hypothesis.
    d. all of the above.
    e. a and b

38. Homogamy refers to our tendency to be attracted to partners who are
    a. close to us.
    b. familiar to us.
    c. similar to us.
    d. different from us.
    e. none of the above.

39. Mildred and Herb have been dating for years. Both are physically unattractive, and one acquaintance wonders what they see in each other. Which of the following factors could contribute to their mutual attractiveness?
    a. Proximity
    b. Similarity
    c. Matching
    d. All of the above
    e. a and c

40. Romantic love
    a. occurs only in certain cultures and at certain periods in history.
    b. is intensified by parental approval.
    c. can be completely explained in terms of sexual arousal.
    d. differs from companionate love in that romantic love depends heavily on similarity.
    e. c and d

41. The Romeo-and-Juliet effect refers to the fact that
    a. opposites attract.
    b. passionate love is most common among young adults.
    c. parental disapproval tends to intensify a couple's romantic passion.
    d. all of the above.
    e. none of the above.

42. Romantic love has been described as having three components: intimacy, passion, and commitment. In comparison, companionate love would differ most from romantic love in that it would have less
    a. intimacy.
    b. passion.
    c. commitment.
    d. b and c
    e. a and c

Answer Key for Self-Test

1. b
2. c
3. d
4. a
5. d
6. d
7. b
8. d
9. d
10. d
11. e
12. b
13. c
14. d
15. d
16. a
17. d
18. c
19. b
20. b
21. d
22. b
23. a
24. a
25. d
26. e
27. a
28. d
29. c
30. b
31. c
32. d
33. e
34. a
35. e
36. a
37. e
38. c
39. d
40. a
41. c
42. b

Investigating Psychological Phenomena

MATCHING FOR INTELLIGENCE AND ATTRACTION

Equipment: None
Number of participants: One, yourself
Time per participant: Twenty minutes
Time for experimenter: Twenty minutes

As described in the text, one of the major features of romantic couples is that they are similar along a wide variety of dimensions. Much of this similarity seems to be a reason for the formation of the relationship, rather than a consequence of it. Although certain characteristics may become more similar the longer a couple is together, this cannot be so for the many characteristics unlikely to change in adulthood, such as height. Furthermore, we are likely to seek a partner with a high rating on characteristics for which there can be a clear positive or negative evaluation (such as intelligence or attractiveness), with competitive selection and fear of rejection tending to sort us out with others at our own level of achievement, ability, beauty, and so forth. Thus, we would expect similar ratings on almost all traits.

This study will demonstrate the principles of homogamy and matching by examining the similarity of couples on two characteristics: physical attractiveness and intelligence. You will be the one participant in this study. First, select 10 heterosexual couples that you know fairly well. The couples should be selected according to the following criteria:

1. The couples should be romantically involved: married or together for at least one year.
2. The couples should be about the same age in two senses: The members of the couple should be no more than 10 years apart in age, and the oldest person should be no more than 20 years older than the youngest person of the same gender on the list. (If you cannot generate the 10 couples that this study calls for, you can ask a friend to generate the data for you.)

DO NOT INCLUDE YOURSELF IN ANY OF THESE COUPLES.

List the couples (by first name of each partner) in the accompanying tables. Now rank the 10 women and the 10 men separately for both physical attractiveness and intelligence. Thus, for physical attractiveness, rank the most attractive man number 1, the next most attractive number 2, and so on until all 10 numbers have been assigned. Rank the women in the same fashion.

Now calculate a rank-order correlation, a statistic that represents the correlation between the ranking for men and women in each couple. (See the Statistical Appendix in the text, but use the formula on p. 164 to calculate the correlation.) If the members of a couple match perfectly on a characteristic (i.e., if the man ranked number 1 for attractiveness is involved with the woman ranked number 1 in this same trait, etc.), the correlation coefficient would equal 1.00—the highest possible value for correlation. If the members of a couple are inversely matched (i.e., if the man ranked number 1 for attractiveness is involved with the woman ranked number 10 on that trait), then the correlation coefficient would equal –1.00 (the lowest possible value). If there is no relation between the ranking of the man and woman in a couple on the trait in question, then the correlation coefficient would be 0.

Couple (man's/woman's name)	Attractiveness			
	Man's Rank	Woman's Rank	Difference	Difference^2
1 ______	______	______	______	______
2 ______	______	______	______	______
3 ______	______	______	______	______
4 ______	______	______	______	______
5 ______	______	______	______	______
6 ______	______	______	______	______
7 ______	______	______	______	______
8 ______	______	______	______	______
9 ______	______	______	______	______
10 ______	______	______	______	______

Correlation for attractiveness = ______________

Couple (man's/woman's name)	Intelligence			
	Man's Rank	Woman's Rank	Difference	Difference^2
1 ______	______	______	______	______
2 ______	______	______	______	______
3 ______	______	______	______	______
4 ______	______	______	______	______
5 ______	______	______	______	______
6 ______	______	______	______	______
7 ______	______	______	______	______
8 ______	______	______	______	______
9 ______	______	______	______	______
10 ______	______	______	______	______

Correlation for intelligence = ______________

Use the formula below to calculate the correlation, *r*.

$$r = 1 - \frac{6\ (\text{sum of the difference in ranking between couple members}^2)}{\text{number of couples (number of couples}^2 - 1)}$$

CHAPTER 14

Intelligence

Learning Objectives

1. Explain the relationship between the rise of mental testing and real-world issues, such as academic and professional careers.

MENTAL TESTS

2. Distinguish between achievement and aptitude tests.

The study of variation

3. Define frequency distribution, mean, median, and variability.
4. Explain the importance of variability in evolution.
5. Explain the meaning of correlation, and describe the correlation coefficient.

Evaluating mental tests

6. Explain the concept of reliability and different measures of reliability.
7. Explain face, convergent, discriminant, and convergent validity.

INTELLIGENCE TESTING

8. Indicate the difficulties in defining intelligence.

Measuring intelligence

9. Describe the origins of intelligence testing.
10. Discuss the strategy behind constructing intelligence tests.
11. Describe a few types of intelligence tests.

Reliability and variability

12. Review the reliability and validity of intelligence tests.
13. Discuss the role of IQ scores as predictors of outcomes.

WHAT IS INTELLIGENCE? THE PSYCHOMETRIC APPROACH

The logic of psychometrics

14. What is the psychometric approach?

Spearman and the concept of general intelligence

15. What is a correlation matrix and what is factor analysis?
16. Define general intelligence, or g.

A hierarchical model of intelligence

17. Describe the hierarchical conception of intelligence.

Fluid and crystallized g

18. Distinguish fluid and crystallized intelligences.
19. What factors can cause impairment in tasks requiring fluid intelligence?

THE INFORMATION-PROCESSING APPROACH

Mental speed

20. Discuss evidence that links intelligence scores to mental speed.
21. Indicate the logic and evidence behind the suggestion that simple cognitive processes, such as performance on simple or choice reaction time tasks or on a lexical decision task, may be components of intelligence.

Working memory and attention

22. Indicate how working memory and attention may be components of intelligence, and describe operation span tasks.

Other contributions to intellectual functioning

23. Summarize the factors that contribute to intelligence.

WHAT IS INTELLIGENCE? BEYOND IQ

Practical intelligence

24. What are the limitations of intelligence tests, in terms of the range of mental abilities measured?
25. Distinguish among practical, analytic, and creative intelligence.
26. What is tacit knowledge, and how does it contribute to practical intelligence?

Emotional intelligence

27. What are the four components of emotional intelligence?
28. What skills and abilities are related to higher levels of emotional intelligence?

The notion of multiple intelligences

29. What are Gardner's multiple intelligences, and what is the evidence for them?

30. What are some problems with the multiple intelligences idea? Refer to interpretations of the savant syndrome.

The cultural context of intelligence

31. How might cultural differences produce different performances on questions on intelligence tests?

32. Explain and evaluate the statement "We may be able to measure intelligence, but we do not really know what it is."

NATURE, NURTURE, AND INTELLIGENCE

Some political issues

33. Review the history of positions on genetic factors in intelligence differences related to racial groups or social class.

Genetic factors

34. Explain why it is not possible for any trait to be determined completely by the genotype.

35. Review basic terms in genetics (*phenotype, genotype*) and the relation between genotype and phenotype.

36. Describe the cause and genetic basis of phenylketonuria, and know how it illustrates the fact that inborn characteristics from heritability of the same trait between groups may be changeable.

37. Explain why studies of the similarity in intelligence of members of the same family cannot be used to distinguish between genetic and environmental factors.

38. Explain how twin and adoption studies can be used to make this distinction. Summarize the results of these studies.

Environmental factors

39. Describe the effects of impoverished or enriched environments on IQ scores.

40. What is the Flynn effect, and why is it evidence for environmental factors?

Heritability

41. Explain the idea of heritability, why it only makes sense to use it to explain differences across individuals, and how it can change markedly over time.

Group differences in IQ

42. Describe the mean differences and overlap in IQ between African Americans and European Americans.

43. Explain how heritability within groups can differ markedly from heritability of the same trait between groups.

44. What is stereotype threat, and how is it demonstrated in the laboratory?

45. Evaluate each of the following explanations of the reported difference between average IQ scores of African Americans and European Americans:
    a. The difference does not exist.
    b. The tests and test situations for African Americans are unfair.
    c. There are differences in environments between the groups.
    d. There are genetic differences between the groups.
    e. There is stereotype threat.

Programmed Exercises

MENTAL TESTS

1. Tests of __________ measure what an individual can do now—his present knowledge and competence in a particular area. — achievement

2. Tests of __________ predict what an individual will be able to do later. — aptitude

3. __________ tests measure general aptitude. — Intelligence

4. The frequency with which individual cases are distributed over different intervals of some measure is called a(n) __________ __________. — frequency distribution

5. The sum of all cases (observations) divided by the number of cases is called the __________. — mean

6. The case located in the middle of the frequency distribution, such that 50 percent of cases are smaller and 50 percent are larger, is called the __________. — median

7. The more that individual cases differ from one another, the higher the __________. — variability

8. In evolution, __________ provides the basis on which natural selection works. — variability

9. Each point in the figure below represents the weight (vertical axis) and IQ (horizontal axis) of one person. This display is called a __________ __________.

scatter diagram

Weight

IQ

10. The __________ __________ is a statistic that describes the relations between two sets of measures.

correlation coefficient

11. The correlation between X and Y is –.70; that is, __________ = –.70. This means that the bigger X gets, the __________ Y gets, on average.

r
smaller

12. The consistency with which a test measures is called its __________.

reliability

13. This can be measured by calculating the __________ between scores on the same test at two different times, or __________-__________ reliability.

correlation
test-retest

14. Reliability can also be measured as the __________ between split halves of the same test.

correlation

15. The extent to which a test measures what it is supposed to measure is called its __________.

validity

16. The higher the positive correlation between the score on a driving test and the number of years driving without an accident, the greater the __________ __________ of this test.

predictive validity

17. A high correlation between two measures designed to assess the same construct suggests high __________ __________.

convergent validity

INTELLIGENCE TESTING

18. The Wechsler Adult Intelligence Scale was in part a response to the emphasis on language in the Binet-Simon IQ tests. The Wechsler test has two types of subtests, namely __________ and __________.

performance
verbal

WHAT IS INTELLIGENCE? THE PSYCHOMETRIC APPROACH

19. In the __________ approach, the results of intelligence tests are studied and analyzed in an attempt to discover the structure of intelligence.

psychometric

20. The fact that scores from a variety of different intelligence tests, specific and general, are positively __________ led Spearman to introduce the factor of __________ __________.

correlated, general
intelligence (g)

21. The technique used to try to extract the structure of intelligence from correlation matrices is called __________ __________.

factor analysis

22. It seems to be the case that as we age, our ability to deal with new problems or to respond rapidly, called __________ intelligence, tends to deteriorate, while our repertoire of basic cognitive skills, knowledge, and strategy, called __________ intelligence, remains intact.

fluid
crystallized

THE INFORMATION-PROCESSING APPROACH

23. One possible cognitive correlate of intelligence is the speed with which a person responds to a stimulus, or __________ __________ __________.

simple reaction time

24. A better cognitive correlate is the speed of response when there are several responses and stimuli, or __________ __________ __________.

choice reaction time

25. The time needed to discriminate between two stimuli, otherwise known as __________ __________, correlates around –.50 with intelligence. — inspection time

26. Working memory and attention ability are measured in __________ __________ tasks. — operation span

27. People with a large __________ __________ capacity perform well on many tests, including the verbal SAT, tests of reading comprehension, and IQ tests. — working memory

28. Intelligent performance depends on a number of factors, including __________ __________, __________, and __________ used for problem solving, learning, and remembering. — crystallized intelligence knowledge, strategies

WHAT IS INTELLIGENCE? BEYOND IQ

29. IQ tests measure principally __________ intelligence. But two other types of intelligence are __________ and __________. — analytic practical, creative

30. __________ __________, derived from experience in specific domains, is an important part of practical intelligence. — Tacit knowledge

31. __________ __________ refers to the ability to understand our own and others' emotions. — Emotional intelligence

32. The MSCEIT, a measure of emotional intelligence, has some level of __________ __________ about how we will perform in social settings. — predictive validity

33. Gardner's theory of __________ __________ holds that there are eight different, __________ mental capacities. — multiple intelligences independent

34. Evidence for these independent capacities is the presence of developmentally disabled people who show outstanding performance on a task related to one of these activities. Such people have what is called the __________ syndrome. — savant

35. Some have argued that it is useful to distinguish intelligence from other __________, such as musical or athletic ability. — talents

36. People from different __________ may know different things, respond to tests differently, and make different interpretations of the meaning of the same question. — cultures

37. An intelligence test that is free of any biases and fair to all would be called __________ __________. — culture free

NATURE, NURTURE, AND INTELLIGENCE

38. The observed characteristics of an organism are called its __________. But its underlying genetic blueprint is called its __________. — phenotype genotype

39. At some level, any trait is a result of __________ between genotype and environment. — interaction

40. A form of mental retardation that is caused by a single gene is __________. — phenylketonuria (PKU)

41. The fact that PKU can be prevented by dietary interventions argues that heredity does not always imply __________. — immutability (unadulterability, impossibility of change)

42. The fact that members of the same family have positively correlated intelligence and often share special abilities can be used as evidence for both __________ and __________ factors. — hereditary (genetic), environmental

43. Two basic methods for estimating the role of inherited factors in intelligence or other traits are __________ and __________ studies. — twin, adoption

44. The pattern of a higher correlation of IQ scores in __________ twin pairs than in __________ twin pairs, argues for a role for heredity in intelligence. — identical, fraternal

45. The fact that the IQ of early-adopted children correlates more highly with the IQ of the biological as opposed to adoptive mother is evidence for __________ determinants of intelligence. — genetic (biological, hereditary)

46. As adopted children grow older, the correlation of their IQ with their *biological* parents' IQ __________. This supports the importance of __________ factors in IQ.

increases, genetic (hereditary)

47. The negative effects of poor environments on IQ are illustrated by data showing that the longer a child is in a deprived environment, the lower her IQ. This appears as a __________ correlation between IQ and age.

negative

48. A number of studies have shown that __________ environments increase IQ.

enriched

49. Evidence for environmental influence on IQ is the __________ effect, the gradual (few points/10 years) increase in worldwide mean IQ.

Flynn

50. __________ is a concept that describes the percentage of the variation in a population that can be attributed to genetic factors. It does not apply to individuals.

Heritability

51. Controversy about intelligence assessments arises primarily from __________ comparisons, which find __________- to __________-point differences in mean IQ between European Americans and African Americans.

group
10, 15

52. Evidence from twin and adoption studies and other sources suggests that heritability of IQ in American whites is about __________.

50

53. We cannot infer that if a trait has high heritability within two populations, then population differences will also be explainable as largely due to __________.

heredity

54. A number of studies indicate that when differences in the environment of African Americans and European Americans during childhood are markedly reduced or equated, the African American and European American IQ difference is markedly __________.

reduced (diminished)

55. As a result of __________ __________, a group tends to perform in accordance with societal and its own expectations about ability in the relevant domain.

stereotype threat

56. Thus, in experiments, if African Americans are reminded of their race, their score on IQ tests becomes __________.

lower

Self-Test

1. Mental testing is primarily an American product, dating from the beginning of the twentieth century. America was a natural place for mental testing because
   a. Americans embraced Freudian theories.
   b. the American idea that all people are created equal required mental tests to show up their subtle differences.
   c. of the high social and occupational mobility in America.
   d. reinforcement was a popular concept in America.
   e. Binet and Simon were Americans.

2. One group of five people gets the following scores on a mathematics test: 85, 85, 90, 95, 95. Another group gets these five scores: 80, 80, 90, 100, 100. Which of the following statements about these groups is true?
   a. Both groups have the same means and different variability.
   b. Both groups have the same means and the same variability.
   c. Both groups have different means and the same variability.
   d. Both groups have different means and different variability.
   e. It is impossible to say which group has a higher mean.

3. The accompanying diagram represents the hypothetical scores of individual participants on an IQ test and on a history achievement test. The correlation displayed would be closest to
   a. +1.00.
   b. +.50.
   c. +0.00.
   d. –50.
   e. –1.00.

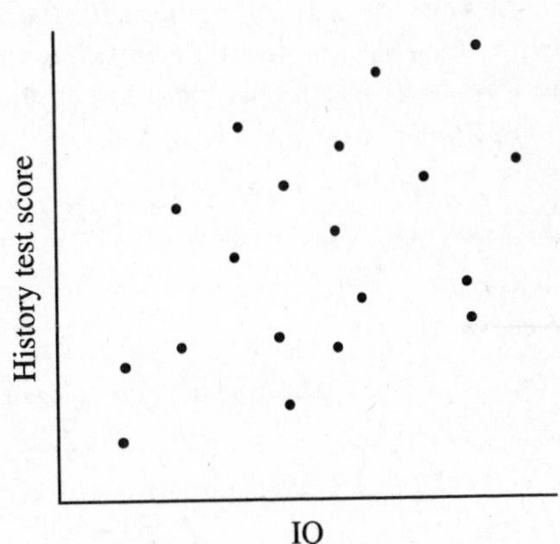

4. For which of the following pairs of variables would one expect to see a negative correlation?
   a. Age and vocabulary
   b. Height and visual acuity
   c. Brain size and intelligence
   d. Long-distance running ability and weight (among adults)
   e. Social security number and intelligence (among adults)

5. If X is correlated with Y, then
   a. if we know X, we can guess better than chance at the value of Y.
   b. if we know Y, we can guess better than chance at the value of X.
   c. there is no variability in X and Y.
   d. X causes Y.
   e. a and b

6. A hypothetical air force needs a test to help select people for training as pilots. There is no adequate theory of the acquisition of flying skills, but air force investigators discover that the speed with which a person can tap with the third finger correlates +.80 with good performance in flying school. On the basis of this observation, we could say that the test had
   a. high reliability.
   b. high predictive validity.
   c. a frequency distribution.
   d. good standardization.
   e. no mean validity.

7. Split-half reliability assesses consistency from one
   a. test question to the next.
   b. test administration to the next.
   c. measure of a construct to the next.
   d. a and c
   e. none of the above.

8. Intelligence testers face special problems because
   a. intelligence changes with age.
   b. intelligence tests are not reliable.
   c. all questions require prior knowledge, so past experience determines the test score.
   d. there is no agreement about what intelligence is.
   e. it is difficult to calculate an intelligence score.

9. A student takes the same test of reaction time at 10:00 a.m. on two consecutive days. She gets very different scores on these two days. If this were true of many other test takers, it would suggest that this test is not
   a. valid.
   b. standardized.
   c. reliable.
   d. all of the above.
   e. none of the above.

10. A test measuring participants' abilities to do jigsaw puzzles would be a __________ test.
    a. performance
    b. verbal
    c. fluid
    d. unreliable
    e. c and d

11. A psychometrician examines a verbal and a spatial intelligence test and finds that the scores on these two tests correlate +.38. From this she might conclude that
    a. performance on both tests is partly determined by g, but mostly by specific factors.
    b. these tests measure very different things, and there is no g component here.
    c. both of these tests are excellent measures of g.
    d. these results constitute proof that g is only a statistical fact.
    e. none of the above.

12. Gordon is really pretty ignorant, but he has a way of seeing relationships among ideas and figures and quickly comes up with new ways of doing things. He could be described as
    a. high in g.
    b. high in fluid and low in crystallized intelligence.
    c. evidence for one-factor theories of intelligence.
    d. someone who would do well on vocabulary tests.
    e. someone who would do poorly on Raven's progressive matrices.

13. Studies indicate that certain types of intelligence decline with age in adulthood and others do not. A type that improves or at least holds its own through most of adulthood is
    a. g.
    b. fluid intelligence.
    c. crystallized intelligence.
    d. b and c
    e. none of the above.

14. Tests looking at how quickly participants respond to a stimulus assess
    a. operation span.
    b. simple reaction time.
    c. choice reaction time.
    d. inspection time.
    e. none of the above.

15. Working memory capacity is
    a. frequently assessed using measures of operation span.
    b. essential for intelligent performance.
    c. positively correlated with scores on many tests.
    d. related to lateral prefrontal cortex function.
    e. all of the above.

16. The hypothetical finding that artists and composers are generally poor at solving everyday problems, like organizing a group of people on a task, would argue in favor of
    a. the distinction between practical and analytic intelligence.
    b. the importance of strategies in intelligence.
    c. the importance of working memory in only some kinds of intelligence.
    d. the separation of practical and creative intelligence.
    e. b and d

17. Cindy has to memorize the names of all of the American vice presidents and the dates that they held office. She considers doing it in alphabetical order, but then decides it would be better to try to remember them in chronological order. She is demonstrating
   a. analogical reasoning.
   b. enhanced working attention.
   c. a psychometric effect.
   d. simple cognitive components.
   e. strategy for using strategies.

18. We occasionally find people who are highly intelligent but terrible at spatial relations. This fact supports
   a. Gardner's theory of multiple intelligences.
   b. practical intelligence.
   c. the concept of g.
   d. the importance of working memory.
   e. a and b

19. We might expect that individuals in non-Western cultures might be superior to Westerners at some types of intelligences and inferior in others. One major variable might be the degree of literacy. Which of the following features of intelligence, broadly conceived, might be relatively unaffected or even improved by an inability to read?
   a. The ability to see spatial relations
   b. The ability to memorize and repeat long narratives
   c. The ability to solve analogy problems
   d. a and b
   e. b and c

20. The observation that people on the political left tend to think of intelligence as more under environmental control, while those on the right tend to think of it as more under genetic control suggests that
   a. we must distinguish between within- and between-group differences.
   b. the study of genetic and environmental influences on intelligence is inherently political.
   c. sociopolitical factors influence judgments about the role of heredity in intelligence.
   d. there is no way to study scientifically the issue of the role of heredity and environment on intelligence.
   e. c and d

21. In the period between the two World Wars, IQ scores of Eastern European immigrant groups improved the longer the immigrants were in the United States. This finding
   a. justified a policy of excluding Eastern Europeans from immigrating to the United States.
   b. raises questions about U.S. immigration policy in the period between the wars.
   c. demonstrates that intelligence is primarily under genetic control.
   d. demonstrates that intelligence is primarily under environmental control.
   e. none of the above.

22. Jane and Phyllis have brown eyes. All of Jane's relatives have brown eyes. Phyllis's father has brown eyes, but her mother has blue eyes (brown eye color is dominant). From this information, we can guess that Jane and Phyllis have
   a. the same genotype and phenotype.
   b. the same genotype and different phenotypes.
   c. different genotypes and the same phenotype.
   d. different genotypes and phenotypes.
   e. c or d

23. A genetic female who is exposed to androgens as a fetus and develops male genitals, and a person with phenylketonuria who is treated at birth and develops no symptoms, both illustrate that
   a. inborn, genetically determined traits can be changed by environmental factors.
   b. sex-linked traits can occur in both sex and intelligence.
   c. behavior is inherited.
   d. environmental factors, under some circumstances, have no influence on behavior.
   e. behavior is related to sex chromosomes.

24. The clustering of specific talents (e.g., music in the Bach family) or high intelligence in particular families, across generations, argues for
   a. a significant role for genetics in these abilities.
   b. a significant role for environment in these abilities.
   c. polygenic inheritance.
   d. both a and b
   e. a and/or b

25. If, counter to the results actually found, it was reported that fraternal and identical twins had the same high correlation in intelligence and that this was higher than the correlation between other siblings (e.g., brothers and sisters of different ages), we would be most justified in concluding that
   a. the higher correlation in twins was due to environmental factors.
   b. the higher correlation in twins was due to genetic factors.
   c. fraternal twins are more closely related genetically than other siblings are.
   d. a and c
   e. b and c

26. Environmentalists explain the significant correlation between the IQ of adopted children and their biological parents in terms of selective placement of these children in adopted homes. (Children with higher-IQ biological parents are placed with higher-IQ adoptive parents.) This argument, however, is significantly weakened by
   a. the studies on identical twins.
   b. the fact that the IQ of adopted children correlates more highly with their biological parents than with their adoptive parents.
   c. the fact that there is a positive correlation between the IQ of adopted children and their adoptive parents.
   d. b and c
   e. none of the above.

27. Which of these findings does *not* support or is *not* consistent with the idea of a hereditary component in intelligence differences?
    a. Higher IQ correlation in identical than fraternal twins
    b. Higher IQ correlation between adoptive children and their biological parents than between these same children and their adoptive parents
    c. Higher IQ correlation between siblings than between half-siblings (sharing only one parent)
    d. Higher correlations on IQ between fraternal twins than between other siblings
    e. The stability of IQ over decades

28. If intelligence (IQ scores) in a particular group showed a heritability of 1.0, this would mean that
    a. existing environments have no effects on intelligence.
    b. while existing environments have no effects on intelligence, presently nonexistent environments might have significant effects.
    c. genetic factors account for most of the variation in IQ in this particular group.
    d. genetic factors account for all of the variation in IQ in this particular group.
    e. none of the above.

29. Which of the following traits would you expect to show the lowest heritability?
    a. Eye color
    b. Height
    c. Length of hair
    d. Visual acuity
    e. Running speed

30. Many have argued that IQ tests and the circumstances under which they are given favor European Americans over African Americans. All but one of the following reported findings argue against this view—that is, all but one indicate that the tests are reasonably culture fair. Select the one reported finding that does not argue in favor of the culture fairness of tests or test situations.
    a. The African American and European American IQ difference remains about the same when the African American version of the test is translated into African American English.
    b. The African American and European American difference is about the same for verbal tests and for the abstract Raven's progressive matrices.
    c. The African American and European American difference remains about the same whether the tester is African American or European American.
    d. The African American and European American difference remains about the same for tests of verbal and tests of spatial intelligence.
    e. The African American and European American difference decreases in the children of families that have children of both races through adoption.

31. In two breeds of cattle, size differences within the breed are completely determined by genes (heritability: 1.0). One breed is found in New Zealand and the other in central Africa, and the New Zealand breed averages about 10 percent bigger than the African breed. What inferences can be made about the origin of this difference between breeds?
    a. It is certainly due to heredity.
    b. It is certainly due to environment.
    c. The heritability of the population difference would be at least .50.
    d. The heritability of the population difference would be at least .10.
    e. No certain inference can be drawn about the original breed differences from this information.

32. It is a fair summary of studies on environmental matching or change, as applied to the African American and European American IQ difference, to say
    a. there is generally a decreased African American and European American IQ difference when attempts are made to equalize environments in the comparison groups, and an improvement in African American IQs when the environment is improved.
    b. appropriate manipulation of environments, to provide African Americans with the full advantages of the European American environment, leads to elimination of the African American and European American IQ difference.
    c. there is very little effect of environmental change or equalization on African American IQ or on African American and European American IQ differences.
    d. a and b
    e. none of the above.

33. Which of the following statements about IQ differences is true?
    a. For European Americans, environment accounts for most IQ differences.
    b. There is no logical relation between with- and between-group heritability.
    c. Twin studies show no effect of environment on IQ.
    d. African American versus European American IQ differences disappear completely when attempts are made to equalize environment.
    e. None of the above.

34. What would be educationally and scientifically appropriate sociopolitical responses to a hypothetical proof that a fair proportion of the difference in IQ scores between African Americans and European Americans could be assigned to hereditary factors?
    a. Curtailment of early enrichment programs
    b. Establishment of racial quotas
    c. Inclusion of race as an important factor in determining the ability of applicants for jobs involving intelligence
    d. Cessation of affirmative action programs
    e. None of the above

Answer Key for Self-Test

1. c
2. a
3. b
4. d
5. e
6. b
7. a
8. d
9. c
10. a
11. a
12. b
13. c
14. b
15. e
16. d
17. e
18. a
19. d
20. c
21. b
22. c
23. a
24. e
25. a
26. b
27. d
28. d
29. c
30. e
31. e
32. a
33. b
34. e

Investigating Psychological Phenomena

INTELLIGENCE TESTS

Equipment: None
Number of participants: One (yourself)
Time per participant: Thirty minutes
Time for experimenter: Thirty minutes

This is an experiment that will help you to understand the construction of intelligence tests. The procedure that you will go through will be like the procedure that might be used in the development of an intelligence test. The main concern is that you understand how a distribution of test scores is generated, and how an individual score is interpreted with respect to that distribution.

For this purpose, rather than making up a so-called intelligence test, we have chosen to try out a measure of a characteristic that is rarely tested: one's knowledge of foods and cooking. In this case, we begin with some idea of the ability or knowledge base that we are trying to assess. Questions or tasks are constructed that seem to measure this. Then, pilot tests, like those we will give you, are distributed to a representative sample of the population for which the tests are intended. In your case, your class might serve as a sample of college undergraduates. Of course, students differ within schools and within different regions, so this would not be anything like the random sample we would need were this a real test.

The results of the test are examined. Typically, most of the questions that all participants get right or all get wrong are discarded, because such questions do not help to measure *differences* among people in the abilities under study. Then, some sort of retest study is done to make sure the test is reliable, and a validity study is done to assure that the test measures what it is supposed to measure.

We will deal only with one phase of test construction here. We have made up a test that has never been used by psychologists before. We ask each of you to take the test. It is brief. The food knowledge test is in the format of a written test, with unlimited time. It is, of course, closed book. Fill it out in a quiet place. Then score your answers, using the list of correct answers at the end of this section.

FOOD KNOWLEDGE TEST

Sex ______________

Listed below are five countries

Italy (southern Italy)
China
India
Mexico
Germany

Each of the following food items (1–14) is particularly characteristic of the cuisines of one of the five countries listed above. Write the name of the appropriate cuisine (country) beside the food item.

1. potatoes ____________
2. corn ____________
3. sesame oil ____________
4. olive oil ____________
5. soy sauce ____________
6. cumin (two possible answers) ____________
7. oregano ____________
8. curry ____________
9. chili pepper (two possible answers) ____________
10. liverwurst ____________
11. turmeric ____________
12. yogurt ____________
13. bean curd ____________
14. ghee ____________

Write in the name of the country associated with each of the following items:

15. sushi ____________
16. lasagna ____________
17. taco ____________
18. paella ____________
19. moussaka ____________
20. goulash ____________
21. sukiyaki ____________
22. mousse ____________
23. sate (pron: sa′ • tay) ____________
24. biryani ____________
25. mole (pron: mo′ • lay) ____________
26. trifle ____________
27. kim chee ____________
28. champagne ____________
29. What is the primary ingredient used in raising (leavening) bread? ____________
30. What is yogurt made from? ____________
31. What are raisins made from? ____________
32. What is meringue made of? ____________
33. What animal does bacon come from? ____________
34. What are prunes made from? ____________
35. What type of fish is lox made from? ____________
36. What vegetable are pickles usually made from? ____________
37. What fruit is wine usually made from? ____________
38. What is sauerkraut made from? ____________
39. What are chitterlings made from? ____________
40. What does caviar come from? ____________
41. What is marzipan made from? ____________
42. What is the primary ingredient in guacamole? ____________

Indicated below are five common cooking methods:

baking
sautéing or pan frying
braising
boiling
broiling

For each dish or food below, indicate by writing in the correct term from those listed above the primary cooking method used.

43. chicken soup ____________
44. bread ____________
45. scrambled eggs ____________
46. pot roast ____________
47. shish-kebab ____________
48. spaghetti ____________
49. soufflé ____________
50. hash-brown potatoes ____________
51. collard greens ____________

TEST RESULTS AND "IQ" CALCULATIONS

The food knowledge test was taken by 153 University of Pennsylvania undergraduates in the introductory psychology course and twenty-one students in a University of Michigan class in learning and memory. The results were

Mean score: 35.9 for 174 participants
Standard deviation: 5.03
Range of scores: 22 (lowest) to 47 (highest)

Females do slightly better than males on this test (mean female score: 36.8; mean male score: 35.1).

CALCULATION OF A "CULINARY IQ"

As we will discuss below, much more work would have to be done with this test before it could actually be used in a meaningful way. For the sake of illustrating the scaling of psychological tests, we will use the data generated by undergraduates taking this test to develop a "deviation" scale like that used in IQ tests. You can then calculate your "culinary IQ."

The basic principle behind scaling of tests is the deviation score. Like a percentile score, it expresses where a particular score stands with respect to all of the other scores. The distribution of scores for tests usually falls into what is called a normal distribution. An ideal normal distribution is drawn in the next column. Normal distributions are typically described by their mean value and their standard deviation, a measure of the spread or variability of the curve (see the statistical appendix to the text). In a normal distribution, 68 percent of all observations fall within one standard deviation of the mean, and 96 percent of all observations fall within two standard deviations of the mean (see the accompanying figure). Test scores are measured in units of deviation from the mean. For all IQ type tests, 100 is set as the mean value and 15 point as the standard deviation. Thus, an IQ of 115 corresponds to the score one standard deviation above the mean (85 to one standard deviation below); 130 corresponds to a score of two standard deviations above the mean (70 to two below), and so on. (An IQ of 105 would then be one-third of a standard deviation above the mean.) In percentile terms, an IQ of 130 would be at the 98th percentile, and an IQ of 85 would be at the 16th percentile (see figure).

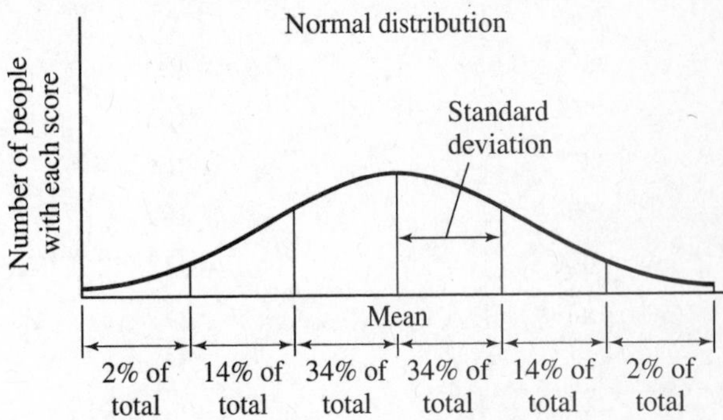

Applying these ideas to our test, the mean score (35.9) on the food test would be assigned a scaled score of 100. Subtracting one standard deviation (5.03) from this score, we get approximately 31, a score that would be assigned a scaled score of 85 (one standard deviation below the mean corresponds to 15 scaled points). We have performed the appropriate arithmetic for the food test, and provided the raw score (your actual score) and scaled score (converted to deviation units) equivalents in the table on the next page. Because the standard deviation for the food knowledge scores is almost exactly 5, each additional point on the test is worth one-fifth of a standard deviation, or 3 "IQ" points.

FOOD TEST

Raw score (your actual score)	Scaled score ("IQ")
18	46
19	49
20	52
21	55
22	58
23	61
24	64
25	67
26	70
27	73
28	76
29	79
30	82
31	85
32	88
33	91
34	94
35	97
36	100
37	103
38	106
39	109
40	112
41	115
42	118
43	121
44	124
45	127
46	130
47	133
48	136
49	139
50	142
51	145

The next step in developing a test would be to improve the first version. For example, in the food knowledge test, there are a number of useless items: these are items that do not contribute to the measurement of differences in people. For three items (number 16—lasagna, 37—wine, and 44—bread), all 174 participants got the right answer. Because of this, these items would normally be discarded. Three additional items were missed by less than 2% of the participants and might also be discarded. There were no questions that were missed by all participants. The "hardest" question was about the country of origin of sate (Number 23—Indonesia), and 8.6% of participants were correct on this item.

We would also eliminate any questions that turned out to be ambiguous. In this test, for example, some of the "What is X made from?" questions need clarification. Thus, for Number 39—chitterlings (chitlings), some people answered "pig," and others said "intestine." We scored both as correct, but should have been more specific in the question. Similarly, for Number 30—what is yogurt made from?—we intended that milk be the correct answer. But bacteria cultures are also components of yogurt. We should have asked, "What is the primary ingredient in yogurt?" See if you can find some other ambiguous questions. Finally, we would examine the correlation of correctness on each question with the total score on the test. Are there any items that don't seem to be measuring the same sort of thing as the rest of the test? (See the experiment on personality testing in the next chapter.) Such items might or might not be included but would at least be reexamined. Along these same lines, one might look at any questions that the top performers on the test all missed. Often such items are badly worded, or perhaps even in error. For the food test, there was no single item missed by all of the six top scorers.

Having streamlined the test, we would then use some type of test-retest procedure to determine reliability. (Will the same person score about the same on two different occasions?) The reliability measures would be complicated, since one would expect improvement on the second time through.

We would then perform some sort of validity test. Is the test measuring what it is supposed to measure? If the food knowledge test is supposed to predict likely candidates for success in a cooking school, does it actually do so?

Finally, having satisfied ourselves that we had a reliable and valid test, we would then administer the test to a large sample of people (hundreds to thousands of people) randomly selected from the population of people for whom the test was designed (e.g., high school seniors, all adults).

Ask yourself whether you believe the food test is meaningful. How would you validate it? What might it be used for? What would it correlate with?

FURTHER ACTIVITIES

Sketch out what you think would be an appropriate test for use in predicting success in a particular profession: for example, fighter pilot, baseball player, or architect. Then ask yourself how you would validate the test.

Answer Sheet

Score one point for each correct answer
(Listed next to each answer are the percentages correct out of 174 students.)

1. potatoes–Germany (83.9%)
2. corn–Mexico (78.7%)
3. sesame oil–China (28.2%)
4. olive oil–Italy (93.7%)
5. soy sauce–China (97.7%)
6. cumin–India or Mexico (78.2%)
7. oregano–Italy (90.2%)
8. curry–India (73.0%)
9. chili–India or Mexico (90.2%)
10. liverwurst–Germany (97.7%)
11. turmeric–India (48.3%)
12. yogurt–India (44.8%)
13. bean curd–China (44.8%)
14. ghee–India (60.3%)
15. sushi–Japan (55.7%)
16. lasagna–Italy (100%)
17. taco–Mexico (98.8%)
18. paella–Spain (40.2%)
19. moussaka–Greece (43.7%)
20. goulash–Hungary (73.6%)
21. sukiyaki–Japan (76.4%)
22. mousse–France (74.7%)
23. sate–Indonesia (8.6%)
24. biryani–India (37.4%)
25. mole–Mexico (14.9%)
26. trifle–England (47.7%)
27. kim chee–Korea (13.2%)
28. champagne–France (80.4%)
29. bread–yeast (97.1%)
30. yogurt–milk (88.5%)
31. raisins–grapes (96.0%)
32. meringue–egg white (74.1%)
33. bacon–pig (99.9%)
34. prunes–plums (77.0%)
35. lox–salmon (66.7%)
36. pickle–cucumber (97.7%)
37. wine–grapes (100%)
38. sauerkraut–cabbage (89.1%)
39. chitterlings–pig or intestine (29.3%)
40. caviar–fish eggs (91.4%)
41. marzipan–almond or sugar (31.0%)
42. guacamole–avocado (48.3%)
43. chicken soup–boiling (96%)
44. bread–baking (100%)
45. scrambled eggs–pan frying (98.3%)
46. pot roast–braising (46.6%)
47. shish kebab–broiling (57.5%)
48. spaghetti–boiling (97.7%)
49. soufflé–baking (83.3%)
50. hash-brown potatoes–pan fry or sautéing (96.6%)
51. collard greens–boiling (55.7%)

CHAPTER 15

Personality

Learning Objectives

THE TRAIT APPROACH

1. What is the trait approach to personality? What does *persona* refer to?

The search for the right taxonomy of traits

2. What was Cattell's approach to developing a taxonomy of personality traits? What modifications of Cattell's analysis have been suggested and why? What are the Big Five?

3. Discuss Eysenck's taxonomy of neuroticism and extroversion-introversion. What personality differences are encompassed by this scheme? Do the two dimensions of Eysenck's classification apply to other cultures?

4. What are the arguments about the validity of a factor-analytic approach to personality?

Traits versus situation: The consistency controversy

5. What is the importance of cross-situational consistency, or inconsistency, in the argument against trait theory? How does this affect the validity of personality tests?

6. What is situationism, and how is it related to personality?

7. Review the evidence on the consistency of behavior across time and situations. Describe how superficially different expressions of a personality trait contribute to apparent behavioral inconsistency. What are the implications for trait theory?

8. Realize that consistency may be a personality trait. How does Snyder's self-monitoring scale measure behavioral consistency in different situations?

Traits and biology

9. What is the definition of the word *temperament,* and what effect does temperament have on a person's personality?

10. Be prepared to discuss how evidence from the study of twins contributes to our understanding of personality traits.

11. Discuss the evidence that personality traits may have a genetic component. What traits are most heritable?

12. What studies have been done to show that between-family differences in environment are not important in determining personality traits? In what situations do between-family environmental differences matter?

13. How can differences within a family environment affect its children?

14. Describe how Eysenck compares introverts and extroverts in terms of their arousal systems. What research on sensation seeking has Zuckerman done that correlates with Eysenck's findings?

15. What is known about the involvement of neurotransmitter systems in sensation seeking?

THE PSYCHODYNAMIC APPROACH: FREUD AND PSYCHOANALYSIS

The origins of psychoanalytic thought

16. Describe the symptoms of hysteria. Why is this illness termed a psychogenic disorder?

17. Describe glove anesthesia.

18. What is free association?

19. What are repression and resistance?

20. What is psychoanalysis, and how does it relate to the understanding of psychopathology and the normal personality?

Unconscious conflict

21. Understand the nature of unconscious conflict and its effect on behavior.

22. What are the three divisions of personality according to Freud? How do these develop, and how do they interact to give rise to conflict and resolution?

23. Be cognizant of the major role of anxiety as a motivating force in keeping unacceptable urges repressed.

24. How does repression affect the realm of thought in addition to that of behavior?

25. What are defense mechanisms?

26. Describe the specific defense mechanisms (repression, displacement, reaction formation, rationalization, and projection).

Unconscious conflict and the formation of personality

27. What are Freud's stages of psychosexual development, and what is the relation of these stages to sexuality and pleasure?

28. What are oral and anal characters, and how, according to Freud, do they relate to psychosexual development?

29. In Freud's view, the Oedipus complex is the most important aspect of psychosexual development. Discuss this theory with respect to both sexes.

30. What are Freud's views of the psychosexual development of girls?

Windows into the unconscious

31. What is the psychopathology of everyday life, and how does it reflect underlying motives and conflicts?

32. Explain Freud's theory of dreams. Understand the motive of wish fulfillment and its symbolic expression, and the difference between the latent and the manifest dream context.

33. How have Freud's theories been used to interpret myths?

A critical look at Freudian theory

34. Recount some of the methodological and conceptual difficulties with Freud's theories.

35. Explain how interpretations of clinical evidence cast doubt on the testability of Freud's theory.

36. Review the evidence on the validity of the existence of anal and oral characters, and their link to childhood toilet training and feeding experiences.

37. How universal is the Oedipus complex? Summarize evidence from the Trobriand Islanders.

38. What evidence militates against Freud's emphasis on wish fulfillment in the interpretation of dreams?

39. Summarize the issues and arguments against and in favor of Freud's reliance on repression in dealing with unconscious conflicts. What is the evidence for repression, as opposed to a less motivation-oriented view of retrieval blocking?

40. What are Freud's major contributions to our understanding of human nature and to the field of psychology? What are the shortcomings of his approach and theory?

THE PSYCHODYNAMIC APPROACH: PERSONALITY DIFFERENCES

41. What are dominant patterns of defense, and what, according to the neo-Freudians, is their role in accounts of personality differences?

Coping patterns and mental health

42. What are coping mechanisms and how do they relate to Freudian defense mechanisms?

43. What do longitudinal studies tell us about the importance and consistency of coping patterns? What child-rearing patterns are associated with the best adjustment?

44. What is the relationship between coping mechanisms and Freud's view of the unconscious?

THE HUMANISTIC APPROACH

The major features of the humanistic movement

45. Describe the basic differences between the humanistic approach and each of the other approaches to personality that have been discussed.

46. Explain the hierarchy of needs, including self-actualization.

47. What is the self-concept according to Rogers?

Evaluating the humanistic approach

48. What are the empirical and conceptual problems of the humanistic approach?

Positive psychology

49. Describe the contributions and weaknesses of positive psychology.

THE SOCIAL-COGNITIVE APPROACH

Behavioral roots of social-cognitive theories

50. What is the central assumption of the social-cognitive approach to personality?

51. What is Bandura's view of personality? How is it based on expectations of outcomes?

Cognitive roots of social-cognitive theories

52. How does the concept of construals govern Kelly's view of personality?

53. Be prepared to describe the five cognitive qualities that Mischel has proposed as dimensions on which people differ.

Control

54. What is the evidence that control over a situation is a cognitive dimension that people seek? What is the role of self-efficacy?

Self-control

55. Describe how self-control is seen as an important personality characteristic. Discuss evidence that children can be influenced in their self-control depending on physical and cognitive factors.

56. How is the early ability to delay gratification related to late coping ability?

Traits and social-cognitive theory

57. How are social-cognitive theorists different from trait theorists? What are working models?

SOME FINAL THOUGHTS: THE NEED FOR MULTIPLE APPROACHES

58. Why are multiple approaches necessary?

Programmed Exercises

1. The way that people differ in their desires and feelings and in the expression of these feelings reflects __________ differences. — personality
2. In the comic dramas that they performed, the Greeks and Romans thought of the different characters and their respective personalities as __________. — types
3. The __________ hypothesis is a widely used personality inventory invented by Cattell. — lexical
4. Tests that assume someone knows a great deal about their own beliefs, emotions, and past actions are called __________-__________ measures. — self-report
5. The idea behind projective techniques is that in structuring unstructured materials, a participant will reveal deeper facets of his __________. — personality
6. The categories used to score the Rorschach are the portion and the __________ of the blot (such as color) used and the __________ of the response. — attribute, content
7. In interpretations of Rorschach inkblots, use of the entire blot is said to reflect __________ thinking, while attention to details is said to suggest __________. — integrative (conceptual), compulsiveness (rigidity)
8. Rorschach responses using the white space as the foreground are interpreted as indicating __________, and those dominated by color as suggesting __________. — rebelliousness (negativism), emotionality (impulsivity)
9. The __________ __________ Test (TAT), in which people tell stories about pictures, places a major emphasis on content. — Thematic Apperception

THE TRAIT APPROACH

10. The major task in determining the proper traits with which to classify personality is the development of a(n) __________ of personality difference. — taxonomy
11. Cattell's taxonomy of personality is based on __________, using factor analysis to discover how __________ terms are interrelated. — language, trait
12. The Big Five dimensions of personality are __________, __________, __________, __________, and __________ to experience. — extroversion, neuroticism, agreeableness, conscientiousness, openness
13. Eysenck's classification scheme included __________ versus __________ stability, and __________ versus __________. — neuroticism, emotional, extroversion, introversion
14. Some psychologists have argued that the reason many tests are not good predictors of future behavior is that most people exhibit a lack of __________-__________ consistency. — cross-situational
15. __________ maintains that human behavior is largely determined by the situation a person is in rather than by the actual, internal traits of the person. — Situationism
16. When a person's reactions cannot be predicted adequately solely by situation or by individual differences, the critical factor may be the __________ of these two. — interaction
17. Since cross-situational consistency varies from person to person, it may be regarded as a __________ that only some individuals possess. — trait
18. We can assess how much a person adjusts her behavior to fit a situation by having that person complete the __________-__________ scale developed by Mark Snyder. — self-monitoring
19. It is believed that a person's __________ ultimately originates from his biological makeup. — temperament
20. Identical twins show more similarity of personality than fraternal twins do, indicating some __________ of personality traits. — heritability

21. It appears that __________-__________ differences in environment are unimportant in determining personality traits such as emotionality and extroversion. However, __________-__________ differences in environment (e.g., birth order and spacing, friends) faced by children in the same family will cause variations in personality between those siblings. — between-family; within-family

22. According to Eysenck, introversion corresponds to a high level of __________; thus, persons of this type are actually more awake than others. — arousal

23. Zuckerman's research on __________ __________ indicates that those people with a higher arousal system (introverts) have higher levels of the neurotransmitter __________ in their brains. Those with lower levels of this neurotransmitter are underaroused, and as a result are likely to seek thrills and take risks. — sensation seeking; norepinephrine

THE SOCIAL-COGNITIVE APPROACH

24. The social-cognitive approach, in contrast to __________ theory, emphasizes the importance of external forces in the determination of behavior. — trait

25. This view is a direct descendent of __________, an important movement early in this century that emphasized the role of learning, and de-emphasized the role of cognition. — behaviorism

26. Kelly called our interpretation of a situation our __________ of it. — construal

27. Patients who are allowed the opportunity to __________ their environments are more active and feel better than patients who are not. — control

28. Our __________ style indicates the extent to which we designate the causes of events as internal or external. — explanatory

29. The __________-__________ questionnaire asks people about situations and what might have caused them. — attributional-style

30. Measures of __________ of gratification in young children show that this characteristic predicts behavior in adolescence. — delay

31. Social learning theorists can still be regarded as behaviorists in that they continue to stress the importance of the __________ in determining behavior, and they insist on the importance of __________ in acquiring various personality characteristics. — situation; learning

THE PSYCHODYNAMIC APPROACH: FREUD AND PSYCHOANALYSIS

32. According to the psychodynamic approach, understanding of human personality requires understanding of __________ psychological forces. — hidden (deep, unconscious)

33. The psychodynamic approach derives from __________, founded by Freud. — psychoanalysis

34. A patient exhibiting partial blindness, glove anesthesia, or memory gaps would likely be diagnosed as suffering from __________. — hysteria

35. If organic damage is ruled out in the above case (question 34), then the origin of the symptoms must be __________. — psychogenic

36. Freud and Breuer believed that crucial memories that were repressed could be recovered through __________ __________. — free association

37. Although Freud began by using hypnosis, he later abandoned this approach, since not all of his patients were hypnotizable and since the same crucial memories could be obtained in the waking state through the method of __________ __________. — free association

38. A patient is told to say anything that enters his mind, yet struggles at times to change the subject or forgets what he was going to say. This subject is demonstrating __________ to the recovery of __________ memories. — resistance; repressed

39. According to Freud's view, forbidden impulses are never completely controlled, despite repressive measures by the individual. This division of the individual (one part fighting another) gives rise to __________ conflicts. unconscious

40. Freud investigated unconscious conflicts: their origin, effects, and removal. He termed his exploration and interpretation of these phenomena __________. psychoanalysis

41. The three distinct systems of the human personality, according to Freud, are the __________, the __________, and the __________. id, ego, superego

42. The most primitive portion of personality is the __________. It operates according to the __________ principle, with the single goal being immediate satisfaction. id, pleasure

43. As id-dominated infants encounter the frustrations of the real world, they develop a(n) __________, which attempts to satisfy the urges of the id according to a __________ principle. ego, reality

44. The young child refrains from doing wrong only through fear of being caught. Because the rules and admonitions of the parents are __________, however, the __________ develops and suppresses forbidden behavior even in the absence of negative consequences. internalized, superego

45. __________ is the crucial factor in the mechanism underlying repression. Internal thoughts and feelings that evoke this state must be escaped and are thus suppressed. Anxiety

46. Repression can be regarded as the primary, initial mechanism of __________. defense

47. When fear of retaliation blocks the expression of anger, a person may vent her feelings on another recipient, resulting in __________ aggression. displaced

48. When a repressed thought or wish manifests itself as a diametrically opposite wish or thought, it is a result of __________ __________. reaction formation

49. __________ is another defense mechanism, in which a repressed thought is reinterpreted in more acceptable terms. Rationalization

50. Cognitive reorganization also plays a role in __________, in which forbidden urges are attributed to others rather than to the self. projection

51. Freud's theory of __________ development postulates biologically determined stages of emotional and sexual development. psychosexual

52. Seeking pleasure through the mouth is characteristic of the __________ stage, which yields to the __________ stage as toilet training begins. The __________ stage focuses on the stimulation of the genitals, while interest in the satisfaction of others as well as one's own satisfaction characterizes the __________ stage. oral, anal, phallic, genital

53. A lingering attachment to pleasure seeking of the type characteristic of a particular psychosexual stage is called a __________. This can sometimes be manifested in terms of opposite characteristics, mediated by the mechanism of __________ __________. fixation, reaction formation

54. The __________ character recapitulates the pleasure and passive dependency of nursing at his mother's breast. oral

55. The __________ character is typically excessively clean, obstinate, and stingy. anal

56. The family drama from which grows the boy's internalized morality and identification with the same-sex parent is called the __________ __________. Oedipus complex

57. According to the theory of the Oedipus complex, the __________ urges of the boy at ages three and four are directed toward the __________ as the source of previous gratification during the oral stage. phallic (sexual), mother

58. The young boy's __________ of the father leads to hostility and a fear of retaliation by the father. jealousy

59. The renunciation of genital pleasures endures from about five to twelve years of age and is termed the __________ __________. latency period

60. The weakest aspect of Freud's theory of psychosexual development concerns the young girl's progression of sexual interests. This is called the _________ complex. Specifically, why does the little girl desire the father instead of the mother? Freud attributed this transference of attachment to _________ _________. — Electra; penis envy

61. Through his study of dreams, Freud came to the conclusion that dreams are an attempt at _________ _________. Desires suppressed by considerations of reality and by the superego emerge and are gratified in dreams. — wish fulfillment

62. The _________ dream content is the disguised expression of the _________ dream content, which represents hidden and forbidden wishes. — manifest, latent

63. Studies of Trobriand Islanders have suggested that the hostility of the young boy toward the father in our culture may be a product, not of sexual _________, but rather of the father's role as an _________. — jealousy; authoritarian

64. The same urge may sometimes be disguised and sometimes be expressed openly in a dream. Freud's assertion that the manifest dream represents a _________ disguise cannot handle this fact. — defensive

65. Despite the criticisms of Freud's theoretical proposals, his conception of _________ conflict and the sheer scope of his ideas rank him as one of the giants of psychology. — internal (unconscious)

66. Mental processes that are not currently in focal awareness, but that could easily be brought to awareness are at the _________ level. — preconscious

THE HUMANISTIC APPROACH

67. In contrast to the behavioristic and psychoanalytic approaches to personality, _________ psychologists describe themselves as having a positive view of human motivation. — humanistic

68. Maslow places the needs referred to above at the bottom of the _________ of _________. At the top is the desire to realize oneself to the fullest, called _________-_________. — hierarchy, needs; self-actualization

69. According to humanistic psychologists, a basic part of one's subjective experience is one's sense of oneself as both agent and object, called one's _________-_________. — self-concept

70. According to Rogers, a solid sense of self-worth depends on a child's feeling of _________ _________ _________. — unconditional positive regard

71. According to Maslow, satisfaction of lower-level needs and a reasonable sense of self-worth allow for the expression of the desire for _________-_________. — self-actualization

72. One problem with the humanistic approach is that there is little _________ to support the assertions made about human nature. — evidence

73. Another problem is that, in an important sense, people like Adolf Hitler fit the description of being _________-_________. — self-actualized

74. The emerging field of _________ psychology is concerned with defining well-being and how it is attained. — positive

75. The phenomenon of _________ refers to the fact that humans grow accustomed to a static stimulus. — adaptation

THE SOCIOCULTURAL PERSPECTIVE

76. The _________-_________ method compares different cultures, with the aim of extracting common themes. — cross-cultural

77. _________ cultures place less emphasis on self-satisfaction, as opposed to _________ cultures. — Collectivist; individualist

Self-Test

1. Personality differences include
   a. intelligence, ability, and insight.
   b. desires, feelings, and modes of expressing these needs and feelings.
   c. a and b
   d. none of the above.

2. States can refer to
   a. unchanging personality traits.
   b. temporary moods.
   c. a and b
   d. none of the above.

3. Data collected on an individual by interviewing people that are acquainted with that person are known as
   a. informant data.
   b. self-reflective measures.
   c. friend-reports.
   d. knowledge database.

4. We seem to behave less consistently than a trait conception would predict. This is known as
   a. the inconsistency paradox.
   b. the personality paradox.
   c. the situation paradox.
   d. none of the above.

5. Situations that produce near-uniform behavior are called
   a. strong situations.
   b. weak situations.
   c. consistent situations.
   d. inconsistent situations.

6. Situations that allow for a wider variety of behavior are called
   a. strong situations.
   b. weak situations.
   c. consistent situations.
   d. inconsistent situations.

7. Inhibited temperament refers to a behavior pattern common in
   a. introverts.
   b. extroverts.
   c. adults.
   d. children.

8. This term refers to the idea that people from different cultures tend to have different personalities:
   a. *national personalities*.
   b. *national pride*.
   c. *national character*.
   d. none of the above.

9. Theorists who hold that relationships with important others constitute a powerful and relatively neglected motive underlying human behavior are called
   a. object relations theorists.
   b. self-reflective theorists.
   c. interpersonal theorists.
   d. cognitive theorists.

10. Which of the following is *not* an established piece of evidence against the validity of the Rorschach inkblot test?
    a. The failure of highly intelligent people to use the entire inkblot more than others do
    b. The lack of relation between Rorschach indices and psychiatric diagnosis
    c. The failure of artists to demonstrate a preponderance of human movement in their perceptions
    d. The fact that individual Rorschach indices show little relation to external validity criteria

11. The primary attachment figure in a child's life is
    a. always the father.
    b. usually the father.
    c. always the mother.
    d. usually the mother.

12. A taxonomy is a
    a. classification system.
    b. rating scale used in psychiatric diagnosis.
    c. type of mental disorder.
    d. class of stable personality traits.

13. Eysenck hypothesized that all personalities can be classified on the basis of a rating on two independent scales, __________ and __________.
    a. paranoid, schizophrenic
    b. shy-outgoing, anxiety
    c. neuroticism, extroversion-introversion
    d. psychopathic deviance, extroversion-introversion

14. Which of the following constitute problems for Eysenck's theory of personality based on neuroticism and introversion-extroversion?
    a. The dependence of factor analysis on the existing data set
    b. The possible nonindependence of these two dimensions
    c. The observation that introverted people tend to be more easily aroused than extroverts are
    d. a and b

15. Walter Mischel found that children are __________ in their behavior in different circumstances. He saw this as evidence __________ the validity of personality traits.
    a. consistent, for
    b. inconsistent, for
    c. consistent, against
    d. inconsistent, against

16. Situationists
    a. deny the existence of individual differences.
    b. believe that social roles play a large role in the situations people get into.
    c. claim that situations themselves are the best predictors of people's reactions.
    d. believe that past situational experiences determine personality traits.

17. In defense of trait theory, we could cite evidence that behavior is
    a. consistent over time.
    b. consistent across situations.
    c. a and b
    d. none of the above.

18. Tom is a gregarious and talkative person. He enjoys organizing activities with friends. Which of the following choices would *not* illustrate a reciprocal relation between Tom and the situation?
   a. Tom gives a party for his birthday.
   b. Tom's job is social director for a large singles' group in his city.
   c. On many evenings Tom likes to sit in his room and videotape sports events.
   d. Tom shares a house with five other guys from his college graduating class.

19. High self-monitors are
   a. not adaptable.
   b. inconsistent.
   c. consistent.
   d. rigid.

20. Which of the following traits is heritable?
   a. Neuroticism
   b. Agreeableness
   c. Extroversion
   d. All of the above
   e. a and c

21. Studies have found that behaviors such as television watching or tendencies toward divorce are partially heritable. These findings need to be interpreted cautiously, however, because
   a. television watching is so recent that it could not have influenced genetic makeup.
   b. divorce, although hundreds of years old, is still too recent to have influenced genetic makeup.
   c. other, more fundamental traits such as extroversion may be the ones that are heritable, and they reveal themselves in such behaviors as television watching.
   d. all of the above.
   e. a and b

22. One line of evidence suggesting a strong heritable component to personality traits is that
   a. identical twins have higher correlations (each to the other twin) in measures of personality traits than do fraternal twins.
   b. identical twins have lower correlations (each to the other twin) in personality traits than do fraternal twins.
   c. identical twins and fraternal twins have equal correlations (each of the pair to the other twin) in personality traits.
   d. fraternal twins have higher correlations (each to the other twin) than to siblings who are not twins.

23. Which of the following statements is true?
   a. Identical twins have less chance of being alike on various personality tests than fraternal twins do.
   b. Fraternal twins raised apart show a lower correlation of personality traits than those raised together do.
   c. Siblings raised in the same family are likely to have different personalities partly because the reciprocal interaction between each child's genetic makeup and his environment will be different.
   d. Identical twins raised together show a higher correlation of personality traits than those raised apart do.

24. Which of the following is true of sensation seekers?
   a. They have underactive norepinephrine systems in their brain.
   b. They are overaroused in certain systems of their brain.
   c. They have a low pain tolerance.
   d. They react more to external stimuli than people who are not sensation seekers.

25. The social-cognitive approach to personality does not attribute differences in personality to
   a. enduring traits in personality that may be a function of hereditary influences.
   b. differences in how a person will behave in different situations.
   c. learning that occurs during the life of an individual that may cause certain behaviors to appear in certain situations.
   d. classical and operant conditioning.

26. Mischel has proposed that people can differ on which of the following characteristics that determine their personality?
   a. Their construal of external experiences
   b. Their beliefs about the world
   c. Their emotional response to situations
   d. Their goals
   e. All of the above

27. The Attributional Style Questionnaire is an important instrument for measuring control because it
   a. assesses the extent to which an individual thinks the causes of events are internal to her or due to external forces.
   b. has value in predicting clinical depression.
   c. is related to the idea of learned helplessness in animals that may be related to depression.
   d. all of the above.

28. The extent to which a child is willing to delay gratification is related to later
   a. academic performance.
   b. social competence.
   c. coping skills in adolescence.
   d. all of the above.

29. Social-cognitive approach is to psychodynamic approach as
   a. psychiatry is to psychology.
   b. normality is to pathology.
   c. surface is to deep.
   d. airplane is to surface transportation.
   e. pleasure is to pain.

30. Which of the following adjectives would *not* be used by Freud to describe basic human nature?
   a. Sexually motivated
   b. Selfish
   c. Pleasure seeking
   d. Conflict free
   e. b and d

31. Freud made a major contribution to the understanding of human nature when he suggested that the apparent irrationality of much human behavior was a symptom of
   a. basic insanity.
   b. severe hysteria.
   c. unconscious conflicts.
   d. wish fulfillment.
   e. internalized standards.

32. Which of the following are symptoms of hysteria?
   i. Partial or total blindness
   ii. Paralysis
   iii. Feelings of helplessness
   iv. Anesthesia of a body part
   v. Uncontrollable urges
   a. i, iii, v
   b. i, ii, iv, v
   c. ii, iii, iv
   d. i, ii, iv
   e. All are symptoms of hysteria.

33. Charcot and Freud believed that hysteria is
   a. inherited.
   b. psychogenic.
   c. the result of physical trauma (injury to the brain).
   d. incurable.
   e. unimportant.

34. A patient is asked merely to say whatever comes to his mind during a therapy session. This psychoanalytic technique is known as
   a. transference.
   b. free association.
   c. resistance formation.
   d. wish fulfillment.
   e. hypnosis.

35. All of the following statements (made by a patient during free association) are examples of resistance *except*
   a. I really can't think of anything right now.
   b. I just forgot what I was about to say.
   c. I'm thinking of something that has nothing to do with my problem.
   d. I just remembered a terrible experience from my childhood.
   e. What I'm thinking about now is too unimportant to tell you.

36. According to Freud, repressed thoughts
   a. are connected to a wish or thought that a person is unable to face without intense anxiety.
   b. are linked to basic biological urges.
   c. often date back to early life.
   d. all of the above.
   e. none of the above.

37. Which of Freud's subsystems would be responsible for a desire to eat or drink?
   a. Ego
   b. Superego
   c. Id
   d. A combination of ego and superego
   e. All of the above

38. If a child wants a drink, we often find that she asks for something rather than just taking it. This is evidence for the operation of
   a. the ego.
   b. repression.
   c. the id.
   d. a and c
   e. b and c

39. When children begin to think of themselves as if they were the parent, the __________ has begun to develop.
   a. ego
   b. superego
   c. id
   d. a and b
   e. It is impossible to tell from this information.

40. Conflicts develop because the __________ and __________ often issue conflicting commands to the __________.
   a. id, ego, superego
   b. id, superego, ego
   c. ego, superego, id
   d. superego, ego, id
   e. All three systems issue commands to both other systems.

41. The mechanism underlying repression is based on
   a. irrationality.
   b. biological urge reduction.
   c. anxiety reduction.
   d. fear reduction.
   e. ego expansion.

42. A child is punished for something she did. She then hits her brother. This is an example of
   a. repression.
   b. transference.
   c. hysteria.
   d. displaced aggression.
   e. anxiety.

43. A child has deeply hidden feelings of hostility toward a younger sibling. However, the child treats his sibling with apparent love. This is an example of the defense mechanism known as
   a. projection.
   b. reaction formation.
   c. rationalization.
   d. displacement.
   e. repression.

44. A child who displays a behavior diametrically opposed to her frustrated true desires is demonstrating
   a. reaction formation.
   b. displacement.
   c. projection.
   d. isolation.
   e. none of the above.

45. After failing to be offered a good job, an applicant decides that he wouldn't have liked the job anyway. This person is displaying a defense mechanism called
   a. rationalization.
   b. projection.
   c. reaction formation.
   d. isolation.
   e. repression.

46. When a person attributes her own thoughts and feelings to someone else, we call this
   a. rationalization.
   b. projection.
   c. reaction formation.
   d. repression.
   e. isolation.

47. Which of the following presents the correct stages of psychosexual development in the right order?
   a. Oral, anal, erogenous, phallic, genital
   b. Oral, anal, phallic, genital
   c. Anal, oral, erogenous, phallic
   d. Oral, anal, phallic, erogenous
   e. None are in the correct order.

48. An adult who dislikes eating, and avoids kissing and smoking, would, according to Freud, be described as
   a. fixated at the anal stage.
   b. showing a reaction formation from the oral stage.
   c. an oral character.
   d. an anal character.
   e. a remnant.

49. If a child experienced severe toilet training, and grew up to be messy, generous, and open minded, a Freudian would account for this by referring to the mechanisms of
   a. fixation and reaction formation.
   b. repression and fixation.
   c. projection and displacement.
   d. isolation and rationalization.
   e. A Freudian could not account for this.

50. The critical component(s) of Freud's theory of personality is (are)
   a. psychosexual stages.
   b. unconscious conflict.
   c. fixation and reaction formation.
   d. all of the above.
   e. b and c

51. The anal and oral characters have in common
   a. reaction formation at a stage of development.
   b. fixation at a stage of development.
   c. a concern for orderliness.
   d. a lack of normal sexual interests.
   e. none of the above.

52. The drama of the Oedipus complex unfolds according to the following progression of events:
   a. identification, love, fear, hate, renunciation.
   b. love, fear, hate, renunciation, identification.
   c. hate, fear, renunciation, identification.
   d. love, hate, fear, renunciation, identification.
   e. none of the above.

53. The stage following resolution of the Oedipus complex comprises
   a. the latency period.
   b. increased masturbation.
   c. puberty.
   d. the genital stage.
   e. all of the above.

54. Freud believed that the basis of every dream was
   a. projection.
   b. schizophrenia.
   c. wish fulfillment.
   d. day residues.
   e. castration anxiety.

55. Freud distinguished between two parts of the dream, which he termed
   a. conscious and unconscious.
   b. latent and manifest.
   c. normal and deviant.
   d. wish fulfillment and disguise.
   e. normal and abnormal.

56. Problems with the psychoanalytic view include
   a. lack of objectivity of clinical practitioners in reporting patients' statements.
   b. so much flexibility that an outcome or its opposite can be predicted.
   c. suggestion or influence of patients to report certain kinds of events or feelings.
   d. all of the above.
   e. a and c

57. For which claim of psychoanalytic theory is there specific positive evidence?
   a. Universality of the Oedipus complex
   b. Link between hostility to the father and his sexual link to the mother
   c. Existence of a cluster of traits predicted by the anal character
   d. Link between toilet training and the anal character
   e. None of the above

58. There is little evidence for the following assertions of psychoanalytic theory *except*
   a. the existence of unconscious conflict.
   b. the general theory of psychosexual development.
   c. the central importance of biology in determining stages of emotional development.
   d. personality is essentially fixed by the age of five or six.
   e. the Oedipus complex.

59. Carl Jung came up with the concept(s) of
   a. archetypes.
   b. the collective unconscious.
   c. a and b
   d. none of the above.

60. Life data accounts for
   a. satisfaction in marriage.
   b. rewarding friendships.
   c. good physical health.
   d. all of the above.

61. Coping is
   a. a conscious mechanism parallel to unconscious defense mechanisms.
   b. somewhat consistent in style across decades in a given individual.
   c. an unsuccessful way of dealing with problems.
   d. all of the above.
   e. a and b

62. The humanistic approach differs from both the social-cognitive and psychoanalytic approaches in all of the following ways *except* the
   a. emphasis on the positive side of human nature.
   b. assumption of a hierarchy of needs.
   c. acknowledgment of the existence of deficiency needs.
   d. emphasis on self-actualization.
   e. emphasis on free choice.

63. In contrast to the social-cognitive approach, the trait, psychoanalytic, and humanistic approaches all
   a. emphasize internal causes of behavior.
   b. focus on the conflict between biological and social needs.
   c. posit a hierarchy of needs.
   d. take a basically statistical approach to personality.
   e. emphasize the role of the environment in shaping personality.

64. Self-actualization is
   a. at the top of the need hierarchy.
   b. associated with a higher frequency of peak experiences.
   c. dependent on the satisfaction of lower-level needs.
   d. all of the above.
   e. a and b

65. Unconditional positive regard in the humanistic scheme and failure to fixate at the oral or anal phases in the psychodynamic scheme are both
   a. features of personality.
   b. contributing factors to adult psychopathology.
   c. dependent on repression.
   d. influenced by genetic predisposition.
   e. conditions for a well-adjusted adult personality.

66. Positive psychology is concerned with
   a. defining the good life.
   b. causes of making people happy.
   c. causes of making people healthy.
   d. all of the above.
   e. none of the above.

67. Humans across cultures show indications of diversity and common elements. Which of the following show marked commonalities across cultures?
   a. Dimensions of personality
   b. Degree of aggressiveness
   c. Degree of cooperation
   d. Frequency of common personality types
   e. a and c

68. Comparing parallel conditions in different cultures allows researchers to
   a. discover dimensions of human diversity.
   b. extract common features of human nature across cultures.
   c. test hypotheses (e.g., about the effect of early experience on later personality).
   d. all of the above.
   e. a and c

69. Collectivist cultures are more committed to
   a. charities.
   b. the extended family.
   c. community.
   d. self-expression.
   e. b and c

70. Dimensions along which the self might vary in different cultures include
   a. degree of belief in situational determinants of behavior.
   b. degree of belief in personality traits.
   c. permanence of personal names.
   d. degree of interdependence with others.
   e. all of the above.

71. Overall, the five approaches to personality each
   a. represent valid alternative perspectives.
   b. present views that cannot, ultimately, coexist with all of the others.
   c. overemphasize the importance of culture.
   d. emphasize reason over feelings.
   e. assign a different role to the function of drama.

Answer Key for Self-Test

1. b
2. b
3. a
4. b
5. a
6. b
7. a
8. c
9. a
10. a
11. d
12. a
13. c
14. a
15. d
16. c
17. c
18. c
19. b
20. d
21. d
22. a
23. c
24. a
25. a
26. e
27. d
28. d
29. c
30. d
31. c
32. d
33. b
34. b
35. d
36. d
37. c
38. a
39. b
40. b
41. c
42. d

43. b
44. a
45. a
46. b
47. b
48. b
49. a
50. d
51. b
52. d
53. a
54. c
55. b
56. d
57. c
58. a
59. d
60. d
61. e
62. e
63. a
64. d
65. e
66. d
67. a
68. e
69. e
70. e
71. a

Investigating Psychological Phenomena

CONSTRUCTING A PERSONALITY INVENTORY

Equipment: None
Number of participants: One (yourself)
Time per participant: Forty-five minutes
Time for experimenter: Forty-five minutes

Constructing a test to assess a personality trait is an involved process. It requires the creation of test items and the validation of these items through the administration of the test to large groups of participants. While it would be impossible to illustrate all the steps in this process in a short exercise such as this, it is possible to provide an idea about some of the issues that are involved. That is the purpose of this demonstration.

A first draft of a test for a particular personality trait has been created.* Before reading on, you should take this test. Listed below are 21 questions for you to answer. Try to put yourself in each of the following situations and on the answer sheet mark the choice that would best describe your reactions. Limit your replies to the choices given and answer every question.

*We thank Lisa Lange, John Prevost, Barb Merriam, Laurie Tunstall, and Julie Nuse for their permission to use the shyness inventory that was prepared as part of a course project supervised by Dr. Charles Morris. We also thank Dr. Morris for kindly supplying the correlational data.

Draft Personality Inventory

		strongly disagree	slightly disagree	slightly agree	strongly agree
1.	I am in a crowded bar sitting with some friends. A good-looking individual comes up to me and asks me to dance. I like to dance but I notice that the dance floor is empty and answer no.	1	2	3	4
2.	I get an important exam back and I disagree with the grading on one of the problems. But I accept my grade, avoiding a confrontation with the professor.	1	2	3	4
3.	I enjoy attending seminars and discussion groups as opposed to large lectures.	1	2	3	4
4.	I'm in a restaurant and receive some bad food. Instead of saying something, I stay quiet but leave a small tip.	1	2	3	4
5.	My family is moving to another state and I will be attending a new school. I look forward to meeting new people and making new friends.	1	2	3	4
6.	I find it easy to liven up a dull occasion.	1	2	3	4
7.	I am required to form groups in a class and interact on a subject. The groups are formed but I tend to listen more than offer information.	1	2	3	4
8.	If I were in the waiting room of a doctor's office and a stranger sat down next to me, introduced himself or herself, and started asking me questions, I would feel nervous and uncomfortable.	1	2	3	4
9.	I can usually enjoy myself at a party even if I know almost no one there.	1	2	3	4
10.	A teacher asks questions to which I know the answers, but I never raise my hand for fear that the answers might not be what the teacher is looking for.	1	2	3	4
11.	I become uncomfortable and at a loss for words, usually blushing, when I am given a compliment.	1	2	3	4
12.	I often find myself taking charge in group situations.	1	2	3	4
13.	I prefer being with people and going to parties rather than spending my spare time alone pursuing personal interests or hobbies.	1	2	3	4
14.	If someone was smoking a cigarette in a nonsmoking section and the smoke was bothering me, I wouldn't hesitate to ask the person to put out the cigarette.	1	2	3	4
15.	I often look back at a situation and think of things I should have done or said.	1	2	3	4
16.	I feel proud to be called on to give a toast at a social gathering.	1	2	3	4
17.	I would go out of my way to make a stranger feel comfortable in a group in which the people are unfamiliar to him.	1	2	3	4
18.	When I've been waiting in line for service for a long time and someone cuts in front of me, I feel angry but don't say anything about it.	1	2	3	4
19.	I prefer not to answer the door when I know it's a salesperson because I have a hard time getting salespeople to leave once they're inside the door.	1	2	3	4
20.	When I've struck up a conversation with the person sitting next to me, a long plane flight seems more enjoyable.	1	2	3	4
21.	I consider myself to be a shy person.	1	2	3	4

Now that you have answered the questionnaire, you are probably aware that it is intended to assess shyness. The questions themselves were constructed as candidates that might have something to do with predicting how shy people are. How can one tell if the questionnaire accomplishes its purpose or which questions are the best predictors of shyness?

One possibility is to examine the face validity of each of the questions. Since you have just completed the questions yourself and since you are now aware that its purpose is to test for shyness, you can do this yourself. Examine each question and decide for yourself whether you think that it would be a good predictor of shyness. That is, does the question ask participants about a reaction that should depend on how shy the participants are? Try to pick out the four questions that you think would best predict shyness and the four that would be least relevant. Note, by the way, that the questions are constructed so that for some (Items 1, 2, 4, 7, 8, 10, 11, 15, 18, 19, and 21) a high score (e.g., 4) would indicate more shyness, while for the rest, a low score (e.g., 1) would indicate more shyness. This is only done to provide variety; your assessment of each question should be independent of this point.

Questions that would best predict shyness	Questions that would least predict shyness
1. ________	1. ________
2. ________	2. ________
3. ________	3. ________
4. ________	4. ________

Your judgment of the quality of a question is a measure of face validity (i.e., the extent to which a question, on the face of it, is a good predictor of shyness), but this is not the only possible measure of validity. Another criterion is to have some independent measure of a participant's shyness and correlate responses to each question with the measure (predictive validity). Presumably, if a question were a good predictor of shyness, it would correlate highly with this measure.

One such measure is a participant's response to Question 21. This question directly asks participants for their own assessment of whether they consider themselves to be shy. In order to determine how well each test question correlates with this self-assessment of shyness, sixty-nine participants were given this questionnaire and correlations of each question with Question 21 were calculated. They are presented in Table 1 below.

TABLE 1

Correlations of each question in the questionnaire with Question 21. A low correlation (a positive or negative value close to 0) indicates that there is little relationship between the answer to that question and the answer to Question 21; a high correlation (a value closer to −1 or +1) indicates a relationship between responses to that question and responses to Question 21. For example, Item 10 has a correlation of .42 with Item 21. This means that participants who tend to agree with the statement in Question 10 tend to agree also with the statement in Question 21. Likewise, participants who tend to disagree with the statement in Question 10, also tend to disagree with the statement in Question 21. A negative correlation, such as in Question 6, indicates that participants who tend to agree with the statement in 6 tend to disagree with the statement in 21. Likewise, those who tend to disagree with the statement in 6 tend to agree with the one in 21 (note that even though a correlation is negative, it still means that there is a relationship between the two items in question, but a reverse relationship).

Question:	1	2	3	4	5	6	7	8	9	10
Correlation:	.23	.08	−.15	−.08	−.20	−.28	.38	−.24	−.24	.42
Question:	11	12	13	14	15	16	17	18	19	20
Correlation:	.29	−.22	−.20	−.27	.32	−.37	−.16	.17	.09	−.07

Compare your judgments of question quality against these correlations to see whether the ones you judged as good have either high positive or high negative values; also, check whether the questions you judged as poor have correlations near 0.

Another validity criterion that may be reasonable is the total score on the test. The logic of using this criterion is that individual questions may vary in how well they indicate shyness, but the test *as a whole* may be a much better indicator. If this were so, then it would be sensible to correlate scores on individual questions with those on the whole test to see which questions best predict the total test score. This was done for the same sixty-nine participants as above; the correlations are presented in Table 2.

TABLE 2

Correlations of each question with the total test score. As in Table 1, a low value means little relationship of that question with the total test score, while a higher value (either positive or negative) means that there is some relationship. For example, the correlation of .55 for Question 10 indicates that participants who tend to agree with the statement in Item 10 tend to have a high total score on the questionnaire, while participants who tend to disagree with the statement in 10 tend to score low on the whole questionnaire. Another illustration is the correlation of –.49 for Question 5. This means that participants who tend to disagree with the statement in 5 tend to get a high total score, while participants who tend to agree with the statement in 5 tend to have a low score.

Question:	1	2	3	4	5	6	7	8	9	10
Correlation:	.45	.41	–.54	.13	–.49	–.44	.46	.42	–.53	.55
Question:	11	12	13	14	15	16	17	18	19	20
Correlation:	.37	–.42	–.35	–.44	.40	–.46	–.27	.35	.25	–.01

Again, see how well your judgments of question quality are related to these correlations. Note also an interesting pattern in the two sets of correlations presented in Tables 1 and 2. Item 10 has both the highest absolute correlation with Question 21 and the highest correlation with the total test score. Also, Item 7 has very high correlations with both criterion measures. This consistency suggests that these two items may well be good, valid indices of shyness. How did you rate these items? Examine the items themselves to see if you can explain why they might be better than others.

Note also that two items, 4 and 20, have very low correlations with both criterion measures. How did you judge these items? Why to you think they have such low correlations?

If we were to continue to develop a "shyness inventory," we might well try to use other validity criteria as well as the three described above. For example, we might try to use the inventory to predict some behavior that is characteristic of shy people. This would allow us to assess the predictive validity of the test. Whatever the criteria, though, the objective of test construction is to find questions that best predict what you are trying to assess. This exercise should have given you some insight into the process by which this objective is reached.

CHAPTER 16

Psychopathology

Learning Objectives

1. What are some of the problems with the notions of normality and abnormality in talking about psychopathology?

DIFFERENT CONCEPTIONS OF MENTAL DISORDER

Early view of psychopathology

2. Give examples from historical sources of the treatment of madness as demonic possession.
3. Describe the early history of the treatment of psychopathology as a disease.
4. Describe the somatogenic view of mental illness, referring to the example of general paresis.
5. Define psychogenic (as opposed to somatogenic) disorders, and explain the historical role of hysteria in clarifying the nature of these disorders.

THE MODERN CONCEPTION OF MENTAL DISORDER

Diathesis-stress models

6. Describe the two-part conception of psychopathology that is commonly referred to as the diathesis-stress model.

Multicausal models

7. What are the claims of multicausal models of psychopathology?
8. Indicate how the multicausal model addresses some of the shortcomings of the single pathology model.
9. What factors are taken into account in a biopsychosocial viewpoint of psychopathology?

CLASSIFYING MENTAL DISORDERS

Assessment

10. Distinguish among symptoms, signs, and syndromes.
11. Describe the basic course of the diagnosis of mental disorders, including integration of information from the clinical interview about symptoms, signs, course, and onset.

The MMPI

12. Describe how the MMPI was developed.
13. How are the MMPI scores and its findings interpreted?

The DSM

14. What has been the emphasis in the most recent editions of the *DSM,* as compared to the original edition?
15. How may the *DSM* have helped increase diagnostic reliability?
16. What are some of the advantages and disadvantages of diagnostic labels?

SCHIZOPHRENIA

17. What are the Greek roots of the term *schizophrenia?*
18. What is the estimated prevalence of schizophrenia?
19. What are some interesting findings with regard to higher prevalence rates of schizophrenia in some populations?
20. What is the prognosis for patients diagnosed with schizophrenia?

Signs and symptoms

21. Describe the major symptoms of schizophrenia in the areas of thought, social relationships, motivation, and behavior.
22. Define delusions, hallucinations, and ideas of reference.
23. What are the most salient symptoms of catatonic and disorganized schizophrenia?
24. Distinguish between positive and negative symptoms of schizophrenia.

The roots of schizophrenia

25. Discuss the influence of heredity in the etiology of schizophrenia.
26. Evaluate the importance of prenatal effects in schizophrenia. Include evidence linking it to prenatal trauma and exposure to viruses.

27. Evaluate the claim that schizophrenia is a neurodevelopmental disorder.

28. Describe the role of environmental effects in schizophrenia, including low social status and family pathology.

29. What is meant by the downward draft observed in patients with schizophrenia?

What causes the symptoms

30. Describe the dopamine hypothesis and indicate the types of evidence in favor of it. What evidence suggests that this hypothesis may be incomplete?

31. What is the structural defect theory of schizophrenia, and what is the evidence for it?

32. Evaluate the idea that the major psychological disorder in schizophrenia is a disruption of cognition.

33. What are some problems with each of the accounts of schizophrenia?

Schizophrenia: A summary and prognosis

34. What findings have led some to propose that we need a new approach to the study of schizophrenia?

35. Review the evidence indicating that schizophrenia is a lifelong disorder.

MOOD DISORDERS

36. Distinguish mood disorders from schizophrenia.

Bipolar and unipolar syndromes

37. Distinguish bipolar disorder from major depression.

38. Describe mixed states.

39. Discuss mania, including hypomania.

40. Describe the symptoms of depression.

41. Are there times when depressive symptoms are good or appropriate? If so, when?

42. What is the relation between suicide and depression?

43. Discuss the gender differences in suicide.

The roots of mood disorders

44. Review the evidence for a genetic involvement in the causation of bipolar and unipolar disorders.

45. What are the biochemical hypotheses to explain depression, and what is the evidence for them?

Psychological risk factors

46. Describe Beck's cognitive theory of depression.

47. Describe the learned helplessness theory of depression, and summarize the evidence in favor of it that comes from both animal and human research.

48. Explain how the idea of despondent explanatory style as a cause of depression grew out of the concept of learned helplessness, and review the evidence for that idea.

49. Indicate features of depression that Beck's and Seligman's theories have difficulty explaining.

The social and cultural context of depression

50. Discuss the socioeconomic correlates of depression and bipolar disorder.

51. How do different cultures advocate different coping styles for men and women? How may this contribute to the etiology of depression?

Mood disorders and multicausality

52. Describe the multiple causes of depression and their interaction.

ANXIETY DISORDERS

53. What defines the anxiety disorders?

54. What is the prevalence of anxiety disorders in the United States?

Phobias

55. Describe phobias, including social phobias, and explain how they can be accounted for in terms of conditioning.

56. Describe the problems with conditioning accounts of phobias, the preparedness theory of phobias, and how it accounts for at least one problem with a conditioning approach.

57. What is panic disorder? How does it relate to agoraphobia? What is the cognitive account of this disorder?

Generalized anxiety disorder

58. Describe generalized anxiety disorder. What impairments are associated with this disorder?

Obsessive-compulsive disorders

59. Describe the symptoms of obsessive-compulsive disorders.

60. What evidence suggests that biology plays more of a role in the etiology of obsessive-compulsive disorders than the other anxiety disorders?

The stress disorders

61. What is acute stress disorder and how does it relate to post-traumatic stress disorder?

62. What is post-traumatic stress disorder? What factors may predispose an individual to develop post-traumatic stress disorder?

DISSOCIATIVE DISORDERS

63. Describe dissociative amnesia, dissociative fugue, and dissociative identity disorder. What do they have in common?

Factors underlying dissociative disorders

64. What is believed to be the psychological function of dissociative disorders?

65. Indicate a suspected predisposition for dissociative disorders and their controversial link to early traumas.

DEVELOPMENTAL DISORDERS

Autism

66. Describe the symptoms of autism. What do we know about possible causes and treatments for the disorder?

Attention Deficit/Hyperactivity Disorder (ADHD)

67. What are the symptoms of ADHD?

68. What evidence points to a genetic basis of ADHD?

69. What is the mechanism of action of Ritalin?

PERSONALITY DISORDERS

Diagnsing personality disorders

70. What distinguishes Axis I and Axis II disorders?

71. Can the diagnosis of a personality disorder make useful predictions about behavior? If so, what is an example of such predictive power?

The slippery slope

72. What are some of the problems with diagnosing someone with a personality disorder?

Programmed Exercises

DIFFERENT CONCEPTIONS OF MENTAL DISORDER

1. Psychopathology is the study of behaviors that fall outside the __________ range.	normal
2. The commonly accepted definition for mental disorders is presented in the __________. It does not require __________ as a condition for the diagnosis of a disorder.	*DSM-IV* abnormality (deviance)
3. Rather, the *DSM-IV* defines mental disorder in terms of __________, __________, or increased risk of __________.	disability, distress harm
4. A dominant early social response to insanity, which resulted in practices such as drilling holes in the skull, was based on the conception of insanity as __________ __________.	demonic possession
5. Prior to the nineteenth century, people with severe mental illness were treated more or less as we currently deal with __________.	criminals (prisoners)
6. The disappearance of the psychological symptoms of __________ __________ following administration of antibiotics provides strong evidence for a view of mental illness as a disease.	general paresis (syphilis)
7. A disorder that is characterized by symptoms that appear to be somatic but have no organic basis was once called __________.	hysteria
8. Mental symptoms that can be directly explained by malfunction at the organic level are called __________. Those, like hysteria, that are best explained at the psychological level are called __________.	somatogenic psychogenic

THE MODERN CONCEPTION OF MENTAL DISORDER

9. According to the __________ model, mental illness has an organic basis, to be treated with somatic therapies. According to the __________ model, mental disorders are, in large part, the result of maladaptive learning. According to the __________ model, mental illness results from psychogenic factors.	biomedical learning psychodynamic
10. According to the __________ model of mental disorders, they result from an accumulation of factors.	multicausal

CLASSIFYING MENTAL DISORDERS

11. In psychopathology, as in physical medicine, the diagnostic process begins with a __________ __________. This elicits a set of complaints, or __________.	clinical interview, symptoms
12. The diagnostician also looks for __________, that is, indications that are not complaints but that are consistent with the symptoms.	signs
13. A __________ is a pattern of signs and symptoms that go together.	syndrome
14. In the course of the __________ __________, the diagnostician integrates information about __________, __________, __________, and __________ to arrive at a diagnosis.	clinical interview symptoms, signs, course, onset
15. As a result of the diagnosis, we can often draw a conclusion about the __________ and __________ of the disorder.	outlook (prognosis), etiology (cause)

16. The MMPI is considered a __________ test. — personality

17. In the most recent classification, or taxonomy, of mental illness, called __________, more emphasis is placed on the description of disorders than on __________ about their cause. — *DSM-IV*, theories

18. The *DSM* guides the clinician in evaluating an individual along five __________. — axes

SCHIZOPHRENIA

19. The worldwide incidence of schizophrenia is about one person out of every __________. — hundred

20. Schizophrenic symptoms include disorders in __________, __________, and __________. — thinking, motivation, behavior

21. Schizophrenic persons often lose contact with other people as a result of social __________. — withdrawal

22. Schizophrenic symptoms include __________ of persecution and hearing voices or other __________. — delusions, hallucinations

23. Schizophrenics typically show low __________. — reactivity (affect)

24. Some schizophrenics begin to believe that external events are specially related to them personally. These beliefs are called __________ __________ __________. — delusions of reference

25. A schizophrenic with unusual motor reactions, such as remaining motionless for long periods, is classified as __________. If the predominant symptoms are extreme incoherence in thought and inappropriateness in behavior, a person is classified as a __________ schizophrenic. — catatonic, disorganized

26. One argument for an organic basis of schizophrenia is the effectiveness of a group of drugs called __________ __________ in its treatment. — classical antipsychotics (major tranquilizers)

27. The __________ hypothesis of schizophrenia holds that it results from too much brain activity caused by the catecholamine neurotransmitter __________, which may cause the overstimulation characteristic of schizophrenia. — dopamine, dopamine

28. In accord with the theory that holds that neurons in the schizophrenic's brain are oversensitive to dopamine, __________, which enhance dopamine activity, make schizophrenics worse, and can induce a schizophrenic-like __________ in nonschizophrenic individuals. — amphetamines, psychosis (syndrome)

29. There are often __________ abnormalities in the brain associated with schizophrenia, and sometimes evidence of less total brain tissue, as indicated by enlarged__________. — structural, ventricles

30. A more modern classification of schizophrenia contrasts abnormal behavior, or __________ symptoms, with the absence of normal behavior, or __________ symptoms. — positive, negative

31. Twin studies indicate that there is a significant __________ factor in the causation of schizophrenia. — genetic (hereditary)

32. Identical twins show a __________ of 55 percent for schizophrenia. — concordance

33. Prenatal factors including __________ and exposure to __________ are linked to the occurrence of schizophrenia. — stress (trauma), viruses

34. According to the view of schizophrenia as a __________ disorder, pathological genes cause brain abnormalities in the fetus, which eventually lead to schizophrenia. — neurodevelopmental

35. Studies indicate that schizophrenia is much more common in the __________ classes and that class status may be both a cause and an effect of schizophrenia. — lower

36. According to the __________ __________ view, there is a higher incidence of schizophrenia in the lower classes because schizophrenia causes lower-class status, rather than lower-class status causing schizophrenia. — downward drift

37. There is evidence that __________ pathology may cause schizophrenia, but there is also evidence that it may be caused by schizophrenia. — family

38. There is no strong evidence for family attitudes and problems as __________ of schizophrenia, but they can affect how well schizophrenics __________. — causes, cope

MOOD DISORDERS

39. While schizophrenia can be regarded as essentially a disorder of thought, in the __________ disorders, the dominant disturbance is one of affect or mood. mood

40. The two major types of mood disorders are __________ disorder and __________ __________. bipolar, major depression

41. In __________ __________, a person shows symptoms of mania and depression at the same time. mixed states

42. __________ is the opposite of depression and is characterized, among other things, by endless talking and overabundance of energy. In a milder form it is called __________. Mania hypomania

43. Depression is commonly associated with symptoms such as weakness, loss of appetite and interest in sex, and sleep disorders. These are called __________. physical manifestations

44. Depression is associated with a high rate of __________. suicide

45. There is evidence that low levels of three neurotransmitters, __________, __________, and __________, may account for depression. serotonin, dopamine norepinephrine

46. Much of this evidence comes from the fact that antidepressant medications __________ the levels of these three neurotransmitters. increase

47. Twin studies indicate a higher role for genetic factors in __________ than in __________ disorders. bipolar, unipolar

48. According to a number of psychogenic approaches to depression, the primary disorder is __________, which leads to changes in __________. cognitive, mood

49. Beck asserts that depression results from a set of negative beliefs, called a __________ __________ __________, and can be treated successfully with __________ therapy. negative cognitive schema, cognitive

50. According to the __________ __________ theory of depression, depression is caused by an expectation that one's actions will have no significant effects. learned helplessness

51. As a result of the difficulty in explaining symptoms such as self-blame in depression, emphasis on __________ psychological causative factors has changed from learned helplessness to pessimistic __________. explanatory style

52. In Western cultures, there is a much higher incidence of __________ __________ in females. major depression

ANXIETY DISORDERS

53. An irrational and intense fear of an object or situation is called a __________. phobia

54. According to a __________ view, phobias are produced by a form of Pavlovian, or classical, __________. conditioning conditioning

55. A fear of embarrassment or humiliation in front of others is called a __________ phobia. social

56. The __________ theory of phobias accounts for why snakes and spiders are more common phobic objects than flowers or pajamas. preparedness

57. In __________-__________ disorders, anxiety is produced by persistent internal events (thoughts or wishes). obsessive-compulsive

58. __________ are persistent thoughts. __________ are acts usually performed in an attempt to deal with these thoughts. Obsessions, Compulsions

59. Obsessive-compulsive disorder (OCD) is associated with overactivity in the __________ __________, __________ __________, and __________ __________. orbitofrontal cortex, caudate nucleus, anterior cingulate

60. OCD is commonly treated with medications that increase levels of __________ in the brain. serotonin

61. In phobias, anxiety is focused on a particular object or situation. In __________ __________ disorders, it is all-pervasive. generalized anxiety

62. __________ disorder is more acute than generalized anxiety disorder, but like generalized anxiety disorder, it does not focus on a particular object or situation. Panic

63. Fear of having panic attacks causes some people not to venture away from their home, a condition called __________. agoraphobia

64. Some have explained panic disorder as an overreaction to the bodily symptoms of __________. fear

65. Recurrent nightmares and flashbacks about a traumatic event characterize both __________ and __________-__________ __________ disorder. The latter has a much longer __________. acute post-traumatic stress, duration

66. The __________ of the trauma and the levels of __________ support following the trauma affect the likelihood that an individual will develop post-traumatic stress disorder (PTSD). severity, social

67. Some have suggested that early adverse experiences may be a cause of PTSD, and that this may be mediated by low __________ levels. cortisol

DISSOCIATIVE DISORDERS

68. In dissociative disorders, a whole set of mental events is removed from ordinary consciousness. These disorders include __________ __________ and __________ __________ (cite two types). dissociative fugue, dissociative amnesia, dissociative identity disorder (any two)

69. Many believe that dissociative disorders are a psychological __________ against something the individual is unable to face. defense

70. According to one formulation, the tendency to be able to be __________ forms part of the predisposition for dissociative disorders, and __________ __________ often triggers the disorder. hypnotized severe trauma (severe abuse, child abuse)

DEVELOPMENTAL DISORDERS

71. __________ is a disorder characterized by a variety of developmental problems affecting language, motor, and social skills. Autism

72. Many autistic children are __________ __________, though a few show islands of preserved or enhanced __________. mentally retarded skills

72. The __________, a brain region involved in emotion and motivation, has been implicated in the etiology of autism. amygdala

74. Attention deficit/hyperactivity disorder (ADHD) is more common in __________ than in __________. boys, girls

75. Some have suggested that ADHD is caused by deficits in __________ circuits in the brain. inhibitory

76. The stimulant __________ is a common treatment for ADHD. Ritalin

PERSONALITY DISORDERS

77. Personality disorders are coded on __________ of the *DSM*. Axis II

78. Axis I disorders are characterized by a well-defined set of __________, while Axis II disorders are characterized by much broader patterns of __________. symptoms behaviors

79. Individuals who show just a few symptoms of a personality disorder are said to have a __________ case of the disorder. subsyndromal

Self-Test

1. Treatment of mental disorders in the past by prayer, music, or flogging is indicative of a conception of these disorders as caused by
   a. microorganisms.
   b. criminal impulses.
   c. degeneration.
   d. demonic possession.
   e. medical malpractice.

2. The discovery of a cure for general paresis gave support to the view of mental illness as
   a. demonic possession.
   b. akin to criminality.
   c. a disease of society.
   d. somatogenic.
   e. resulting from medical malpractice.

3. If a specific enzyme lack was pinned down as the cause of a previously poorly understood severe mental illness, it would change its classification from __________ to __________.
   a. psychosis, neurosis
   b. disease, pathology
   c. psychoanalytic, medical
   d. psychogenic, somatogenic
   e. minor, serious

4. Psychodynamic models claim that mental disorders are manifestations of
   a. unconscious psychological conflicts.
   b. maladaptive thoughts.
   c. organic abnormalities.
   d. all of the above.
   e. none of the above.

5. Which of the following goes along with symptoms, course, and onset in forming a mental disorder diagnosis?
   a. Signs
   b. Labeling
   c. Deviance determination
   d. Neurosis evaluation
   e. Psychogenic evaluation

6. The diagnosis often leads to information about the
   a. signs.
   b. deviance.
   c. outlook.
   d. etiology.
   e. c and d

7. In the *DSM* a global assessment of functioning is coded on
   a. Axis I.
   b. Axis II.
   c. Axis III.
   d. Axis IV.
   e. Axis V.

8. The two-part model of depression claims that the __________ creates the disposition for the disorder, while __________ provides the trigger that turns the potential into an actual disorder.
   a. stress, diathesis
   b. neurosis, psychosis
   c. diathesis, stress
   d. genetic makeup, environmental influence
   e. psychosis, neurosis

9. Protective factors
   a. have the opposite effect of the diathesis.
   b. increase resilience.
   c. decrease the risk for psychopathology.
   d. all of the above.
   e. none of the above.

10. A model that acknowledges the many factors that contribute to the etiology of mental disorders is referred to as
    a. multicausal.
    b. diathesis-stress.
    c. biological.
    d. psychoanalytic.
    e. learning.

11. The MMPI was designed to
    a. assess patient profiles along 10 separate scales.
    b. determine causes of psychopathology.
    c. differentiate among patient groups.
    d. a and b
    e. a and c

12. The general idea that schizophrenics have difficulty distinguishing between personal (internal) and external events can be used to explain some of the symptoms of schizophrenia. Which of the following schizophrenic symptoms can be explained in this manner?
    a. Delusions
    b. Hallucinations
    c. Catatonic immobility
    d. a and b
    e. All of the above

13. Delusions differ from hallucinations in that delusions
    a. are associated with ideas of persecution.
    b. are based on interpretations of real events.
    c. are primarily visual while hallucinations are auditory.
    d. are associated with apathy (indifference).
    e. cause social withdrawal.

14. The prevalence of schizophrenia
    a. is around 1 to 2% of the general population.
    b. varies significantly from one nation to another.
    c. is higher in people with parents who suffer from schizophrenia.
    d. is similar in men and women (though severity levels differ).
    e. all of the above.

15. Thorazine is a drug in the classical antipsychotic (major tranquilizer) family and is effective as therapy for schizophrenia. Antipsychotics are known to block the action of dopamine at the synapse. Dopamine is a neurotransmitter. Low levels of dopamine in animals lead to the neglect of stimulation. Taken together, these findings suggest that
    a. schizophrenia results from an excess of dopamine, leading to overstimulation or overload.
    b. there is a strong, enzyme-based hereditary deficit in dopamine in schizophrenics.
    c. schizophrenics have too little dopamine, leading to cognitive and affective symptoms.
    d. there is probably no direct relation between dopamine levels and schizophrenia.
    e. drugs should be given simpler names.

16. Antibiotics are to general paresis as __________ is (are) to schizophrenia.
    a. dopamine
    b. amphetamines
    c. antipsychotics (major tranquilizers)
    d. norepinephrine
    e. genetics

17. According to the dopamine hypothesis of schizophrenia, a drug that opposes the effect of amphetamines would
    a. be likely to reduce positive symptoms of schizophrenia.
    b. be likely to reduce negative symptoms of schizophrenia.
    c. cause schizophrenic symptoms in normal people.
    d. oppose the effect of antipsychotics.
    e. a and b

18. Bizarre behaviors in catatonic schizophrenics are examples of
    a. syndromes.
    b. signs.
    c. ideas of reference.
    d. negative symptoms.
    e. positive symptoms.

19. Cognitive deficits in schizophrenia include
    a. abnormalities in sensory processing.
    b. problems with reasoning.
    c. an inability to focus on a goal while carrying out tasks.
    d. an inability to inhibit habitual responses.
    e. all of the above.

20. The concordance rate among identical twins for schizophrenia is estimated to be as high as 50%, while the comparable figure for fraternal twins is 15%. These results suggest that
    a. genetic factors predominate as causes of schizophrenia.
    b. there is a very weak genetic component in the causation of schizophrenia.
    c. schizophrenia is essentially caused by environmental factors.
    d. the primary cause of schizophrenia is probably lack of a neurotransmitter rather than a genetic effect.
    e. both genetic and environmental factors play important roles in the causation of schizophrenia.

21. Evidence that schizophrenia may be caused or promoted by a virus is that
    a. it is more common in twins connected by a single placenta.
    b. in the temperate parts of the world, it is more common in children born during the winter.
    c. in the tropics, there is no relation between season of birth and incidence of schizophrenia.
    d. all of the above.
    e. a and b

22. The incidence of schizophrenia is higher in the lower classes. This suggests that
    a. social class is a causal factor in schizophrenia.
    b. schizophrenics are lower in social class because they are schizophrenic.
    c. schizophrenia does not have a strong organic component.
    d. all of the above.
    e. a and b

23. Manic-depressive illness is now known as
    a. unipolar depression.
    b. bipolar depression.
    c. schizophrenia.
    d. general paresis.
    e. none of the above.

24. Grandiosity and racing thoughts are symptoms of
    a. a depressive episode.
    b. a manic episode.
    c. a mixed episode (or mixed states).
    d. a and b
    e. b and c

25. Manic disorders share with some forms of schizophrenia the symptoms of
    a. hallucinations.
    b. social withdrawal.
    c. shifting from one subject to another in conversation.
    d. blunted affect in response to stimuli that would normally elicit affective responses.
    e. enormous amounts of energy.

26. A person shows little interest in the world around him. He shows little emotional response and has disconnected thoughts. On this basis, the most likely guess for a diagnosis would be
    a. mania.
    b. major depression.
    c. bipolar disorder.
    d. schizophrenia.
    e. a or c

27. A common physical manifestation of depression is
    a. fatigue.
    b. loss of appetite.
    c. loss of interest in sex.
    d. disturbed sleep.
    e. all of the above.

28. According to the biochemical hypothesis, abnormalities in levels of dopamine, norepinephrine, or serotonin are implicated in
    a. mania.
    b. depression.
    c. schizophrenia.
    d. all of the above
    e. a and c

29. Bipolar disorder is thought to
    a. involve some of the same neurotransmitter systems as unipolar depression.
    b. involve very different neurotransmitter systems than unipolar depression.
    c. be caused by mitochondrial abnormalities.
    d. a and c
    e. b and c

30. In terms of the hypothesis that holds that high levels of norepinephrine (or serotonin) cause mania, an effective therapy for mania should be
    a. a drug that mimics norepinephrine.
    b. amphetamine.
    c. a drug that increases reuptake of norepinephrine by the presynaptic neuron.
    d. a drug that decreases the rate of breakdown of norepinephrine in the synaptic gap.
    e. a drug that increases the rate of synthesis of norepinephrine in the synaptic terminals.

31. Depression is accompanied by psychosis in
    a. about 20% of all patients.
    b. about 50% of all patients.
    c. about 70% of all patients.
    d. bipolar patients only.
    e. none of the above.

32. Parents with bipolar disorder tend to have children with bipolar disorder, and parents with unipolar disorder tend to have children with unipolar disorder. This suggests that
    a. parents are a stress.
    b. bipolar and unipolar disorders have a different basis.
    c. bipolar and unipolar disorders share a common cause.
    d. environmental events are the primary cause of mood disorders.
    e. bipolar disorder is more likely to be inherited than unipolar disorder.

33. According to Seligman's helplessness views, the low affect of depression results from
    a. low levels of norepinephrine.
    b. negative cognitions that produce affective changes.
    c. a tendency toward suicidal thoughts.
    d. bipolar mood change.
    e. self-hatred.

34. Which of the following symptoms of depression would be particularly difficult to explain for both the biochemical and psychogenic (learned helplessness) theories?
    a. Negative affect
    b. Inactivity
    c. Responsiveness to antidepressant drugs
    d. Self-hatred
    e. None of the above

35. According to the learned helplessness theory of depression, of the following the most relevant cause for depression would be
    a. depletion of norepinephrine or serotonin.
    b. past experiences in which a person could not control her environment.
    c. genetic factors.
    d. parents who gave the person too much responsibility as a child.
    e. c or d

36. The advantage of the explanatory style explanation of depression over the learned helplessness explanation is that the former can explain
    a. inactivity.
    b. suicidal thoughts.
    c. self-blame.
    d. global depression.
    e. low levels of norepinephrine.

37. Which of the following hypothetical findings would oppose the organic explanations of a higher incidence of depression in adult females?
    a. Equal incidence of schizophrenia in both sexes
    b. Equal incidence of depression in both sexes in traditional cultures
    c. Lower levels of brain norepinephrine in females
    d. Lower levels of activity in adult females
    e. a and b

38. Which of the following lists of disorders is arranged in order of increasing importance of psychogenic causative factors?
    a. Schizophrenia, depression, bipolar disorder
    b. Schizophrenia, general paresis, phobias
    c. Phobias, depression, bipolar disorder
    d. General paresis, depression, phobias
    e. Schizophrenia, phobias, general paresis

39. One effective treatment for specific phobias is to expose the phobic person to weak instances of the phobic object while the person relaxes. The strength of the stimulus is gradually increased. Under these conditions, many phobias disappear, and no undesirable symptoms seem to replace them. This therapeutic success is an argument in favor of
    a. the conditioning view of phobias.
    b. preparedness.
    c. genetic factors in phobia.
    d. a biological basis for social phobias.
    e. none of the above.

40. A disorder in which anxiety is handled by repetitive and ritualistic acts is called
    a. phobia.
    b. psychogenic fugue.
    c. obsessive-compulsive disorder.
    d. conversion disorder.
    e. generalized anxiety disorder.

41. OCD has been linked to overactivity in the
    a. orbitofrontal cortex.
    b. caudate nucleus.
    c. anterior cingulate.
    d. all of the above.
    e. a and c

42. If phobias are often about objects, and obsessions are about thoughts, then panic disorders can be said to be about
    a. physiological symptoms.
    b. lack of ability to escape.
    c. sexual objects.
    d. denial of fear.
    e. sympathy.

43. Posttraumatic stress disorder and specific phobias share
    a. a conditioning explanation.
    b. causation by a traumatic event.
    c. dissociation.
    d. low anxiety.
    e. ritualistic behaviors.

44. Amnesia, fugue, or multiple identities may be symptoms of
    a. obsessive-compulsive disorders.
    b. psychoses.
    c. conversion disorders.
    d. dissociative disorders.
    e. none of the above.

45. Autism is
    a. not common.
    b. more prevalent in boys than in girls.
    c. commonly diagnosed in early childhood.
    d. all of the above.
    e. a and b

46. ADHD is thought to be caused by
    a. biological factors.
    b. a virus.
    c. prenatal trauma.
    d. bad parenting.
    e. all of the above.

47. A person who displays a long-standing pattern of preoccupation with receiving attention is likely to be diagnosed with
    a. paranoid personality disorder.
    b. narcissistic personality disorder.
    c. antisocial personality disorder.
    d. avoidant personality disorder.
    e. none of the above.

48. A person who displays a long-standing pattern of lack of moral concern is likely to be diagnosed with
    a. paranoid personality disorder.
    b. narcissistic personality disorder.
    c. antisocial personality disorder.
    d. avoidant personality disorder.
    e. none of the above.

49. A person who displays a long-standing pattern of suspiciousness and lack of trust in others is likely to be diagnosed with
    a. paranoid personality disorder.
    b. narcissistic personality disorder.
    c. antisocial personality disorder.
    d. avoidant personality disorder.
    e. none of the above.

Answer Key for Self-Test

1. d
2. d
3. d
4. a
5. a
6. e
7. e
8. c
9. d
10. a
11. e
12. d
13. b
14. e
15. a
16. c
17. a
18. e
19. e
20. e
21. e
22. e
23. b
24. e
25. c
26. d
27. e
28. d
29. d
30. c
31. a
32. c
33. b
34. d
35. b
36. c
37. b
38. d
39. a
40. c
41. d
42. a
43. b
44. d
45. d
46. a
47. b
48. c
49. a

Investigating Psychological Phenomena

DEPRESSION AND NEGATIVE EXPERIENCES

Equipment: Pencil, paper, and stopwatch or watch with second indicator
Number of participants: One (yourself; you will need the cooperation of a friend to serve as a timer for about five minutes)
Time per participant: Twenty minutes
Time for experimenter: Twenty minutes

Depression is a very common disturbance. It can vary from almost universal blue moods to a serious, chronic, and incapacitating disorder. Because at least some of the characteristics of deep (psychotic) depression occur occasionally in most people, it is possible to study depression in a general population. In any population, there seems to be a more or less continuous distribution of people along a dimension running from depression to elation.

Severe depression is characterized by depressed mood; loss of interest in others and normally desirable things (such as food); feelings of hopelessness, helplessness, and worthlessness; and slowed-down thought and motor activity. Many of these symptoms appear in mild forms in the general population. It is reasonable to expect that mildly depressed people will show some of the same bases or causes of their symptoms as severely depressed people.

A number of theories of depression are outlined in the text. These include biochemical explanations (e.g., depletion of norepinephrine) and psychological theories emphasizing hopelessness or learned helplessness. In this study we will explore a particularly simple additional theory: people are depressed because bad things happen to them. Clearly, some people get depressed in the face of success and others remain nondepressed following a series of adverse events. Nonetheless, it seems very reasonable that negative experiences would contribute to the causation of depression. We will test the hypothesis that people who are more depressed have had relatively more adverse experiences in the recent past.

A major purpose of this exercise is to illustrate some of the difficulties that arise in the scientific study of psychopathology. More than in previous studies in this *Study Guide,* we want to make you aware of the problem of making definitive measurements that clearly support a particular hypothesis. We want you to appreciate the difficulty of research and at the same time realize that progress can be made.

The first problem that we face is this: How do we measure depression? A basic issue that arises is the matter of subjective or objective measurement. In the case of a mood disorder, we might be inclined to subjective measurement, and indeed, much of the diagnosis of depression is concerned with what people say about how they feel. More objective measurements would involve observation of people (facial expression, level of activity) or having people report on their activities (e.g., how many hours they sleep each night). In this study we look at a totally subjective measure, the participant's rating of his or her mood. Remember that we are dealing with the range of depression and elation seen in the general population, and not with people actually diagnosed as depressed. In the case of diagnosis, interview and observation by an experienced clinician is involved, sometimes along with administration of a question inventory. We will use only self-ratings of mood and will collect two such ratings: one for the participant's momentary mood (how depressed he or she feels now) and the other for how depressed he or she has felt, in general, over the past year.

The second problem is this: How do we develop a measure of the incidence of negative and positive events in the recent life of each participant? We will use as our measure the participant's recall of negative and positive events over the past year. There are many problems and alternative interpretations of the results of this procedure. We will discuss them after you have served as a participant in this study.

Fill out the two rating scales that follow and enter your self-ratings on the answer sheet at the end of this section. Then continue to the recall task.

Rate what you judge to be your mood, right now. Circle the most appropriate number.

Extremely depressed 9	Very depressed 8	Moderately depressed 7	Slightly depressed 6	Neither depressed nor happy 5
Slightly happy 4	Moderately happy 3	Very happy 2	Extremely happy 1	

Rate what you judge to have been your mood, on the average, over the last twelve months.

Extremely depressed 9	Very depressed 8	Moderately depressed 7	Slightly depressed 6	Neither depressed nor happy 5
Slightly happy 4	Moderately happy 3	Very happy 2	Extremely happy 1	

RECALL OF NEGATIVE AND POSITIVE EVENTS

For this measure you will need the assistance of a friend who will time two separate two-minute intervals for you. No one but you will see what you write down.

You will go through two recall tasks, in order. Get a pen or pencil and sit at a table. When you are comfortable, ask a friend to say "Go" when the second hand of a watch crosses 12. When your friend says "Go," turn to the next page, read the sentence at the top, and follow the instructions. Ask your friend to say "Stop" when two minutes have elapsed. You should then stop the task.

The next time the second hand passes 12 (i.e., a minute after you complete the first part of the task), have your friend time another two minutes. When he or she says "Go," turn to the page after the one you have just written on, read the instructions, and follow them for two minutes.

Do not read on until you have completed the above task.

You are asked to perform the following task for exactly two minutes.

Someone will time the two minutes. When he or she says "Go," read the sentence below and follow the instructions. Continue until you hear "Stop" at two minutes.

List below all of the negative things that have happened to you in the last twelve months.

You are asked to perform the following task for exactly two minutes.

Someone will time the two minutes. When he or she says "Go," read the sentence below and follow the instructions. Continue until you hear "Stop" at two minutes.

List below all of the positive things that have happened to you in the last twelve months.

Add up the number of negative and the number of positive events that you remembered. Put these numbers on the answer sheet at the end of this section. Also enter the difference between the number of negative events and the number of positive events (# negative events minus # positive events), and the total # of events recalled (# negative events plus # positive events).

ANALYSIS OF DATA

We obtained these same data (depression ratings and event scores) from sixty-four undergraduate students at the University of Michigan. We will present these data here. You will add your own results to theirs, and we will then discuss the results.

MEASURES OF DEPRESSION

We used two measures of depression: rated mood now and rated mood over the last twelve months. You might expect that momentary and long-term mood would be related but that the two could sometimes be different. That, in fact, is just what our data show. Below is a scatter plot that presents the data from all sixty-four participants (see the statistical appendix to the text to learn more about scatter plots). Each point on the plot represents the two mood scores for one participant. Enter your own data point.

There is a positive relation between the two measures of depression. All relations described in these results will be expressed as correlation coefficients (see the statistical appendix). A value of +1.00 indicates a perfect positive correlation; a value of –1.00 a perfect negative correlation, and a value of 0.00 indicates no relation at all.

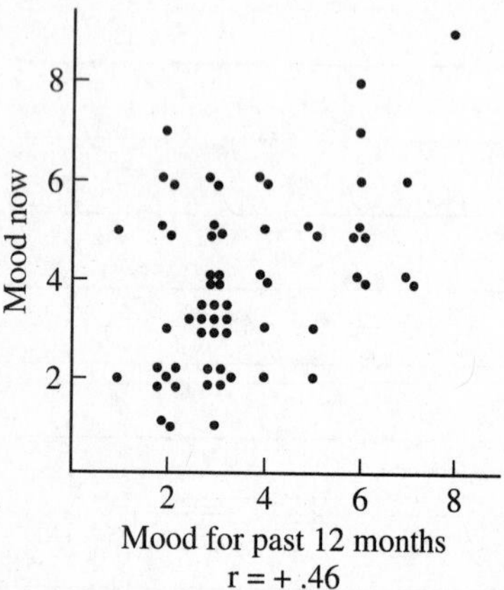

Our measure of "mood now" correlates +.46 with the measure of "mood over one year."

Looking at the scatter plot, you can see that there is some relation between the two mood measures. The general pattern of dots goes from lower left (happy on both scores) to upper right (depressed on both scores). But there are some exceptions. The correlation is positive, but far from perfect. Mark your point on the graph. Does your point fit in with the general pattern, or is it something of an exception? If an exception, can you explain this (e.g., it has been a very good year for you, but something unpleasant just happened to you)?

EVENT SCORES AND DEPRESSION

Before we test the major hypothesis (relatively more negative events in more depressed people), we can examine another prediction that can be made from the symptoms of seriously depressed people. Such people are characterized by a slowing down of action and thought. If this symptom also appears in milder form, in the low levels of depression in the student population, we would expect slowdown in memory search, along with other mental events. Therefore, we would expect that more depressed students would recall fewer events, positive or negative. (This type of finding would surely be true in a comparison of seriously depressed hospitalized patients versus "normal" participants.) We can test for this possibility by computing the correlation between self-rated depression (mood now) and the total number of events recalled (positive plus negative events). Note that because high scores on the depression rating mean more depression and high scores also represent large numbers of events recalled, we would expect a negative correlation: high depression scores go with low event recall scores.

For our sixty-four participants, the correlation between "mood now" and the total events is –.05: There is no evidence of any relation. Enter your score on these two measures in the scatter plot on the next page. You can see by examining the scatter plot that the two measures do not seem to be related. The relations between "mood over one year" and total events is also small. The correlation is +.14 (this is very small, but also in the direction opposite to the direction we predicted). There are two possible interpretations of our result. One is that our sample is not representative of the population, and that there actually is a negative depression–total event relation. Given the data we have, there is no reason to believe this. Another interpretation is that there is no relation, but that there might well be such a relation if we looked at severely depressed people as well—that is, the slowdown of mental function may only be marked in severe depression.

We now ask whether increased depression goes with a higher relative incidence of negative events. If this were true, we would expect a positive correlation between either depression score and the difference between number of negative and number of positive events recalled. We present below the scatter plot for both depression scores. Enter your own points on each of these plots. Just by inspecting these scatter plots you should be able to see that there is a positive relation: higher depression scores *tend* to go with higher negative minus positive event scores. In fact, the correlations are

Mood now versus negative–positive events r = +.46
Mood over one year versus negative–positive events r = +.32

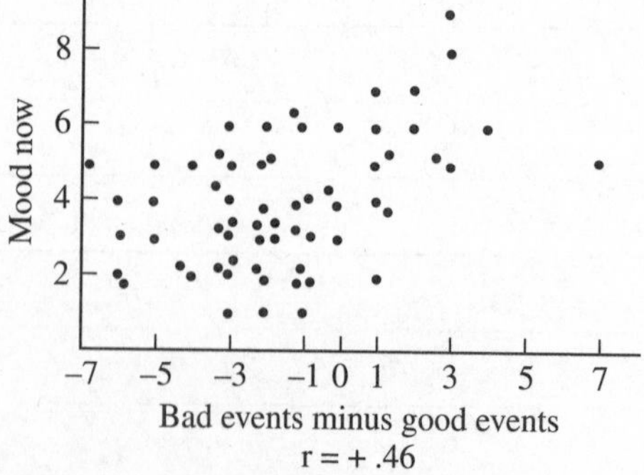

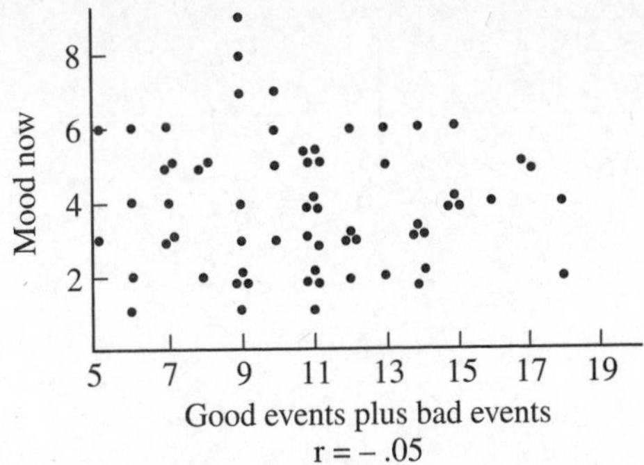

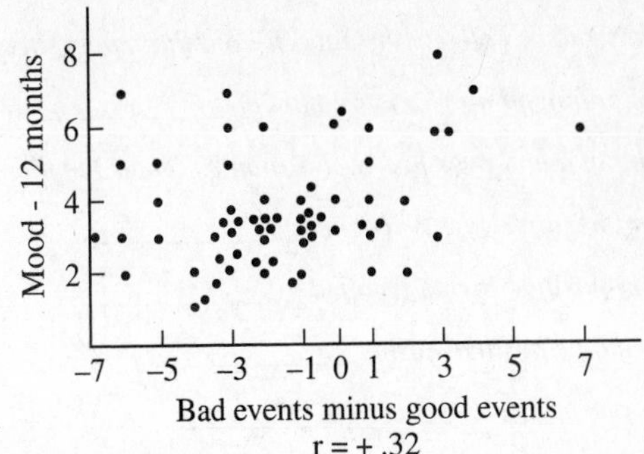

The relations are not overwhelming, but there is a clear relation. For example, the .46 correlation is significant at more than the .001 level: this means that a correlation this high could come about less than one chance in 1,000 if there were no relation between mood now and negative–positive events in the population (see the statistical appendix).

DISCUSSION AND COMMENTS

Our hypothesis—that in college populations, depression as measured by self-rating is positively related to relative recall of recent negative events—has been confirmed. We will now discuss a few problems in interpreting these results in order to make you more aware of the type of thinking that must go into research in general, and especially in this area.

First, our measure of events can be interpreted in a number of ways. We did not actually measure the number of positive and negative events that our participants experienced. We measured their *recall* for these events. A predominance of negative events could mean either that the participant experienced more of them or that the participant selectively remembers them . . . presumably because she is depressed. Remember that correlations show relations, but not causes (see the statistical appendix). Our hypothesis was that negative events cause depression. But the results of our study could be taken to indicate that in a relatively depressed mood, a person is more likely to remember negative events. The fact that the correlation was bigger between negative minus positive events and mood now, as opposed to mood over the last year, suggests that current mood may well influence what one thinks about. Of course, it is also possible that both effects exist: negative events lead to depression and depression leads to selective memory for negative events. There is some evidence in the literature for both of these effects. Under further activities, we will discuss ways of finding out whether both of these effects actually occur.

Second, even if more negative events do occur in more depressed people, the events may not be a cause of depression. Because a person is depressed, more negative events may occur to that person. For example, a depressed student will be less active, will be less inclined to study, and will probably not perform as well as he could in school.

Third, the same event that is evaluated as negative by someone who is depressed may not be considered negative by that same person when he is in a good mood (or by another person in a better mood). Many events may be both positive and negative (e.g., receiving a B in a course when one hoped for an A but did very little work and actually worried about getting a C, or the breakup of a relationship that had been unsatisfactory for some years). Read through your own events and decide how many could be seen as both positive and negative.

We have just begun to scratch the surface, but we hope that you can appreciate the fact that a study like this would be just a beginning and that many more studies would have to be done to clarify the relation between negative events and depression. It should also be clear that whatever that relation is, there are many factors that influence depression. After all, the correlations we do have between depression and events are significant, but they are not that high. We might improve the correlations by getting better measures of depression and negative and positive events. But we also know from other studies, including those dealing with levels of catecholamines in the brain and specific types of past experiences (e.g., helplessness), that other factors are involved.

FURTHER ACTIVITIES

Try to think of some ways in which you could pull apart the effects of actual negative experiences and selective recall of them. After you decide on a few methods, read our suggestions below.

One approach is to get a more objective measure of the actual negative and positive events that a person has experienced. It is not practical to follow someone around for a year. But you could get a fair measure by giving the person a checklist of rather objective events, that are clearly negative or positive. Thus you could ask someone whether over the past year

A close relative or friend died
A course was failed
A job was lost
A favorite team had a disappointing season
A close relationship was broken

and so on, and, of course, a set of positive events.

You could then compare the negative minus positive recall score to the results of the checklist. What would you administer first to the participants: the free recall or the checklist? Why? You could try to make up an appropriate checklist for college students. It isn't easy.

A second approach is to test whether depressed people selectively remember negative events. For example, you could write a story that included a number of negative and positive events. It could be read to participants, and you could measure their recall for the story, say one hour later. You could look at whether people who are more depressed remember relatively more of the negative events.

ANSWER SHEET

(If your instructor collects the data, fill out the report sheet in Appendix 2.)

Self-rating of mood now (enter number) ___________

Self-rating of mood over last twelve months (enter number) ___________

Number of negative events recalled ___________

Number of positive events recalled ___________

Negative minus positive events ___________

Negative plus positive events ___________

CHAPTER 17

Treatment of Mental Disorders

Learning Objectives

BIOLOGICAL THERAPIES

1. Describe some early precursors to therapy for psychological disorders.

Pharmacotherapies

2. Discuss the effects of the classical antipsychotic medications, such as Thorazine, on schizophrenia. What symptoms do they affect and what symptoms do they leave largely untouched? What are the side effects?

3. Discuss the pharmacological effects of the atypical antipsychotics, such as Clozaril. How are they similar to more established antipsychotics, and how are they different?

4. What are the social side effects of treating schizophrenia with drugs, and why do they occur?

5. Discuss the effects of the monoamine oxidase inhibitors and the tricyclic antidepressants on the treatment of depression. How do the selective serotonin reuptake inhibitors differ from these? Why are they widely prescribed?

6. What are the atypical antidepressants, and how do they work?

7. What is the effect of lithium salts and other antimanics?

8. What is the action of the anxiolytics, and for what maladies are they prescribed?

Evaluating a medication

9. What are the drawbacks to using a before-and-after method to evaluate the effect of a therapy?

10. Describe placebo effects and discuss how they can have an impact in the evaluation of a drug therapy. What might cause placebo effects? How prevalent are they?

11. Discuss the randomized clinical trial and its usefulness in overcoming expectation effects. What are the limitations of this technique? How are these overcome when the goal of a study is to compare a new treatment with an existing one?

12. How is improvement assessed in the current medical climate?

13. Be aware of the limitations of pharmacotherapy and its impact on mental hospitals.

Psychosurgery

14. What has been the history of psychosurgery? When is it used today?

Electroconvulsive therapy

15. What is electroconvulsive therapy used for, and how effective is it? What are its side effects?

PSYCHOTHERAPY

16. What are the different types of psychotherapy, and what are the theoretical underpinnings of each?

Classical psychoanalysis

17. What is the theory underlying classical psychoanalysis? What investigative techniques are used in classical psychoanalysis? Of what relevance is transference?

Psychodynamic therapy

18. What are the modern variations on traditional psychoanalysis that have been made by neo-Freudians? How do they differ from Freud's techniques? How are women now viewed?

Imterpersonal therapy (IPT)

19. What is the underlying rationale for IPT?

20. Describe the areas of interpersonal relationships that IPT addresses.

Behavior therapy

21. What basic assumptions are made by behavior therapists? How are these assumptions translated into treatment techniques?

22. How does systematic desensitization use response incompatibility to eradicate phobias? How does an anxiety hierarchy figure into this therapy?

23. Describe aversion therapy and modeling, and give examples of the use of each.

24. What is the major approach used in the application of operant techniques?

Cognitive therapy

25. How do cognitive therapies differ from traditional psychoanalysis? What are the assumptions of cognitive therapy?

26. How does confrontation figure into cognitive therapy? How is stress-inoculation therapy used to overcome stress in cognitive therapy?

Some common themes

27. What common themes underlie the various therapeutic schools?

Extensions of psychotherapy

28. How has psychotherapy been extended in recent years?

29. Understand the reasons for the development of group therapy. What are shared-problem groups? Give examples.

30. What are the advantages of therapy groups for the patients who join them?

31. Describe meta-analysis, and its role in answering question 30.

32. Describe the goals and techniques of couples and family therapy. How are they related to the relationship rather than to the individual?

Comparing different therapies

33. How has psychotherapy reached beyond the original goals envisioned by Freud?

34. Describe the dodo bird verdict.

35. Describe how knowledge of and sensitivity to the cultural background of a patient can enhance the course of therapy.

36. What is an externalizing disorder? What does the emergence of psychological disorders in children mean for psychotherapy?

EVALUATING THERAPEUTIC OUTCOME

Does psychotherapy work?

37. What is the evidence concerning the effectiveness of psychotherapy?

38. Why should there be a deterioration effect?

39. Are there differences in the effectiveness of the various therapies? How do placebo effects bear on this question?

40. What factors do the various psychotherapies have in common? Are there specific effects of individual therapies that go beyond their common effects?

41. How has the implementation of psychotherapy been influenced by practical considerations of accountability?

42. What are the issues surrounding discussions of whether a therapy is effective?

43. What are shadow syndromes? How can they be addressed?

44. What does *evidence-based practice* refer to?

45. What is the difference between efficacy and clinical utility?

46. What does comorbidity mean? How might this complicate the diagnosis of a mental disorder?

Programmed Exercises

BIOLOGICAL THERAPIES

1. Until the Middle Ages, __________ (the removal of pieces of skull bone) was a popular treatment for mental disorders. — trephining

2. __________ medications have their effects predominantly on mental conditions. — Psychotropic

3. __________ are drugs that have an effect on mental illness, and the effectiveness of these was among the first lines of evidence of the biochemical basis of schizophrenia. — Antipsychotics

4. Effective drug treatments for schizophrenia include __________ and __________. — Thorazine, Haldol

5. The advent of antipsychotic drugs led to the big movement in the 1960s to __________ mental patients. — deinstitutionalize

6. Atypical antipsychotic drugs, such as __________, have effects on both the positive and negative symptoms of schizophrenia. — Clozaril (Risperdal)

7. The effects of the atypical types of antipsychotics seem to be lodged in their impact on the neurotransmitter __________, as well as its impact on the __________ system, which is affected by antipsychotics. — serotonin, dopamine

8. An individual feels extremely depressed most of the time. We would expect one of two types of drugs to have an effect on her: the __________ __________ __________ and the __________ antidepressants. — monoamine oxidase inhibitors, tricyclic

9. Drugs such as Prozac have been developed for the specific treatment of depression. These drugs are called __________ __________ __________ __________. — selective serotonin reuptake inhibitors

10. Salts of __________ have an effect on bipolar disorder, both in causing manic episodes to subside and in preventing depressive episodes. They are called __________. — lithium, antimanics

11. Valium and other __________ have become commonplace in treating anxiety in that they increase the transmission of the inhibitory neurotransmitter GABA. — anxiolytics

12. The major weakness of using before-and-after assessment techniques to evaluate the effect of a drug treatment is that the patient may __________ spontaneously. — improve

13. Sometimes merely giving patients what they think is a drug will cause an improvement in their condition; this is called a __________ effect. — placebo

14. A __________ __________ __________ involves random assignment of participants to groups. — randomized clinical trial

15. The biggest cost associated with drug therapy is the likelihood of unpleasant __________ effects. — side

16. In evaluating the effectiveness of a drug, if they provide symptom relief, they can be considered at least somewhat __________. — effective

17. In a prefrontal lobotomy, the connections between the __________ and the __________ lobes are severed. — thalamus, frontal

18. Electroconvulsive shock treatment (ECT) is most effective in the treatment of __________; however, repeated shocks may cause __________ damage and __________. — depression, brain, amnesia

PSYCHOTHERAPY

19. According to the __________ school, neurotic ills stem from unconscious defenses against unacceptable urges. — psychoanalytic

20. Freud thought patients needed to work through their __________ as part of their therapy. — conflicts

21. Freud insisted on __________ therapy sessions per week. — three

22. While Freud wanted patients to gain insight into their motives, he did not want these insights to be merely __________, because __________ involvement is necessary for genuine self-discovery. — intellectual, emotional

23. Freud considered __________ as the means for producing emotional involvement. — transference

24. The __________-__________ view emphasizes interpersonal and cultural factors rather than psychosexual development. — neo-Freudian

25. Behavior therapists hold that the condition Freud called neurosis is caused by maladaptive __________, which can be corrected through reeducation. — learning

26. The major goal of behavior therapists in treating phobias is to break the link between the __________ stimulus and the __________ response. — conditioned, fear

27. Sequential tensing and relaxing of the major muscles produces muscular relaxation, which is considered incompatible with the fear response. Pairing the former with fear-evoking stimuli in order to eradicate phobias is part of the systematic __________ paradigm. — desensitization

28. Since fear-evoking stimuli can seldom be brought into the treatment room, systematic desensitization must depend on the patient's imagination of fear-evoking situations according to a(n) __________ __________. — anxiety hierarchy

29. In order to break compulsive fingernail biters of their habit, we coat their nails with a harmless but extremely bitter liquid so that they experience an unpleasant taste each time they bite their nails. This is an example of __________ therapy. — aversion

30. A __________ __________ uses operant reinforcement techniques to change patients' responses. This technique is usually most effective with in-patients. token economy

31. One operant technique is __________ management, in which the patient learns of the consequences of his actions. contingency

32. In contrast to behavior therapists, some therapists dispense with all conditioning techniques and, instead, help the patient acquire more appropriate ways of thinking. This is known as __________ therapy. cognitive

33. __________ therapy is a technique for treating depression based on the idea that the disease stems from social isolation. Interpersonal

34. One common feature of various therapies is the creation of a(n) __________ alliance in which the patient feels as if she has a friend working with her. therapeutic

35. One common element of all therapists is __________ __________, in which the patient is encouraged to rid himself of intense and unrealistic fears. emotional defusing

36. An important part of therapy helps show patients how they react to others and is called __________ __________. interpersonal learning

37. One of the important components of psychotherapy is __________-__________, which may mean different things for different schools; for psychoanalysis, for example, it means insight into the patient's past. self-knowledge

38. A deliberate weaving together of various traditions is called __________ __________. multimodal therapy (technical eclecticism)

39. A new trend in psychotherapy is __________ __________, doing whatever works. multimodal therapy (technical eclecticism)

40. In recent years, there has been a large shift in the delivery of therapeutic services from the one therapist–one patient model to __________ therapy. group

41. One example of __________ therapy is the __________-__________ group, in which a common affliction is present for all the patients. group, shared-problem

42. A form of group therapy that concentrates on the relationship of the attendees rather than on them as individuals is __________ therapy. couples

43. An important issue in therapy is the recognition that the __________ background of the patient may have an important effect on what techniques are likely to affect her. cultural

EVALUATING THERAPEUTIC OUTCOME

44. A valuable recent technique for investigating treatment effectiveness is __________, in which a comparison is made of studies that investigate those receiving treatment and those who have not been treated. meta-analysis

45. In general, a treatment group's scores on a test of emotional well-being will be more __________ following treatment than will a control group's, indicating a __________ effect in addition to improvement. variable deterioration

46. The __________ __________ verdict is that all therapies are equivalent in their effects. dodo bird

47. By and large, while __________ have an effect on outcome, genuine psychotherapy seems to have more of an effect. placebos

48. __________ therapy is therapy that follows a specific set of guidelines, not allowing the therapist room for improvisation. Manualized

Self-Test

1. Classical antipsychotic drugs typically have effects on all of the following symptoms *except*
   a. delusions.
   b. hallucinations.
   c. apathy.
   d. none of the above.

2. Beta-blockers are usually prescribed to treat
   a. anxiety disorders.
   b. schizophrenia.
   c. depression.
   d. none of the above.

3. One of the important drawbacks to the antipsychotic drugs is that they
   a. have serious side effects such as the production of apathy.
   b. must be administered in a hospital setting only.
   c. produce side effects that keep patients from taking them.
   d. all of the above.

4. The new generation of atypical antipsychotic drugs, such as Clozaril, is an advance on standard ones because they
   a. work on more than one neurotransmitter system.
   b. work on both positive and negative symptoms.
   c. are effective with a larger percentage of patients.
   d. all of the above.

5. All of the following are effective treatments for depression, either alone or in combination with manic episodes, *except*
   a. monoamine oxidase inhibitors.
   b. tricyclic antidepressants.
   c. lithium carbonate.
   d. selective serotonin reuptake inhibitors.
   e. all of the above.

6. The action of Thorazine that makes it an effective drug for the treatment of schizophrenia is that it blocks dopamine receptors. This must mean that schizophrenia could be caused by too
   a. much dopamine being taken up by receptors at synapses.
   b. little dopamine being taken up by receptors at synapses.
   c. little dopamine being produced at synapses.
   d. much dopamine being produced at synapses.

7. Antipsychotic drugs (e.g., Thorazine) reduce many symptoms of schizophrenia. Below are characterizations of five patients suffering from some form of mental illness. Which patients would be expected to improve with Thorazine treatment?
   i. This patient suffers from bizarre thoughts and beliefs.
   ii. This patient is withdrawn and noncommunicative.
   iii. This patient has frequent hallucinations.
   iv. This patient is easily agitated.
   v. This patient is deeply depressed.
   a. All of the above
   b. i, ii, v
   c. i, ii, iii, iv
   d. ii, iv, v

8. It has been suggested that lithium carbonate may
   a. be a general cure for forms of mental illness.
   b. be useless, acting only as a placebo.
   c. have a general activation and arousal effect rather than a specific treatment effect.
   d. effectively treat bipolar disorder.

9. Some drugs used to treat mental conditions have their action by increasing the amount of GABA that is released at synapses. This neurotransmitter is largely inhibitory in the nervous system, so we might assume that it would reduce the amount of activity to the neurons with which it synapses. In view of this, which of the following drugs do you think have this action?
   a. Valium
   b. Xanax
   c. Anxiolytics
   d. All of the above

10. Which of the following would be convincing evidence that antidepressants do more than just produce euphoria to counteract the depression that they are meant to treat?
    a. If they did not produce euphoria in normal individuals
    b. If they acted on normal people to increase euphoria
    c. If they had specific action on neurotransmitters
    d. If they had an influence on other illnesses such as panic disorder

11. The main problem in using a before-and-after design to evaluate the effectiveness of a drug treatment is the
    a. placebo effect.
    b. effect of expectation.
    c. effect of spontaneous improvements.
    d. dodo bird effect.

12. A researcher finds that after drinking nothing but milk for three months, three patients (out of nine) report that they no longer suffer from migraine headaches. The researcher proclaims the curative powers of milk. What critical questions cannot be answered due to the absence of a control group?
    a. What is the spontaneous recovery rate without treatment?
    b. How did the milk cure the headaches?
    c. Why were only one-third of the patients cured?
    d. Can this finding be repeated?

13. A motorist takes her car to the garage for a tune-up. Unbeknownst to her, the mechanic is dishonest and tells her that he tuned the car when, in fact, he did not. The motorist feels that the car runs better. This is an example of
    a. the placebo effect.
    b. schizophrenia.
    c. a double blind.
    d. desensitization.

14. A new drug is believed to alleviate the symptoms of bipolar disorder. The drug is tested in the following manner: one group of patients receives the drug in pill form, and another similar group receives a sugar pill. The patients are assigned to these groups in a random fashion. This is an example of
    a. a placebo effect.
    b. simultaneous control.
    c. a randomized clinical trial.
    d. transference.

15. Which of the following is *not* a type of humanistic therapy?
    a. Client-centered therapy
    b. Existential therapy
    c. Gestalt therapy
    d. None of the above

16. The original idea behind psychosurgery was to "liberate the patient's thoughts from the pathological influence of his or her emotions." This required
    a. localizing the area of the brain concerned with thought.
    b. localizing the area of the brain concerned with emotion.
    c. disconnecting the area of the brain concerned with thought from that concerned with emotion.
    d. all of the above.

17. A treatment that was designed to liberate the patient's thoughts from her pathological emotions, but which produced ambiguous results and may impair foresight and attention, is
    a. electroconvulsive shock treatment (ECT).
    b. prefrontal lobotomy.
    c. lithium treatment.
    d. catharsis.

18. ECT was originally used to treat schizophrenia but was later found to be more effective in treating
    a. depression.
    b. mania.
    c. compulsive behavior.
    d. It is still most effective in treating schizophrenia.

19. Electroconvulsive shock treatment
    a. is faster than many antidepressant drugs.
    b. can produce severe memory impairment.
    c. is generally used only after drug therapy has been tried.
    d. all of the above.

20. In contrast to pharmaceutical approaches to mental illness, psychotherapy
    a. is much more effective.
    b. involves interpersonal interaction.
    c. is more relevant to the nature of psychopathology.
    d. none of the above.

21. Orthodox (classical) psychoanalysis
    a. states that illness is a result of unconscious defenses against unconscious urges.
    b. states that most problems date back to childhood.
    c. was developed by Freud.
    d. all of the above.

22. According to classical psychoanalysis, the cure for mental illness can be achieved by
    a. the victory of reason over passion.
    b. a complete suppression of bad memories.
    c. a reenactment of the cause of the problem.
    d. none of the above.

23. When a patient confronts his phobia in a real-world situation, this is called
    a. classical conditioning.
    b. phobia confrontation.
    c. in vivo desensitization.
    d. fear avoidance.

24. Psychoanalysts believe the emotions are a principal part of therapy. One means for bringing emotions into play involves the relationship between the patient and therapist. The patient begins to behave as if the analyst were an important figure in her life. This is known as
    a. blinding.
    b. transference.
    c. resistance.
    d. intellectualization.

25. Modern-day practitioners of psychoanalysis
    a. emphasize interpersonal factors rather than sexual development.
    b. subscribe to neo-Freudian views.
    c. focus on the patient's present rather than his or her past.
    d. all of the above.

26. Behavior therapists argue that
    a. the theoretical notions of psychoanalysis are untestable.
    b. the therapeutic effectiveness of psychoanalysis is unclear.
    c. neurosis is caused by maladaptive learning.
    d. all of the above.

27. The behavior therapist tends to emphasize
    a. giving the patient insight into the origins of his problems.
    b. righting improper behavior patterns without regard for underlying causes.
    c. curing the patient by a variety of means, including free association.
    d. enabling the patient to reach a full realization of his human potentialities.

28. For behavior therapists, fear
    a. is a classically conditioned response.
    b. has its roots in early childhood.
    c. is a manifestation of emotional traumas.
    d. is an operantly conditioned response.

29. In systematic desensitization, the patient first learns muscular relaxation and then constructs an anxiety hierarchy of fear-evoking situations. The next step is to have the patient
    a. imagine the least fearful situation while relaxed.
    b. experience the least fearful situation while relaxed.
    c. imagine the most fearful situation and then relax as the conditioned link is extinguished.
    d. given homework assignments involving exposure to fear-evoking stimuli.

30. Systematic desensitization relies on
    a. extinction.
    b. operant conditioning.
    c. counterconditioning.
    d. none of the above.

31. The pairing of an unpleasant stimulus with an undesirable behavior is known as
    a. paired associate learning.
    b. cognitive therapy.
    c. response-produced anxiety.
    d. none of the above.

32. Token economies are
   a. ineffective with inpatients.
   b. a form of instrumental conditioning.
   c. a form of classical conditioning.
   d. based on the use of extinction.

33. All of the following are operant techniques used in therapy *except*
   a. token economies.
   b. aversion therapy.
   c. systematic desensitization.
   d. contingency management.
   e. b and d
   f. b and c
   g. a and d

34. A therapist confronts a depressed patient with the irrationality of his belief that he cannot get a good job because he thinks he is incompetent despite evidence to the contrary. This therapist is most likely to be a proponent of
   a. modeling.
   b. cognitive therapy.
   c. desensitization.
   d. any of the above.

35. Cognitive therapies
   a. focus on the patient's beliefs and attitudes.
   b. are not primarily concerned with the patient's history.
   c. do not rely heavily on behavior modification.
   d. all of the above.

36. One of the features on which cognitive therapies concentrate is
   a. the behaviors exhibited by patients.
   b. the automatic thoughts that patients seem to have.
   c. the irrationality of beliefs that patients have.
   d. more than one of the above.

37. Interpersonal therapy concentrates on the treatment of __________ by addressing the __________ relationships of patients.
   a. schizophrenia, intellectual
   b. schizophrenia, emotional
   c. depression, intellectual
   d. depression, social
   e. all of the above

38. It seems as if the different forms of psychotherapy concentrate on different aspects of the problem. In particular,
   a. cognitive therapy concentrates on the patient's thoughts.
   b. psychoanalysis concentrates on the patient's understanding of her past.
   c. humanistic therapy concentrates on the patient's feelings.
   d. all of the above.

39. Psychoanalysis can be summarized by the word *unconscious* in the same way that behavior therapy can be represented by *conditioning*. What word best summarizes humanistic therapy?
   a. *Cause*
   b. *Feeling*
   c. *Directive*
   d. *Rational*

40. All of the following are common to the various therapeutic schools *except*
   a. interpersonal learning.
   b. self-knowledge.
   c. emotional defusing.
   d. therapy as an all-or-none process.

41. Recently psychotherapists have been advocating the use of technical eclecticism in treating patients, which amounts to
   a. token economies.
   b. doing what works.
   c. psychoanalysis.
   d. behavior therapy.
   e. none of the above.

42. A major difference between shared-problem groups and group therapy is that shared-problem groups
   a. involve more interpersonal interaction.
   b. work on a single problem that is common to the group members.
   c. incorporate a greater amount of self-knowledge of the problem in question.
   d. involve a more gradual therapeutic process.

43. One of the differences between family therapy and classical psychoanalysis is that family therapists
   a. deal with a group of individuals, not just one.
   b. concentrate on relationships, not individual mental health.
   c. do not concentrate on the developmental history of each individual.
   d. all of the above.

44. Evaluating couples therapy is difficult because
   a. the patients who decide to see a therapist may not be the most troubled.
   b. the patients who decide to see a therapist may need the most individual therapy.
   c. the individuals will not get therapy on their own, just in a group.
   d. group sessions do not allow us to separate out the effect that the therapist has on any single person.

45. Relative to an untreated control group's scores on a test of emotional well-being, the scores of a post-treatment group are
   a. always at least slightly better.
   b. seldom significantly different.
   c. more variable.
   d. less variable.

46. Meta-analysis provides a way to compare effectiveness across a wide variety of different treatments and outcomes by comparing the percentage(s) of
   a. patients who benefit from the treatment of each different kind.
   b. treated patients who fall above the average of untreated patients.
   c. success of each of the treatment regimens.
   d. treated individuals who fall above the treatment average.

47. A patient gets worse following therapy. This is known as
    a. spontaneous remission.
    b. a deterioration effect.
    c. the placebo effect.
    d. desensitization.

48. One reason there are deterioration effects is that
    a. the variability in post-treatment scores is larger than the variability in pretreatment scores.
    b. the variability in pretreatment scores is larger than the variability in post-treatment scores.
    c. the mean of post-treatment scores is higher than the mean of pretreatment scores.
    d. any of the above.

49. Evidence that psychotherapies are effective not merely because patients expect them to be effective includes the fact that
    a. patients given placebos score worse than the average score of patients given psychotherapy.
    b. patients given one form of psychotherapy improve about as much as patients given another form of psychotherapy.
    c. behavioral and cognitive therapies seem to produce more improvement than other techniques.
    d. there are no significant placebo effects when it comes to psychotherapies.

50. If psychotherapy's only effect is nonspecific, it
    a. may nevertheless have value in providing a shoulder to lean on.
    b. will have proved largely an ineffective treatment course.
    c. will then, by definition, be just a placebo effect.
    d. will be more effective than if its effect had been specific.

51. Combining different types of therapies during treatment is known as
    a. technical eclecticism.
    b. multimodal therapy.
    c. a and b.
    d. none of the above.

Answer Key for Self-Test

1. c
2. a
3. c
4. d
5. c
6. a
7. c
8. d
9. d
10. a
11. c
12. a
13. a
14. c
15. d
16. b
17. d
18. a
19. d
20. b
21. d
22. d
23. c
24. b
25. d
26. d
27. b
28. a
29. a
30. c
31. d
32. b
33. f
34. b
35. d
36. d
37. d
38. d
39. b
40. d
41. b.
42. b
43. d
44. a
45. c
46. b
47. b
48. a
49. a
50. a
51. c

Investigating Psychological Phenomena

DEMONSTRATION OF ROLE PLAYING

Equipment: None
Number of participants: Yourself and one other
Time per participant: Thirty minutes
Time for experimenter: Thirty minutes

All of the treatment options discussed in the text, whether behavior therapy, cognitive therapy, psychodynamic therapy, or drug therapy, require a trained and skilled practitioner to administer. Because of this, it is impossible to conduct an exercise that illustrates any of these treatments. However, one technique that is sometimes employed by therapists can be illustrated: role playing. Therapists use this technique to educate their patients about various aspects of interpersonal relations. This technique requires at least two people to assume the roles of individuals other that themselves in a particular social situation. In so doing, the hope from the treatment is that the participating individuals will gain some insight about the feelings, emotions, and cognitions of the persons whose roles are being played.

Although the technique sounds simple enough in principle, in actual practice it is a bit tricky. As the following quote illustrates, role-playing participants frequently lapse back into their own personalities and have to be reminded about their role-playing activities.

[The therapist] says "Tom, do you really care for me?" Tom says "I would say to her that I do, but she'd complain." Therapist: "Don't tell me what you *would* do. I'm Jane. Talk to me. Tom, do you really care for me?" Tom (turning away, looking slightly disgusted): "Yes." Therapist (still as Jane): "You don't say it like you mean it." Tom: "Yeah, that's what she says, and I usually . . ." Therapist (interrupting): "You're again telling me *about* what you'd say. I'm Jane: 'Tom, you don't say it like you mean it.'" Tom: "It's very hard for me to answer her when she says that." Therapist: "OK, I'm Jane. Tell me how you feel." Tom: "Jane, when you do that it really turns me off. Maybe if you didn't ask me so often, I'd be able to say it spontaneously without feeling like a puppet. . . . (Then, in a tone that indicates he is now talking to the therapist as therapist) Gee, I wonder what would happen if I really said that to her?" (Wachtel, 234–35).

You can try role playing on your own to discover some of its features. Solicit from your introductory psychology class the participation of a fellow student of the opposite sex and set up the following situation:

The two of you are married and have just graduated from college. Each of you has very well defined career plans, and you have each been skillful and lucky enough to have been offered very attractive first jobs that fit precisely the career lines that you have planned. The problem is that your job offers are in cities 1,000 miles apart. How do you decide what to do?

You should go through two sessions: first, have a discussion about this problem with your partner with each of you playing yourselves. Write down each of your responses on paper. Second, switch roles and try having the discussion again. In each case, put yourselves in the other's situation. Again, write your responses on paper.

After you have finished playing both roles, talk about differences in the conversations that resulted from your playing the male versus the female role. Compare the transcripts of each session. Did this help you gain a different perspective on the problem?

At this point, you might want to try another role-playing exercise in which the two roles are quite different from one another. This will allow you to take two very different perspectives on a scene. Try out the following scene:

One of you should assume the role of an instructor for a course you are both taking (perhaps introductory psychology) while the other plays the role of a student. The issue is that the student has scored poorly on the midterm examination, but feels that at least part of the reason for his or her poor performance is that he or she was graded unfairly by the instructor. In addition, the student was faced with taking four midterm exams within three days, so his or her performance was bound to suffer. Now imagine that the student has come in to talk with the instructor about these issues. The person playing the role of the instructor should really try to assume the personality and attitudes of the real instructor in the course as much as possible. After you have acted out a scene, switch roles. This time, to add some variety, have the student role be one of a very aggressive student who is determined not to leave the instructor's office without a change of grade. Again, after each scene, write down your impressions so that you can later discuss and evaluate them.

Having finished this scenario, think about some of the following questions: Was it more difficult to assume the role of the instructor or student? Was it difficult to stay in character without lapses? What insights have you gained about instructor-student relationships? Would this be a useful exercise for students and instructors to try in general? How was this role-playing exercise different from the first one?

Reference

Wachtel, P. L. (1979). *Psychoanalysis and behavior therapy: Toward an integration*. New York: Basic Books.

APPENDIX 1

Statistics: The Description, Organization, and Interpretation of Data

Learning Objectives

1. What is the topic of statistics about? Why are statistical tests needed in psychological research?

DESCRIBING THE DATA

2. What is scaling? Why is it important to understand the types of number scales?

Categorical and ordinal scales

3. Understand what categorical and ordinal scales are. Be able to describe the arithmetic operations permitted and not permitted with each. Give examples of these scales.

Interval scales

4. What is the important feature of an interval scale? Give examples.

Ratio scales

5. What defines a ratio scale? What are some examples of ratio scales?
6. How do interval and ratio scales differ? What arithmetic operation is permitted with ratio scales?

ORGANIZING THE DATA

The frequency distribution

7. How is a frequency distribution created from the raw scores in an experiment? To get practice in constructing a frequency distribution, plot one for the following heights (in inches) of males in a small class: 72, 72, 68, 66, 74, 73, 69, 69, 70, 67, 66, 73, 72.

Measures of central tendency

8. What is a measure of central tendency and why is it useful? Describe the three measures of central tendency that are commonly used. Calculate these three quantities for the scores given above.
9. What does it mean for a distribution to be skewed or symmetrical?

Measures of variability

10. Describe what the range of a group of scores is, and describe why the range has limited utility. What is the range for the scores given in Question 7 above?
11. What is the variance of a set of scores? Why is it a useful measure of variability? Calculate the variance and standard deviation of the scores given above.

Converting scores to compare them

12. How are percentile ranks calculated, and how do they permit comparison of scores obtained from different distributions?
13. What is a z-score? Why is it useful for comparing scores from two distributions?
14. How are z-scores and percentile ranks similar?

The normal distribution

15. What are the characteristics of a normal distribution?
16. Be able to convert a z-score into a rank for a variable that has a normal distribution.
17. Understand the principle that can explain when a variable will be distributed normally. To do this you should roughly understand how a repeated two-alternative event will approximate a normal distribution.

DESCRIBING THE RELATION BETWEEN TWO VARIABLES: CORRELATION

Positive and negative correlation

18. What is the meaning of positive and negative correlation?
19. How is a scatter plot constructed? What does it show? What does a line-of-best-fit have to do with a scatter plot?

The correlation coefficient

20. Understand what various values of r mean.
21. How is a correlation coefficient computed? Do you understand the logic of this computation?

Interpreting and misinterpreting correlations

22. Give examples of cases for which a correlation cannot be interpreted in terms of one variable causing changes in another. What is the danger in interpreting correlations in terms of cause-effect?

INTERPRETING THE DATA

Accounting for variability

23. What does it mean to account for variance?
24. Understand how variance is acounted for in actual experiments, such as the examples given in the text.
25. How does one account for variance in correlational data?

Hypothesis testing

26. Describe the procedure by which you could determine whether a particular test score does or does not belong to a distribution of scores.
27. What are null and alternative hypotheses? How do critical ratios allow us to rule out one of these hypotheses?
28. What trade-off is involved in the decision about where to set the cut-off for the critical ratio?
29. Be able to describe how hypotheses about differences between means can be tested using a critical ratio.
30. What is the relationship between a sample mean and a population mean?
31. What is a standard error, and what role does it play in testing hypotheses about sample means?
32. Be sure to follow the statistical analysis of the imagery experiment presented in the text.
33. Explain what it means to be reasonably confident that the mean of the population will fall within a specified interval.

Some implications of statistical inference

34. Explain how statistical conclusions are probabilistic. How does this affect these conclusions both about population means, and about individuals?
35. Based on your knowledge of how to compute a critical ratio, describe how sample size affects a statistical conclusion. When may statistical and psychological significance differ?

Programmed Exercises

1. The collection, organization, and interpretation of numerical data comprise the topic of ___________. — statistics

DESCRIBING THE DATA

2. When all subjects in a group perform differently, or when the same subject performs differently on different occasions, we say that the data contain ___________. — variability
3. Differences among subjects ___________ groups and ___________ groups are the two sources of variability that are analyzed by statistical methods. — between, within
4. The assignment of numbers to events is called ___________. — scaling
5. The type of ___________ that numbers represent is defined by which arithmetic operations are permitted on those numbers. — scale
6. The assignment of students in a school to the first, second, or third of three kindergartens would involve the use of a(n) ___________ scale. — categorical (nominal)
7. If you ask someone to rank order four cola drinks from most to least preferred, you would be using a(n) ___________ scale. — ordinal
8. The Fahrenheit scale of temperature is a(n) ___________ scale as indicated by the fact that the difference between 30° and 35° equals the difference between 75° and 80°. — interval
9. The scale of length in feet is a(n) ___________ scale; thus, we can say that a board of four feet is twice as long as a board of two feet. — ratio

ORGANIZING THE DATA

10. A ___________ ___________ of birthweight could be represented by a ___________, a graph of the numbers of people in a sample who are born at various weights in the range to be studied. — frequency distribution, histogram
11. Investigators often organize data into ___________ so that groups of observations that fall within a small interval are counted as the same value for a frequency distribution. — bins
12. There are three major measures of central tendency, the ___________, ___________, and ___________. — mean, median mode
13. The distribution of reaction times in an experiment is likely to be ___________, since there will be none below 0, many short ones, and fewer and fewer long ones. — skewed
14. The distribution of heights of males is ___________ because there are just as many males with heights above the mean as there are males with heights below the mean. — symmetrical
15. The ___________ is a measure of variation that is defined as the difference between the highest and lowest scores. — range

16. The ___________ is a measure of variation that takes account of each score's deviation from the mean. Its square root is called the ___________ ___________. — variance, standard deviation

17. The ___________ ___________ of a score is the percentage of scores that lie below it. — percentile rank

18. A ___________-___________ expresses scores in terms of units of standard deviations from a mean. — z-score (standard score)

19. The heights of females in a population form a ___________ ___________, one in which there are equal frequencies of heights on both sides of the mean. — normal distribution

DESCRIBING THE RELATION BETWEEN TWO VARIABLES: CORRELATION

20. If two dependent variables are related to one another, they are said to be ___________. — correlated

21. If we ranked the top 10 runners in the world so that the top runner was ranked 1 and the 10th runner was ranked 10, and if we based these ranks on time to run the 1500 meter race, there would by definition be a ___________ correlation between rank and time. — positive

22. On the average, the faster one can complete each item on an aptitude test, the higher will be one's score, assuming that one doesn't sacrifice accuracy. There is thus a ___________ correlation between time per item and test score. — negative

23. Plotting two dependent variables, one on the abscissa and one on the ordinate, yields a graph that shows the relationship between the variables. This is called a ___________ ___________. — scatter plot

24. A line fit to the points of the graph described in Question 22 is called a ___________-___________-___________-___________. — line-of-best-fit

25. A ___________ ___________ of –1 indicates that there is a perfect ___________ correlation between two variables. — correlation coefficient, negative

INTERPRETING THE DATA

26. We say that we have ___________ variance when we can attribute some of the variability in a set of scores to a particular factor. — explained (accounted for)

27. Squaring a correlation coefficient yields a proportion of ___________ that is explained. — variance

28. The ___________ ___________ of a test statistic is usually set at 2 so that the probability of choosing the alternative hypothesis when the null hypothesis is, in fact, correct is quite small (one chance in twenty). — critical ratio

29. The standard deviation of a distribution of sample means is called the ___________ ___________. — standard error

30. The ___________ ___________ is the range within which we can be fairly confident the actual population mean will fall. — confidence interval

31. There are two important characteristics of statistical conclusions: they are affected by sample ___________, and they are ___________. — size, probabilistic

Self-Test

1. If there are 100 questions on a test, with each question worth one point, then the set of scores from 0 to 100 constitutes
   a. a nominal scale.
   b. an ordinal scale.
   c. an interval scale.
   d. a ratio scale.

2. Suppose you have three children and measure their heights: 49, 47, and 40 inches. These measurements constitute
   a. a nominal scale.
   b. an ordinal scale.
   c. an interval scale.
   d. a ratio scale.

3. If you assert that a jar has twice as much orange juice as another jar, you are making an implicit assertion about
   a. a categorical scale.
   b. an ordinal scale.
   c. an interval scale.
   d. a ratio scale.

4. There are ten digits on a touch-tone phone. If we compare two phone numbers, say 784-5183 and 982-2161, we must use which of the following scales to make that comparison?
   a. nominal scale
   b. ordinal scale
   c. interval scale
   d. ratio scale

5. The results of an examination are graphed so that each score is listed in order on the abscissa, and the number of students receiving that score is plotted on the ordinate. Such a graph
   a. is a frequency distribution.
   b. is a histogram of the scores.
   c. is not a scattergram.
   d. could be a normal distribution.
   e. all of the above.

6. Suppose the graph in Question 5 turned out to look like the graph below. From this we could conclude that

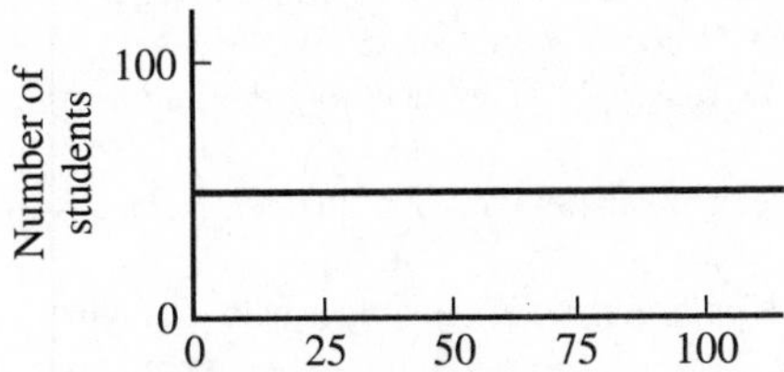

   a. the mean is greater than the median.
   b. the mode is 50.
   c. the variance is 0.
   d. the test was statistically significant.
   e. none of the above.

7. Suppose the graph in Question 5 turned out to look like the graph that follows. From this we could conclude that

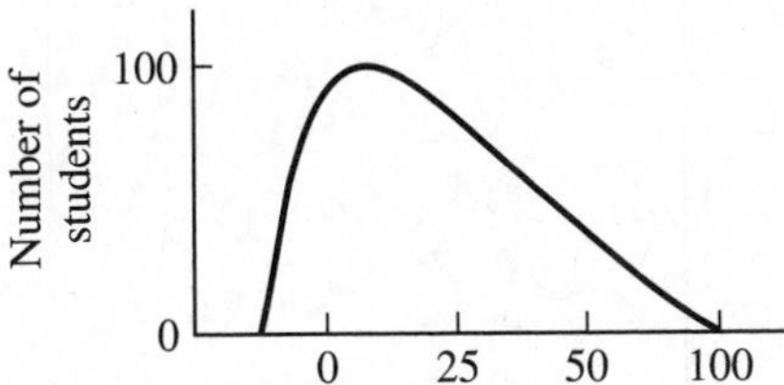

   a. the distribution is normal.
   b. the median is lower than the mean.
   c. the students with a score of 75 are in the 75th percentile.
   d. the mode is 100.
   e. none of the above.

8. For the following five scores, 1, 2, 3, 4, 5,
   a. the median is 3.
   b. the mean is 3.
   c. the variance is 2.
   d. all of the above.
   e. a and b but not c

9. Variability is to central tendency as variance is to
   a. correlation.
   b. z-score.
   c. mean.
   d. standard deviation.

10. All of the following could be measures of variation in a set of scores except
    a. mean-median.
    b. highest score-lowest score.
    c. sum of (each score-mean)^2.
    d. average of highest two scores-average of lowest two scores.

11. Consider two examinations: on one, the mean is 50, the standard deviation is 5, and your score is 65. On the other, the mean is 50, the standard deviation is 2, and your score is 60. Which of the following is true?
    a. Your percentile rank is higher on the second test.
    b. Your z-score is higher on the second test.
    c. You can meaningfully compare your z-scores on the two tests.
    d. You cannot meaningfully compare your raw scores on the two tests.
    e. All of the above.

12. If a set of scores on an exam has a mean of 75 and a standard deviation of 10, then
    a. the distribution must be normal.
    b. the distribution must be symmetric.
    c. a score of 50 corresponds to a z-score of –2.5.
    d. a z-score of 1.0 equals a test score of 75.

13. If SAT scores have a mean of 500 and a standard deviation of 100, and if IQ scores have a mean of 100 and a standard deviation of 15, then with an SAT score of 650 and an IQ score of 115
    a. the z-score for IQ will be higher than the z-score for SAT.
    b. the percentile score for IQ will be higher than the percentile score for SAT.
    c. both of the above.
    d. the percentile score for IQ will be 84.
    e. the scores on the two tests will not be comparable since the tests differ.

14. If we found a correlation coefficient of –.88 between reaction time and performance on a test of motor skill, we could conclude that
    a. a high score on the test of motor skill predicts a fast reaction time.
    b. a high score on the test of motor skill predicts a slow reaction time.
    c. motor skill causes people to have faster reaction times.
    d. reaction time and motor skill are largely unrelated.

15. In the scatter plot shown below

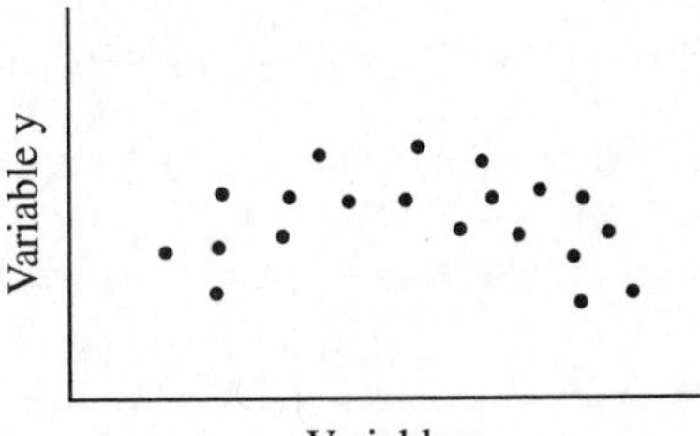

    a. there is no relationship between x and y.
    b. the correlation coefficient is statistically significant.
    c. the correlation coefficient is close to 0.
    d. variable x is the independent variable.

16. If a line-of-best-fit for a scatter plot were flat, then
    a. the correlation would be 1.
    b. the correlation would be 0.
    c. the correlation would not be significant.
    d. we know nothing about the correlation until we calculate it.

17. Which of the following correlation coefficients shows the strongest inverse relationship between variables x and y?
    a. .82
    b. –.74
    c. 0
    d. –1.14

18. If the correlation between a parent's and his children's scores on a test of motor skills were .70, then we would know that
    a. 70 percent of the variability of the children's score is accounted for by the parent's scores.
    b. 70 percent of the variability of the parent's score is accounted for by the children's scores.
    c. children's motor skills are caused by the skills of their parents.
    d. none of the above.

19. An experiment is performed to determine whether eating breakfast improves one's test performance. Two groups are given tests, one group after eating a good breakfast, one after no breakfast. Consider the following hypothesis: eating breakfast has no effect on test performance. This hypothesis
    a. can be evaluated only probabilistically.
    b. is called the "alternative" hypothesis.
    c. cannot be evaluated in this experiment.
    d. is assessed by examining within-subject variability.

20. In the experiment of Question 19 which of the following would be necessary in order for us to believe that eating breakfast enhances test performance?
    a. The sample must be normal.
    b. The sample must be statistically significant.
    c. The between-subject variance must be larger than the within-subject variance.
    d. All of the above.
    e. None of the above.

21. Suppose you were to discover a hospital in which there were eight new births each day, and you wished to test the hypothesis that this hospital had more births per day than the average hospital of its size. To do this we would need to know
    a. the correlations among births at all the hospitals in question.
    b. the mean, standard deviation, and number of hospitals in the comparison group.
    c. only the standard error of the births in the comparison group.
    d. none of the above.

22. Two hospitals report eight births per day average with a standard deviation of ten births. For hospital A, this average was computed over 25 days; for hospital B, it was computed over 400 days. The standard errors of births in these hospitals
    a. are equal.
    b. are 2 in hospital A and .5 in hospital B.
    c. are not comparable because of the difference in number of days.
    d. none of the above.

23. If a sample mean is 20, its standard deviation is 30, and the number of participants in the sample is 9, then
    a. you can be fairly confident that the sample is normal.
    b. a participant with a score of 25 is in the fifth percentile.
    c. a score of 17 would be equal to a z-score of 1.
    d. you can be fairly sure that the population from which this sample was drawn has a mean greater than 0.

24. Suppose you're trying to predict whether a Republican or Democratic candidate will win a particular senatorial race. You conduct a poll of the relevant voters and discover that 53 percent would vote for the Republican and 47 percent for the Democrat. Who do you think will win?
    a. You can be reasonably confident that the Republican will win.
    b. You can be reasonably confident that the Democrat will win.
    c. Given the polling data, it's not clear who will win.
    d. There isn't enough information to make a prediction one way or the other.

Answer Key for Self-Test

1. d
2. d
3. d
4. a
5. e
6. e
7. b
8. d
9. c
10. a
11. e
12. c
13. d
14. a
15. c
16. b
17. b
18. d
19. a
20. c
21. b
22. b
23. d
24. d

Investigating Psychological Phenomena

APPLYING STATISTICAL CONCEPTS

This exercise provides an opportunity for you to apply some of the statistical concepts described in the text. Reconsider the experiment described in the text in which participants are tested for recall performance on lists of twenty words with and without instructions to form images. Imagine that twenty participants had been run in this experiment—the ten described in the text plus ten others. The data of all these participants are presented in Table 1 below. In the first column are the recall scores with imagery instructions; the second column contains recall scores when no imagery instructions were provided; the third column is the difference between the first two, the amount of improvement. Finally, the fourth column contains the results of a test of imagery ability that was given to each of the participants in this hypothetical experiment (scores on this test could range from 0 to 40). Using the data in this table, perform the following tabulations and analyses.

TABLE 1

Participant	Score with imagery	Score without imagery	Improvement	Test of imagery ability
Alphonse	20	5	15	30
Betsy	24	9	15	26
Cheryl	20	5	15	27
Davis	18	9	9	21
Earl	22	6	16	33
Fred	19	11	8	26
Germaine	20	8	12	32
Hortense	19	11	8	38
Imogene	17	7	10	30
Jerry	21	9	12	27
Kerry	17	8	9	29
Linda	20	16	4	24
Moe	20	10	10	26
Nicolas	16	12	4	22
Orry	24	7	17	36
Penelope	22	9	13	32
Quarton	25	21	4	23
Ronald	21	14	7	26
Steven	19	12	7	24
Terry	23	13	10	28

1. Create frequency histograms for the recall data on the two unlabeled sets of axes below. The left graph is for the recall scores with imagery instructions, and the right is for recall scores without imagery instructions. Note that you must decide what specific values to place on each axis for each graph.

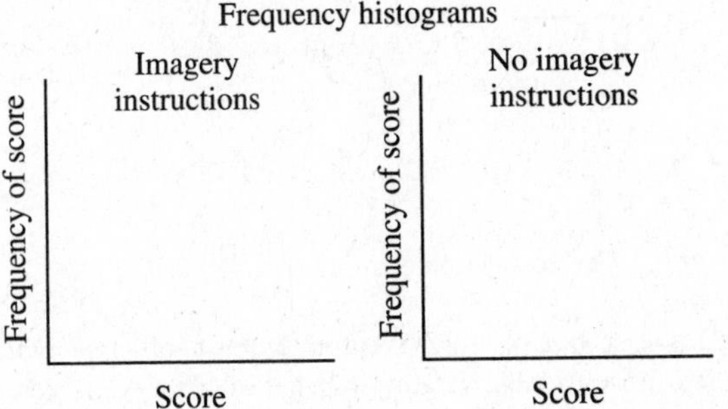

2. Calculate the mean, median, and mode of each of the distributions whose scores you have plotted above.

3. Calculate the range and standard deviation of each of these distributions.

4. Analyze the improvement scores to test the hypothesis that imagery instructions lead to better recall performance than no imagery instructions. To do this, you must compute a critical ratio that evaluates the sample mean of the improvement scores against the population mean for the null hypothesis (no improvement). Is this critical ratio larger than 2.0? If so, how do we interpret the improvement scores?

5. Examine the relationship between the improvement scores and performance on the test of imagery ability in two ways. First, create a scatter plot on the axes presented below. Second, compute a correlation coefficient between these sets of scores. Is there a relation between the variables? How would you interpret this relation psychologically?

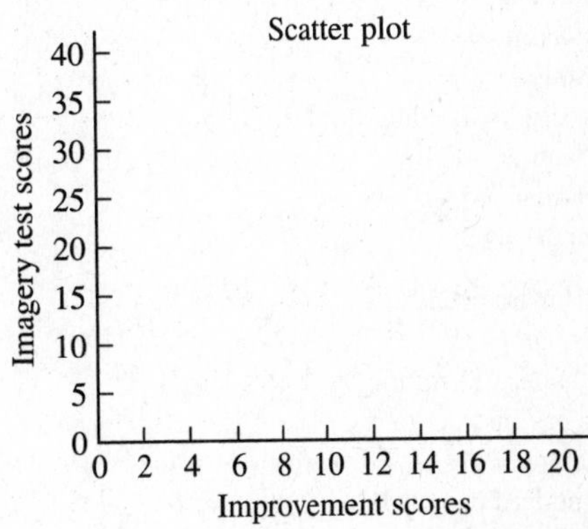

Now that you have completed your analyses, you should turn to the next page to examine the correct answers and compare them to your own answers.

Answers to Statistical Exercise

1.

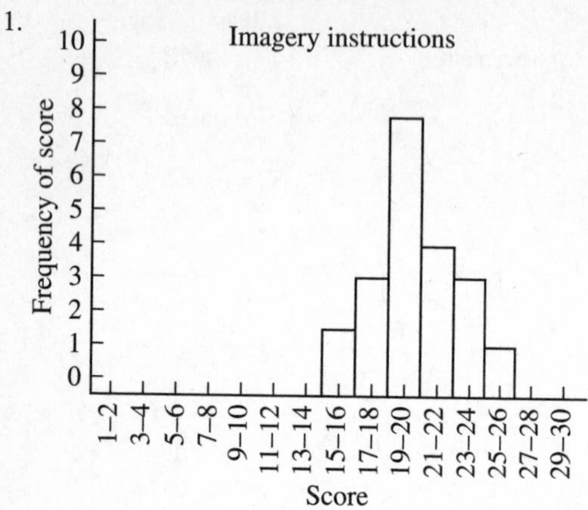

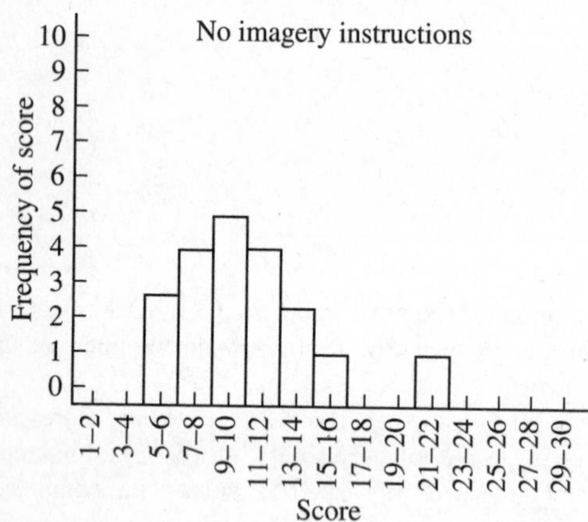

2. Imagery instructions
   - Mean = 20.35
   - Median = 20
   - Mode = 20

   No imagery instructions
   - Mean = 10.10
   - Median = 9
   - Mode = 9

3. Imagery instructions
   - Range = 9
   - Standard deviation = 2.46

   No imagery instructions
   - Range = 16
   - Standard deviation = 3.89

4. Critical ratio =

$$\frac{\text{sample mean} - \text{population mean by null hypothesis}}{\text{standard error of the mean}}$$

standard error of the mean

$$= \frac{\text{standard deviation}}{\sqrt{N}}$$

$$= \frac{4.05}{\sqrt{20}}$$

$$= .91$$

$$\text{critical ratio} = \frac{10.25 - 0}{.91}$$

$$= 11.26$$

This critical ratio is much larger than 2.0; therefore, we may conclude that there is a statistically significant improvement in recall scores comparing no imagery to imagery instructions.

5. Scatter plot

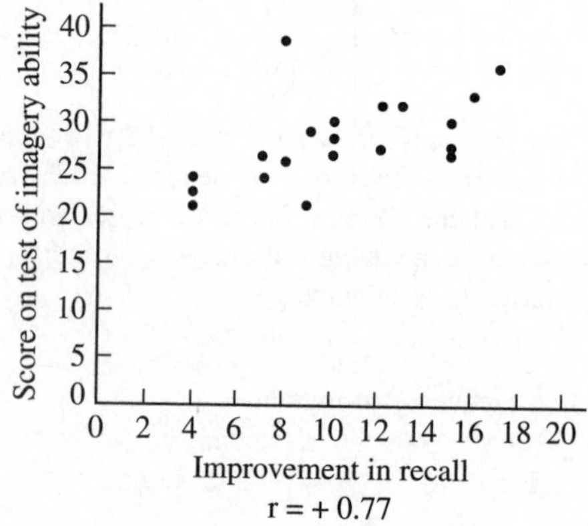

The correlation coefficient, r, is +0.77.

Both the scatter plot and the correlation coefficient indicate that there is substantial relationship between the variables. We might propose the following hypothesis to account for this relationship. Participants with a better imagery ability are better able to form mental images in the memory task, and thus perform better. Our hypothesis must remain tentative, however, since we are not permitted to draw cause-effect conclusions from correlational data.

APPENDIX 2

Report Sheets

On this and the following pages you will find report sheets for several of the experiments in the preceding chapters. If your instructor wants to collect the data for these experiments, use these report sheets. You can cut them out and hand them in to your instructor.

Chapter 1

REPORT SHEET—CONSISTENCY OF JUDGMENTS OF FACIAL EXPRESSION

	Female Subjects	Male Subjects
Female ecstatic		
Female happy		
Female sad		
Female shocked		
Female frightened		
Female disgusted		
Female calm		
Female resigned		
Female disappointed		
Female angry		
Female resolute		

	Female Subjects	Male Subjects
Male ecstatic		
Male happy		
Male sad		
Male shocked		
Male frightened		
Male disgusted		
Male calm		
Male resigned		
Male disappointed		
Male angry		
Male resolute		

Chapter 2

REPORT SHEET—HEART RATE

Data from three participants (a, b, and c)

Instruction and time	A	B	C
"Begin and relax"			
00:00–0:30			
0:45–1:15			
"Increase physical activity"			
1:30–2:00			
2:15–2:45			
"Relax"			
3:00–3:30			
3:45–4:15			
"Increase mental activity"			
4:30–5:00			
5:15–5:45			
"Relax"			
6:00–6:30			
6:45–7:15			

List for each participant the basic situation that he or she imagined in the "increase" minutes.

	Physical	Mental
A	____________	____________
B	____________	____________
C	____________	____________

Chapter 3

REPORT SHEET—NERVE IMPULSE

Practice Trial 1 ankle = Time in seconds*

Part I
Trial 1 ankle = ____________
Trial 2 ankle = ____________
Trial 3 ankle = ____________
Trial 4 ankle = ____________
Trial 5 ankle = ____________

Part II
Trial 1 upper arm = ____________
Trial 2 upper arm = ____________
Trial 3 upper arm = ____________
Trial 4 upper arm = ____________
Trial 5 upper arm = ____________

Test
Part III
Trial 1 ankle time = ____________
÷ 25 = ____________ (a)
Trial 2 upper arm time = ____________
÷ 25 = ____________ (b)
Trial 3 upper arm time = ____________
÷ 25 = ____________ (c)
Trial 4 ankle time = ____________
÷ 25 = ____________ (d)

$\frac{a + d}{2}$ = ____________ (average ankle time)

$\frac{b + c}{2}$ = ____________ (average upper arm time)

Average ankle time – average upper arm time = ____________ (difference 1)

(1) Distance of ankle to base of neck (for third tallest person) = ____________

(2) Distance of upper arm to base of neck (for third tallest person) = ____________

Distance 1 – distance 2 = ____________ (difference 2)

$\frac{\text{difference 2}}{\text{difference 1}}$ = (speed of nerve impulse)

*Record time accurate to .1 second.

Chapter 4

REPORT SHEET—MEASURING BRIGHTNESS CONTRAST

Background values:	1	3	4	5	7	10
Matching value 1:	______	______	______	______	______	______
Matching value 2:	______	______	______	______	______	______
Matching value 3:	______	______	______	______	______	______
Total matching value:	______	______	______	______	______	______
Average matching value:	______	______	______	______	______	______

Chapter 6

REPORT SHEET—LEARNED TASTE AVERSIONS

Number of participants questioned ________

Number of participants with aversions ________

Number of participants who confirm Garcia's notions ________

Summarize the results from all of your participants below. Decide which questions are relevant to each feature of learned taste aversion, and summarize your results with respect to each of the features listed below.

BELONGINGNESS Relevant questions (Nos.)

____

____

____

ONE-TRIAL LEARNING Relevant questions (Nos.)

____

____

____

LONG CS-US INTERVAL Relevant questions (Nos.)

____

____

____

NOVELTY EFFECT Relevant questions (Nos.)

____

____

____

"IRRATIONALITY" Relevant questions (Nos.)

____

____

____

OTHER INTERESTING RESULTS

____

____

____

Chapter 6

REPORT SHEET—MAZE LEARNING

Trial	Time	Number of errors
1	________	________
2	________	________
3	________	________
4	________	________
5	________	________

(using paper
with cut-out hole)

Chapter 7

REPORT SHEET—IMAGERY INSTRUCTIONS

Answer sheet for List 1	Answer sheet for List 2
1. ________	1. ________
2. ________	2. ________
3. ________	3. ________
4. ________	4. ________
5. ________	5. ________
6. ________	6. ________
7. ________	7. ________
8. ________	8. ________
9. ________	9. ________
10. ________	10. ________
11. ________	11. ________
12. ________	12. ________
13. ________	13. ________
14. ________	14. ________
15. ________	15. ________
16. ________	16. ________
17. ________	17. ________
18. ________	18. ________
19. ________	19. ________
20. ________	20. ________

Chapter 8

REPORT SHEET—THE STROOP EFFECT

Experiment 1

Color patch list

List 1 ________ sec. __________ errors

List 3 ________ sec. __________ errors

List 5 ________ sec. __________ errors

List 7 ________ sec. __________ errors

List 9 ________ sec. __________ errors

Average = __________ sec.

Total errors = __________

Letter string list

List 2 ________ sec. __________ errors

List 4 ________ sec. __________ errors

List 6 ________ sec. __________ errors

List 8 ________ sec. __________ errors

List 10 ________ sec. __________ errors

Average = __________ sec.

Total errors = __________

Experiment 2

Neutral words

List 1 ________ sec. __________ errors

List 3 ________ sec. __________ errors

List 5 ________ sec. __________ errors

List 7 ________ sec. __________ errors

List 9 ________ sec. __________ errors

Average = __________ sec.

Total errors = __________

Color words

List 2 ________ sec. __________ errors

List 4 ________ sec. __________ errors

List 6 ________ sec. __________ errors

List 8 ________ sec. __________ errors

List 10 ________ sec. __________ errors

Average = __________ sec.

Total errors = __________

Experiment 3

Neutral words

List 1 ________ sec. __________ errors

List 3 ________ sec. __________ errors

List 5 ________ sec. __________ errors

List 7 ________ sec. __________ errors

List 9 ________ sec. __________ errors

Average = __________ sec.

Total errors = __________

Color referent words

List 2 ________ sec. __________ errors

List 4 ________ sec. __________ errors

List 6 ________ sec. __________ errors

List 8 ________ sec. __________ errors

List 10 ________ sec. __________ errors

Average = __________ sec.

Total errors = __________

Chapter 9

REPORT SHEET—IMPLICIT LEARNING

1. ______	9. ______	17. ______
2. ______	10. ______	18. ______
3. ______	11. ______	19. ______
4. ______	12. ______	20. ______
5. ______	13. ______	21. ______
6. ______	14. ______	22. ______
7. ______	15. ______	23. ______
8. ______	16. ______	24. ______

Participant's statement of rule: ______________________

____

____

____

____

____

____

____

____

Number of correct responses out of 24: ______________

Chapter 10

REPORT SHEET—CONSERVATION OF NUMBER

1. More blue ______
   More red ______
   Both equal ______
2. More blue ______
   More red ______
   Both equal ______
3. More blue ______
   More red ______
   Both equal ______
4. More blue ______
   More red ______
   Both equal ______
5. More blue ______
   More red ______
   Both equal ______
6. More blue ______
   More red ______
   Both equal ______
7. More blue ______
   More red ______
   Both equal ______
8. More blue ______
   More red ______
   Both equal ______

Chapter 11

REPORT SHEET—SEX DIFFERENCES

	Your data* (combined with classmates' data)			
	Males		Females	
Item	#	%	#	%
1. Killing cockroach	_____	_____	_____	_____
2. Queen Anne's lace (correct answer: flower)	_____	_____	_____	_____
3. Using word "shit" (fewer than 5 times)	_____	_____	_____	_____
4. Sew clothes	_____	_____	_____	_____
5. Intercourse only after spiritual love	_____	_____	_____	_____
6. Nude in locker room	_____	_____	_____	_____
7. Crying frequently (very often, often, or only with good reason)	_____	_____	_____	_____
8. Feel like smashing things	_____	_____	_____	_____
9. Chest measurement	_____	_____	_____	_____
10. Change tire	_____	_____	_____	_____
11. Playing radio	_____	_____	_____	_____
12. Prefer dominance in relationship	_____	_____	_____	_____
13. Overweight	_____	_____	_____	_____
14. Washing hair when depressed	_____	_____	_____	_____
15. Sleep in nude	_____	_____	_____	_____
16. Closest parent (mother)	_____	_____	_____	_____
17. Keep room neat	_____	_____	_____	_____

*Tabulate your results below in the following way. For the "yes" or "no" questions (e.g., Item 1), add up the number of participants who answered "yes." Then calculate what percentage answered "Yes." For the "true" or "false" questions (e.g., Item 8), record those who answered "True." For other items (e.g., Item 2), add up the number of participants whose answers are the same as those indicated in parentheses under "Item" (e.g., Item 2—flower).

List the femaleness scores of all of your participants:

Males: _____ _____ _____ _____ _____ _____ _____ _____ _____ _____

_____ _____ _____ _____ _____ _____ _____ _____ _____ _____

Females: _____ _____ _____ _____ _____ _____ _____ _____ _____ _____

_____ _____ _____ _____ _____ _____ _____ _____ _____ _____

Chapter 12

REPORT SHEET—IMPRESSIONS

Percent of participants checking favorable adjective at left

	Asch's data		Your data	
Adjective pair	Group A (24 students)	Group B (34 students)	Group A (__ students)	Group B (__ students)
generous	24	10		
wise	18	17		
happy	32	5		
good-natured	18	0		
humorous	52	21		
sociable	56	27		
popular	35	14		
reliable	84	91		
good-looking	74	35		
serious	97	100		
restrained	64	9		
honest	80	79		

Chapter 16

REPORT SHEET—DEPRESSION

Self-rating of mood now (enter number) ___________

Self-rating of mood over last twelve months (enter number) ___________

Number of negative events recalled ___________

Number of positive events recalled ___________

Negative minus positive events ___________

Negative plus positive events ___________